I0113477

Photo by Denis Reggie. Used with permission of Hachette Book Group.

Edward M. Kennedy

S. Doc. 111–6

Memorial Addresses and Other Tributes

HELD IN THE SENATE
AND HOUSE OF REPRESENTATIVES
OF THE UNITED STATES
TOGETHER WITH MEMORIAL SERVICES
IN HONOR OF

EDWARD M. KENNEDY

Late a Senator from Massachusetts

One Hundred Eleventh Congress
First Session

U.S. GOVERNMENT PRINTING OFFICE
WASHINGTON : 2010

Compiled under the direction
of the
Joint Committee on Printing

CONTENTS

BIOGRAPHY

EDWARD M. KENNEDY was the third longest serving Member of the U.S. Senate in American history. Voters of Massachusetts elected him to the Senate nine times—a record matched by only one other Senator. The scholar Thomas Mann said his time in the Senate was "an amazing and endurable presence. You want to go back to the 19th century to find parallels, but you won't find parallels." President Obama has described his breathtaking span of accomplishment: "For five decades, virtually every major piece of legislation to advance the civil rights, health, and economic well-being of the American people bore his name and resulted from his efforts."

Senator KENNEDY fought for and won so many great battles—on voting rights, education, immigration reform, the minimum wage, national service, the Nation's first major legislation to combat AIDS, and equality for minorities, women, the disabled, and gay and lesbian Americans. He called health care "the cause of my life," and succeeded in bringing quality and affordable health care to countless Americans, including children, seniors, and those with disabilities. Until the end he was working tirelessly to achieve historic national health reform. He was an opponent of the Vietnam war and an early champion of the war's refugees. He was a powerful yet lonely voice from the beginning against the invasion of Iraq. He stood for human rights abroad—from Chile to the former Soviet Union—and was a leader in the cause of poverty relief for the poorest nations of Africa and the world. He believed in a strong national defense and he also unceasingly pursued and advanced the work of nuclear arms control.

He was the conscience of his party, and also the Senate's greatest master of forging compromise with the other party. Known as the lion of the Senate, Senator KENNEDY was widely respected on both sides of the aisle for his commitment to progress and his ability to legislate.

Senator KENNEDY was chairman of the Senate Health, Education, Labor, and Pensions Committee. Previously he was chairman of the Senate Judiciary Committee and served on that committee for many years. He also served on the Senate Armed Services Committee and the Congressional Joint Economic Committee. He was a leader of the Congressional Friends of Ireland and helped lead the way toward peace on that island.

He was a graduate of Harvard University and the University of Virginia Law School. He lived in Hyannis Port, MA, with his wife Vicki. He is survived by her and their five children: Kara; Edward, Jr.; Patrick; Curran; and Caroline; and his sister Jean Kennedy Smith.

MEMORIAL ADDRESSES

AND

OTHER TRIBUTES

FOR

EDWARD M. KENNEDY

Proceedings in the Senate

PRAYER

The Chaplain, Dr. Barry C. Black, offered the following prayer:

O merciful Lord, we thank You for the refreshment and accomplishments of our time away and for Your clear, shining inward light that directs our steps. May the Members of this body feel Your peace and power today. Restrain wandering thoughts and break in pieces those temptations that lead them away from Your will. Lord, join our Senators to Yourself with an inseparable bond of love, for You alone truly satisfy. Grant that their love may abound more and more in knowledge and depth of insight, so that they may be able to discern what is best, and may be pure and blameless when they stand before You.

Lord, this is the first time in nearly 50 years that the Senate will convene without Senator EDWARD KENNEDY as one of its Members. Thank You for his life and legacy.

We pray in Your sovereign name. Amen.

MOMENT OF SILENCE IN HONOR OF THE LATE SENATOR EDWARD M. KENNEDY

Mr. REID. I ask unanimous consent that the Senate now observe a moment of silence in memory of our friend and departed colleague, the late Senator EDWARD KENNEDY.

The ACTING PRESIDENT pro tempore. Without objection, it is so ordered.

[Moment of silence.]

Mr. REID. Mr. President, I have to acknowledge that as I came into the Chamber this afternoon, I came upon Senator KENNEDY's desk, which is covered with the traditional black velvet, with the flowers and his favorite poem on the desk. I read the poem and a tear came to my eye. ...

Mr. McCONNELL. Mr. President, the Senate grieves the loss of one of its giants and one of our great friends. All of us were, of course, moved by the many tributes that have poured in since Senator KENNEDY's passing. We will make time later in the week for Senators, including myself, to deliver tributes of our own on the Senate floor.

Mr. KYL. Mr. President, I want to speak to the same issue my colleague Senator McCain spoke to in a couple minutes. First I wish to make some brief comments about two of our colleagues who will no longer be with us—of course, our friend and colleague, Senator KENNEDY, and Senator Martinez.

Let me, first of all, speak to Senator KENNEDY's departure from this body due to his untimely death.

During his five decades of public service, Senator KENNEDY served with diligence, tireless passion, and, of course, vigor—the word that immediately evokes the Kennedy spirit.

Because of who he was, he could have gotten by without a lot of hard work. But that was not his way. He believed deeply, so he worked hard—as hard as any Senator I have known.

One thing that has been commented on by many who worked with Senator KENNEDY was his willingness to compromise. I have characterized Senator KENNEDY as a legislator's legislator, often a results-oriented pragmatist, who knew that clashes between the two parties are inevitable and, in fact, an integral part of our political system, and that it was important to reach across the aisle if you wanted to get things done. He believed that people with dramatically different points of view could usually find some common ground.

While Senator KENNEDY and I did not share a perspective on very many issues, and he was always ready to make an ideological or political point, my colleagues and I appreciated his efforts to actually legislate as well. His dedication, his hard work, humor, and high spirit will always be remembered. My wife Caryll and I extend our thoughts and prayers to his family.

Mr. WHITEHOUSE. ... In closing, let me just say this is the first time I have spoken on the Senate floor since our colleague, Senator KENNEDY, has left us. His desk is three down from me. I don't know if the camera shows it now, but there is a black drape over it and some flowers and a copy of Robert Frost's "The Road Less Traveled." I know this poem meant a lot to him, and he certainly meant a lot to me as a very gracious mentor with vast experience who could easily have ignored a new colleague. But he took an interest, and I will never forget his kindness to me.

We all will miss his booming voice. He could fill this Chamber with his voice. We will miss his rollicking good humor. No one enjoyed life and enjoyed his colleagues more than the senior Senator from Massachusetts. We will miss his masterful legislative skills as we try to work our way through the obstructions the other side will be throwing up against progress on health care reform. His wise voice and counsel will be missed.

Finally, we will miss his lion's heart. He knew when the fight was right, he knew when it was worth fighting for, and he was in it to win it.

TED, God bless you. We miss you.

I yield the floor.

The PRESIDING OFFICER. The Senator from North Dakota.

Mr. DORGAN. Mr. President, let me follow on the remarks of my colleague from Rhode Island as he discussed briefly at the end of his remarks the loss of our colleague and friend, Senator TED KENNEDY.

The desk that is now cloaked in black and adorned with flowers is a desk that was once occupied by Senator John F. Kennedy, then occupied by Senator Robert Kennedy, and for many years occupied by Senator TED KENNEDY.

He was an extraordinary friend to all of us, a remarkable legislator. This is not a case of the Senate just losing one Senator. He was such a much larger presence than that in the public life of our country and particularly in the workings of this Congress.

My thoughts and prayers have been with TED KENNEDY and his family over these many months as he has battled brain cancer. Now, since his death, we have all reflected on what he meant to us and to this country.

Today it seems inappropriate to take the floor of the Senate without at least acknowledging the absence of our friend, TED KENNEDY, and to send our prayers to his family.

Mr. President, when Senator KENNEDY would come to the floor with a booming voice, full of passion about an issue, it was an extraordinary thing to watch and to listen to. He had that kind of passion. ...

[5]

Mr. FEINGOLD. Mr. President, today I rise to bid farewell to TED KENNEDY, a man who spent so many hours on this floor. It was here that he engaged in the cause that shaped his life, and now shapes our memories—his commitment to everyday people in their pursuit of the American dream.

It is hard for me, as it is for all my colleagues, to imagine this place without TED KENNEDY. To serve here with him was a great honor. At the age of 14, I was already wearing a TED KENNEDY for President button. Then when I arrived here, this man, this lion of the Senate, was so friendly and funny and generous. He helped to teach me the ropes in the Senate, and I felt so fortunate to know him as a person, not just to admire him from afar.

He and his family are one of the reasons I stand here today. His work in the Senate, his brother John's call for a new generation to serve their country, and his brother Bobby's call for social justice—all these inspired me to run for office to in some way serve my country as Senator KENNEDY and his family had. One of the greatest honors of my life was winning the Profiles in Courage Award with Senator McCain, and being recognized by members of the Kennedy family for our work on campaign finance reform.

Having Senator KENNEDY there that day was part of what made that such an honor. There was no one else like him; he was truly one of a kind. Who else could be such a fierce advocate, and at the same time such a skilled negotiator? Who else could engage in such heated debate, but still count so many of us, on both sides of the aisle, as devoted friends? No one but TED KENNEDY could do that.

His qualities were legendary—he was the hardest worker, he was the quickest debater, and he was the guy who lit up a room with his warmth and wit. It was all there in one extraordinary man, who became one of the greatest U.S. Senators in our Nation's history. Even putting aside TED's legendary personal qualities, his legislative record speaks volumes about how effective he was. It is a record for the ages, with hundreds of his legislative efforts becoming law.

His achievements in civil rights, education, health care, and workers' rights speak to the absolute commitment he had to the people he saw who struggled to live the American dream; the dedicated people who are the lifeblood of this country, but who struggle—especially in times like these—when they lose their job, or their health insurance, or their home. In TED KENNEDY, those Americans found their champion, and we thank him for everything he achieved on their behalf.

I admired so many things TED KENNEDY did, but most of all I was inspired by his work on civil rights. His commitment, through his 47 years in the Senate, to the cause of equality for every American, was perhaps his greatest achievement of all. In his very first speech on the Senate floor, just 4 months after his brother John's assassination, he called for the passage of the Civil Rights Act of 1964. He played a key role in the Voting Rights Act of 1965, was the chief sponsor of the Voting Rights Amendments Act of 1982, and just a few years ago was a key co-sponsor of the Fannie Lou Hamer, Rosa Parks, and Coretta Scott King Voting Rights Act Reauthorization and Amendments Act of 2006. He was one of the chief co-sponsors of the Americans with Disabilities Act of 1990, the chief sponsor of the Civil Rights Restoration Act of 1988, and a key proponent of the Civil Rights Act of 1991. And the list goes on, Mr. President. There simply is no doubt that he was the most important legislative architect of the expansion of civil rights in the last half century. I am committed to helping to continue that work here in the Senate in his memory.

TED was also someone who suffered many personal tragedies, but he bore those burdens with a quiet dignity that came from his tremendous inner strength. You couldn't know him without being awed by that strength, and sensing it whenever he entered the room, or when he took up an issue. When he spoke, his words echoed not just in this Chamber, but across the country and around the world. This was a man who could change the momentum on a bill or an issue just through his own personal will. He was a powerful person determined to help the powerless in our society, and we loved him for it.

I think "beloved" is the best word to describe how we felt about him here in the Senate, and how so many Americans felt about him around the country. We are grateful that he lived to achieve so much, and to inspire so many.

And now we wish, as he did when he laid his brother Robert Kennedy to rest, that "what he wished for others will someday come to pass for all the world." And now we pledge, as he did at the Democratic Convention in 1980, that "the work goes on, the cause endures, the hope still lives and the dream shall never die." And now, as we grieve his loss, we say goodbye to our friend, Senator EDWARD M. KENNEDY. We thank him for his lifetime of service to our country, and for

[7]

his profound commitment to the cause of justice here in the United States and throughout the world.

SENATE RESOLUTION 255—RELATIVE TO THE DEATH OF EDWARD MOORE KENNEDY, A SENATOR FROM THE COMMONWEALTH OF MASSACHUSETTS

Mr. REID (for himself, Mr. McConnell, Mr. Kerry, Mr. Dodd, Mr. Akaka, Mr. Alexander, Mr. Barrasso, Mr. Baucus, Mr. Bayh, Mr. Begich, Mr. Bennet, Mr. Bennett, Mr. Bingaman, Mr. Bond, Mrs. Boxer, Mr. Brown, Mr. Brownback, Mr. Bunning, Mr. Burr, Mr. Burris, Mr. Byrd, Ms. Cantwell, Mr. Cardin, Mr. Carper, Mr. Casey, Mr. Chambliss, Mr. Coburn, Mr. Cochran, Ms. Collins, Mr. Conrad, Mr. Corker, Mr. Cornyn, Mr. Crapo, Mr. DeMint, Mr. Dorgan, Mr. Durbin, Mr. Ensign, Mr. Enzi, Mr. Feingold, Mrs. Feinstein, Mr. Franken, Mrs. Gillibrand, Mr. Graham, Mr. Grassley, Mr. Gregg, Mrs. Hagan, Mr. Harkin, Mr. Hatch, Mrs. Hutchison, Mr. Inhofe, Mr. Inouye, Mr. Isakson, Mr. Johanns, Mr. Johnson, Mr. Kaufman, Ms. Klobuchar, Mr. Kohl, Mr. Kyl, Ms. Landrieu, Mr. Lautenberg, Mr. Leahy, Mr. Levin, Mr. Lieberman, Mrs. Lincoln, Mr. Lugar, Mr. Martinez, Mr. McCain, Mrs. McCaskill, Mr. Menendez, Mr. Merkley, Ms. Mikulski, Ms. Murkowski, Mrs. Murray, Mr. Nelson of Nebraska, Mr. Nelson of Florida, Mr. Pryor, Mr. Reed, Mr. Risch, Mr. Roberts, Mr. Rockefeller, Mr. Sanders, Mr. Schumer, Mr. Sessions, Mrs. Shaheen, Mr. Shelby, Ms. Snowe, Mr. Specter, Ms. Stabenow, Mr. Tester, Mr. Thune, Mr. Udall of Colorado, Mr. Udall of New Mexico, Mr. Vitter, Mr. Voinovich, Mr. Warner, Mr. Webb, Mr. Whitehouse, Mr. Wicker, and Mr. Wyden) submitted the following resolution; which was considered and agreed to:

S. RES. 255

Whereas the Honorable EDWARD MOORE KENNEDY was elected to the Senate in 1962 and served the people of Massachusetts in the United States Senate with devotion and distinction for nearly 47 years, the third longest term of service in Senate history;

Whereas the Honorable EDWARD MOORE KENNEDY became the youngest Majority Whip in Senate history at the age of 36;

Whereas the Honorable EDWARD MOORE KENNEDY served as Chairman of the Senate Judiciary Committee from 1979–1981 and as Chairman of the Senate Health, Education, Labor and Pensions Committee for nearly 13 years between 1987–2009;

Whereas the Honorable EDWARD MOORE KENNEDY made the needs of working families and the less fortunate among us the work of his life, particularly those of the poor, the disenfranchised, the disabled, the young, the old, the working class, the servicemember and the immigrant;

[8]

Whereas his efforts on behalf of the citizens of Massachusetts and all Americans earned him the esteem and high regard of his colleagues;

Whereas more than 300 laws bear his name and he co-sponsored more than 2000 others covering civil rights, health care, the minimum wage, education, human rights and many other issues; and

Whereas with his death his State and the Nation have lost an outstanding lawmaker and public servant: Now, therefore, be it

Resolved, That the Senate has received with profound sorrow and deep regret the announcement of the passing of the Honorable EDWARD MOORE KENNEDY, the great Senator from the Commonwealth of Massachusetts.

Resolved, That the Secretary of the Senate communicate these resolutions to the House of Representatives and transmit an enrolled copy thereof to the Kennedy family.

Resolved, That when the Senate adjourns today, it stand adjourned as a further mark of respect to the memory of the deceased Senator.

Mr. UDALL of Colorado. Mr. President, I ask unanimous consent that the Senate proceed to the immediate consideration of S. Res. 255, submitted earlier today.

The PRESIDING OFFICER. The clerk will state the resolution by title.

The legislative clerk read as follows:

A resolution (S. Res. 255) relative to the death of the Honorable EDWARD MOORE KENNEDY, a Senator from the Commonwealth of Massachusetts.

There being no objection, the Senate proceeded to consider the resolution.

Mr. UDALL of Colorado. Mr. President, I ask unanimous consent that the resolution be agreed to, the preamble be agreed to, and the motion to reconsider be laid upon the table, and that any statements be printed in the *Record*.

The PRESIDING OFFICER. Without objection, it is so ordered.

The resolution (S. Res. 255) was agreed to.

The preamble was agreed to.

Mr. UDALL of Colorado. If there is no further business to come before the Senate, I ask unanimous consent that it adjourn under the provisions of S. Res. 255 as a further mark of respect for the memory of our late colleague, Senator EDWARD MOORE KENNEDY.

There being no objection, the Senate, at 7:06 p.m., adjourned until Wednesday, September 9, 2009, at 10 a.m.

Mr. DURBIN. Mr. President, we knew it was coming. Yet the sight of Senator EDWARD KENNEDY's desk draped in the black velvet of mourning is painfully sad.

America and the world have lost a great champion of civil rights, human rights, and fairness. As President Obama said so well, Senator KENNEDY was not only historic, he was heroic.

We will have more time later this week to talk about his extraordinary life and the honor those of us who served with him enjoyed during his life. Today, I wish to say what a great honor it was to have worked alongside TED KENNEDY.

On his desk today is a copy of one of his favorite poems, "The Road Less Traveled" by Robert Frost.

There is another Frost poem that is identified with the Kennedys that TED KENNEDY loved as well. It is called "Stopping by Woods on a Snowy Evening." It is the story of a man who pauses to admire the simple serene beauty of a New England woods filling softly with snow and wishes he could stay longer. It reads:

But I have promises to keep,
And miles to go before I sleep,
And miles to go before I sleep.

Unlike his beloved brothers, Senator KENNEDY's life was not one of promise cut short but a life of promises kept. He loved America, and his life's work made us a better and more just Nation.

If TED KENNEDY were here today, I feel absolutely certain that he would be on the floor at this moment talking about health care. It really was the hallmark of his public career. From the beginning, he understood this was one of the most fundamental things when it came to justice and fairness in America. ...

Mr. MARTINEZ. ... We did also strive mightily in this body to seek a solution to immigration reform, something I felt very strongly about. And being the only immigrant in this body, I believed I was dutybound to try to advance that cause. I am proud to say our efforts for immigration reform gave me the opportunity to work very closely with Senator TED KENNEDY, whom we are honoring today, with nearly a half century of service in the Senate.

I can recall reminiscing with him one day near his desk. He came to the Senate in 1962. That was the same year I came here from Cuba. It was also immediately after we had a very serious confrontation involving Cuba—the Cuban missile crisis. I remember discussing with him how his family will be tied to that period of time, to the history of Cuba, and how deeply that had touched my life as well. In addition to the many opportunities to reminisce about things such as that with him, I hold dear the opportunity to have sat at a table and negotiated with him what I thought would have been a very good immigration reform package—a bill that I believed would be good for our country and good for many people in our country.

We didn't always agree. We didn't always have the same point of view. But we always found a way to get along and be very civil about our differences, and I admired greatly his ability to put differences aside and his desire to find consensus. What was most telling about working with Senator KENNEDY is that he was committed to reaching an outcome. He wanted a solution, which then meant—and this might be a lesson for current issues today—that he could put aside the whole banana in order to get what he could. ...

PRESIDENT'S ADDRESS DELIVERED TO A JOINT SESSION OF CONGRESS ON
SEPTEMBER 9, 2009

The PRESIDENT ... That is why we cannot fail. Because there are too many Americans counting on us to succeed—the ones who suffer silently, and the ones who shared their stories with us at townhall meetings, in emails, and in letters.

I received one of those letters a few days ago. It was from our beloved friend and colleague, TED KENNEDY. He had written it back in May, shortly after he was told that his illness was terminal. He asked that it be delivered upon his death.

In it, he spoke about what a happy time his last months were, thanks to the love and support of family and friends, his wife, Vicki, and his children, who are here tonight. And he expressed confidence that this would be the year that health care reform—"that great unfinished business of our society," he called it—would finally pass. He repeated the truth that health care is decisive for our future prosperity, but he also reminded me that "it concerns more than material things." "What we face," he wrote, "is above all a moral issue; at stake are not just the details of policy, but fundamental principles of social justice and the character of our country."

[11]

I've thought about that phrase quite a bit in recent days—the character of our country. One of the unique and wonderful things about America has always been our self-reliance, our rugged individualism, our fierce defense of freedom, and our healthy skepticism of government. And figuring out the appropriate size and role of government has always been a source of rigorous and sometimes angry debate.

For some of TED KENNEDY's critics, his brand of liberalism represented an affront to American liberty. In their mind, his passion for universal health care was nothing more than a passion for big government.

But those of us who know TEDDY and worked with him here—people of both parties—know that what drove him was something more. His friend, Orrin Hatch, knows that. They worked together to provide children with health insurance. His friend John McCain knows that. They worked together on a patient's bill of rights. His friend Chuck Grassley knows that. They worked together to provide health care to children with disabilities.

On issues like these, TED KENNEDY's passion was born not of some rigid ideology, but of his own experience. It was the experience of having two children stricken with cancer. He never forgot the sheer terror and helplessness that any parent feels when a child is badly sick; and he was able to imagine what it must be like for those without insurance; what it would be like to have to say to a wife or a child or an aging parent—there is something that could make you better, but I just can't afford it.

That large-heartedness—that concern and regard for the plight of others—is not a partisan feeling. It is not a Republican or a Democratic feeling. It, too, is part of the American character. Our ability to stand in other people's shoes. A recognition that we are all in this together; that when fortune turns against one of us, others are there to lend a helping hand. A belief that in this country, hard work and responsibility should be rewarded by some measure of security and fair play; and an acknowledgement that sometimes government has to step in to help deliver on that promise. ...

But that's not what the moment calls for. That's not what we came here to do. We did not come to fear the future. We came here to shape it. I still believe we can act even when it's hard. I still believe we can replace acrimony with civility, and gridlock with progress. I still believe we can do great things, and that here and now we will meet history's test.

[12]

Because that is who we are. That is our calling. That is our character. Thank you, God Bless You, and may God Bless the United States of America.

Mr. REID. "A freshmen Senator should be seen, not heard; should learn, and not teach."

Mr. President, that is a quote from Senator TED KENNEDY. These are the very first words he spoke on the floor of this Chamber. He was hesitant to rise and speak that April day when he said those words. He had been a Senator for less than 18 months. The country was still reeling from President KENNEDY's death just months before.

But the question before the Senate was the Civil Rights Act of 1964, and Senator KENNEDY knew he could hold his tongue no longer.

He rose to speak because he loved his country. He waited as long as he did to give that maiden speech because he loved this institution. In that speech, he said a Senator of his stature at the time should be seen and not heard. But 45 years later, we can still hear his great booming voice. He said young Senators should learn and not teach. But who can list all we learned from his leadership?

It was a thrill to work with TED KENNEDY personally. He was a friend, the model of public service, and an American icon. He was a patriarch of both the Kennedy family and the Senate family. Together we mourn his loss.

At so many difficult times in their family's history, the Kennedys have turned to their Uncle TEDDY for comfort. At so many critical times in our country's history, America has turned to TED KENNEDY for the same.

We can all remember how he walked solemnly with the grieving First Lady at Arlington National Cemetery. We can remember how his deep love for his brother helped him somehow summon the strength to deliver a defining eulogy in New York. We can all remember how, as patriarch, he memorialized his nephew off the shores of Massachusetts.

For decades, TED KENNEDY was a rock to his family. The impact he has etched into our history will long endure. It is now left to us to remember the man who helped remember the lives of so many others. He was a very famous man. If you take the subway, people would always come up to Senator KENNEDY. I would joke with him, "TED, are they coming

[13]

for me or for you?" It was obvious whom they were coming for. It was a joke.

TED was so good. When he thought you did something well, he would drop you a note or give you a call. It meant a lot to me that he would take the time to do that. I have come to learn since his death that he did that for so many people. You didn't have to be a Senator. He would do that for anybody whom he thought deserved a pat on the back. It is up to us to celebrate a Senator who helped so many live better lives.

I have long been a devotee of the Kennedys and an admirer of their service to our Nation. As a student at Utah State University, I founded the first Young Democrats Club—in that bastion of Republicanism. I worked for President KENNEDY's election in 1960.

A week before President Kennedy took the oath of office and implored us to ask what we can do for our country, John Kennedy sent me a personal letter of thanks. He had won the election, but he had not yet been inaugurated.

That letter still hangs at the doorway of my Capitol office, just a few feet off the Senate floor, where the three youngest Kennedy brothers ably served. That letter he sent me was for the work I did out West for that campaign.

Many times, TED would come to my office, and he would stop and look at that letter. He would always say, "That's his signature," indicating that some staff hadn't signed it or some machine hadn't signed it. He was proud that his brother had done what he learned from his brother to do—send these very meaningful letters. He was proud of his brother. He was proud of his own work in the Western States during the 1960 race and proud that I kept that memento in such a prominent place.

President-elect KENNEDY's letter was short, but it overflowed with optimism. He wrote to me that the incoming era would allow us to "make our country an even better place for our citizens to live, as well as to strengthen our country's position of leadership in the world." Think how I felt getting that letter. I was still a student.

TED KENNEDY shared the dream his brother had, and he never stopped working to realize it.

TED KENNEDY's legacy stands with the greatest, the most devoted, the most patriotic men and women to ever serve in these Halls. Because of TED KENNEDY, more young children could afford to become healthy. Because of TED KENNEDY, more young adults could afford to become college students.

Because of TED KENNEDY, more of our oldest and poorest citizens could get the care they need to live longer, fuller lives. Because of TED KENNEDY, more minorities, women, and immigrants could realize the rights our founding documents promised them. Because of him, more Americans could be proud of their country.

TED KENNEDY came from a family of great wealth and status. He didn't need to work hard for himself. So he chose a life of working hard for others. When he was admitted to the Massachusetts bar in 1959, the application asked him to state his main ambition. TED KENNEDY answered: "The public service of this State."

To quote one of his favorite poems—the Robert Frost verses that now rest on his desk on the Senate floor—"that has made all the difference."

TED KENNEDY's America was one in which all could pursue justice, enjoy equality, and know freedom. That is TED KENNEDY.

TED's life was driven by his love of a family who loved him and his belief in a country that believed in him. TED's dream was the one for which the Founding Fathers fought and which his brothers sought to realize.

The liberal lion's mighty roar may now fall silent, but his dream shall never die. One of his older brothers was killed in World War II. He was a pilot going into a mission, and he recognized going into it he would probably never come back. His other brother—the President—was assassinated. His other brother, as a Senator running for President, was assassinated.

Again, Senator KENNEDY's dream shall never die.

The ACTING PRESIDENT pro tempore. The Republican leader is recognized.

Mr. McCONNELL. Mr. President, I, too, would like to speak of our departed colleague, TED KENNEDY, whose passing last month focused the attention of the Nation and whose extraordinary life has been memorialized over these past weeks in so many poignant stories and heartfelt expressions of gratitude and grief.

Today, the Senate also grieves—not only because he was a friend but because the Senate was so much a part of who he was and because he became so much a part of the Senate.

The simplest measure is sheer longevity. At the time of his death, TED could call himself the third longest serving Senator in history, having served almost one-fifth of the time the

Senate itself has existed. Or consider this: When I was an intern here in the sixties, TED was already a well-known Senator. When I was elected to the Senate nearly a quarter of a century ago, TED had already been here for nearly a quarter of a century. He served with 10 Presidents or nearly 1 out of every 4 of them.

No one could have predicted that kind of run for TED on the day he became a Senator back on November 7, 1962— no one, that is, except maybe TED. TED had signaled what his legacy might be as far back as 1965, when he spoke of setting a record for longevity. Mike Mansfield saw a glimpse of it, too, a few years later. When somebody mentioned TED as a possible Presidential candidate, Mansfield responded:

He's in no hurry. He's young. He likes the Senate. Of all the Kennedys, he is the only one who was and is a real Senate man.

As it turned out, Mansfield was right. But TED knew even then that his legacy as a lawmaker would not come about just by sitting at his desk; he would have to build it. And over the course of the next 47 years, that is exactly what he did, slowly, patiently, doggedly, making his mark as much in tedious committee hearings as on the stump, as much in the details of legislation as in its broader themes.

TED's last name ensured he was already one of the stars of American politics even before he became a Senator. To this day, he is still the only man or woman in U.S. history to be elected to the Senate while one of his relatives sat in the White House. But to those who thought TED, even if elected, would avoid the rigors of public life, he became a living rebuke. In short, he became a Senator.

He surprised the skeptics, first of all, with his friendliness and his wit. When he made his national political debut in 1962 on "Meet the Press," a questioner asked him if maybe there were already too many Kennedys. His response: "You should have talked to my mother and father ..."

Russell Long was an early admirer. In what has to go down as one of the falsest first impressions in modern politics, Long spoke approvingly of the new Senator from Massachusetts as "a quiet ... sort of fellow."

TED got along with everybody. The earliest memories family members have are of TED laughing and making other people laugh. His secret weapon then, and years later, as Chris Dodd rightly pointed out at one of the memorial services, was simply this: People liked him, so much so that he could call people such as Jim Eastland, somebody with whom he had absolutely nothing in common, a friend.

TED had learned early on that he could be more effective through alliances and relationships than by hollering and carrying on. We all know he did a fair amount of that as well. He provided some of the best theater the Senate has ever known. But once he left the Chamber, he turned that off. He sought out allies wherever he could find them—Strom Thurmond, Dan Quayle, Orrin Hatch, John McCain, and even George W. Bush—and he earned their cooperation by keeping his word and through thousands of small acts of kindness. Senator McCain has recounted the birthday bash TED threw 10 years ago for his son Jimmy's 11th birthday. Senator Barrasso remembers the kindness TED showed him as a new Senator. And Senator Barrasso's family will long remember how much time Senator KENNEDY spent sharing stories with them at the reception after the swearing in and that he was one of the last ones to leave.

Like so many others, I have known TED's graciousness first hand. Anyone who watches C–SPAN2 could see TED railing at the top of his lungs against my position on this policy or that policy. What they didn't see was the magnificent show he put on a few years ago in Kentucky at my invitation for students at the University of Louisville or the framed photo he gave me that day of my political role model, John Sherman Cooper. I interned for Cooper as a young man. TED knew that, and he knew Cooper was a good friend and neighbor of his brother Jack's.

TED's gregariousness was legendary, but his passion and intensity as a lawmaker would also reach near-mythic proportions in his own lifetime. Even those of us who saw the same problems but different solutions on issue after issue, even we could not help but admire the focus and the fight TED brought to every debate in which he played a part. Over the years, we came to see what he was doing in the Senate.

When it came to TED's future, everyone was always looking at it through the prism of the Presidency. They should have focused on this Chamber instead. It was here that he slowly built the kind of influence and voice for a national constituency that was common for Senators in the 19th century but extremely rare in the 20th.

He became a fiery spokesman for liberals everywhere. TED and I would have had a hard time agreeing on the color of the carpet when we were in the Chamber together. Yet despite his public image as a liberal firebrand, he was fascinated by the hard work of creating consensus and jumped into that work, even toward the end, with the enthusiasm of a young staffer. TED's high school teammates recall that he never walked to the huddle; he always ran. Anyone who ever sat across from TED at a conference table believed it.

TED realized Senators could do an awful lot once they got past the magnetic pull Pennsylvania Avenue has on so many Senators. His brother Jack once said that as a Senator, he thought the President had all the influence, but it wasn't until he was President that he realized how much influence Senators had. It was a similar insight that led TED to tell a group of *Boston Globe* reporters in 1981 that for him, the Senate was fulfilling, satisfying, challenging, and that he could certainly spend his life here, which, of course, he did. Then, when it was winding down, he saw what he had done as a Senator and what the Senate had done for him. He wanted others to see it too, so he set about to establish the Edward M. Kennedy Institute for the United States Senate, a place that would focus on this institution the way Presidential libraries focus on Presidents.

The Founders, of course, envisioned the legislative and executive branches as carrying equal weight. Article I is about Congress, after all, not the Presidency. His life and legacy help restore that vision of a legislative counterweight of equal weight. That is an important institutional contribution every Senator can appreciate. It is something he did through hard work, tenacity, and sheer will. It was not the legacy most expected, but it is the legacy he wrought, and in the end he could call it his own.

Toward the end of his life, one of the great lawmakers of the 19th century, Henry Clay, was asked to speak to the Kentucky General Assembly. Thanks to Clay's efforts, the Compromise of 1850 had just been reached, and Clay had become a national hero through a job he had spent most of his career trying to escape. His speech received national coverage, and, according to one biographer, all acknowledged his privileged station as an elder statesman.

For years, Clay had wanted nothing more than to be President of the United States. But now, after this last great legislative victory, something else came into view. Clay told the assembled crowd that day that in the course of months and months of intense negotiations leading up to the Great Compromise, he had consulted with Democrats just as much as he had with Members of his own party and found in them just as much patriotism and honor as he had found with the Whigs. The whole experience had moved Clay away from party rivalry, he said, and toward a new goal. "I want no office, no station in the gift of man," he said, "[except] a warm place in your hearts."

Every man has his own story. TED KENNEDY never moved away from party rivalry. He was a fierce partisan to the end. But over the years, he reminded the world of the great potential of this institution and even came to embody it. We will never forget the way he filled the Chamber with that booming voice, waving his glasses at his side, jabbing his fingers at the air, or the many times we saw him playing outside with his dogs. How many times did we spot him coming through the doorway or onto an elevator, his hair white as the surf, and think: Here comes history itself.

As the youngest child in one of the most influential political families in U.S. history, TED KENNEDY had enormous shoes to fill. Yet in nearly 50 years of service as a young Senator, a candidate for President, a legislative force, and an elder statesman, it is hard to argue that he didn't fill those shoes in a part he wrote all by himself.

It is hard to imagine the Senate without TED thundering on the floor. It will be harder still, I am sure, for the Kennedy family to think of a future without him. You could say all these things and more about the late Senator from Massachusetts, and you could also say this: EDWARD MOORE KENNEDY will always have a warm place in our hearts.

Mr. President, I yield the floor.

Mr. KERRY. Mr. President, I thank Majority Leader Reid and Minority Leader McConnell for the time they have set aside for us today to remember TED KENNEDY, our beloved colleague, my senior Senator for nearly a quarter of a century, a friend, a man I met first and who had great influence on me in politics back in 1962 when, as a young, about-to-be college student, I had the privilege of working as a volunteer in his first campaign for the Senate.

It is difficult to look at his desk now cloaked in the velvet and the roses, a desk from which he championed so many important causes, a desk from which he regaled us, educated us, and befriended us for so many years, and even more difficult for us to think of this Chamber, our Nation's Capital, or our country without him.

On many occasions in the Senate, he was the indispensable man. On every occasion in this Chamber and out, he was a man whose heart was as big as heaven, whose optimism could overwhelm any doubter, and whose joy for life was a wonderfully contagious and completely irresistible thing.

TED loved poetry, and though the verse was ancient, the poet could have had TED in mind when he wrote: "One must wait until the evening to see how splendid the day has been."

Our day with TED KENNEDY was, indeed, splendid, its impact immeasurable. Just think for a moment what a different country we lived in before TED KENNEDY came to the Senate in 1962 and what a more perfect Union we live in for the 47 years he served here. Before TED KENNEDY had a voice in the Senate and a vote in the Senate, there was no Civil Rights Act, no Voting Rights Act, no Medicare, no Medicaid, no vote for 18 year olds, no Martin Luther King, Jr. holiday, no Meals on Wheels, no equal funding for women's collegiate sports, no State Health Insurance Program, no Family Medical Leave Act, no AmeriCorps, no National Service Act. All of these are literally just a part of TED's legislative legacy. It is why the *Boston Globe* once wrote that in actual measurable impact on the lives of tens of millions of working families, the elderly, and the needy, TED belongs in the same sentence with Franklin Roosevelt.

TED's season of service spanned the administrations, as we heard from the minority leader, of 10 Presidents. He served with more than 350 Senators, including those for whom our principal office buildings are named: Richard Russell, Everett Dirksen, and Philip Hart. He cast more than 16,000 votes. He wrote more than 2,500 bills. He had an important hand in shaping almost every single important law that affects our lives today. He helped create nearly every major social program in the last 40 years. He was the Senate's seminal voice for civil rights, women's rights, human rights, and the rights of workers. He stood against judges who would turn back the clock on constitutional freedoms. He pointed America away from war, first in Vietnam and last in Iraq. And for three decades, including the last days, he labored with all his might to make health care a right for all Americans.

Through it all, even as he battled, he showed us how to be a good colleague, always loyal, always caring, always lively. His adversaries were never his enemies. And his friends always came first.

In my office there is a photograph of the two of us on day one—1985—my first day in the Senate. TED signed it: "As Humphrey Bogart would have said: 'This is the beginning of a beautiful friendship.'" For almost 25 years it was a beautiful friendship, as I worked at his side learning from the best. And, yes, like any colleague in the Senate, there were moments when we had a difference on one issue or another, but we always found a way to move forward in friendship and in our efforts to represent the State.

TEDDY was the best natural teacher anyone in politics could ask for. I may not always have been the best student, but he never stopped dispensing the lessons. I came to the Senate out of an activist grassroots political base, where the coin of the realm was issues and policy positions. Activists are sometimes, as I learned, so issue focused and intent that they can inadvertently look past the personal touch or the emotional connection for fear that it somehow distracts from the agenda. But TEDDY, through his actions, showed us how essential all of those other elements of political life are.

Yes, Tip O'Neill taught a generation of Massachusetts politicians that all politics is local. It was TEDDY who went beyond that and taught us that all politics is personal. All of us knew the kindness of TED KENNEDY at one time or another, Mr. President.

During my first term in the Senate, I came down with pneumonia. I was then single and tired and TED deemed me not to be getting the care I ought to get. So the next thing I knew, he literally instructed me to depart for Florida to stay in the Kennedy home in Palm Beach and be cared for until I got well. Indeed, I did exactly that.

He also showed up at my house the evening of Inauguration Day 2005, and together with Chris Dodd, we shared laughter and stories from the campaign trail. We were loud enough and had enough fun that someone might have wondered if we were somehow mistaken and thought we had won. He understood the moment. He knew the best tonic was laughter and friendship. Many times that is all he needed to do, just be there. You couldn't help but feel better with him around.

All of us who served with him were privileged to share TED's incredible love of life and laughter. In the Cloakroom, sometimes the roars of laughter were so great they could be heard out on the Senate floor. Once I remember TED was holding forth—I will not share the topic—and the Presiding Officer pounded the gavel and demanded, "There will be order in the Senate and in the Cloakroom." It was the first time I ever heard that call for order.

His pranks were also works of art and usually brilliantly calculated. One night after a long series of Thursday night votes that had pushed Senators past the time to catch commercial flights home to the Northeast, Senator Frank Lautenberg had arranged for a private charter for himself in order to get up to Massachusetts. It turned out a number of Senators needed to travel in that direction, and when Frank learned of it, he kindly offered Senator Claiborne Pell, TED, and myself a ride with him. There was no discussion of sharing the cost. Everyone thought Frank was being very generous.

But the next week, when we were reassembled on the floor of the Senate, official-looking envelopes were delivered to each of us under Frank Lautenberg's signature with exorbitant expenses charged for this flight. Senator Pell roared down the aisle, came up to me sputtering about this minor little aircraft and how could it possibly cost so much money. Senator Lautenberg was red-faced, protesting he knew nothing about it, when out of the corner of my eye I spotted TED KENNEDY up there by his desk with this big Cheshire cat grin starting to split a gut, so pleased with himself. The mystery was solved. TED had managed to secure a few sheets of Lautenberg stationery, and he sent false bills to each of us.

He once told me his earliest recollections were of pillow fights with his brother Jack and, in the years following, sailing with Jack. At the end of the day TED's job was the long and tedious task of folding and packing the sails away. In politics and in the great progressive battles that were his life's work, TED never packed his sails away. Were he here today, he would exhort us to sail into the wind, as he did so many times. There is still so much to do, so much that he wanted to do, and so much that he would want us to do now, not in his name but in his spirit.

When TED was 12 years old, he spent hours with his brother Jack taking turns reading the epic Civil War poem "John Brown's Body," by Stephen Vincent Benet. It is book length and filled with great and terrible scenes of battle and heartbreaking vignettes of loss and privation and home. It surprises me to read it now and find so much in it that in fact reminds me of TED. Benet wrote:

> Sometimes there comes a crack in time itself. Sometimes the Earth is torn by something blind. Sometimes an image that has stood so long it seems implanted on the polar star is moved against an unfathomed force that suddenly will not have it anymore. Call it the mores, call it God or Fate, call it Mansoul or economic law, that force exists and moves. And when it moves it will employ a hard and actual stone to batter into bits an actual wall and change the actual scheme of things.

TED KENNEDY was such a stone who actually changed the scheme of things on so many issues for so many people. Over the years, I have received hundreds of handwritten notes from TED—some funny, some touching, all of them treasures.

Just before Thanksgiving TED sent me a note that he would be spending the holiday with his beloved sailboat, the *Mya*. He added: "If you are out on the sound, look for the *Mya*. She will be there." Indeed, I will never sail the sound again without thinking of the *Mya* and her big hard skipper.

There is an anonymous quote that I once read, which because of TED's faith—which was grounded and deeply important to him—I think describes how we should think of his departure from the Senate. It says:

I am standing upon the seashore. A ship at my side spreads her white sails to the morning breeze and starts for the blue ocean. She is an object of beauty and strength. I stand and watch her until at length she hangs like a speck of white cloud just where the sea and sky come down to mingle with each other. Then, someone at my side says; "There, she is gone!" "Gone where?" Gone from my sight. That is all. She is just as large in mast and hull and spar as she was when she left my side and she is just as able to bear her load of living freight to her destined port. Her diminished size is in me, not in her. And just at the moment when someone at my side says, "There, she is gone!" There are other eyes watching her coming, and other voices ready to take up the glad shout; "Here she comes!" And that is dying.

That is the way TED KENNEDY will live in the Senate—his spirit, his words, and the fight that still comes.

Mr. President, I yield the floor.

The ACTING PRESIDENT pro tempore. The Senator from New Mexico.

Mr. BINGAMAN. Mr. President, first, let me thank my colleague from Massachusetts for his eloquent statement which I have had the privilege to hear. Let me make a short statement myself about my friend and colleague, TED KENNEDY.

I came to the Senate in January 1983, and my first real opportunity to work with TED came in the Armed Services Committee at the beginning of that service. Although he had already been in the Senate for 20 years, he had chosen that year to go on the Armed Services Committee. Since we were both going on that year, in 1983, we were considered the two freshmen committee members. TED and I were able to work together on the Armed Services Committee for many years.

He has been described as a visionary leader, a great orator, the keeper of the faith for the liberal wing of the Democratic Party. All of those descriptions, of course, are true. But the TED KENNEDY I came to know and with whom I had the great opportunity to work was a passionate, committed advo-

[23]

cate and was the workhorse of the Senate. Frankly, TED KENNEDY set a very high standard for himself in the effort that he made on each and every issue that came up for debate. He set a high standard for the homework he did in preparation for that debate. All of us who served with him found ourselves trying to meet a similar standard. The result was that he raised the level of performance for those of us who served with him by the example he set.

In addition to serving with TED KENNEDY on the Armed Services Committee for many years, in May 1990, following the death of Senator Matsunaga, I had the good fortune to be assigned to what was then called the Labor and Human Resources Committee—TED's committee. As chairman, TED gave a whole new meaning to the word "proactive" in that committee. The volume of useful legislation he was able to move forward through the committee was truly impressive. A major key to his success was the way he found to underscore for all members the importance of what the committee was working on. As chairman, he rightly saw it as his job to put together the agenda and the priorities for the committee's work. But before doing that he would sit down with the rest of us over dinner at his house to get our views on what those priorities needed to be. The serious approach he took to the committee's work inspired those of us who served there to elevate the importance of that work in our own minds as well.

During the course of our work in the Senate, each of us gets the opportunity to interact with many colleagues, to form judgments about those colleagues. During my 27 years I have served with many capable and dedicated public servants who deserve recognition and praise. But it is clear to me none of us exceeds TED KENNEDY in our passion or commitment for accomplishing the work we have been sent to do.

Hendrick Hertzberg wrote a short piece in the *New Yorker* last week that captures well the TED KENNEDY with whom I was privileged to know and serve. Mr. Hertzberg wrote:

The second half of his 47-year senatorial career was a wonder of focused, patient, unwavering service to a practical liberalism that emphasized concrete improvements in the lives of the poor, the old, the disabled, children, the uninsured, the undocumented, the medically or educationally disadvantaged.

That phrase—focused, patient, unwavering service—is a good description of the TED KENNEDY I knew as my chairman and my friend, and I will miss him very much.

The ACTING PRESIDENT pro tempore. The Senator from Connecticut.

Mr. DODD. Mr. President, I also want to rise this morning to share some brief thoughts about our colleague from Massachusetts. I want to commend John Kerry and Jeff Bingaman for their comments capturing the good qualities of the Senator from Massachusetts.

This is a hall noted for a robust amount of noise, and it seems quiet today because TEDDY is not here. So we gather to share a few thoughts.

Mr. President, I ask unanimous consent to have printed in the *Record* some remarks I made at the memorial service for Senator KENNEDY at the John F. Kennedy Library.

There being no objection, the material was ordered to be printed in the *Record*, as follows:

[Mr. Dodd's remarks can be found on page 258.]

Mr. DODD. I was very honored to be asked by Mrs. Kennedy and her family to share some thoughts that evening, and I was proud to do so.

I commend my colleague from Rhode Island, Patrick Kennedy, for his comments at his father's funeral, and TEDDY's son Edward Kennedy, as well, who made wonderful comments about their father at that funeral service.

A few short thoughts this morning, and a proposal I wish to make to our colleagues as we recognize the contribution of Senator KENNEDY. When we consider how to pay tribute to our colleagues, we often try to devise monuments to celebrate the work of those who served here and made a significant contribution to our country. It is not an easy task. I have tried to think about what would be an appropriate way to celebrate, in some concrete way, the work of TED KENNEDY. He certainly has been, as our colleagues and others have pointed out over these last couple of weeks, one of the greatest Members to ever serve in this body.

I had the distinction and honor of serving as the chairman of the Rules Committee a few years ago. I was asked to complete some of the ovals in the Reception Room. For those who have not been to Washington, or to the Capitol, there is a room a few feet from where I am speaking here this morning called the Reception Room. It was designed by the great artist, Brumidi, and he intended that work to celebrate the work of the Senate.

In the mid-1950s, John Fitzgerald Kennedy, then a freshman Senator from Massachusetts, was asked by the leadership of this body to form a committee to identify the five most significant Senators who had served up until the 1950s. Then-Senator John Kennedy of Massachusetts went to work, reviewing the contributions of the people who served in this body since the founding of our Republic in 1789. He concluded there were five Members who deserved recognition. The first three were the obvious ones: Clay, Calhoun, and Webster. The last two, Senator LaFollette of Wisconsin and Senator Taft of Ohio, were more controversial, but were accepted as fine contributions to that room that celebrates those who have contributed the most to this body and our country.

I was asked a couple of years ago to help add a couple more names to that honor roll of renowned Members of this body. We concluded that Senator Vandenberg, who made such a contribution to the post-World War II foreign policy of our Nation, along with Senator Wagner of New York, who back in the 1920s, 1930s, and 1940s, was the author of much of the social legislation that we celebrate in this country today, were fine additions to those who had already been recognized in this Reception Room just off the floor of the Senate.

One day it will be appropriate to add our colleague and friend from Massachusetts, who deserves to be in that hall of celebrated heroes, having made a significant contribution to this institution and to the people of our country.

But there are other ways to celebrate him as well. I suspect that Senator KENNEDY, if he had a chance to weigh in on how he would like to be recognized and remembered, might choose other means.

There are very few issues over the last half century on which Senator KENNEDY did not leave his mark, and a good many of the most significant pieces of legislation that passed this Senate in his time not only bear his mark but bear his name as the author. That, in a sense, is a monument, one with a meaning far broader than anything we might inscribe on any wall.

Across America there are people who might have lacked for an advocate had TED KENNEDY not stood up for them, people who can now stand up for themselves with dignity and hope and a chance to make it in America because they had a friend by the name of EDWARD MOORE KENNEDY.

These Americans are also a monument that I think Senator KENNEDY might say is fitting enough—that there are people today doing better, living more secure lives, growing up with a sense of confidence and optimism about their future and the future of our country because of his contribution. That in itself is a great monument.

Perhaps we could consider the flood of tributes that have come from across the aisle as well as across the globe, from those who shared in his crusade for social justice and those who spent their careers opposing him, and those who never enjoyed the privilege of working alongside him. All understood how important Senator KENNEDY was, not only to this Nation but to millions of people around the globe who today lead better lives because he stood up for them even though they were not citizens of our own country.

He understood that the Founders of our Republic, when they talk about inalienable rights, were not limiting those rights in our minds to those who happen to enjoy the privilege of being citizens of our country but knew that they were God-given rights that every human being is endowed with upon birth, regardless of where they live. TED KENNEDY understood that intuitively, deeply, and passionately. That in itself, I suppose, could be a great tribute, knowing there are people whom he never met, never even knew what he looked like, who lead better lives today because of his contribution.

Then perhaps we might consider these tributes offered by our colleagues here and others, the literally thousands who lined up in those long hours to pay tribute to their Senator from Massachusetts at the John F. Kennedy Library, the more than 50,000 people in Massachusetts who had known and respected, elected and reelected and reelected and reelected, over and over again, their Senator. They appreciated him immensely for the work he did for them and their Commonwealth for almost 50 years. In itself that is a great tribute. It would be enough, I think, for many of us, being recognized by the people of your State for having fought on their behalf.

TEDDY's monument can be found in his talented and wonderful family as well. Joe Biden talked about this in the memorial service in the John F. Kennedy Library. When you consider this remarkable family of Senator KENNEDY and those of his brothers, their children, their nieces and nephews, it is a source of inspiration when you think of what each of them has done, the contributions they have made.

A few short weeks prior to TEDDY's passing, he lost his sister Eunice, who was a wonderful friend of mine over many years. She did remarkable things as an individual. To think, millions of people who suffer from mental disabilities enjoy a greater respect today because of one individual, Eunice Kennedy Shriver. TEDDY's brother Joe lost his life in World War II, defending our country and fighting for freedom. His sister Jean has done a remarkable job with the Very Special Arts in her contribution to the country. And then look at his wonderful wife Vicki, who was such an incredible source of strength and inspiration for him during their life together and particularly over the last 15 months. There is no doubt in my mind TEDDY lived as long as he did with brain cancer because Vicki was at his side and took such nurturing care of him and has done a remarkable job providing all of us the opportunity to celebrate his life as we all wished to do.

His children, grandchildren, nieces, nephews—all are following TEDDY's example by making a difference in this country. His son Patrick I mentioned already, serves in the other body. His son Teddy is a great friend of mine, lives in Connecticut and is making a significant contribution as a citizen of our State. He holds no office, doesn't have any title. He and his wife make a wonderful difference on many issues in our State every single day, and his daughter Kara, for whom he has such great affection, has also made her contributions as well. That in itself can be a monument. How many would say if your children and family do well and stand up and make a difference in the lives of other people, what better tribute, what higher form of compliment, could you have, or form of flattery, than to know that your children, your family, your nieces or nephews, your sisters and brothers, are out making a difference in the lives of others?

In a way, it is hard to decide what is an appropriate way to celebrate the life of someone who filled the room on so many occasions, not only with his booming voice—as we all are familiar with here, particularly the staff of the Senate who would, many times, be the only ones in this room as TED KENNEDY would be pounding that podium back in that corner, expressing his passionate views about some great cause of the country. But we remember also his determination that this country live up to its expectations, that it become the more perfect union that our Founders described more than two centuries ago.

Today, I wish to make a suggestion to my colleagues. I talked to the leadership about it and to the Republican leadership as well. Never before in the history of this country have three brothers served in this Chamber: Jack Kennedy, Robert Kennedy, and, of course, TEDDY KENNEDY. That has never happened before in the history of our Nation. One of the rooms that has been of similarly historic significance to our Nation is the Caucus Room in the Russell Office Building. It has been the site of remarkable hearings and meetings. Since its building almost a century ago, that room has been very important. The hearings on the *Titanic* were held in that room; the Watergate hearings, going back years ago, were held in that room. It is there that we have commemorated tragedies. We have met to celebrate triumphs in that room. We have gathered as Members with our spouses from time to time to share some quiet moments with each other as we reflected on our responsibilities here as Senators. We have held some of the greatest debates that have ever occurred in that room. It is there that Senator KENNEDY's Health Committee, in which I was privileged to act as sort of a fill-in for him over the last number of months, held 5 weeks of hearings and debate and markup of a bill that concluded in the adoption of the health care reform legislation that he authored.

It is in that room that Senator KENNEDY's brothers each announced their candidacies for the Presidency of the United States. Both Jack Kennedy and Robert Kennedy, in that very room, announced that they intended to seek that office. And it is there that I propose we affix the Kennedy name, not just as a monument to the things these three brothers did as Senators and as colleagues of ours here, but in the spirit of compassion and compromise, the fierce advocacy and tender friendship that TEDDY and his brothers brought to this body.

This was TEDDY's wish and desire. I asked him what could we do to recognize him, and he said, "I would like to have you recognize my brothers as well for their contribution."

TED KENNEDY believed in impassioned debate. He believed in pounding that podium when it was appropriate. But he also believed that at the end of the day we best serve the people of our great Nation when we respect each other and work together in common cause to solve the problems of our day. Whatever history is made in the Caucus Room of the Russell Senate Office Building in the next century, I would like to believe it will be guided by that spirit of respect and good humor that TEDDY KENNEDY brought to this institution for almost a half century. Thus, may the Kennedy Caucus Room stand as one monument to the contribution of a family that has made such a difference to our country. They devoted their considerable talents and energy and their lives to serving our Nation that they loved and that loved them back.

I yield the floor.

The ACTING PRESIDENT pro tempore. The Senator from Rhode Island is recognized.

Mr. REED. Mr. President, I rise along with my colleagues to pay tribute to an extraordinary American, probably the greatest Senator to serve in this body. I think time will confirm that as we go forward. I particularly want to express my deepest sympathy to Vicki and Kara and Patrick and Ted, Jr. I have had the privilege now of serving not only with Senator TED KENNEDY but also with Congressman Patrick Kennedy, and both of these gentlemen have demonstrated zeal for public service and commitment and passion to help people that has been emblematic of the Kennedy family.

I particularly am proud of Patrick, and his words at his father's funeral. His continued dedication to the people of Rhode Island is not only commendable but inspiring to me and to all of us.

Like so many of my generation, I grew up with the Kennedy family. In 1960, John Kennedy carried the banner of the Democratic Party as the Presidential candidate. He won, but, as we understood then and now, we got the whole family, not just President John Kennedy, and it was a remarkable family—his brother Robert, the Attorney General and later the U.S. Senator from New York, and then, of course, TED KENNEDY.

His contribution to the country and to the world is probably unmatchable as we go forward in every area: health care, which was his particular passion and on which President Obama spoke so movingly last evening about his commitment to moving forward in this Congress and finally achieving a dream that has eluded our country for years; his work with his son Patrick on mental health parity, which is so important.

On education, I had the privilege of serving with him on the Education Committee and as a Member of the House to collaborate with him on education bills, and every major education initiative in this country bears his stamp, his input, his inspiration. He worked very closely with my predecessor, Senator Claiborne Pell, for the creation of the Pell grants and for so many other initiatives in education. He not only worked with Senator Pell, they developed a very deep and abiding friendship.

[30]

One of the impressive things about TED KENNEDY is that the public persona was impressive, and the private persona was equally impressive and extraordinarily endearing. He was someone who had a great sense of camaraderie and friendship and good humor.

I can recall being invited to join Senator KENNEDY at the Pell's home in Newport after Senator Pell retired. Every year, unannounced, without any fanfare, Senator KENNEDY would sail his boat up into Newport and insist on taking Senator Pell out for a cruise, and then they would all retire to the Pell home for a delightful supper. I was privileged to be there on a couple of occasions.

Toward the end of his life, Senator Pell had difficulty moving around, but Senator KENNEDY would insist on coming every summer. The last outing, we literally had to carry Senator Pell aboard. Senator Pell at that time was not communicating as effectively as he was previously, but he didn't have to because Senator KENNEDY could take both parts of the conversation—in fact, he could take multiple parts of the conversation. There was never a lost word or a dull moment. It was a great opportunity to see an extraordinary statesman and at the same time an extraordinary gentleman.

He said famously about his brothers that they lived to see the American dream become reality, and he said famously that the dream lives on. But he also, more than dreaming, tried to give substance, shape, and texture to that dream effectively, to try to ensure that opportunity was available to every American family, that they could use their talent to build their family and to secure their future and to contribute to a better America. That was why he led on health care, because without adequate health care, you cannot realize your talents, your potential, and you cannot contribute as much to this great country. He led on education, because it is the great engine that pulls this Nation forward and individually gives people an opportunity to move up and to help their families move forward.

On civil rights, he was a strong advocate. In fact, I think it is fair to say that his first major speech was in favor of the 1964 Civil Rights Act because he understood that the talent of America was not restricted to any group and that to meet the challenges of this Nation and this world, we need the contribution and the participation of every American, regardless of race, regardless of gender.

He also was someone who understood that for the working men and women of this country, they needed help, they needed to share in the bounty of this country. What we have seen over the last decade has been growth, up until the crisis of last September, but that growth was not shared fairly or evenly, executives getting huge salaries and bonuses and working men and women were barely keeping up. In order to have a strong, prosperous economy, we need a strong, prosperous middle class. His work in terms of education and health care and labor—all of that had a purpose not only of helping individuals but, wisely, trying to establish an environment for economic growth that we all could share.

He also served on the defense committee with me. And he was very perceptive. He had spent many years viewing the world, and his understanding of not only the military but the forces, economic and cultural, that shape our interaction with other countries was profound in its insights. He was, very clearly, opposed to the operation in Iraq because he understood that it was a strategic deviation from the real task, which continues in Afghanistan, to root out Al Qaeda, to stabilize the region, the most volatile region in the country. That is just one example of his insight into the international arena.

There is a story, and it is attributed to either his brother John or to Senator KENNEDY, but I think it might be apropos for both. It might be slightly apocryphal, but either John or TED, according to the story, was standing outside a factory and a worker came up and said, "They tell me you have never worked a day in your life."

And KENNEDY was taken aback.

Then shortly, the worker said, "Don't worry, you haven't missed anything."

A family of great privilege, of great opportunity, in fact, worked every day of their lives, and particularly TED KENNEDY, hard, relentlessly to ensure that person coming out of the factory had a chance.

Finally, what I sensed when I was at the funeral service—which was extraordinarily moving and inspirational, the outpouring of affection and regard for Senator KENNEDY not only by the dignitaries who assembled but by ordinary citizens of Massachusetts—and here lining the route to Arlington, bespeaks a connection and a validation by the American people of an individual who had trials and tribulations but rose above it in constant service to the country, in constant service to the people who do not have a voice, and constant service to those who need a chance to help themselves, to help their family, and to make the Nation a better place. It reminded me of words spoken about Franklin Delano Roosevelt. His cortege was moving through Washington, DC, and a man was visibly shaken and weeping.

A reporter went up to him and said, "You know, you are so upset, did you know the President?"

He said, "No, I did not know him, but he knew me."

TED KENNEDY knew us all. He knew our strengths, he knew our weaknesses, he knew that this government could make a difference, a positive difference in the lives of people. He had shared the same difficulties and challenges we face: children stricken with cancer, the loss of one of his sisters in an airplane crash, the loss of his brothers, and the human reality.

And because he knew us, he never stopped working for us.

His legacy is extraordinary. It will inspire and sustain us as we go forward. His loss, not just to his family, which is considerable, but for all of us, is balanced by how much he made us better, more attuned to the challenge of serving America and leading the world. We will miss him. But our task now is to take up his work, to continue his effort. That is the greatest tribute we can pay. Let us begin with this debate on health care.

I yield the floor.

The PRESIDING OFFICER (Mrs. Gillibrand.) The Senator from Kansas.

Mr. BROWNBACK. Madam President, I rise to add my voice to those who have already paid tribute to our friend and colleague, the late Senator TED KENNEDY, who passed away this last month after a courageous battle with cancer.

He was quite an institution. I came into this body in a seat held by an individual who was quite an institution as well. Bob Dole was in this seat. So I know that when people look to the person who follows after TED KENNEDY, you just can't replace an individual like that who was such a towering figure in this body, who was the lion of the Senate, as many have noted, and certainly deserved that topic and that accolade.

While Senator KENNEDY and I did not see eye to eye on most political issues, I admired him greatly as a colleague and certainly as a dedicated public servant. TED KENNEDY fought for what he believed and did so with passion and conviction and incomparable ability. When he was your opponent on an issue, you knew you had a fight on your hands, and when he was on your side, you knew you had an advocate who worked hard and effectively.

His skills as a legislator were unmatched. I think what was at the core of that was he really enjoyed working with other people. He had built relationships across the aisle with individuals, so that he could personally go to other individuals with that relationship he had built. Even though there were huge disagreements on policy issues on many other fronts, he had the personal relationships. To him, I think, in many cases, it was a lot more about the person rather than policy. I think that is a good lesson for many of us to learn. He mastered the legislative process, became one of the most effective Members of this body and that this body has ever known. One of the keys of his effectiveness was his tenacity and perseverance in attending to, in many cases, the unglamorous details and the sometimes tedious work that goes into crafting and passing a bill.

He also understood that getting things done as a politician means compromise. He had a great sense of when to fight on principle and when to reach out to the other side and arrive at an agreement in order to advance the cause for which he was fighting. I think you can probably look back over the last decade or 15 years of this body and no major piece of legislation passed without TED KENNEDY's fingerprints somewhere around or on that piece of legislation.

Despite our political differences, I always found him to be professional, courteous, thoughtful, and a caring individual. He was always looking for ways to find common ground and had a wonderful ability to win others over to his side with that charm, Irish wit, fellowship, and gregarious nature. And once he made an agreement, you could depend on him to be true to his word, and to honor in public an agreement he had made in private.

Over the years I had the opportunity to work on several legislative issues with Senator KENNEDY. As many testified, he was the best ally one could ever hope for.

Most recently we worked together to pass the Prenatally and Postnatally Diagnosed Conditions Awareness Act, a pro-life piece of legislation. When I would travel around the country saying that TED KENNEDY and I had introduced a pro-life piece of legislation together, many people would be quite startled. I would explain what this was. It was a piece of legislation that would encourage people, once they had a diagnosis that their child had Down syndrome in utero, not to abort the child but instead to have the child. It put together an adoption registry of individuals who were willing to adopt children with Down syndrome. We have this terrible plague in the country where 90 percent of our children who are diagnosed with Down syndrome never get here; they are aborted.

In our office we went to the disability community. We went to his sister Eunice and talked with her about it. And I went to TED. I remember how effective his sister Eunice would be on lobbying TED on this piece of legislation. Just this past year, when we were able to move things forward with it, I met with Eunice. She was obviously getting more difficult and failing of health at that point. She said, "Is TEDDY being helpful? Is TEDDY working with you and helping?" I would say, "Yes, he is, but you can always help us more and push him more." And she did. What an effective team that was on providing help for those especially with mental disabilities, even on this pro-life piece of legislation that I hope will result in more people getting here who have disabilities so that they are not killed in utero but instead get here and, if people can't handle that issue in their families, that they put them up for adoption. We have adoption registries ready to go for people who want to adopt a child who may have more difficulties. Working together we were able to find common ground on protecting the dignity of these precious Americans by providing parents who receive a pre- or postnatal diagnosis of genetic disability with resources, information, and a network of support.

I am so pleased to know Senator KENNEDY lived to see this bill passed and signed into law. It stands as an example of how we can find common ground to advance the interests of all Americans in spite of differences. This body truly will not be the same place without TED KENNEDY, without his rhetoric and his strong voice, his abilities as a legislator.

My thoughts and prayers go out to him and his family and friends.

I yield the floor.

The PRESIDING OFFICER. The Senator from Michigan.

Mr. LEVIN. Madam President, I join today with colleagues to pay tribute to the life and legacy of Senator TED KENNEDY. Each of us has lost a friend with his passing, and all Americans—but especially those in need—have lost a champion of government's ability to bring light to dark places. All of us stand in awe of the lengthy record of accomplishment Senator KENNEDY leaves us. It was a great privilege to serve many years with TED KENNEDY on the Armed Services Committee and to witness first hand the traits so well known to Members of the Senate: the tireless preparation, the intimate knowledge of the legislative process, the relentless focus on justice and equality.

Today our citizens are safer, our military more capable, our troops better equipped because of his service.

Senator KENNEDY approached his work with diligence and dedication. But he also knew that work goes more smoothly when it is accomplished with friendship and good humor. It was possible to disagree with TED KENNEDY but never to dislike him. His sense of humor was contagious, and his concern for those around him, from fellow Senators to staff, to the many often unheralded people who make the Senate function, ensured that he was loved as well as respected throughout this body. That love extends across lines of party and ideology, in part because of that good humor and genuine concern for others for which he is so rightly known.

But it was not just these qualities that endeared TED KENNEDY to figures of all political persuasions. It was the seriousness and good faith with which he approached ideas that differed from his own. In 1983, this liberal Catholic from Massachusetts traveled to the conservative Liberty Baptist College in Virginia where he told the students:

The more our feelings diverge, the more deeply felt they are, the greater is our obligation to grant the sincerity and essential decency of our fellow citizens on the other side.

TED KENNEDY lived out that sentiment every day. We salute his ability to work across party lines to achieve consensus, to work on a piece of legislation until doubters became enthusiastic supporters. He excelled in transforming nays to yeas. Senator KENNEDY was a master of our own specialized world, and his legislative legacy stands with those of the giants of this Chamber. He tackled what some see as the great game of politics with gusto.

But TED KENNEDY's life's work was not a game. Politics was not a contest staged for its own sake or in pursuit of power or prestige. TED KENNEDY was a master not of the politics of the moment but of the politics of meaning.

TED KENNEDY's task was to touch lives. He touched the family whose children have health insurance because of the Children's Health Insurance Program he helped establish; the child who has a better chance at an education because of his work on the No Child Left Behind law. More Americans can fully participate in our democracy because of the civil rights and voting rights legislation he pushed forward.

We saw TED KENNEDY's passion for justice, tolerance, and understanding again recently when we were working on the Matthew Shepard Local Law Enforcement Hate Crimes Prevention legislation. I quoted him during that debate on that legislation when the defense authorization bill was on the floor, and I quote him again now. He said:

We want to be able to have a value system that is worthy for our brave men and women to defend. They are fighting overseas for our values. One of the values is, we should not, in this country, in this democracy, permit the kind of hatred and bigotry that has stained the history of this Nation over a considerable period of time.

The children of our men and women in uniform have some of the best child care available, thanks to the National Military Child Care Act TED KENNEDY championed in 1989. He was actively involved more recently following the outrages at Walter Reed Army Medical Center when we passed the wounded warrior legislation in 2008.

The lesson of TED KENNEDY's life and career is that politics at its best is not a game to be refereed by TV pundits. It is not a contest of poll numbers or a scorecard of grievances to nurse and favors to return. Senator KENNEDY struck many deals. He brokered many compromises. He won many votes. But the true majesty of his career is not to be found in this Chamber, though his work was done here. His lesson for us is that democracy is best understood in the homes and lives of its citizens. It is in the homes of families less burdened by want. It is in the minds of children freed by education. It is in the relief of parents who no longer fear for a child in need of medical care. It is in the souls of Americans who find inspiration in his triumph over tragedy and over his own shortcomings. It is in the hearts of the colleagues he leaves behind who will be inspired to rededicate ourselves to a politics that recognizes our common humanity and seeks common ground in the pursuit of justice.

My wife Barbara and I will always keep in our hearts Vicki, the love of TED's life, and we will always remember TED's love affair with the American people.

I yield the floor.

The PRESIDING OFFICER. The Democratic whip.

Mr. DURBIN. Madam President, there was a historic moment on Capitol Hill last night. The President of the United States asked for a joint session of Congress to address one of the most important and controversial issues of our time. Emotions were running high in the House Chamber as Members of the House and Senate gathered to hear the President. We know they ran high because there were expressions of support and disapproval during the President's speech. I sat with Harry Reid and other leaders from the Democratic side in the Senate and watched carefully as the speech unfolded. I thought the President was at his best, even under fire, with the high emotions in the Chamber. I wondered what the ending would be and how it would be received.

If Members will recall, at the end of the speech, the President referred to a letter that had been sent to him by the late Senator TED KENNEDY to be read after the Senator had passed away. As the President referred to that letter, an amazing thing happened in that Chamber filled with hundreds and hundreds of people. The emotions quieted down. At one point, one could have heard a pin drop in the House Chamber as President OBAMA recalled the legacy and the promise of the life of Senator EDWARD KENNEDY.

I came today to this seat on the Senate floor. It is not my ordinary desk, but it is the row where I sat for a number of years as a new Member of the Senate. It was a particularly good assignment to sit in this row because behind me was Paul Wellstone and then TED KENNEDY. One never had any better back-benchers than those two men. Now they are both gone.

As I reflect on the absence, particularly of Senator KENNEDY, I recall for history his first speech on the floor of the Senate. It was April 9, 1964. Here is the amazing fact: This speech took place 16 months after he took his Senate seat. That booming voice and presence, which was so dominant in the Senate for decades, waited patiently for his turn, 16 months after the special election in Massachusetts that gave him the Senate seat once held by his brother John. When he rose to make his first speech on April 9, 1964, he said he planned "to address issues affecting the industry and employment in my home state [of Massachusetts]," a thoughtful decision by someone recently elected, to make sure that your first speech touches issues important to the friends at home. He said he would make that speech one day. But he decided his first speech would be much different.

On that day, with his first speech, conscience and the cause of freedom compelled TED KENNEDY to speak instead in eloquent support of the bill the Senate was then debating. It was a measure President KENNEDY proposed nearly a year earlier. Now, less than 5 months after that terrible day in Dallas, TX, when his brother was assassinated, the youngest Kennedy brother stood at the same desk his brother John had used when he served the Senate, the same desk TED KENNEDY used for the nearly 47 years he served in the Senate. He presented more than a dozen letters he had received from religious leaders all urging Congress to pass the Civil Rights Act and end the evil of segregation in America. That was TED KENNEDY's first speech in the Senate.

He said:

When religious leaders call on us to urge passage of this bill, they are not mixing religion and politics. This is not a political issue. It is a moral issue to be resolved through political means.

He continued:

Religious leaders can preach, they can advise, they can lead movements of social action. But there comes a moment when persuasion must be backed up by law to be effective. In the field of civil rights, that point has been reached.

He concluded by saying:

My brother was the first President of the United States to say publicly that segregation was morally wrong. His heart and soul are in this bill. If his life and death had a meaning, it was that we should not hate but love one another; we should use our powers not to create conditions of oppression that lead to violence, but conditions of freedom that lead to peace. It is in that spirit that I hope the Senate will pass this bill.

That first speech by TED KENNEDY bore so many of the qualities that would define his public career. The moral courage to take on the most urgent moral question of his time no matter how controversial, the determination to pick up his brother's fallen standard, the prodigious amount of work behind the scenes building alliances, and an optimist's unshakable faith that his beloved America would become an even more just and decent Nation.

Listening to Senator KENNEDY's speech that day were some of the giants of the Senate—Hubert Humphrey, a man who more than anyone brought me to public life when he allowed me to serve as an intern in his Senate office. The first to speak was a man whom I would come to know well, Senator Paul Douglas of Illinois. He said:

I have never heard an address of a more truly noble and elevated tone.

He called the young Senator from Massachusetts:

A worthy continuer of the great traditions of the seat which he occupies in the Senate, beginning, I believe, with John Quincy Adams, Daniel Webster and Charles Sumner and through ... to his beloved and lamented brother ...

[39]

Senator WAYNE Morse stood to speak as well, and he made a prediction on the first day TED KENNEDY spoke in this Chamber. He said:

[I]n my judgment, the junior Senator from Massachusetts has already demonstrated that before he leaves the U.S. Senate, he will have made a record in this body that will list him among the great Senators in the history of the Senate.

That prediction was made 45 years ago by Senator Wayne Morse of Oregon.

EDWARD MOORE KENNEDY was one of the greatest Senators not only of our time but of all time. There was no better advocate and no more determined fighter for civil rights and human rights. He was a son of privilege, but he was a man, despite that background, who identified with the poor and the dispossessed and the voiceless in America.

His fingerprints can be found on significant legislation of the last half century: health care, voting rights, women's rights, gay rights, immigration reform, worker safety, fair housing, consumer protection, campaign finance reform, sensible gun laws, national service, minimum wage—the list goes on and on.

He was a protector of the vulnerable—of widows and orphans, the wounded and maimed, the grieving and dispossessed. He was a champion of people with disabilities. He believed we should all be judged by what we can do, not by what we cannot do.

When I was asked by my local media in Illinois, after TED KENNEDY's passing, if there was something about him that I knew that other people did not know, I said there was one thing most people did not know. As a result of an airplane crash early in his Senate career, when his broken body was dragged out of the plane by his Senate colleague, Senator Birch Bayh of Indiana, whose son now serves in this Chamber, TED KENNEDY, with a broken back and ribs, went through a long period of convalescence and a lifetime of problems as a result of that almost fatal accident.

Those of us who were around him every day knew that TED was in pain a lot of the time—physical pain—because of his back problems. If you had a press conference with TED KENNEDY, you brought a little stool that he could perch on because standing caused pain. You watched him as he labored to get out of a chair trying to make sure he could stand and speak. But never a word of complaint—not one. A physical condition that might have created a total disability for some other people did not stop him. In addition to the intellectual part of this man, there was this physical commitment that he would give whatever it took to serve his people in Massachusetts and serve the causes and values which motivated his public life.

He was an advocate for the elderly throughout his career. Little did he realize his passion would eventually affect him personally, as he served long enough to qualify for Social Security and Medicare.

He believed education was the key to the American dream and he worked tirelessly to extend it, helping to create programs from Head Start for preschoolers to the Direct Lending Program for college students.

He helped bring an end to apartheid in South Africa and violence in Northern Ireland.

His office wrote more than 2,500 bills and more than 300 of them became law. In addition, some 550 bills he co-sponsored became law. Nearly every major legislative achievement of his was advanced with a Republican partner.

He was a genius at compromise, principled compromise. As someone said, he was able to maintain a sense of idealism in setting goals and realism in achieving them. He had an optimist's willingness to settle for progress, not perfection.

It was from his bother Jack, he said, that he learned the most important lesson: that you have to take issues seriously, but do not take yourself too seriously. As we all know, he was gracious and generous in sharing credit for success. But he also, because of the suffering in his life through his family and personally, developed this heart of gold, this empathy for other people and their own misfortunes.

If one of his colleagues in the U.S. Senate had something bad come their way, you could almost bet the first call they would receive would be from TED KENNEDY, regardless of which side of the aisle you were on. He would be the first to talk about some misfortune or illness in your family. How he learned this so quickly we never figured out, but the Kennedy network was there gathering that information, making certain he always offered a helping hand and a pat on the shoulder if you needed it.

Health care was such an important part of his public career—decent, affordable health care, as a right but not as a privilege. And he did more than anyone in our Nation's history to advance that noble cause.

He voted to create Medicare and Medicaid, protecting those programs for decades. Community health centers were a Kennedy initiative in 1966. How much good that has done for America is incalculable.

He was the chief architect of the WIC Program, the COBRA law, and the Ryan White Act. Fewer Americans are forced to make the agonizing choice of keeping their job or caring for a loved one who is sick because TED KENNEDY helped pass the Family and Medical Leave Act.

Eleven million children of low-income working parents are able to see a doctor this year—11 million of our young kids in America—because TED KENNEDY helped create the Children's Health Insurance Program.

He was the driving force behind cancer research and speedier approval of drugs. He helped lead the fight to end discrimination by insurance companies against people with mental illness and addiction. His son Patrick has managed to pick up that standard and help, with his father, pass that legislation, a bill which meant so much to Senator Paul Wellstone and so many others, Pete Domenici included.

During the last few months of his life, he expended what little energy he had left to urge us to pass health care, and that is why the President's speech last night struck a chord with so many people. He continued to work hard at his job, even on the phone, during the last days of his life.

His son Patrick said that while his father was hospitalized this last year for treatment in North Carolina and Massachusetts, he would roam the halls of the hospital—you can just see him—asking other cancer patients and their families how they were doing and how they were managing their bills. Some of the answers, they said, broke his heart.

He was ready to come back and vote on health insurance reform if the vote was needed. Even in the closing days of his life, Senator Reid, reaching out to Vicki, knew that TED would be there if his vote made the difference, even if it was the last physical act of his life.

Just as he implored the Senate in his first speech so many years ago to pass the civil rights bill in honor of his brother, the fallen President, we all know that Senator KENNEDY, were he here today, would urge us to finish the cause of his life and make affordable health care for every American a right, not a privilege.

It is our obligation to search in good faith, as he did so often, for the principled compromise that will enable us to finish this urgent moral challenge of our time in the name of TED KENNEDY.

I was fortunate to attend the memorial service in Boston at Our Lady of Perpetual Help—a packed church with hundreds standing in the rain outside, wishing they could attend. Thousands had passed by to see his remains and to pay a tribute to him over the final days. It was a great send-off to a great man.

I was so touched by his family—that extended Kennedy family—starting with Vicki, his best ally in his life, a woman who stood by him through those tough times in the closing months of his life, his children, nephews, nieces, grandchildren. All of them gathered. As they went to take Communion, John McCain leaned over to me and said, "You can see the map of Ireland on all those faces." And you could. It was a great gathering of the Kennedy clan.

I want to express my condolences not only to the family but to the great Kennedy staff, always regarded as the best on Capitol Hill. TED KENNEDY not only did great work, he helped build great people, who continue to serve us in public careers. They have done so much for this Nation. They will continue to do so, inspired by his example.

We are saddened by his passing, but we are determined to carry on. We know if he were here today his voice would be booming on this floor for the extension of unemployment benefits, making sure COBRA deductions are still there for those who have lost work, not forgetting to increase the minimum wage, making sure health care does not forget the tens of millions who are being left behind without health insurance in this country.

We are going to miss that booming voice, but he is going to continue to be an inspiration to all of us.

Last year at the Democratic National Convention in Denver there was a little breakfast for TED. He gave a great speech at the convention, even though there was a question at the last moment as to whether he would be able to physically do it. At that breakfast, Vicki, his wife, came up to me and she handed me this little plastic bracelet, and she said, "I thought you might want to have this. It has written on it one word: 'Tedstrong.'"

Well, I put that bracelet on, and I just took it off for the first time since then at this moment. I will not be wearing this bracelet, but it will be in my Senate desk, and each time I open it, I will remember that great man, TED KENNEDY.

Thank you, Madam President.

The PRESIDING OFFICER. The Senator from Tennessee.

Mr. ALEXANDER. Madam President, the assistant Democratic leader, in his eloquent remarks, mentioned TED KENNEDY's maiden address, which is a tradition we have here in the Senate. We try to wait for an appropriate time before we say much, and then we try to say something we think makes a difference.

I waited an appropriate time and made some remarks on the floor in support of legislation that would help put the teaching of American history and civics back in its rightful place in our schools so our children could grow up learning what it means to be an American. I know the Presiding Officer has a great interest in that subject as well, and she and I have worked on that together. I proposed that we create summer academies for outstanding teachers and students of U.S. history.

TED KENNEDY was on the floor. He was the chairman or ranking member of the committee that handled that at the time. He came over afterward and said, "I will get you some co-sponsors. The next thing I knew, he had 20 Democratic co-sponsors for my little bitty bill that I had introduced. However well I thought of him before that, I thought even better of him after that. I think it is a small example of why he was so effective here in what he cared about.

I remember him talking about taking his family—his extended family—once a year to some important place in America, some place that made a difference. He was especially taken with their trip to Richmond, I believe it was, where they went to the place where Patrick Henry went down on one knee and made his famous address. I guess one reason he was so interested in U.S. history was because he and his family were and are such a consequential part of it, but he made a big difference in what we call the teaching and learning of traditional American history.

On another occasion, he called me up to his hideaway—he had been here long enough to have a great room somewhere; I do not know where it is, but it has a great view of the Capitol—to talk about Gettysburg and what we could do to preserve that.

Then, we were working together, when he died, with Senator Byrd, who has been such a champion through U.S. history, on legislation that would tie the teaching of American history to our national parks, which we are celebrating this year, with Ken Burns' new movie, and with other ways to try to help use those nearly 400 national park sites we have to teach American history.

He and I and David McCullough had breakfast, for example, and talked about David McCullough teaching a group of teachers about John Adams at the John Adams House in Massachusetts, as one example. Then, of course, that turned to what was TED KENNEDY going to do about finding an appropriate place to honor John Adams in Washington, DC. That was another piece of unfinished business TED KENNEDY left that others of us will have to continue to work on. That is why he got along so well here.

When he cast his 15,000th vote, I remember saying the sure-fire way to bring a Republican audience to its feet was to make an impassioned speech against high taxes, against more Federal control, and against TED KENNEDY, and he laughed that great big laugh of his. But it was true. But almost everyone on this side will say there was no one on that side who we would rather work with on a specific piece of legislation because no matter how much we might disagree with him—and we certainly did on many issues—when it got to the point where it was time to decide, Can we do something?, he was ready to do something. His word was good. And his ability to help pass an important piece of legislation was unquestioned. Plus, we liked him. We liked his spirit, and we liked his personality.

My first engagement with Senator KENNEDY was as a very young man when I came here in 1967 as a young aide to then-Senator Howard Baker. Senator Baker, who was the son-in-law of Senator Dirksen, then the Republican leader, teamed up with TED KENNEDY, the younger brother of the former President, and they took on the lions of the Senate, Sam Ervin of North Carolina and Everett Dirksen, and won a battle over one man, one vote. I was the legislative assistant on this side and Jim Flug, the longtime friend and aide of Senator KENNEDY, was the legislative assistant on that side.

I am here today, as we all are, to pay our respects to Senator KENNEDY. Maybe some of us can help with that unfinished business, such as helping to make sure we expand the idea of teaching American history in our national parks to larger numbers of outstanding teachers and to outstanding students of U.S. history; and continuing the effort to do something about the long lines of adults in America who are waiting to learn our common language—English. TED was very interested in that, as I am. But most of all, what I wish to say is what I believe most of us feel: We will miss him.

We will miss his big voice, we will miss his big smile, and we will miss his big presence.

Thank you, Madam President. I yield the floor.

The PRESIDING OFFICER. The Senator from California.

Mrs. BOXER. Madam President, I am deeply honored to pay tribute to TED KENNEDY today and to honor his extraordinary legacy.

I will always think of TED KENNEDY as many think of him—as the lion of the Senate. From that seat, in that seat in the back of this beautiful Senate Chamber, he used his powerful voice to speak out for those whose voices were rarely heard. I also have described TED as the drummer in a large orchestra. TED KENNEDY was a steady drumbeat for justice, for fairness, for compassion, and for progress. On days when the Senate wasn't that interested in listening; on days when maybe the polls were against him; on days when his compassion might not have been in fashion, that drumbeat got louder and louder because TED KENNEDY knew that at the end of the day, the values he stood for would be embraced again.

TED never let us forget why we are here—never. He always reminded us to be courageous. He always reminded us to be strong in fighting for the causes we believe in, not by lecturing us about it but by being brave, being strong, being courageous, taking on the tough issues. He spent 9 long years standing in the back of the Chamber talking about raising the minimum wage and explaining why people needed it—9 long years—but he knew the drumbeat would go on until we passed it. And we did.

TED KENNEDY had genuine and deep friendships in the Senate on both sides of the aisle. His greatest legislative skill was to know every Senator and to know their passions. When I first came to the Senate in the early 1990s, I had spent 10 years in the House and Senator KENNEDY was already an icon, but he knew I was passionate about health issues and, in particular, women's health issues. So even though I was new to the Senate, he came to me when he was managing a bill on the floor to protect the rights of women who were trying to get into reproductive health care clinics. At that time, protesters were blocking the entrances to the health care clinics so the women could not get in and get treated. So Senator KENNEDY wrote a bill that simply said: It is fine to express your views, but you cannot block women or individuals from entering those clinics. It is dangerous, it is wrong, and you are denying women health care. Senator KENNEDY asked me if I would be his lieutenant—that was his word, his "lieutenant"—and help him manage that bill on the floor of the Senate. Well, clearly, I was so pleased. It was such a thrill to watch him work and, as did so many of TED KENNEDY's bills, it passed and it became the law of the land and women can get health care without being intimidated and frightened and harmed.

Later, when he was championing the bill to increase the minimum wage—and he did it year after year after year—he asked me and the other women of the Senate to come to the floor and to organize and speak about the impact raising the minimum wage would have on women and families across the country. He said, "Barbara, you know, 60 percent of the people earning minimum wage are women. A lot of our colleagues think it is teenagers. That is not true. It is women. They are supporting their families. Can you help me with this?" I said, "Senator, I am all over it. I am with you."

The women of the Senate had a special role to come to the floor—unfortunately, for 9 years in a row—until we made the case that it was important that America's families, working so hard, can actually afford to live in this, the greatest country of all.

Although TED had deeply-held views, he worked beautifully with Members across the aisle. We have colleague after colleague coming down to speak about their experiences. He was an expert at finding the thread of common ground. Sometimes it was just a tiny little strand of commonality, but he could weave it into something bigger and bigger and come to an agreement without losing his principles.

TED's legislative work has touched the lives of every American, and I think it is going to take 5, 6, 7, 10 of us to pick up this void he has left. I am so proud that Tom Harkin, who has come to the floor, will be the chairman of the HELP Committee—because Tom shared with TED those deep feelings about us being here not to champion the voices of those who have a strong voice and are heard but for those who don't have a strong voice: the middle class, the workers, the working poor, the families, the children. They don't have a voice here.

TED KENNEDY worked to help get 18 year olds the right to vote. He made it easier for Americans to change jobs and keep their health insurance. He expanded Head Start programs. He wrote the law creating Meals on Wheels. He was a driving force behind the Civil Rights Act of 1964, the Americans with Disabilities Act, and the Family and Medical Leave Act. Many of these Senator Harkin and he partnered up on. He led efforts to reform the Nation's immigration system—never a popular issue, a tough, hard issue. He worked to increase competition in the airline industry. He worked to protect women from violent crime.

Virtually every major health care advance of the last four decades bears his mark—whether it is the CHIP Program, the Ryan White CARE Act, COBRA, the mental health parity bill or increased funding for cancer research. The list goes on and on.

Senator KENNEDY was once asked what his best quality was as a legislator, and he answered with a single word: "Persistence." Persistence. That is a message to all of us on both sides of the aisle. If you believe something in your heart is right, you don't give up. You don't give up because progress takes time. Piece by piece, every year, for almost half a century, he advanced the causes he believed in: expanding access to health care, educating our children, extending civil rights, helping our society's least fortunate.

I will say, if we were in danger of losing our way in the Senate, Senator TED KENNEDY held steady. He stayed true to his ideals. That is why it is fitting that his new biography is entitled "True Compass." In many ways, he was a compass in the Senate.

I wish to thank the people of Massachusetts for sending TED KENNEDY to us for these last nearly 47 years. He loved his State. He fought for you and he fought for all Americans.

I wish to thank his wife Vicki, who gave him so much joy, and the entire Kennedy family for sharing TED KENNEDY with us.

I will miss his warm and engaging presence, his sense of humor, his bellowing laughter, and the way he reached out to all Senators in friendship. No one person will ever be able to fill his shoes. No one. He was one of a kind and irreplaceable. But we know how to honor his legacy. We know how to fill this void and that is by continuing his life's work. I believe the most fitting tribute we can give him is to carry on his fight for a quality education for all our children, affordable health care our families can rely on, and an economy that works for everyone.

TED KENNEDY came from a privileged and renowned family, but he saw so much suffering in his lifetime, so much loss. He saw what happens in your family when two of your three children have cancer. Even though you have every bit of financial stability to give them what they need, he saw how hard it was. And then to have another child with an addiction and the pain of that. So what Senator TED KENNEDY understood is, if it is so hard for me to see my children suffer, what must it be like for someone without the financial resources or someone who had an insurance company walk away from them at the time they needed it the most.

TED KENNEDY could put himself in other people's shoes, and that is what he did every single day. Even when it was hard for him to get up from his chair, he stood and he fought. As he said during his concession speech at the 1980 Democratic National Convention:

For all those whose cares have been our concern, the work goes on, the cause endures, the hope still lives, and the dream shall never die.

I say to TED and to his family, I believe these words are true. The hope still lives and the dream shall never die.

Thank you.

The PRESIDING OFFICER. The Senator from Mississippi.

Mr. COCHRAN. Madam President, it is difficult to imagine or accept the fact that TED KENNEDY is no longer serving in the Senate. He was such a presence here, a big man with a big smile and a bigger heart. He was sympathetic to those in need and willing to do all he could to address their needs. He got results, improving and expanding Federal programs to make available education and nutrition benefits to more Americans than ever before.

I first met the Senator from Massachusetts when he was running in his first campaign for the Senate in 1962. It was a happenstance meeting. I was an instructor at the Naval Officer's Candidate School in Newport, RI, and a friend had invited me up to Hyannis Port during the weekend. I ended up at TED and Joan Kennedy's house. He was there working with his friends from Massachusetts on fundraising activities. We exchanged greetings. He asked, "You are in law school?"

I said, "Yes, I am."

He said, "It is hard as hell, isn't it?"

I said, "It sure is."

Well, that was about all the conversation we had that day and I had no idea, first of all, how his campaign would turn out and certainly the most remote thing in my mind would have been my being a Member of the Senate. But he and his wife Joan were spending the summer in Hyannis Port near the other Kennedy family members, so I was getting to see some of them as well as enjoying the New England weather; the ambiance in the summer was a real treat. But instead of politics, we talked about how hard law school was.

I didn't think I would ever see him again. I had no reason to think I would, much less end up serving in the Senate with him and serving the day he took charge as chairman of the Judiciary Committee from my predecessor in the Senate, James O. Eastland. It was a day that attracted a lot of attention. The hearing room was absolutely full of people. As a matter of fact, the news media was all over the place. It was hard to get near the seats of the committee members.

I remember when Alan Simpson and I were the two most junior Republicans, and as we were trying to get situated there at the end of the row of seats of committee members, one of the cameramen bumped Al's head with his camera, and Al told him he should not do that again because he might have a hard time finding his camera—or some words to that effect.

But what a day of excitement and interest. That is the kind of excitement TED KENNEDY brought not only to the Judiciary Committee and his leadership as a brand-new chairman, but his entire career reflected that kind of exuberance. People responded and reacted to him in a very positive way in the Senate.

We could make a long list of the things he did in terms of legislative accomplishments and political leadership in the Senate. He was a good person. He was a thoughtful person and generous with his house. He invited all the members of the Judiciary Committee to come out for dinner at his house in Washington. What a nice, thoughtful thing to do, and what an exciting evening it turned out to be. Everyone enjoyed it enormously.

TED KENNEDY became a very determined advocate for serious reforms, and he left an impressive record of legislative accomplishments and protecting and enlarging the civil rights of ordinary citizens.

I came to respect Senator KENNEDY and appreciate his friendship over the years we served together in the Senate. His personal qualities, his generosity, and his serious commitment to fairness and assistance for those who needed help from their government will long be remembered and appreciated.

May he rest in peace.

The PRESIDING OFFICER. The Senator from Vermont is recognized.

Mr. LEAHY. Madam President, I thank my dear friend from Mississippi for his kind words. I know they will be appreciated by the Kennedy family.

Madam President, when I heard the Senator from Mississippi, and before him the Senator from Illinois, the Senator from California, the Senator from Massachusetts, and others who have spoken, it brought back so many memories. On August 26, very early in the morning, we heard the news about Senator KENNEDY. Marcelle and I knew that day was coming. We knew the day was coming and that we would lose a close friend of over 35 years, but our farmhouse in Vermont was still filled with grief upon the learning of the news. We walked back and forth on the road in front of the house, looking out over the mountains and finding it hard to put into words how we felt.

We left Vermont to come down and join Vicki, such a dear and wonderful person, and all of Senator KENNEDY's family at the memorial service in Boston, where so many offered touching stories of how they remembered Senator KENNEDY.

Ted Kennedy, Jr., gave an incredibly moving tribute to his father. I told him afterward that was the kind of eulogy Senator KENNEDY would have liked. It was so Irish. Ted Kennedy, Jr., made us all laugh, and he made us all cry, almost in the same sentence. How Irish, how KENNEDY, but how true were the emotions of every man and woman in that church—from the President, to the Vice President, to former Presidents, to Senators, to Members of the House, to close friends, and to so many of the Kennedy family.

I think of being sworn into this body as a 34-year-old nervous Senator. One of the first people who came up to shake my hand after being sworn in was TED KENNEDY, then Mike Mansfield and Howard Baker. I was awed to think I was in the presence of such people.

After serving with TED for 35 years and speaking with him almost every single day, I look over at his desk, at something I have seen over the 35 years when we have lost colleagues, but I don't know of any time it has hurt so much to see the black drape across the desk, to see the vase of white flowers. I went by there yesterday and just put my hand on the desk. I will admit I was overcome with emotion and left the floor.

I have so many memories, as we all do, of my friendship with TED. Senator Durbin spoke about how TED KENNEDY had a way—no matter who you were, if you had tragedy in your family or an illness or something had happened, he would call or write, and he would offer help. It made no difference who you were.

I was very close to my father. He had met TED a number of times. When my father passed away, virtually the first telephone call my mother received that morning was from TED KENNEDY. I remember my mother taking comfort in that.

Senator KENNEDY's office is just one floor below mine in the Russell Senate Building. We both have stayed there all these years. On many occasions, especially when he was going for a vote, we could hear his great laugh echoing down the halls, and it would change our whole mood, our whole day. We often talked about the bond of the New England Irish and spoke about that again when we came back from Pope Paul John II's funeral and refueled the plane in Ireland. It was like following the Pied Piper at Shannon Airport. There were paintings of President Kennedy there. The Senator from Iowa remembers that.

As we walked through, TED KENNEDY and Chris Dodd were telling Irish stories. There are memories of when TED was walking the dogs outside of the Russell Building, and we would talk and chat, saying, "How is your family? How is this one or that one?"

After TED died, one of our newspapers in Vermont had a front-page picture that my wife Marcelle had taken back in 1968. It showed a young TED KENNEDY in Vermont campaigning for his brother Robert and talking with an even younger State attorney. We talked about Robert Kennedy—the two of us—and I gave that photograph to TED a few years ago because I found it in my archives. He chuckled and talked about how young we looked, and then he asked for another copy so he could sign one to me. That day we sat there and talked about his brothers—obviously, the President, John Kennedy; Senator Robert Kennedy; and also his brother, Joe Kennedy, who had died. I talked about being interviewed by Robert Kennedy, who was Attorney General, when he invited me down to the Department of Justice. I was a young law student, and he talked to me about the possibility of a career in the Department of Justice. That talk meant so much to me, and his brother told me how independent the Department of Justice must be, even from the President of the United States. We never have enough time in this body, and a roll call started and that conversation stopped. But I remember every bit of that so much.

I remember after that time we campaigned for Robert Kennedy, the next time I saw him was here when I was a Senator-elect. As a former young prosecutor, I walked into his office with trepidation and almost thinking I was going into the inner sanctum. I was going to talk with him about what committees I might go on. This great voice said, "Good morning, Senator."

Coming from him, I turned around, assuming another Senator was walking in behind me, and I realized he was talking to me.

TED's wonderful wife Vicki was part of a small book club, and my wife Marcelle was in that. The days they would meet, TED would come up and put his arm around my shoulder and say, "Patrick, we are in trouble today. Our wives are meeting, and tonight we are going to get our marching orders." You know what, Madam President. He was right.

All of the years I served on the Judiciary Committee, until this past year, I sat beside him. I am going to miss him on that committee. I am going to miss his help and advice. I am going to miss him on the Senate floor because not having him with us in the Senate is going to make a huge difference in negotiations on legislation, whether it is on the current issue of health care reform or any other issue.

I remember one meeting with Ronald Reagan when he was President. The President turned to TED—and several of us, Republicans and Democrats, were meeting with him—and said, "Thank goodness you're here, TED. You are bringing us together."

That difference extended beyond our shores. He personally made such a difference in bringing peace to Ireland and ending apartheid in South Africa. I remember going with President Clinton after the peace agreement, and everybody— while they would thank the Prime Minister of Ireland and Great Britain and President Clinton, they all wanted to come over and thank TED KENNEDY.

His sense of history and of our country and his firm and constant belief in America's promise and America's future were inspiring. His willingness to spend time with the most junior Senators, as with all others of both parties, made him a Senator's Senator. I think every single Senator, Republican or Democrat, would agree he was a Senator's Senator.

It is easy in politics to appeal to the self-interests in each of us. TED KENNEDY appealed to the best in us, to the American verities that are written not on water but in stone. He appealed to our sense of justice, to our sense of responsibility to each other, and to our uniquely American sense of hope and possibility. In the Senate, he labored to help reach bipartisan progress on health care, education, civil rights, voting rights, immigration reform, and so much more.

Madam President, the powerful have never lacked champions. TED KENNEDY was a champion for ordinary Americans and for those who struggle, those who do not have a champion. He believed everyone in this great land deserved the opportunity to pursue the American dream.

I thought last night at the President's speech—I talked before the speech with Mrs. Kennedy and after the speech with Senator KENNEDY's three children. It was just impossible to fully put into words how much I miss him.

Marcelle and I miss our friend dearly, but we know it was a privilege to call him our friend. It was a privilege to serve alongside such a public servant dedicated as he was to making the lives of millions of his fellow Americans better.

It is a sad passing of an era, but TED KENNEDY would also tell us it is a time to look to the future.

Madam President, I close with this. I always thought when I left the Senate I would say farewell to this body and TED KENNEDY would be here to wish me Godspeed. I wish him Godspeed.

The PRESIDING OFFICER. The Senator from Utah.

Mr. HATCH. Madam President, I thank all of our colleagues who have taken the time to come to the floor to speak for and on behalf of our great friend and colleague, Senator TED KENNEDY. I particularly enjoyed the remarks of the distinguished Senator from Vermont who served with him for 35 years. I only served 33 years with TED. I thank them for the remarks and the reverence most everybody has had for our departed colleague.

I rise today to offer my remarks on the passing of my dear friend and colleague, Senator TED KENNEDY. Over this past recess, America lost one of its greatest leaders and this Chamber lost one of its most dynamic and important Members. I mourn the loss not only of a respected colleague but of a dear personal friend. I think I speak for all my colleagues when I say that Senator KENNEDY will be missed and that the Senate is a lesser place without him here.

People have often remarked about the working relationship I had with Senator KENNEDY, oftentimes calling us the "odd couple." We used to laugh about that. But the truth be told, he and I really didn't agree on a lot of things. Over the years, Senator KENNEDY and I were on opposite sides of some of the fiercest battles in this Chamber's history. While we have long been good friends, we did not pull any punches on one another. If we were opposing one another in a debate, Senator KENNEDY would come to the floor and, in his classic style, he would lay into me with his voice raised—and he had a terrific voice—and his arms flailing. Of course, I would let him have it right back. Then, after he finished, he would finally come over and put his arm around me and say, "How was that?" I would always laugh about it, as we did. We laughed at each other all the time.

That is what set Senator KENNEDY apart from many in Washington. For him, politics rarely got personal. He was never afraid to voice his disagreement with the views of a fellow Senator. But, in the end, I believe he always maintained a warm and cordial relationship with almost every one of his colleagues. That is difficult to do sometimes, particularly when partisan tempers flare up, but it always seemed to come easy for Senator KENNEDY.

Despite our tendency to disagree on almost everything, Senator KENNEDY and I were able to reach common ground on many important occasions and on some important issues.

As I mentioned at the recent memorial service, one of my defining moments as a Senator came when I met with two families from Provo, UT. The parents in these families were humble and hard working, and they were able to provide food and clothing and shelter for their children. But the one necessity they could not afford was health insurance. Their children were children of the working poor. The struggles of this family touched me and inspired me to work with Senator KENNEDY to create SCHIP, which continues to provide health care coverage to millions of children of the working poor and others throughout the country, and which passed with broad bipartisan support.

Over the years, Senator KENNEDY and I worked successfully to get both Republicans and Democrats on board for a number of causes. We drafted a number of pieces of legislation to provide assistance to AIDS victims, including the Ryan White AIDS Act. I named that bill right here on the floor with Mrs. White sitting in the audience. We worked together, along with Senator Harkin, to craft and pass the Americans with Disabilities Act. There was also the Orphan Drug Act, as well as the FDA Modernization Act, and a whole raft of other bills that would take too much time to speak about, all of which bear the Hatch-Kennedy, Kennedy-Hatch name.

Our final collaboration came just this year in the form of the Edward M. Kennedy Serve America Act, which I was pleased to name after Senator KENNEDY right here on the floor. He came up afterward, and we hugged each other. Then we went back to the President's Room, and he had pictures taken, even though he was not feeling well. He had so many pictures with so many people who were involved.

All of our bills passed because of the willingness of Senator KENNEDY and myself to put consensus ahead of partisanship—something we see far too infrequently in Washington.

It is axiomatic in politics that timing is crucial. No one understood or practiced that principle better than Senator KENNEDY. He had a sixth sense and an open mind to notice when the time was ripe for the key compromise. He knew when to let events sit and when it was time to close the deal. More important, he knew when he should stick to his guns and when he needed to reach across the aisle to get the help of his Republican colleagues. He was always able to recognize and work with those who shared his goals, even if they had different ideas on how to achieve them.

I will never forget, after I had made the deciding vote on civil rights for institutionalized persons—it was a Birch Bayh-Hatch bill, and Birch had led the fight on the floor, and so did I.

Later came the Voting Rights Act. I felt very strongly about not putting the effects test in section 2. I had no problem with it in section 5, but I did not want it in section 2 so that it applied to all the other States. I lost in committee. I voted for the bill out of committee because I considered the Voting Rights Act the most important civil rights bill in history.

The day they were going to have the bill signed at the White House, he caught me right inside the Russell Building where we both had offices, and he said, "You are coming with us, aren't you?"

I said, "Well, I was against the change in section 2."

He said, "You voted for it and were very helpful in getting that bill passed, and I know how deeply you feel about it."

I did go down with him. I would not have gone without Senator KENNEDY recognizing I did feel deeply about the Voting Rights Act. And even though I lost on what I thought was a pivotal constitutional right, the fact is I voted for the bill.

At the risk of riling my more liberal colleagues in the Senate, I would like to point out that Senator KENNEDY shared an utterly optimistic view of the American experiment with President Ronald Reagan. They both deeply believed that whatever the current trials or challenges we must face as a Nation, America's best days were ahead of her. That is something many people do not appreciate well enough about Senator KENNEDY.

Because of his optimism and hope for our Nation's future, Senator KENNEDY was, throughout his career in the Senate, a great practitioner of the Latin motto "*carpe diem*," "seize the day." Few worked harder day in and day out than Senator KENNEDY. As a result, every Senator had to work a little bit harder, either to follow his lead if you were on the same side of the issue or to stand in his way if you were in the opposition. I have been in both positions. I am not saying it was inherently difficult to work with Senator KENNEDY. But as anyone who has negotiated a tough piece of legislation can tell you, it can be sheer drudgery, even when you agree on most issues. But Senator KENNEDY brought a sense of joy even to the most contentious negotiating sessions. And when you were working with Senator KENNEDY, you knew he would keep his word. If after these long sessions an agreement was reached, he would stick by it no matter how much heat he would have to take.

All this was no doubt the result of his love for this great institution and his commitment to the American people. Political differences notwithstanding, there can never be any doubt about Senator KENNEDY's patriotism.

Few had a presence in the Senate as large as Senator KENNEDY's. More often than not, you could hear him coming down the hall—a mini-hurricane with a bevy of aides in tow, a batch of amendments in one hand and a stack of talking points in the other. He was almost always effective but seldom very quiet.

I also want to share a few thoughts about his staff. While at the end of the day the full responsibility of the Senate falls squarely on the shoulders of each Senator, it is also true that during the day and often long into the night and on many weekends, much of the work of the Senate is conducted by a group of the most committed team of staff members of any institution anywhere. Throughout his career, it was known that the Kennedy staff was comprised of one of the most formidable and dedicated collections of individuals of the Senate. Many of them have gone on to have distinguished careers, including now-Justice Stephen Breyer; Dr. Larry Horowitz, who managed his health care right up to the end and loved TED KENNEDY deeply; Nick Littlefield, who ran the Labor Committee for Senator KENNEDY and was an adviser right up to the time Senator KENNEDY passed away; and, of course, Michael Myers—just to name four, with no intention of leaving out the others. Senator KENNEDY would be the first to recognize how their efforts contributed to his success. I salute them for their hard work over the years. I cannot exactly say I have always been totally pleased with all of the Kennedy staff all of the time, but, as was true of their boss, while we might have been frequent adversaries, we were never enemies.

I am saddened by the loss of my dear friend Senator KENNEDY. I will miss him personally. I will miss the fights in public. I will miss his sense of humor in private and public. And perhaps more significantly, I believe this Chamber will miss his talents as a legislator and, most of all, his leadership.

While I cannot say I hope more of my colleagues will adopt his views on policy, I hope more of us can adopt his approach to the legislative process.

I was in California giving a speech at a fundraiser when they came in with a cell phone and said, "Senator KENNEDY is on the line, and he sounds very agitated."

So I went out on the plaza and I said, "TED, what is the matter?"

He said, "Oh, I have great news for you."

I said, "What is that?"

He said, "I am going to get married again."

I said, "Do I know her?"

He said, "No, but you would love her. She is a wonderful person, and she has two wonderful children. I am going to adopt them and treat them as my own. And I am so happy."

I said, "TED, why would you call me in California?"

He said, "Well, her daughter was bragging to her elementary school teacher at that time that her mother was going to marry TED KENNEDY."

The elementary school teacher was married to a *Washington Post* reporter.

So he said, "I wanted you to become one of the first to know. I am very happy. I am going to marry Vicki Reggie."

I have come to know Vicki very well. She has made such a difference in his life and in his family's life. She is a tremendous human being, as are his children. They are terrific.

I was happy to be in the Catholic Church where TEDDY went to pray for his daughter every day he could when she was suffering from cancer. I know how deeply he feels about Patrick and Teddy, Jr. I thought they did a terrific job at the mass at his funeral. He has to be very proud of them. I am very proud of them.

I think Vicki Kennedy deserves an awful lot of credit for all of the later happy years of my friend TED KENNEDY. I want her to know that I love her dearly for what she did and as an individual herself.

I love TED KENNEDY's entire family. A number of them have come to me at times where I was able to help them because he could not as a member of the family. I have to say that I was close to a great number of the members of his family, and I really appreciate them as well and the influence they had on him and he had on them.

He had a great influence on me as well. I want to personally thank him for it and say to my dear friend and colleague, as I look at his desk over there with the flowers and the drape, rest in peace, dear TED, and just know that a lot of us will try to carry on, and hopefully, with some of the things you taught us and helped us to understand, we can do it better than we have in the past.

I yield the floor.

The PRESIDING OFFICER (Mr. Burris). The Senator from Maryland.

Ms. MIKULSKI. Mr. President, I wish to speak about Senator TED KENNEDY. Clearly, I would have been proud to be on my feet to give such a testimonial, but as many of my colleagues know, I had a fall a few weeks ago coming out of church. I am ready to be at my duty station, but I can't quite stand to be 4'11" and give these remarks.

I do wish to speak and speak from my heart, speak from my memory, and speak with my affection. I have known TED KENNEDY a very long time. He has been my friend, my pal, my comrade in arms. I have enjoyed everything from working with him on big policy issues to sailing off the coast of Hyannis. I have been with him in his hideaway while we strategized on how to move an agenda of empowerment, and I have danced at his famous birthday parties. We have had a good time together.

I remember one of the first parties was a theme from the 1960s, and I came with a big wig, hoping I would look like Jackie Kennedy. TED was a chunky Rhett Butler because

Vicki and he were coming as Rhett Butler and Scarlett O'Hara. As we jitterbugged, I said, "Do you think I look like Jackie?" He said, "Well, nice try."

The last party we went to was a movie theme, and I came with one of those big bouffants. It was to be a movie theme, as I say, and I looked like something out of "Hair Spray." I will not tell you his comments, but, again, he said, "Your hair gets bigger with every one. I can't wait until my 80th."

Well, unfortunately, there will not be an 80th birthday party, but we will always carry with us the joy of friendship with TED KENNEDY.

It is with a heavy heart that I give this salute to him. I first met him as a young social worker. I testified before his committee. As a young social worker, I was there to talk about a brand-new program called Medicare, about what was working, what were the lessons learned—once again from being on the ground; what was happening in the streets and neighborhoods—and how to help people get the medical and social services they needed. He listened, he was intent, and he asked many questions. Little did I know I would join him in the Senate to fight for Medicare, to fight for health care, and to fight for those senior citizens.

Similar to so many others of my generation, I was inspired by the Kennedys to pursue a life in public service. I chose the field of social work and then went into politics because I saw politics as social work with power. As a Congress-woman, I was on the Energy and Commerce Committee. That was a counterpart to what TED was doing in the Sen-ate. We got to know each other at conferences working to-gether. Those were the great days of bipartisanship. As we would come in from the Energy and Commerce Committee, there would be TED KENNEDY and Jacob Javits working to make sure we could pass good legislation. I saw there that good legislation came from good ideas that could be pursued with good humor in an atmosphere of civility.

As we got to know each other, I admired his verve, his te-nacity, and he admired me because I could dish it out with the best of them as well. When he ran for President in 1980, he asked me to nominate him at the Democratic Convention. I was thrilled and honored to do so. Remember the drama of that? Jimmy Carter was an incumbent President. TED KENNEDY was an upstart. I backed KENNEDY. Well, it didn't work out and TED called me and said, "I am withdrawing from the race. We are going to support President Carter 100 percent. But though you are not going to nominate me for

President, I hope you will still introduce me at the convention." I said, "Absolutely. But one day I hope to be able to nominate you."

That night, as I took the podium, it was the famous speech that everyone remembers—TED KENNEDY talking about the work going on, the cause enduring, the hope still living, and the dream never dying. What was amazing about that speech was the way TED KENNEDY used a moment in his life—which some viewed as a defeat—as a time to redefine himself in public service and to claim the mantle of being one of the best Senators America has ever seen. He used that speech not as a retreat but as a reaffirmation and a recommitment of what he would do.

That night I did introduce him. While all my colleagues were in Boston, and I watched the funeral from my rehabilitation room, mourning his death and feeling sad that I could not join with my colleagues there, I had that speech and I read it then and, as I looked at it, I realized I could give it again and again. Because when I took the floor of the 1980 convention, I first said, "I am not here for Barb Mikulski. I am here today for all those people who would like to say what they knew about TEDDY KENNEDY." I am going to say some of those words I said then that would be appropriate for now.

I said, "I am here on behalf of a lot of people who want to be here but can't: Old women desperately trying to use their Social Security checks to pay for food and medicine and yet frightened about their energy bills. Students whose tuition has gone up so much they are going to have to work two jobs just to stay in school."

I spoke of small business people trying to just keep their doors open and the returning war vet who is unemployed. While his brother has signed up for a tour of duty, he is standing in the unemployment line.

I said during that speech that, day after day, EDWARD KENNEDY has spoken out for those people; that he has been there talking about the economy, energy policy, and jobs, long before many others. I talked about how EDWARD KENNEDY said that when Black freedom riders were being attacked and beaten, he was the one who fought for racial justice and helped to get the Voting Rights Act through. I said that as a young social worker, working in the neighborhoods during the dark Nixon years, and wondering how old people were going to get the services they needed, TED KENNEDY introduced the first nutrition program for the elderly—a program that guaranteed senior citizens at least one hot meal a day. It was TED KENNEDY, I said, who won the passage of programs such as neighborhood health centers, who fought the war on cancer, who led the fight to save nurses' scholarships and save them he did. In his fight for legislation, he was always there.

In my fight to help battered women, Senator KENNEDY was one of the first to be a strong and active ally. He said he knew very early on that all American women work but that too many women work for too little or are paid unequal pay for their work. I said then, and I say again, TED KENNEDY wanted to change Social Security to make it fairer for women and to extend the Equal Rights Amendment so we would be included in the Constitution.

It was amazing the issues he fought for then and that he continued to fight for all his life. In the time I knew him, I knew him not just as a newsclip, but I found him to be truly gallant in public and in private—caring about others and modest about himself, always about grace, courage, and valor.

When I came to the Senate, I was the only Democratic woman, and he was there for me, but I saw how he was there for so many other people. In 2004, when we were in Boston, TED KENNEDY and I had lunch in the North End. It was one of our favorite things, to get together for a meal and for conversation. What I realized then—as we enjoyed ourselves with big plates of antipasto, always vowing that we would eat more of the salad and less of the pasta, as we got up and left and walked around the North End—is that his best ideas came from the people. It was his passion for people. I knew he represented those brainy people in Cambridge who went to Harvard and who often came up through the Kennedy School with those great ideas. But as I walked around the neighborhoods with him, I saw he actually listened to people, trailed by a staff person who was actually taking notes.

As we walked down the street, there was the man who came up and who talked about his mother's problem with Social Security. "Take it down," he said. "Let's see what we can do." We walked down a few feet more. "Oh, my grandson wants to go to West Point; how does he apply?" He said, "He is going to love it and he is going to love my process. Let's see how we can do that." A few feet on down, the small business guy said, "Keep on fighting, TED. You know, I can't buy this health insurance. Can I call you?" "Always call me," he said. "And by the way, don't forget to call Barbara"—the legendary Barbara Souliotis. And all of us know TED KENNEDY had an outstanding staff, whether it was the staff in Massachusetts, who took care of casework and projects and day-to-day needs, or the staff in Washington who helped TED KENNEDY take the ideas that came from the people, their day-to-day struggles, and converted them into national policy. That is what it was—people, people, people.

When I came to the Senate, it was only Nancy Kassebaum and I. We were the only two women. He was a great friend, along with Senator Sarbanes. They were people I called my Galahads—people who helped me get on the right committees, show me the inner workings of the Senate. TED was determined I would be on his Committee on Health and Education to get the ideas passed, but he also was determined I would get on the Appropriations Committee to make sure we put those ideas into the Federal checkbook. He was my advocate.

One of the things that was clear is, he was the champion for women. He was a champion for this woman in helping me get on those committees. And during those sometimes rough days getting started, he would take me to La Colline with Senator Dodd, and while he drank orange juice with a little vodka—so no one would know he had a little vodka—he was giving me shooters of Chardonnay to boost my spirits. He and Chris would give me a pep talk, and I felt like I was Rocky. They would say, "Get out there, fight; don't let it get you down. Pick yourself up." I felt like I was going to spit in the bucket and get back on the floor. He lifted my spirits, just like he lifted the spirits of so many.

The story I wish to conclude with—because there are so many issues we worked on together—is when I went to him and said, "TED, did you know that women are not included in the protocols at NIH?" He said, "What do you mean?" I said, "In all the research we do, women are not included in the protocols. They just finished a famous study which said to take an aspirin a day, keep a heart attack away. It included 10,000 male medical students and not one woman." I said, "I want to change that." Teaming up with Nancy and Pat Schroeder and Olympia Snowe and Connie Morella, who were in the House, he helped me create the Office of Women's Health at NIH so women would always be included in those protocols.

Then I spoke out and said, "TED, the health care research for breast cancer is low. That is why they are racing for the cure." He helped us, working with Tom Harkin, to boost the money for research and to also get mammogram quality standards through so that when a woman would get her mammogram, it would be safe.

But here is one of the most profound things we did, again working on a bipartisan basis. Dr. Bernadine Healy, who was the head of NIH, wanted to do a study on the consequences of hormone therapy. TED and I and Tom did not believe we should earmark NIH—and I believe that today— but we made sure we put money and a legislative framework in place so Dr. Healy could institute the famous hormone therapy study. Well, let me tell you the consequences of that. That study has changed medical practice. That study has resulted in breast cancer rates going down 15 percent.

So when someone says: What did TED KENNEDY do to help women? What did TEDDY KENNEDY do to work with Barbara Mikulski? Tell them we worked together, and we worked to save the lives of women, 1 million at a time.

This is my final salute to Senator KENNEDY on the floor, but I will always salute him every day in the Senate to make sure we continue what he said about how the dream will continue on.

I ended my speech at the Democratic Convention in 1980 when I said this—and I end my remarks today by saying this: EDWARD KENNEDY has kept his faith with the American people. He hasn't waited for a crisis to emerge or a constituency to develop. He always led, he always acted, he always inspired.

God bless you, TED. And God bless the United States of America.

The PRESIDING OFFICER. The Senator from Alabama is recognized.

Mr. SESSIONS. Mr. President, I would like to take a moment to join with my colleagues, and I see quite a number on the Senate floor now, to pay tribute to TED KENNEDY. He was a truly remarkable force in the Senate, a champion of liberalism—perhaps the Nation's leading champion of liberalism. He believed government could serve the people, and it ought to do more to serve people. On that we sometimes disagreed, but he believed it with a sincerity and he battled for it with a consistency that is remarkable. He constantly sought to utilize the ability of government to do good for the American people, and that is admirable.

[64]

He also was a champion of civil rights. He was a force during the civil rights movement, and his activities, his personal leadership, truly made a difference in making this a better country. Without his leadership, things would have been much more difficult for sure.

I have a vivid memory of him—presiding as I did when I first came to the Senate, a duty given to the younger, newer Members—in the night, TED KENNEDY, alone on the Senate floor, roaring away for the values he believed in. It was just something to behold, in my view. I saw nothing like it from, maybe, any other Member. He had served so many years in the Senate—and I learned today from our chairman on Judiciary, Senator Leahy, that he served on the Senate Judiciary Committee longer than any other Senator in history. But even as his years went by, many years in the Senate, he did not lose the drive, the will, the energy, the commitment to give of himself for the values he believed in.

As I told one reporter after his death, I would just hope to be somewhat as effective in promoting the values I believed in as he was in promoting those values. If we disagreed, and sometimes we certainly did, people continued to admire him, I think, to a unique degree. There were no hard feelings. You would battle away, and then afterward it would be a respectful relationship between Senators. I think that is pretty unusual and something that is worthy of commenting on.

He talked to me about being a co-sponsor, his prime co-sponsor on a bill. He said he wanted to work with me on something important. It was a bill we commonly referred to as the prison rape bill. There was a lot of concern that in prisons, people who are arrested were subjected to sexual abuse. That, in my view, is not acceptable. I know the Presiding Officer, a prosecutor, knows people deserve to do their time in jail, but they should never be subjected to those kinds of abuses. So we passed a pretty comprehensive bill. I was proud of it and proud to be with him at the signing ceremony.

I also talked to him and we met and talked at some length about a major piece of legislation to increase savings in America, savings for the average working American who had not been able to share in the growth of wealth that so many have been blessed with in this country. I thought we had some pretty good ideas. Savings at that time had fallen below zero—actually 1 percent negative use of people's savings which were going away. I guess now we are at a 5 or

6 percent savings rate after this turmoil we have had economically. I do not think the idea should go away. Maybe it lost a little steam in the fact that we have seen a resurgence of savings today, but I was very impressed with his commitment to it, the work of his fine staff, and his personal knowledge of the issue.

I see my other colleagues. I will join with them in expressing my sincere sympathy to Vicki and their entire family for their great loss. The Senate has lost a great warrior and a great champion of American values.

I yield the floor.

The PRESIDING OFFICER. The Senator from Iowa is recognized.

Mr. HARKIN. Mr. President, I ask unanimous consent the period of morning business be extended to 2:30 p.m., with Senators permitted to speak therein for up to 10 minutes each.

The PRESIDING OFFICER. Without objection, it is so ordered.

Mr. HARKIN. Mr. President, as I look around this Chamber, I see men and women of remarkable talents and abilities. I also have a strong sense, we all do, that there is a tremendous void now in our midst. A very special Senator, a very special friend, a Member who played a unique role within this body for nearly a half century is no longer with us.

We have had many glowing and richly earned tributes to Senator TED KENNEDY over these last couple of weeks. He was not only the most accomplished and effective Senator of the last 50 years, he was truly one of the towering figures in the entire history of the Senate. Yet for all his accomplishments, for all the historic bills he authored and shepherded into law, for all the titanic battles he fought, I will remember TED KENNEDY first and foremost as just a good and decent human being.

I remember his extraordinary generosity, his courage, his passion, his capacity for friendship and caring, and, of course, that great sense of humor. I remember one time I was in my office, and we had a phone conversation. It was about a disagreement we had. It was right at St. Patrick's Day, so we were having this discussion on the phone and tempers got a little heated. I think I was holding the phone out about like this. He probably was too. I think our voices

[66]

got raised to a very high decibel level, sort of yelling at each other, and pretty soon we just hung up on each other.

I felt very badly; I know he did too. So several hours later, when I came on the Senate floor and I saw TED at his desk, I went up to him and pulled up a chair next to him. He would get that kind of pixie smile on his face, have a twinkle in his eye.

I said, "TED, I'm sorry about that conversation we had. I should not have lost my temper as I did." I said, "My staff is a little concerned about our relationship."

He sort of got that great smile and chuckled. "Well," he said, "forget about it. I just told my staff that is just the way two Irishmen celebrate St. Patrick's Day."

That is just the way he was. He could disarm you immediately, and you would move on. He had a great disarming sense of humor.

TED came from a remarkable family—so many tough breaks, so many triumphs, so many contributions to our Nation—both in war and in peace. TED and his siblings were born into great wealth. They could have lived lives of luxury and leisure, but they chose instead to devote themselves to public service. They devoted themselves to making the world a better place for others, especially those in the shadows of life.

There are so many things I could focus on this morning in my brief remarks, but I want to focus on just one aspect of TED KENNEDY: all that he did to improve the lives of people with disabilities in our country. I thought about this: With the death of Eunice Kennedy Shriver on August 11, and all she did to found the Special Olympics now being carried on by her son Tim, then the death of TED on August 25, people with disabilities in this country lost two great champions.

Their sister Rosemary lived her entire life with a severe intellectual disability. The entire Kennedy family is well acquainted with the joys and struggles of those with disabilities. Those of us who were in the church in Boston at the funeral—and those probably watching on television—heard the very eloquent speech by Teddy, Jr., about his battle with cancer at a young age, losing his leg and confronting his disabilities, and how TED helped him get through that.

In 1975, Senator KENNEDY helped to pass what is now called the Individuals with Disabilities Education Act—IDEA. In 1978 he passed legislation expanding the jurisdiction of the Civil Rights Commission to protect people from discrimination on the basis of disability. In 1980 he introduced the Civil Rights for Institutionalized Persons Act, protecting the rights of people in government institutions, including the elderly and people with intellectual and mental disabilities.

Nineteen years ago he was one of my most important leaders and partners in passing the Americans with Disabilities Act—1990. I will never forget, after I had been in the Senate for 2 years, Republicans were in charge, and then in 1986 Democrats came back, took charge, and Senator KENNEDY wanted me on his Education and Health Committee. I sort of played a little hard to get.

I said, "Well, maybe, but I am really interested in disability issues." He knew about that. He knew about my work on some of the stuff I had done in the House before I came here, especially for people with hearing problems. I said I would like to come on his committee, but I said I would be interested in working on disability issues.

He got back to me and said, "Tell you what, I have the Disability Policy Subcommittee, and you can chair it."

I am a freshman Senator. He didn't have to do that for me. I was astounded at his great generosity. So I have always appreciated that. He already had this great, extensive record on disability issues. Yet he let me take the lead. Then when the Americans with Disabilities Act came up, he could have taken that himself. He was the chairman of the committee.

As I said, he had this long history of championing the causes of people with disabilities. Yet he knew how passionately I felt about it, and he let me author the bill. He let me take it on the floor. He let me be the floor manager of it and put my name on it. He didn't have to do that. He was the chairman. He could have had his name on it. He could have floor-managed it. But he let me do it in spite of the fact that I was just a freshman Senator.

He was an indispensable leader in bringing disparate groups together to get the Americans with Disabilities Act passed. I will never forget that great act of generosity on his part in letting me take the lead.

TED always insisted that our focus should be not on disability but on ability; that people with disabilities must be fully included in our American family. Americans with disabilities had no better friend, no tougher fighter, no more relentless champion than TED KENNEDY.

Yesterday I accepted the chairmanship of the Senate HELP Committee, the Health, Education, Labor, and Pensions Committee. It is a great honor and a great challenge and, I must add, somewhat daunting to carry on the legacy of Senator TED KENNEDY. He dedicated his life to making our economy work for all Americans, to secure a quality education for every child and, of course, securing quality, affordable health care for every citizen as a right and not a privilege.

In the Democratic Cloakroom, there is a page from the *Cape Cod Times* with a wonderful picture of TED and a quote from him. Here is the quote:

Since I was a boy I have known the joy of sailing the waters of Cape Cod and for all my years in public life I have believed that America must sail toward the shores of liberty and justice for all. There is no end to that journey, only the next great voyage.

We have heard many eloquent tributes to Senator KENNEDY. But the tribute that would matter most for him would be for his colleagues to come together, on a bipartisan basis, to pass a strong, comprehensive health reform bill this year.

It is time for us to sail ahead on this next great voyage to a better and more just and more caring America. So as we sadly contemplate the empty desk draped in black, we say farewell to a beloved colleague. He is no longer with us, but his work continues. His spirit is here. And as he said, the cause endures.

May TED KENNEDY rest in peace. But may we not rest until we have completed the cause of his life—the cause he fought for until his last breath—ensuring quality, affordable health care for every American.

I yield the floor.

The PRESIDING OFFICER. The Senator from South Carolina.

Mr. GRAHAM. Mr. President, today is a day to remember a colleague, a friend, someone whom it was a challenge to oppose and a joy to work with, and I wish we were not here today talking about the passing of Senator KENNEDY.

We disagreed on most things but found common ground on big things. And everyone has a story about Senator KENNEDY. There has been a lot of discussion about his life, the legacy, his human failings, which we all have, his self-inflicted wounds, and his contribution to the country. But I want to talk about what will be missing in the Senate.

We had a giant of a man who was very principled and understood the Senate as well as anyone I have ever met; he understood the need to give and take to move the country forward.

[69]

My experience with Senator KENNEDY was, I used his image in my campaign to get elected, like every other Republican did. We do not want another person up here to help TED KENNEDY. And he loved it. He got more air time than the candidates themselves. He loved it.

I remember him telling me a story about Senator Hollings. The tradition in the Senate is when you get reelected, you have your fellow Senator from that State follow you down to the well. He went over to Senator KENNEDY and said, "I want you to come down and escort me."

He said, "Why? I am not from South Carolina."

Senator Hollings said, "In my campaign you were. You were the other Senator from South Carolina."

TED got a lot of fun out of that. I think he appreciated the role he played, and Republicans, almost to a person, would use Senator KENNEDY in their campaigns.

But when they got here, they understood Senator KENNEDY was someone you wanted to do business with. If you had a bill that you thought would need some bipartisan support, Senator KENNEDY is the first person you would think of. And you had to understand the limitations on what he could help you with. He was not going to help you with certain things, because it ran counter to what he believed in. But where you could find common grounds on the big issues, you had no better ally than Senator KENNEDY.

We met in the President's Room every morning during the immigration debate, and at night he would call me up and say, "Lindsey, tomorrow in our meeting you need to yell at me because you need to get something. I understand that. I will fight back. But you will get it."

The next day he would say, "I need to yell at you." It was sort of like all-star wrestling, to be honest with you, and that was fun. Because he understood how far I could go, and he challenged me to go as far as I could. But he never asked me to go farther than I was capable of going. And, in return, he would walk the plank for you.

We had votes on the floor of the Senate on emotion-driven amendments designed to break the bill apart from the right and the left. I walked the plank on the right because I knew he would walk the plank on the left. He voted against amendments he probably agreed with, but he understood that the deal would come unraveled.

The only thing I can tell you about Senator KENNEDY, without any hesitation is if he told you he would do something, that is all you needed to hear. A handshake from him was better than a video deposition from most people. I do not know how to say it any more directly than that.

Opposing him was a lot of fun because he understood that a give-and-take to move a ball forward was part of democracy, but standing your ground and planting your feet and telling the other side, in a respectful way, to go to hell, was also part of democracy. And he could do it with the best of them. He could also take a punch as well as give one.

So what we are missing today in the Senate is the spirit of TED KENNEDY when it comes to standing up for what you believe and being able to work with somebody who you disagree with on an issue very important to the country.

If he were alive today, the health care debate would be different. That is not a slam on anybody involved, because this is hard. I do not know if he could deliver, but I think it would be different, and I think it would be more hopeful.

The immigration bill failed. But he told me, "I have been through this a lot. Hard things are hard for a reason, and it will take a long time." He indicated to me that the immigration debate had all the emotion of the civil rights debate. And that was not something he said lightly.

We sat in that room with Senator Kyl and Senator Salazar and a group of Senators who came and went, and the administration officials, Homeland Security Secretary Chertoff, and Commerce Secretary Gutierrez, and we wrote it line by line with our staffs sitting by the wall.

It was what I thought the government was supposed to be like in ninth grade civics. It was one of the highlights of my political life to be able to sit in that room with Senator KENNEDY and other Senators and literally try to write a bill that was difficult.

We failed for the moment. But we are going to reform our immigration system. And the guts of that bill, the balance we have achieved, will be the starting point for a new debate. Most of it will become law one day, because it is the ultimate give and take and it made a lot of sense.

I say to his wife Vicki, "I got to know TED later in his life. Through him I got to know you. I know you are hurting now. But I hope that all of the things being said by his colleagues and the people at large are reassuring to you, and that as we move forward as a Senate, when you look at the history of this body, which is long and distinguished, around here there are all kinds of busts of people who have done great things during challenging times."

I will bet everything I own that Senator KENNEDY, when the history of this body is written, will be at the top echelon of Senators who have ever served. The point is that you can be as liberal as you want to be, you can be as conservative as you want to be, and you can be as effective as you want to be. If you want to be liberal and effective, you can be. If you want to be liberal and ineffective, you can choose that route too. The same for being conservative. You do not have to choose. That is what Senator KENNEDY taught this body, and, I think, what he demonstrated to anybody who wants to come and be a Senator. So if you are a left-of-center politician looking for a role model, pick TED KENNEDY. You could be liberal, proudly so, but you also could be effective.

What I am going to try to do with my time up here is be a conservative who can be effective. That is the best tribute I can give to Senator KENNEDY—being somebody on the right who will meet in the middle for the good of the country.

TED will be missed, but he will not be forgotten.

I yield the floor.

The PRESIDING OFFICER. The Senator from New Jersey.

Mr. LAUTENBERG. Mr. President, this corner of the Senate has become a lonely place. I sat next to TED KENNEDY here for a number of years. We miss him. We miss his camaraderie, his humor, his candor, most of all his courage. And though he will not be here to join us in the future, the things he did will last for decades because they were so powerful. He was a constant presence here. It is hard to imagine the Senate without TED KENNEDY's vibrant voice resounding throughout this floor or his roaring laughter spilling out of the Cloakroom.

Without doubt he was one of the finest legislators ever in this Chamber's history. Throughout his more than 46 years of service, TED introduced 2,500 bills and co-sponsored more than 550 of those into law. He was a man of many gifts, but his greatest had to be his remarkable affinity for ordinary people.

I saw that gift first hand in 1982 when I was making my first run for the Senate. A rally was being held for me in Newark, NJ, and it drew a crowd of thousands. I wanted to think that they were there for me, but it was obvious that they were there for TED KENNEDY.

The warmth, the affection with which he was received in this city far from the borders of Massachusetts, far from the halls of power in Washington, was amazing to witness. It was fitting that TED came to Newark to help me campaign because he inspired me to devote myself to public service. He encouraged my entry into the Senate.

As soon as I joined the Senate, TED KENNEDY became a source of knowledge, information, and wisdom. He was a seatmate of mine here in the Senate, and freely offered ideas on creating and moving legislation that I thought of or sponsored.

Even though he was born into privilege and was part of a powerful political family, his fight was always for the workers, for justice, and for those often forgotten. He was never shy to chase you down and demand your vote or to call you on the phone and insist on your support. Sometimes he would try to bring you to his side through reason, other times it was through righteous fury. TED was such a tenacious fighter for a cause in which he believed that he would often put on the gloves no matter who the opponent might be.

But he never let disagreement turn into a personal vendetta. No matter how bitter the fight, when it was done, he could walk across the Chamber ready to shake hands with his opponents, and was received with affection and respect.

Despite his reputation as a divisive figure, he was at the top of the list of popular Senators beloved by both Republicans and Democrats. He carried a great sense of humor. He liked to play pranks, one of which I saw up close and personal. One Thursday night after a long series of votes, we chartered an airplane to take TED KENNEDY, John Kerry, Senator Claiborne Pell, and me north to join our vacationing families in the area.

A week later we were here in the Chamber, and Claiborne Pell came over to me, hands shaking, with a letter in his hand. I looked at the letter. It was my stationery. On that stationery it asked for Claiborne Pell, a frugal man, to pay a far greater share of the total than was originally agreed to. I was embarrassed, mortified. I quickly declared that it was wrong and apologized profusely. And then I went to TED to assure him that if he got a letter such as that, the letter was incorrect. TED turned belligerent. He reminded me of the help he provided in my first election and asked: How could I nickel and dime him after all of that help? He turned on his heel, walked away red-faced, and then I realized it was part of the creation of a plot to embarrass me. The two of us broke into laughter so loud, so boisterously, that the Presiding Officer demanded that we leave the Chamber.

TED KENNEDY's love of life was always obvious in the Senate. Even though he could rise above partisan division, his life's work was deeply personal. It was TED KENNEDY who inherited the family legacy when two brothers were slain by assassins' bullets. He met that challenge by battling the powerful special interests to pass the Gun Control Act of 1968, which made it illegal for criminals and the mentally ill to buy guns.

Together, TED and I joined the fight to keep our streets safe from the scourge of gun violence. For decades, he was a force that shaped the national political landscape. He crafted life-changing legislation year after year, always fighting to shape public opinion toward his causes. He believed public service was a sacred mission, and the role of a leader was to make progress. No matter how hard, no matter how long the journey, he persisted.

In fact, TED KENNEDY's signature talent was his precise, unmatched ability to get legislation passed. And he did that through the timeless requirements of this profession: preparation, integrity, fairness, patience, hard work, a little bit of table pounding and a profound respect for his colleagues and his constituents.

I had the privilege of working with TED KENNEDY on many pieces of groundbreaking legislation. We worked closely on fighting big tobacco and their attempts to seduce children into a lifetime of addiction. We reached the high-water mark in that struggle earlier this year, when a law was passed that gives the FDA the power to regulate tobacco. It was something we worked on together for a long time. We stood together on other struggles, from the creation of the Children's Health Insurance Program to the Ryan White Act, to the Family and Medical Leave Act.

Think about it: Without TED KENNEDY, nearly 7 million children would not have health insurance. Think about it: Without TED KENNEDY, half a million Americans suffering with HIV would not be receiving vital services to cope with their disease. Think about it: Without TED KENNEDY, more than 60 million workers would not have the right to take time off from their job to care for a baby or a loved one or even receive personal medical treatment.

And he did more. He gave people assurance that the government was on their side.

TED KENNEDY was the guardian of opportunity. Look at his decades-long campaign to increase the minimum wage.

He will forever be remembered as a leader who persevered despite some frailties, who remained a tower of strength despite crippling personal tragedy.

Nothing symbolized his fortitude more than his first major speech on the Senate floor, which came on the heels of President KENNEDY's assassination.

Then, despite all he was facing personally, he fought for passage of the Civil Rights Act of 1964 to outlaw discrimination in employment, education, and public accommodations.

From there, TED KENNEDY became inextricably tied to the struggle for equal rights.

He was the chief sponsor of the Civil Rights Act of 1991.

TED KENNEDY was also a leader in the passage of the Voting Rights Act of 1965.

This law abolished literacy tests at the polls and guaranteed the protection of all Americans' right to vote.

In 1982, he was the chief sponsor of the Voting Rights Amendments Act which led the way to greater minority representation in Congress and State legislatures.

That law, in no small way, made it more likely that Barack Obama would become President of the United States. We are grateful the last Kennedy brother had a chance to see America rise above racism, above prejudice. He had a chance, the last of the Kennedy brothers in office, to see President Obama take that oath. It was a proud moment for him and for all of us.

As his life came to an end, TED said he saw a new wave of change all around us. He promised us that if we kept our compass true, we could reach our destination. In the days and the weeks and the months to come, the years to come, and the decades to come, we have to keep TED KENNEDY's cause alive. It is the cause of breaking gridlock to get things done. It is the cause of expanding health care as a right and not a privilege. It is the cause of bringing hope and justice and prosperity to all.

We are likely never to see the likes of a TED KENNEDY again. But I am confident we can rise to the challenge the people's Senator set for us and carry on for those who remember him, for those, yes, who miss him, for those who loved him, and for those who will always need a champion like TED KENNEDY.

Finally, if there was a demonstration of his humanity, the funeral tribute was one of enormous love and respect. It was enunciated particularly, because I rode with other Senators on the bus, by the hordes of people standing by the curbside with signs of gratitude for his contribution to the life and well-being of America. We are thankful for that.

I yield the floor.

The PRESIDING OFFICER. The Senator from West Virginia.

Mr. BYRD. I thank the Chair.

Mr. President, on August 25, a towering figure on our national political landscape left us. EDWARD MOORE KENNEDY succumbed to a malignant brain tumor after an 18-month battle for his life. As I look now at his desk, draped with black cloth and covered with flowers, I still have difficulty believing that he is gone. My ebullient Irish-to-the-core friend has departed this life forever. How bleakly somber. How utterly final. How totally unlike TED KENNEDY in life.

TED KENNEDY in life was a force of nature—a cheerful, inquisitive, caring man, who never accepted somberness for long or the finality of anything. His energetic adherence to perseverance, his plain dogged determination, his ability to rise from the ashes of whatever new horrific event accosted him, always with grace, and usually with a liberal dose of humor, were his trademarks. It was almost as if TED KENNEDY were at the top of his form when coping with adversity. Life itself inspired him. He believed that life was a contact sport, but that it should never be played without joy in the game itself. That is how he saw politics as well.

TED KENNEDY and I were friends and, yet, we were the oddest of odd couples. He was the scion of a wealthy and storied family. I am a coal miner's son who had no bottom rungs in my ladder. In earlier years we were rivals.

What TED and I discovered, though, was that somehow we had many things in common—a love of history; an affection for poetry; a fondness for dogs; a commitment to the less fortunate in our society. Many will speak of TED's stunning Senate career, his huge and lasting impact on our culture, his domination of the political scene for so many decades. By all means, let us never forget TED KENNEDY's extraordinary contribution to this great country. It is largely unmatched.

But I will especially cherish the personal side of this big man, with his infectious laugh, his booming voice, and his passion for the things and the people that he cared about. I will remember the dog lover who brought Sunny and Splash to my office to visit. I will recall a considerate friend who sent dozens of roses to mark my wedding anniversary or a special birthday. I will again enjoy a very special recitation of the "Midnight Ride of Paul Revere." By habit, I shall immediately look for TED KENNEDY whenever I enter this Chamber. In a thousand ways, large and small, he will simply be deeply, deeply missed.

My heart goes out to his steadfast wife Vicki and to his wonderful family. His spirit surely lives on in all of you.

Not long ago, I picked up a book of poetry which TED KENNEDY had given to me in July 1996. It bore this inscription: "To Bob, the master of our legislative poetry who has already left so many extraordinary Footprints on the Sands of Time." After that, TED had written, "See page 371."

I close with a few stanzas from "A Psalm of Life" on page 371 of TED's gift to me:

Life is real! Life is earnest!
And the grave is not its goal;
Dust thou art, to dust returnest,
Was not spoken of the soul ...

Lives of great men all remind us
We can make our lives sublime,
And, departing, leave behind us
Footprints on the sands of time;

Footprints, that perhaps another,
Sailing o'er life's solemn main,
A forlorn and shipwrecked brother,
Seeing, shall take heart again.

Let us, then, be up and doing,
With a heart for any fate;
Still achieving, still pursuing,
Learn to labor and to wait.

The PRESIDING OFFICER. The Senator from Georgia.

Mr. CHAMBLISS. Mr. President, I have been very fortunate in my life in public service to witness a lot of historical events, but none parallels the tribute that was just paid by one icon of the U.S. Senate to another Member of the U.S. Senate.

I rise to pay my respects to the late Senator TED KENNEDY. As one of my colleagues said earlier, it is a little bit ironic, when you come to the Senate you find out that those with whom you have significant political disagreements are folks you get to know well and you have the opportunity to work with.

I am sure during my political campaign for the U.S. Senate TED KENNEDY raised a lot of money for me by virtue of the fact that I would cite him in my fundraising mailouts because, coming from a very conservative part of the country, it was popular to cite the liberal Members of the Senate and say you needed to be there to counteract them. But when I came to the Senate—and certainly Senator KENNEDY and I do come from opposite ends of the political spectrum—I learned very quickly from Senator KENNEDY what the Senate is all about.

I was here about, gee, it could not have been but a couple of days—something less than 48 hours—when I was notified that I was going to be on the Judiciary Committee and that I would be the chairman of the Immigration Subcommittee on Judiciary and my ranking member would be TED KENNEDY.

Senator KENNEDY came to me on the floor, within a few hours of me being notified of that, and he said, "Saxby, you and I need to sit down. Let's discuss some immigration issues that we want to accomplish during the next 2 years. I just want to talk with you about it, get your thoughts and give you my thoughts."

I said, "Well, sure, TED, that will be great. I will be happy to come to your office and sit down with you."

He said no. He said, "Saxby, that is not the way the Senate works. You are the chairman. I will come to your office."

So the next day, a Senator who had been in office for well over 40 years came to the office of a Member of the Senate who had been here a little over 40 hours and sat down and had a conversation. That was a lesson about the way the Senate works that I will never forget.

We began working together on the Immigration Subcommittee, and we worked for about a year—it was in excess of a year, I guess—on an issue we talked about the very first day in my office. It involved the expansion of the L–1, H–1B visas. At that time, our economy was booming and businesses across our country needed access to more employees who had a specialized expertise.

We were successful in ultimately striking a compromise. It was difficult for TED because the left wing of his party was very much in opposition to what we were doing, and it was somewhat, although a little bit less, difficult for me because the right wing of my party was in opposition to what we were doing.

TED called me up one day after we had finished our negotiations, and he was laughing, and he said, "Saxby, I have to tell you, we have entered into an agreement on this, and I am going to do exactly what I told you I would do, but, boy, am I ever getting beat up by the far left in my party. They are just killing me." He said, "It is to the point where I am up for reelection next year, and you may have to come to Massachusetts and campaign for me."

We kind of laughed about that.

Well, 2 days later, I had been besieged with phone calls from ultraconservative folks from my State, and I called TED up, and I said, "Well, TED, you will not believe this, but I am getting beat up over that same issue by ultraconservatives in my party. But don't worry, I don't need you to come to Georgia to campaign for me."

Well, he laughed about that like I had never heard him laugh. The very last conversation I had with him to any extent was when he was here for President Obama's inauguration, and he reminded me of that story. He never forgot that.

I also have a very fond memory of TED by virtue of the fact that my grandchildren were 8 and 6 years old when I first came to the Senate, and we had this ice cream social out in the park across from the Russell Building where his office was and my office is. In fact, his office was directly below mine. I am walking back from the ice cream social with my grandchildren—who were here for that because it happens at the same time as the White House picnic—and TED is driving off in his car, and he sees me coming across with my grandchildren. He stops the car, gets out, and he says, "Saxby, these must be your grandchildren."

I said, "They are."

He said, "Well, I want my dogs to see them and them have a chance to meet my dogs."

So he got out of the car and got the dogs out, and my grandchildren just loved playing with those dogs.

Every year after that—I never called him—he called me because he knew that when the White House picnic was going on, my grandchildren would be here, and he would insist on bringing the dogs up when the grandchildren were here so they would have a chance to play with them. That is just the kind of guy TED was. It was a much softer side than what we have seen so many times with TED with his passionate debates and whatnot.

Last, let me mention another anecdote I will always remember. I was going down to speak to the Hibernian Society in Savannah, which has the second largest St. Patrick's Day parade in the United States. It is a big deal. We have about 1,000 folks who are at the Hibernian Society dinner that I was going to speak to. All you do is you go in and you tell jokes.

Well, I needed a bunch of Irish jokes, so I called up TED and I told him what I was doing, and I said, "I know you must have a book of Irish jokes."

He said, "I do. I am going to send it to you." And he said, "I will tell you something else you need to do. I know Savannah is a very conservative part of the world, and you are going to see in these jokes that you will have an opportunity to point out somebody to kind of poke fun at." He said, "Every time you have an opportunity in telling these jokes, you use my name."

Well, I took him at his word, and I did. And, boy, did I ever get a rousing welcome from all those Irishmen in Savannah, GA.

So I have very great and fond memories of a man who certainly came from a different part of the country than where I come from, who came from a very different political background than where I come from, and somebody who certainly had much more political experience than I will ever have. But the thing I appreciated in TED KENNEDY was—and I have said this often—he was the best legislator in this body. When TED KENNEDY told you something, you could take it to the bank. You never had to worry about it thereafter.

While we disagreed on many things, we agreed on some things and were able to work together in a very unusual way. Even when we disagreed, we were able to walk out of this Chamber and still be friends.

To Vicki and Patrick and the children, TED was a great American, a great guy, and he is going to be missed in this body. He was a true inspiration to a lot of us, and we are going to miss that compromising aspect of TED KENNEDY that will not be here, even though someone else will take up the mantle.

With that, Mr. President, I yield back.

The PRESIDING OFFICER. The Senator from California is recognized.

Mrs. FEINSTEIN. Mr. President, as I sit here and listen to the remarks of my colleagues and I look over at that black velvet-draped desk, with the pristine white roses, and the poem by Robert Frost, and I think about the past 17 years I have been here and have looked up—and perhaps it is late at night, perhaps it is in the morning, perhaps it is in the afternoon—and Senator KENNEDY is at his desk and he is talking about a bill he cares a great deal about—and, as Senator Lautenberg had said earlier, he co-sponsored 550 bills that became law. Around here, you can introduce a bill, and maybe it goes somewhere and maybe it does not. You can introduce a bill, and maybe it is a small bill, but introducing a big bill that goes somewhere, that passes the House and is signed by the President of the United States, is not a small feat.

I listened to Senator Byrd, and in the past he has spoken about lions of the Senate. TED KENNEDY was a lion of the Senate.

During 47 years—and this morning in the Judiciary Committee, we learned he had been the longest serving member—during 47 years, if you look at the big bills: the Mental Health Systems Act of 1980, which enabled people with mental illnesses to live in their communities with minimal hospital care; the Children's Health Insurance Program, which has been spoken about, which provided health insurance to uninsured children of low-income families; the commitment to health care reform that did not diminish even as he suffered through terminal illness; his dedication to education; he was a leader in the landmark Elementary and Secondary Education Act, which established the Federal Government's commitment to fund school for poor children in public schools; No Child Left Behind, widely hailed as the greatest example of bipartisan cooperation during the Bush administration; the bill he did with Orrin Hatch, the Serve America Act, the greatest expansion of national service since the New Deal—it goes on and on, big bills, bills that changed people's lives, not just in a county or a city but all across this great land.

In civil rights, as you look across at that desk, he had no peers. He would stand up, and I would watch. The lower jaw would quiver slightly, and he would begin, and there would be the thunderous tones, either in the Judiciary Committee or here on the floor, that would fill the room, filled with passion, filled with conviction, filled with determination.

He played a major role in every civil rights battle in this Congress for 40 years. Who else can say that? He fought for people of color, for women, for gays and lesbians, for those seeking religious liberty. His amendments to the Voting Rights Act in 1982 led to significant increases in minority representation in elective office. He was a major sponsor of the Americans with Disabilities Act to ensure that millions of disabled Americans could live productive lives. These are not small bills; these are big bills—the Civil Rights Act of 1991, which strengthened civil rights protections against discrimination and harassment in the workplace; again, a big bill that became law.

I was part of that small group of Senators who met on immigration reform hour after hour in small hot rooms. I watched Senator KENNEDY with his sleeves rolled back, when he would sit back and wait for just the right time to move or change the tenor of the discussion. True, that was one that was not successful, but it wasn't because he did not try.

Seventeen years ago, Joe Biden asked me if I would be the first woman on the Senate Judiciary Committee. I had the honor of doing it. TED KENNEDY was No. 2 in seniority sitting on that committee. I saw his commitment first hand. It was very special. You see, I was a volunteer in the campaign for John Fitzgerald Kennedy. I was a full-time volunteer for Bobby Kennedy for his campaign. I saw the Nation ripped apart by these double assassinations. I saw Senator KENNEDY, in addition to being a lion in the Senate, become a surrogate father to nieces and nephews. I saw him accept this mantle with great enthusiasm, with great love, and with a commitment that spanned the decades. That is very special. It is a very special human dimension of a great individual.

I lost my husband Bert to cancer, and I know well what the end is like. I know the good times that grow less and less and the bad times that become more and more. TED KENNEDY's life was enriched by a very special woman, and her name is Vicki Kennedy. For me, she is a mentor to others of what a wife should be. I have watched her sitting with him, writing speeches. I have watched her at weekend retreats. I have watched her fill his life with love, companionship, understanding.

I know a little bit about what the last months of a cancer victim are like. I can only say to her that we will do everything we can in this body to end cancer in our lifetime.

Yes, TED KENNEDY leaves very big shoes, shoes that probably will never be filled in quite the same way, from a family that will probably never be replicated.

I wish to end my remarks with a passage in the Prayer Book of the High Holy Day services for Reform Judaism. It was written when I was a teenager by a young rabbi I very much admired, and I wish to share it at this time:

Birth is a beginning and death a destination.
And life is a journey:

From childhood to eternity and youth to age;
From innocence to awareness and ignorance to knowing;
From foolishness to discretion, and then, perhaps, to wisdom;
From weakness to strength or strength to weakness—and, often, back again;
From health to sickness and back, we pray, to health again;
From offense to forgiveness, from loneliness to love, from joy to gratitude,
     from pain to compassion, and grief to understanding—
From fear to faith; from defeat to defeat to defeat—
Until, looking backward or ahead, we see that victory lies not in some high
     place along the way, but in having made the journey, stage by stage,
     a sacred pilgrimage.
Birth is a beginning and death a destination.
And life is a journey, a sacred pilgrimage—
To life everlasting.

TED KENNEDY leaves a giant legacy in this body and we should not forsake it.

Thank you very much, Mr. President. I yield the floor.

The PRESIDING OFFICER (Mr. Udall of New Mexico). The Senator from Montana is recognized.

Mr. BAUCUS. Mr. President, following the passing of President John F. Kennedy, Senator Mike Mansfield said, "He gave us of his love that we, too, in turn, might give."

These words ring true today as we remember the life of our late colleague, Senator TED KENNEDY.

So much of this country's history in the past half century can be attributed to this one man. But TED KENNEDY was also a modest man, and he would not have put it that way.

Speaking almost 30 years ago at the 1980 Democratic National Convention, he quoted Tennyson:

I am a part of all that I have met ...
Tho much is taken, much abides ...
That which we are, we are—
One equal temper of heroic hearts ...
Strong in will
To strive, to see, to find, and not to yield.

In the more than 46 years that Senator KENNEDY served this body, he did not yield and, in turn, he affected each and every American.

During his career in the Senate, Senator KENNEDY authored thousands of bills, and hundreds of them became law. From championing civil rights to advocating equal opportunity and higher education, to fighting for access to affordable health care for all Americans, Senator KENNEDY's work has quite simply improved the quality of life for millions of Americans. Over the past 2 weeks we have heard many speak of his accomplishments.

It didn't take long for me to realize when I came to this body, and more and more as each year passed, that TED KENNEDY was probably the greatest legislator in modern American political history. The guy was amazing, absolutely amazing; an inspiration for me personally to try to be a very good legislator. Many people have also said that. I am not the only one who has recognized his talents and that he is probably the best legislator in modern American political history.

Let me just say why that was true for me. First of all, it was the passion of his convictions. His moral compass was set so true: for the average person, the little guy, the person who didn't have representation, health care, the poor, civil rights. He just believed so passionately, so steadfastly. His moral compass was just so firmly set. There is no question of what TED KENNEDY was and what he believed in, and it made him alive. It was his dream to fulfill the lives of the people he worked so hard for.

All of us remember TED KENNEDY working so hard to fulfill his dreams. From his desk over here, he would stand up and he would thunder, red-faced. He would get so involved, so passionate, speaking so loudly, almost shouting what he believed in. You couldn't help but know that here was a guy who believed what he said and, by gosh, let's listen to him. He also had terrific staff. TED KENNEDY's staff had him so well prepared. All of these briefing books—I will never forget the briefing books TED took, and he read them. He studied them. He was so well prepared. Along with his passion was his preparation, and his staff just helped him prepare because they were all one team. They were working so closely together for the causes they believed in.

I also was impressed and found him to be such a great legislator because after the speeches he believed in so thoroughly and passionately, he would sit down with you and start to negotiate, try to work out an agreement, try to work out some solution that made sense for him and made sense for you if you happened to be on the other side. It was amazing to sit and watch him work, a different demeanor, a different temperament. He would sit there and cajole, talk, tell jokes, all in good spirit, all in an attempt to try to get to the solution.

On the one hand he would be here in the Chamber and he would be thundering, but in the conference room he would be saying, "OK, let's figure out how to do this. How do we get this done?" It was amazing. It was such a lesson to learn, just watching him legislate.

I think he is also one of the best legislators in modern American political history because he had such a light touch. He really cared individually for people, not just groups but individually. We have heard references to a book he gave Senator Byrd, a poetry book, and how Senator KENNEDY would bring his dogs over to Senator Byrd's office; and listening to Senator Chambliss, how Senator KENNEDY made sure he knew when Senator Chambliss' grandchildren would be here so the grandchildren could see his dogs. He loved his dogs, and he had that very light touch.

I remember not too long ago—and Senator Byrd referred to it—I think it was Senator Byrd's 67th wedding anniversary, and Senator KENNEDY had the foresight and the caring to send 67 roses to Robert Byrd and Erma Byrd. It was one of the things he just did, as well as all the letters he wrote, the handwritten letters he wrote.

Here is this wonderful guy who probably never used a BlackBerry; didn't know what they were. We know what they are. We use them. He wrote notes, hundreds of notes, thousands of handwritten notes, tens of thousands of handwritten notes. It was incredible. He would write a note to anybody at any time—just a light touch—on their birthday or call them on their birthday or call somebody who was in the hospital. He would just do that, more than any other Senator here I can think of, and I would venture to say probably more than most Senators combined. He was just that way.

Let me give one small example. Several years ago, in my hometown of Helena, MT, I was at a meeting and came back late at night after the meeting, and my mother said, "Max, TED KENNEDY called."

"Really?"

"Yes," Mom said. "Well, I told him you were out, but we had a nice chat, TED KENNEDY and I."

"What did you talk about?"

"We talked about the Miles City bucking horse sale." It is an event in Montana that comes up every year. TED came and rode a horse at the Miles City bucking horse sale back in 1960.

A few days later I was back on the floor of the Senate, and I walked up to TED and I said, "TED, I understand you talked to my mother."

[85]

"Oh," he said. "Sometimes on the telephone you are talking to somebody, you can tell who the person is. Your mother, she is such a wonderful person, so gracious," on and on, talking about my mother and the conversation the two of them had.

They had never met before. My mother is a staunch Republican, and here is TED KENNEDY.

So I went back home a few days later, and I told my mother, I said, "Mom, TED was sure impressed with the telephone call you had."

"Oh, gee, that is great. That is wonderful."

My mom wrote TED a note thanking him for being so—for praising her so much to me, her son, just a few days earlier.

Well, the next thing I knew, my mother and TED were pen pals. TED wrote a letter back to my mother, and they were back and forth and back and forth. I would be at a committee hearing someplace and TED would say, "Hey, Max, look. Here is the letter I am writing your mother." Just out of the blue. Basically, they were just reminiscing about Montana and again about the bucking horse sale, which is another reason TED was such a great guy.

He lived life so fully. He just loved life. He embraced life in all of the ways that life is available to a man. He was just wonderful that way.

Back in 1960 when his brother was running for President, TED was assigned the Western States in the 1960 Presidential campaign. So TED was out in Montana, and they went to a Democratic gathering. There wasn't anybody there, so he went to the Miles City bucking horse sale. We in Miles City, MT, have this bucking event. We take these horses off the prairie and buck them. You bid on the horses and, obviously, the best bucking horses get the highest bid and go off with the rodeo operators and they use them.

Anyway, the long and the short of it is, TED was there and he went to the bucking horse sale and got in the booth because he wanted to speak on behalf of his brother. The announcer said, "Well, young man, if you want to speak, first you have to ride a horse."

TED said, "Why not?"

So TED got on a horse, and there is this wonderful photo of TED at the Miles City bucking horse sale in Montana that somebody took. So there is TED on his bronco. I don't think he made the full 8 seconds, but he sure had a great time on that horse.

The long and short of it is, he is a great man for so many reasons, and we love TED for all he was. Again, I think he was the greatest legislator I think, in modern American political history.

I am touched by what a family man he was. As the years went by, after his brothers were tragically lost and all that happened in the Kennedy family, TED was a rock to others in the family. He experienced so much and he went through so much tragedy and it has built so much character.

TED was more than a Senate icon who fought for causes, more than a voice for the Commonwealth of Massachusetts. As I mentioned, he was a loving son, brother, husband, father, uncle, grandfather, and friend. Working with him for the past 30 years is one of the greatest honors I have had as a Senator.

TED, as far as I am concerned, we are going to take up your last great cause, health care reform. We are, in the Senate, doing all we can to get it passed. I, personally, pledge every ounce of energy at my command to help get health care reform passed for all the American people and for TED KENNEDY.

He was a wonderful man, and he will be sorely missed. I don't think there is going to be another man or woman in the Senate who will be a giant such as TED KENNEDY. He was that great a guy.

I yield the floor.

The PRESIDING OFFICER. The Senator from Wyoming is recognized.

Mr. ENZI. Mr. President, I appreciate having this opportunity to join in the celebration of the life of TED KENNEDY. His loss was deeply personal to all of us because he was a strong and vital presence not only in the day-to-day work of the Senate but in our day-to-day lives as well. He was interested and concerned not only about his colleagues but our staffs and all those with whom he worked on a long list of issues that will continue to have an impact on our Nation for many generations to come. That was the kind of individual TED was—active and completely involved in all things that had to do with the work of the Senate.

For my part, I have lost a Senate colleague who was willing to work with me and with Senators on both sides of the aisle. He was my committee chairman and my good friend.

For those across the country who mourn his passing, they have lost a trusted and treasured voice in the Senate, a champion who fought for them for almost 50 years.

The political landscape of our country has now been permanently changed. I think we all sensed what his loss would mean to the country as we heard the news of his passing. Now we take this time to look back to the past and remember our favorite stories and instant replay memories of the Senator from Massachusetts.

In the more than 12 years I have had the privilege of serving Wyoming in the Senate, I had the good fortune to come to know TED on a number of levels. As a Senator, he was a tremendous force to be dealt with on the floor. If you were on his side, you knew you had a warrior fighting alongside you who went to battle without the slightest fear of failure or defeat. If you had to face him from the other side of the arena, you knew you had a tremendous battle on your hands because, when it came to the principles he believed in, no one said it better or with more passion or more depth of understanding of the issues involved. As a result, he was able to notch an impressive list of legislative victories.

During his long and remarkable career, there were few initiatives that didn't attract his attention and his unique spirited touch that often turned them from faint hopes for change to dreams at long last come true. Whether it was an increase in the minimum wage, equal rights for all Americans or the effort to reform our Nation's health care system, which was his greatest dream, TED operated at one speed and one direction—full speed ahead—and it always found him making progress on the task at hand.

Over the years I was fortunate to have an opportunity to work with him on a number of issues of great importance to us both. He knew what he had to have in a bill to get his side to agree on it, and I was fortunate to have a sense of what it would take to get votes from my side. So, together, we were able to craft several bills that we moved through committee and to the Senate floor.

When I served as the chairman of the Health, Education, Labor, and Pensions Committee, the partnership we had forged over the years helped us to compile a record of which we were both very proud. We passed 35 bills out of committee, and 27 of them were signed into law by the President. Most of them passed unanimously. I remember attending a bill signing during which the President remarked, "You are the only committee sending me anything." We checked, and he was right, and that was due, in large part, to TED's willingness to work with us to get things done.

I will always remember two stories about TED. One was a time when we were working together on a mine safety law. Nothing had been done in that area for almost 30 years. The average bill takes about 6 years to pass around here. Thanks to TED, we got that one done in 6 weeks, and it has made a difference.

Another had to do with my first legislative initiative after I arrived as a newly sworn-in freshman Senator. I knew TED had quite a good working relationship with my predecessor, Alan Simpson. So as I began to work on an OSHA safety bill, I started to discuss the bill with TED and other colleagues and go through it section by section. I knew TED's support would be instrumental if my efforts to pass the bill would be successful. So I arranged to meet with him.

TED opened our meeting by presenting me with some press clippings he had collected for me about my mother's award as "Mother of the Year." That impressed me and showed me how he kept up on anything that was of importance to those people he worked with—members and staff.

Then he spent a great deal of time going over the bill with me section by section. He helped me to make it a winner. Although the bill, as a whole, didn't pass, several sections made it into law. I found out later that this wasn't the way things are usually done around here, and in all the years TED had been in the Senate, nobody had gone over a bill with him a section at a time. I probably didn't need to.

That started a friendship and a good working relationship with him we both cherished. I tried to be a good sounding board for him, and he always did the same for me. Our friendship can best be summed up when TED came to my office and presented me with a photo of a University of Wyoming football helmet next to a Harvard football helmet, with the inscription, "The Cowboys and the Crimson make a great team." We did, and I will always remember his thoughtfulness and kindness in reaching out to me.

TED was one of those remarkable individuals who made all those he worked with more productive. He was a man of exceptional abilities, and he was blessed to have a truly remarkable helpmate by his side. Vicki is a woman of great strength, who brought a renewed focus and direction to TED's life. She was his most trusted confidant, his best friend, and a wellspring of good advice and political counsel. He would have never been all that he was without her, and she will forever be a special part of his life's story.

For the Enzis, we will always remember how thoughtful he was when my grandchildren were born. He was almost as excited as I was. He presented me with a gift for each of them that will always be a cherished reminder that TED had a great appreciation for all of us, and he treated both Members and staff with the same kindness and concern.

Actually, we got Irish Mist training pants for each of them as they were born.

When TED was asked, during an interview, what he wanted to be most remembered for, he said he wanted to make a difference for our country. He was able to do that and so much more. He will be missed by us all, and he will never be forgotten. All those who knew and loved him will always carry a special memory with them of how he touched their lives as he tried to make our Nation and the world a better place.

Now he has been taken from us, and it will always feel like it all happened too soon. He has a record of achievements and success that will probably not be matched for a long time to come. He was a special friend and a mentor who had a lot to teach about how to get things done in the Senate. I know I will miss him and his willingness to sit down and visit about how to get something through the Senate and passed into law. Now he is at peace and with God. May God bless and be with him and continue to watch over his family for years to come.

The PRESIDING OFFICER. The Senator from Washington is recognized.

Mrs. MURRAY. Mr. President, when I was young, TED KENNEDY was larger than life. I was just 12 years old when he was first elected to the Senate as the youngest son of a political dynasty that seemed to dominate the television each night in my house and the newspapers every day.

At first, he served in the shadow of his older brothers. But as I grew up, the youngest brother of the Kennedy family did, too—in front of the entire Nation.

For me and so many others, TED KENNEDY became a symbol of perseverance over tragedy—from his walk down Pennsylvania Avenue at the side of Jacqueline Kennedy, to the heartbreaking speech he delivered at his brother Bobby's funeral, to his pledge to carry on the causes of those who had championed his bid for the Presidency.

TED KENNEDY routinely appeared before the American people with great courage at the most trying times. And all the while, he was also standing in this Chamber each day with that same grit and determination to fight for the people of Massachusetts and the Nation.

On issues from protecting the environment, civil rights, increasing the minimum wage, and health care, he was a passionate and unmatched advocate and leader.

So it was with a lifetime of watching Senator KENNEDY with admiration from afar that I arrived here as a freshman Senator in 1993. By the time I was elected, TED was already on his way to becoming one of the most powerful and influential Senators of all time. So I couldn't believe it when I first walked out onto this floor, and he walked over to personally welcome me. For me, that would have been enough—the lion of the Senate reaching out to a rookie—but to TED KENNEDY it wasn't.

Through calls to my office, discussions on the floor, and by taking me under his wing on the HELP Committee, he became a friend, a mentor, and sooner than I could have ever imagined, a courageous partner on legislation that I cared deeply about.

As a State senator in Washington, I had worked very hard before I got here to successfully change the State laws in Washington on family and medical leave. It was an issue that was extremely personal to me. My father had been diagnosed with multiple sclerosis when I was very young. Since that time, my mother had always been his primary caregiver. But a few years before I ran and became a senator, my mother had a heart attack and had to undergo bypass surgery.

Suddenly, my six brothers and sisters and I were faced with the question of who was going to take time off to care for the people we loved the most, the people who cared for us for so long.

A family leave policy would have allowed any of us just a few weeks necessary to see them through their medical crisis. But at the time, none was available.

So after running and winning and coming to the Senate, the Family and Medical Leave Act was a bill I wanted to stand and fight for. As it turned out, it was the first bill we considered.

Senator KENNEDY was here managing that bill on the Senate floor, and I found out that he, too, had a personal connection to that bill.

I well remember one day when Senator KENNEDY pulled me aside to tell me about how he had spent a lot of time with his own son in the hospital fighting cancer and how he met so many people at that time who could not afford to take time off to care for their loved ones and how some were forced to quit their jobs to take care of somebody they loved because they were sick. He told me that, together, we were going to work hard and get this bill passed. Then he showed this rookie how to do it.

Week after week, he fought against bad amendments to get the votes we needed to pass it.

He blended the right mix of patience and passion. He spoke out loudly in speeches when he needed to, and he whispered into the ears of colleagues when that was called for. A few days after Senator KENNEDY pledged to me we would get it done, we did.

Through that effort, and many more battles on this floor, I learned so much from him and so have all of us because, more than almost anyone, Senator KENNEDY knew the Senate. He knew how to make personal friends, even with those he didn't agree with politically. He knew how to reach out and find ways to work with people to get them to compromise for the greater good. He knew when not to give up. He knew when to change the pace or turn the page to get things done. He knew when to go sit down next to you or pick up the phone and call you. He knew how to legislate. Because of that, he built an incredible legacy.

It is a legacy that will not only live on in the Senate Chamber, where he was so well loved and respected; it is a legacy that will live on in the classrooms across America, where kids from Head Start to college have benefited from his commitment to opportunities in education; on manufacturing floors, where he fought for landmark worker safety protection; in our hospitals, where medical research that he championed is saving lives every day; in courtrooms, where the legacy of discrimination was dealt a blow by his years of service on the Judiciary Committee; in voting booths, where he fought for our most basic rights in a democracy to be protected and expanded for decades; and in so many other places that were touched by his service, his passion, and his giant heart.

Senator KENNEDY fought for and won so many great battles. But for many of us who worked with him every day, it may be the small moments that will be remembered the most—the personal touch he brought, not only to legislating but to life.

As I mentioned a moment ago, my mom had to take care of my dad for most of his life. His multiple sclerosis confined him to a wheelchair and she could not ever leave his side. One of the few and maybe the only time she did leave my dad is when I was elected to the Senate and she flew all the way from Washington State to Washington, DC, to see me be sworn in.

To my mom, TED KENNEDY and his family were amazing individuals whom she followed closely throughout their lives, through their triumphs and, of course, through tragedy. After I was sworn in, and my mother was up in the gallery watching, we walked back through the Halls of Congress to my office. Shortly after that, we had a visitor. Senator KENNEDY unexpectedly came over to my office and gave my mom a huge hug. I will never forget the look on her face, the tears in her eyes, the clear disbelief that she had met TED KENNEDY, and it was overpowering. It was a moment with my mom I will never forget, and it is certainly a moment I will never forget with my friend TED KENNEDY.

I am going to miss him. I know our country is going to miss him. But as he reminded us in his courageous speech that he delivered last summer in Denver, the torch has been passed to a new generation, and the work begins anew.

So today, as we honor all of his contributions to the Senate and the Nation, we must also remember to heed that brave final call and continue his fight for all of those who cannot fight for themselves.

Mr. President, I yield the floor.

The PRESIDING OFFICER. The Senator from New York.

Mr. SCHUMER. Mr. President, first, I thank my friend and colleague Senator Murray for her heartfelt words, and all of my colleagues. The love we all felt and feel for TED KENNEDY is genuine. It is person to person because that is how he was.

There is so much to say. I know we are limited in time. We could speak forever. I think every one of us could speak forever about TED KENNEDY because he had so many interactions with each of us. It is amazing that every person in this body has a long list of stories and thousands of people in Massachusetts and thousands more throughout America. One would think there were 20 TED KENNEDYs. He had so much time for the small gesture that mattered so much, such as the hug, going out of his way to go to a reception and hug Patty Murray's mom. It happened over and over again. So we could each speak forever.

I know time is limited. My colleague from Oregon is waiting. We are going to shut off debate soon, and others want to speak. I will touch on a few things.

I could speak forever about TED KENNEDY. I thought of him every day while he was alive; I think of him every day that he is gone. I had a dream about him the other night where typically he was taking me around to various places in Boston and explaining a little bit about each one with a joke, with a smile, with a remembrance.

There is also nothing we can say about TED KENNEDY because no one is going to replace him. No words can come close to equaling the man.

You read about history, and you read about the great people in the Senate—the Websters, the Clays, the LaFollettes, the Wagners. What a privilege it was for somebody such as myself, a kid from Brooklyn whose father was an exterminator, never graduated from college, to be in the presence of and was actually a friend to a great man. I don't think I can say that about anyone else. It is amazing.

What I want to tell the American people—you all read about him. There were the good times and the bad times and the brickbats that were thrown at him, not so much recently but in the early days. But here in the Senate, when you get to know people personally and when you are in our walk of life, being a Senator, you get to know a lot of people personally. You get to meet a lot of famous people. Some of them, frankly, are disappointing. The more you see them, the less you want to know them. But with TED KENNEDY, the more you got to see him, the closer you got, the better he looked.

He had flaws, but he was flawless. He was such a genuine person and such a caring person and such an honorable and decent man that I wish my children had gotten to know him, that my friends had gotten to know him, that all of my 19 million constituents had gotten to know him a little bit the way I did.

What a guy. There are so many stories and so many memories. One day TED and I sat next to each other—I used to sit over there. I think it was one of the vote-aramas, a long session. We occasionally would go up to his hideaway to talk. I said, "Why don't we bring some of the freshmen?" This was a couple of years ago. I regret that you, Mr. President, and the Senator from Oregon in the class of 2008 did not have that experience. We would go up to his hideaway, and he would regale us with stories. He would talk about the pictures on the wall and tell each person in caring detail what each picture meant, what each replica meant. He would tell jokes and laugh. His caring for each person in that room, each a new freshman, was genuine, and they knew it. We would go up regularly. It sort of became a thing, freshman Members of the Senate. TED didn't need them. He could get whatever he had to get done, and they would support him. But he cared about them as if they were almost family.

Whenever we had a late night, we would sort of gather—I would be the emissary and I would go over to TED and say, "Can we go upstairs?" "Of course." Amy Klobuchar, Sherrod Brown, Claire McCaskill, Bobby Casey—their faces would light up, and there we would go to hear more stories about the past, the Senate, the individuals. It is a memory none of us will forget.

TED KENNEDY would size people up early on, and he would care about them. He was very kind to me, but he also knew I was the kind of guy you had to put in his place a little bit. I would get hazed by TED KENNEDY. Jay Rockefeller told me he went through the same thing when he got here. He knew who I was but would deliberately not mention my name. He would be standing there saying, "Senator Mikulski, you will do this, and Senator Harkin, you will do this; Senator Conrad, you will do this—I was the last one—and the others will do this." It was fun. He did it with a twinkle in his eyes. We loved, he and I, the give and take, Brooklyn-Boston.

The first year I was here, the Red Sox were playing the Yankees in the playoffs. TED and I made a bet. He said, "The loser will have to hold the pennant of the winning team over his head and recite 'Casey at the Bat' on Capitol Hill." We had a bet. The Yankees won. I went over to him—and he was feigning fear, this man who had been through everything. When we went out on the steps, he was hiding behind me. I have a picture of it on my wall. We were joking and laughing. And then he did his duty.

I was only a freshman Senator, sort of like Patty or anybody else. He went out of his way for all of us. He would tell me to remember the birthdays and the individual happenings in each person's life, in each Senator's life, and go over and say something to them. It was his way of teaching me. It was done like a father. An amazing person.

As I said, the closer you got to him, the better he looked. As a legislator and as a giant in our history—and all the history books record it—people have referred to all his accomplishments. But I want to share with people how it was in person, one on one. You could be a Senator or you could be two guys on a street corner. He was fun and he was caring and he was loving. He was a big man, but his heart was much bigger than he was.

He loved almost everybody. He saw the good in people and brought it out. He saw the faults in people, and in a strong but gentle way tried to correct them. He was great on the outside, and he was even more great on the inside.

Again, I see my colleagues are waiting. I will part with this little memory that I will never forget. TED and I became good friends. We spent time together in many different ways. When he got sick, I felt bad, like we all did. I would call him every so often. This was October of last year. He was ill, but he was still in strong health. I called him a couple of days before it was October. I said, "We have a DSCC event a couple days from now in Boston." I thought I would call and say hello, let him know I was going to be in his State, his territory.

He said, "What are you doing before the event? Why don't you come out to the compound at Hyannis?" I did. He picked me up at the airport. I flew in on a little plane. I will never forget, he had his hat on. He was happy as could be, pointing out everything, full of vim and vigor.

It is obvious why the man was not afraid of death. When you know yourself and you know you have done everything as he did on both a personal basis and as a leader, you are not afraid of death. Anyway, he was not at all talking about that.

We were supposed to go out sailing, but it was too windy. So we had lunch—he, Vicki, and I—clam chowder and all the usual stuff. Then he said, "I want to show you something." He lived in the big house on the compound, the one you see in the pictures. He took me to the house by the side. That was the house where President Kennedy lived because when President Kennedy was President, Joseph P. Kennedy, TED's father, lived in the big house.

For about 3 hours, he opened all these drawers and closets, things on the walls, and with each one in loving, teaching detail talked to me about the history of the family and of Boston, what happened from Honey Fitz, the mayor, through his father, and TED growing up in all these pictures, laughing and reminiscing, and then about President Kennedy as he was growing up, and then as President in this little house and through to TED. He was sort of passing on the memories. He did it again out of generosity, spirit, love, and friendship.

As I say, he was a great man and every one of us knows his greatness was not only in the public eye but in the private one on one. A great man. The term is overused. There are not many. He was one. I was privileged to get to know him, to get to be his friend, to stand in that large shadow, learn from him, enjoy it, and to love him.

So, TED, you will always be with us. They may take those flowers off that desk, and they may take the great black drape off the desk, but you will always be here for me, for all of us, and for our country.

I yield the floor.

The PRESIDING OFFICER (Mr. Brown). The Senator from Oregon is recognized.

Mr. MERKLEY. Mr. President, I rise today to remember and honor our colleague Senator EDWARD KENNEDY. I first had the pleasure of hearing Senator KENNEDY speak in 1976. I wanted to come out to Washington, DC, to see how our Nation operated. I had the great privilege of serving as an intern for a Senator from my home State, Senator Hatfield. My father had always talked about Senator KENNEDY as someone who spoke for the disenfranchised, someone who spoke for the dispossessed, someone who cared about the working man. So I was looking forward to possibly meeting him or at least hearing him, when lo and behold, I found out he was scheduled to speak as part of a series of lectures to the interns that summer. So I made sure to get there early, and what followed was exactly the type of address you might anticipate—a roaring voice, a passionate spirit, a principled presentation of the challenges we face to make our society better. I walked out of that lecture and thought: Thank goodness we have leaders like Senator KENNEDY fighting for the working people, the challenged, the dispossessed in our society.

Through that summer, each time I heard Senator KENNEDY was on the Senate floor I tried to slip over and go up to the staff section so I could sit in and see a little bit of the lion of the Senate in action. During that time I never anticipated that I would have a chance to come back and serve in the Senate with Senator KENNEDY. But 33 years later, this last January, when I was sworn in, that unanticipated, miraculous event of serving with him occurred.

I wanted to talk to him about the possibility of joining his Health, Education, Labor, and Pensions Committee—a committee where so many battles for working Americans, so many battles for the disenfranchised Americans are waged. So with some trepidation I approached him on the Senate floor to speak with him and asked if he thought I might be able to serve on that committee, if he might whisper in the ear of our esteemed majority leader in that regard, if he thought I might serve well. It was with some pleasure that weeks later I had a message on my phone in which he went on at some length welcoming me to that committee. That was the first committee to which I received an assignment here, and I couldn't have been more excited and more pleased.

I didn't have a chance to have a lot of conversations with Senator KENNEDY. I was very struck when a bit more than a month ago his staff contacted me and said, in conversation with Senator KENNEDY, they were wondering if I might like to carry on the torch on the Employment Non-Discrimination Act, a civil rights measure he cared a great deal about. They were asking me because it was a battle I had waged in the Oregon Legislature. It had been a hard battle, fought over a number of years, and a battle we had won.

I was more than excited, more than honored to help carry the torch on such an important civil rights measure, and I hope I will be able to do that in a way he would have been satisfied and pleased.

The Senator from New York, Mr. Schumer, talked about the many conversations that took place in Senator KENNEDY's hideaway with freshmen Senators and the stories that were passed on. I didn't get to share much in those types of conversations, but as we were working on health care, Senator KENNEDY invited a group of us to his hideaway to brainstorm. Through the course of about 2 hours, we went through many of the features and many of the challenges and how we might be able to go forward and finally realize that dream of affordable, accessible health care for every single American.

When the meeting concluded, I had a chance to speak with Senator KENNEDY about the picture he had on his wall of his beautiful yacht—the *Mya*. Senator KENNEDY and I both have a passion for sailing. It connected us across the generations, it connected us from the west coast to the east coast, it connected us between the son of a millwright and the son of a U.S. ambassador. It was magic to see the twinkle in his eye

as he started to talk of his love of sailing and some of the
adventures he had on various boats over time and with family.

I asked him if he was familiar with one of my favorite stories—an autobiography written by Captain Joshua Slocum.
Joshua Slocum had been raised in a large family and, to my
recollection, a family of no great means. He had gone to sea
when he was a young boy—as a cabin boy or a deckhand—
and he learned to sail the tall ships. Over time he advanced
through the ranks until eventually he was the captain of a
merchant tall-masted ship. He had amassed some considerable amount of investment through loans to put up his share
of that ship. When the ship went down, he lost everything.
He saved his life, but he lost all of his possessions.

He was up in New England wrestling with how to overcome this tragedy and what to do with his life, and Captain
Slocum had a kernel of an idea. He was offered the gift of
a ship. Not really a ship, a modest boat between 20 and 30
feet long, single-masted. He later overhauled it and added an
after-mast. But he thought: I can rebuild this ship. He said
he rebuilt it, in his story, Captain Slocum. He rebuilt it, all
but the name. The *Spray* stayed from the beginning to the
end. He rebuilt it and went to sea to fish. But it wasn't much
to his liking, and so Captain Slocum had an idea that he was
going to perhaps sail around the world.

He thought: Why not just sail right out across the Atlantic.
It was a revolutionary idea because no one had ever tried to
sail around the world by themselves, just a single person.
But he set off and he went to Europe.

I tell you this story at some length because Senator KEN-
NEDY knew this story well, and we enjoyed sharing pieces of
it back and forth.

He had gone forth in 1895 and taken 3 years to cir-
cumnavigate the globe and came back to New England 3
years later, in 1898. So this was well more than a century
ago, and people around the world were astounded to see him
sail into a harbor all by himself having crossed the broad ex-
panse of an ocean.

In some ways, the life of Captain Slocum represents a
version of the life of Senator KENNEDY—someone who faced
great adversity, who faced great tragedy, but looked at all of
it and said: "I am going to go forward and do something bold,
something important."

For Senator KENNEDY, it wasn't literally sailing around
the world but it was sailing through a host of major issues

that affect virtually every facet of our lives—certainly the issue of public service, the National Service Act, the issue of mental health, and the issue of health care, and the issue of education.

Others who have served with him have spoken in far greater detail and more eloquently than I ever could, but I just want to say to Senator KENNEDY: Thank you for your life of service. Thank you for overcoming adversity to undertake a bold journey, a journey that has touched every one of our lives. Thank you for reaching out to converse with this son of a millworker from Oregon who felt so privileged to be on the floor of the Senate and to have had just a few months with this master of the Senate and who will hopefully carry forward some of the passion and the principle he so embodied.

The PRESIDING OFFICER. The senior Senator from North Dakota is recognized.

Mr. CONRAD. Mr. President, I rise today to remember our colleague, Senator KENNEDY. There is a newspaper in the Cloakroom that has TED's picture, and it has a quote from TED. It reads this way:

Since I was a boy, I have known the joy of sailing the waters off of Cape Cod. And for all my years in public life, I have believed that America must sail toward the shores of liberty and justice for all.

He went on to say:

There is no end to that journey, only the next great voyage.

I like to think that TED is on that next great voyage now. What a man.

I remember so well being elected in 1986 to the Senate and being sworn in in 1987. I held a reception in a little restaurant close by with friends and family from North Dakota. I will never forget it. It was packed. You couldn't move; so many people had come from North Dakota to be with me, family members from all over the country, and a cousin of mine came up to me, so excited, and he said to me, "Senator KENNEDY is here." I hadn't known he was coming. But that was so typical of TED, reaching out to the most junior of us because he knew what his presence would mean. My family had been longtime supporters of the Kennedys, and it meant so much to my family for him to be there that day. That was so typical of him, taking time to do things he knew would mean a lot to others, even when it was inconvenient for him.

The thing I remember and will remember most about TED is his humanity: that smile, that twinkle in his eye, that kind of mischievous grin that would come over his face when he would be commenting on what was going on here, late at night sometimes—you know this place defies description. Yet he always maintained that sense of humor, that joy in life. He communicated it. He made all of us feel as if we were part of something important, something big.

When somebody in this Senate family had a problem, had a challenge, had a medical issue, very often TED was the first to call. I had someone in my family who had health issues, and somehow TED found out and kind of sidled up to me one day on the floor and said, "You know, I heard you have somebody who has a serious health issue. I suppose you already have doctors, but if you are looking for additional assistance or a second opinion and you want to find people who are experts in this area, I would be glad to help." That was TED KENNEDY, over and over reaching out to others, trying to help, trying to provide encouragement, trying to provide the lift. That was TED.

I remember so well about a decade ago when we were engaged in legislation on tobacco, we had a circumstance in which there was an important court decision, and there had to be laws passed to deal with it. I was asked to lead a task force here in the Senate to try to bring together different sides to deal with that legislation. Of course, for a long time TED KENNEDY had been a leader on those issues, as was Senator Frank Lautenberg, and there were others as well. TED far outstripped me in seniority. Yet I was asked to lead this task force. He came to me and said, "Sign me up as a soldier in your effort." We had dozens of meetings, and TED was always there, pitching in, helping to make a difference even when he was not the person leading the effort—it was somebody much more junior. Of course, he had many other responsibilities, but over and over, he was coming up, stepping up, helping out.

There was nothing small about TED KENNEDY. He had big plans, big ambitions, big hopes, and a big spirit. He was always reaching out to even the most junior of us to help out, to connect, to be supportive, and to show how much he cared about what we were doing and to give us a sense of how we were fitting into making history. TED also had a big view of the importance of the role of the Senate in making history and a sense of how critically important the decisions were that were being made in this Chamber. There was nothing small about TED KENNEDY.

When he was engaged in negotiations—I will never forget him saying to me, "Keep your eye on what is possible. You know, we might want to accomplish more, but take what you can get to advance the cause, to make progress, to improve the human condition, to make this a better place." That is what TED KENNEDY had in mind.

I want to close. I see colleagues who are here wishing to speak as well.

My favorite lines from a speech by TED KENNEDY are from the 1980 convention, when he closed with these words:

For all those whose cares have been our concern, the work goes on, the cause endures, the hope still lives, and the dream shall never die.

TED, the dream will never die. You are always in our thoughts.

I yield the floor.

The PRESIDING OFFICER. The Senator from Michigan is recognized.

Ms. STABENOW. Mr. President, I appreciate the opportunity to be here with colleagues, and I so appreciate the words of the Senator from North Dakota and those of the Senator from New York and all of our other colleagues who have been here, talking about our friend and colleague, the great Senator from Massachusetts.

I think for me, being in my second term and still a relative newcomer here, one of the greatest honors of my life was the opportunity to work and become friends with Senator TED KENNEDY.

I often have been asked what was the most surprising or exciting thing about being in the Senate. I always referred to TED KENNEDY, not only knowing him and the larger-than-life way he has been described, which was also true, but for me the images are of sitting in a small room going over amendments on the patients' bill of rights when I was in my first term and having the great TED KENNEDY—not his staff but TED KENNEDY—sitting in a room with advocates talking about how we needed to mobilize and get people involved and what we needed to do to get votes or how to write something—doing the work behind the scenes.

TED KENNEDY, because of who he was—his family, his certainly great leadership and knowledge, and his length of time here—could have simply stood on the floor and made eloquent speeches, which he always did—the booming voice in the back that would get louder and louder as he became more involved in what he was talking about. He could have just done that, and that would have been an incredible contribution to the Senate. But that is not what he did. He was as involved behind the scenes in getting things done, more so than in the public eye. He worked hard and showed all of us an example of someone who was dedicated to the details, to the advocacy as well as to what was happening on the floor of the Senate. It was a very important lesson for all of us.

As chair of the Steering and Outreach Committee for our Senate majority, one of my responsibilities is to bring people with various interests together, usually on a weekly basis, to meet with Members on issues from education to health care, clean energy, civil rights, veterans. People always wanted to have TED KENNEDY in the room. Again, as a very senior Member with tremendous responsibilities, chairing the HELP Committee and all of the other responsibilities he had, he could have easily said to me, "You know, I am just not going to be able to do that. We will have more junior Members come and join in these meetings." But he came, over and over again.

One of the things we joked about all the time was that he would see me coming and say, "I know, there is a meeting tomorrow. I will be there."

He was someone who gave his all at every moment. He also understood that people needed and wanted to see him, to hear him, with the important leadership role he had here. It was important to people. And he treated everyone the same.

He was committed to a vision of making America the best it could be, where every child would have the chance to grow up and be healthy, succeed in life, have a job, at the end of life a pension and retirement, and be able to live with dignity. His service was great, but his legacy is even greater.

I believe his challenge to each of us is even greater. It is true that nearly every major bill that passed in the last 47 years bears some mark from Senator TED KENNEDY—the Civil Rights Act; the Voting Rights Act; Meals for the Elderly; the Women, Infants, and Children Nutrition Program; the Violence Against Women Act; Title IX, which is giving so many women and girls the opportunity to participate and move through education's highest levels, including the U.S. Supreme Court, as well as the wonderful athletic abilities we have seen; the Children's Health Insurance Act; AmeriCorps;

the National Health Service; the American Health Parity Act; legislation to allow the FDA to regulate tobacco; the Ryan White Comprehensive AIDS Act; the Americans with Disabilities Act—it goes on and on. These are just a few of the hundreds of bills Senator KENNEDY sponsored or co-sponsored during his time in the Senate, and each and every one of those bills made America a little bit better.

His commitment to achieve the best for America, for every child, every family, every worker was unmatched. We have lost the lion of the Senate, and he will be sorely missed. Personally, I have lost a friend, someone for whom I had the highest personal respect and someone I cared deeply about as a person.

To Vicki, to the family, we give our love and affection and thanks for sharing him with us. In his maiden speech in the Senate, Senator KENNEDY spoke of his brother's legacy. Today, the same words can be spoken about him. "If his life and death had a meaning, it was that we should not hate but love one another; we should use our powers not to create the conditions of oppression that lead to violence, but conditions of freedom that lead to peace."

TED, we will miss you.

Mr. BURRIS. Mr. President, it is with a heavy heart that I take to the floor of the U.S. Senate today. For each of the past 47 years, this Chamber has rung with the words of a man who came to be known as the lion of the Senate. But today, that familiar voice has fallen silent.

For the first time in half a century, this Senate returns to its work without EDWARD M. KENNEDY. With his passing, our country has lost a true giant—a compassionate public servant who became a legend in his own time, a man whose legacy is bound up in the history of the U.S. Senate, whose life and works have touched everyone in America since the day he entered public service almost 50 years ago.

Over the course of his career, he influenced more legislation than just about anyone in history. He argued passionately for voting rights and helped extend the promise of our democracy to a new generation. He spoke out in defense of our Constitution and the principles of fairness we hold so dear. Time and again, he raised his booming voice on behalf of the less fortunate. He protected the rights and interests of the disabled. He extended health insurance coverage to children and fought to improve the American health care system, a struggle that would become the cause of his life. But perhaps his greatest single achievement came early in his career when he stepped to the center of the national debate and led the fight against segregation. He became a champion of the civil rights movement, lending his full compassion to a difficult and divisive issue.

Today, we live in a Nation that is more free, more fair, and more equal because of EDWARD KENNEDY. He was the single most effective U.S. Senator of our time. He did more good for more people than anyone in the Senate has done before. And it will be a very long time before we see the likes of him again. TED KENNEDY reminded us of the greatness that lives in our highest aspirations. He enjoyed wonderful triumphs and endured terrible tragedy. Through it all, he taught us to keep the fire burning, to confront every challenge with passion and hope and with undying faith in the country we love so much.

He reached across the aisle time and again. When everyone said compromise was impossible, TED KENNEDY did the impossible. When partisan politics divided conservatives from liberals and Republicans from Democrats, TED KENNEDY was always there to bring us together in the service of the American people.

I first met TED KENNEDY in 1962 when his brother was President and TED was a young man running for the U.S. Senate. I was a legal intern at the White House and a second-year law student at Howard University. For me, the chance to serve the Kennedy administration—and meet all three Kennedy brothers—was a remarkable and inspiring part of my early career in public service.

I had the good fortune to meet Senator KENNEDY one more time when I was running for reelection as State comptroller of the State of Illinois, having become the first African American ever elected statewide to office in my State. I was up for reelection, and I had a major fundraiser and I needed a big draw to come and help me raise funds.

Someone said, "Well, there is a Senator from Massachusetts named TED KENNEDY. He will come and help you."

I said, "No, no Senator of his caliber would come down to our capital for a fundraiser for a person who is running for State comptroller."

Needless to say, I contacted the Senator's office. Without hesitation, Senator TED KENNEDY appeared at the fundraiser in our State capital to help me maintain my seat as State comptroller.

During that same time, we had a little tragedy taking place that evening when our 15-year-old son in Chicago had been admitted to the hospital, and it was a question of whether I would be there at the fundraiser or go to Chicago to be with my son because my wife, his mother, was in Minnesota. So Senator KENNEDY understood the dilemma but went on with the fundraiser. We got our son taken care of, but after my son was out of the hospital and home, guess who I got a call from days later wondering how my son was doing? It was TED KENNEDY. You just don't see a man of this caliber each and every day in this country.

After I came to the U.S. Senate myself, I had the honor to serve with TED only briefly. In all the time I knew Senator KENNEDY, I came to see him as more than a living legend, more than a senior statesman, more than the lion he had become. For me, and for all who were fortunate enough to meet him over the years, he was a genuine human being, a remarkable ally, and a compassionate friend. He displayed nothing but kindness and respect for everyone he met, from his good friends to his bitter opponents.

But for his many accomplishments and for all that he accomplished over the course of a lifetime in public service, there was at least one victory that eluded him. As I address this Chamber today, we stand on the verge of health care reform only because we are standing on TED KENNEDY's shoulders.

And when the time comes, I plan to honor his legacy and pay tribute to his service by casting the vote he did not live long enough to see.

When Senator KENNEDY departed this life on August 25, he left more than an empty desk in this Senate Chamber. He left a fight for us to finish—a standard for us to bear. Long ago, he picked up the legacy of his fallen brothers and carried it forward into a new century.

Ronald Reagan once said:

Many men are great, but few capture the imagination and the spirit of the times. The ones who do are unforgettable.

He was talking about President Kennedy. But his words ring just as true when applied to John Kennedy's youngest brother.

They speak to TED's enormous vitality—to his towering impact on the lives of so many for so long. He is gone now, but his presence lingers in these halls.

In the many Senators to whom he has been a friend and mentor, in the dedication, faith, and love of country that he inspired, in the wood and stone and soul of this Senate Chamber, his legacy is very much alive.

Now, that legacy has been passed to each of us. And it is time to take up the standard once again. This is a moment to look to the future, not the past—to meet difficult problems with bold solutions.

As the lion of the Senate told us a year ago, at the Democratic National Convention, "the work begins anew, the hope rises again, and the dream lives on."

Mr. President, no single voice can fill this Chamber as his once did. But together, we can carry this refrain.

Mr. President. I yield the floor.

Mr. BROWN. I heard the eloquent speeches of Senators Stabenow, Schumer, Conrad, and Senator Merkley also about Senator KENNEDY.

I wish to tell two quick stories about him. I had the pleasure of serving on his committee from 2007 on. But early in my first year in the Senate, the Senators, as some know around the country, certainly all Members of the Senate know, we choose our desks on the Senate floor by seniority. And so in the first month or so of 2007, the freshmen, the other 9 members of my class, the 10 of us were choosing our seats on the Senate floor. You can look around the Senate Chamber. There is no bad place to sit.

I heard from a senior Member that Senators carve their names in their desk drawers; sort of like high school, perhaps. So I began to pull the drawers open in some of the desks that had not yet been chosen. I pulled open this drawer, and it had Hugo Black of Alabama, who was FDR's favorite Southern Senator, who introduced legislation for the 8-hour workday, making President Roosevelt's 8-hour workday bill seem a little less radical, and successfully made its way through the Senate; Senator Green from Rhode Island, who came here in the 1960s and served more than two decades; Senator Al Gore, Sr., from Tennessee. And then it just said "Kennedy," without a State and without a first name. So I asked TED to come over, and I said, "TED, which brother is this?"

He said, "It's Bobby's desk, I have Jack's desk."

And I, of course, fell in love with this desk and got the opportunity to sit here for the last 3 years.

The other real quick story about Senator KENNEDY: I know Senator Kyl is scheduled to speak. I and others were invited, from time to time, to go up to his study just off the Senate floor, one floor above us outside the Chamber, and to talk to him and hear him tell stories late in the evening as we were voting sometimes until midnight or 1 or 2 a.m.

What struck me about his study were the photos on the wall. The photos were pictures we all recognized: President Kennedy, Joe Kennedy, Rose Kennedy, Ethel Kennedy, Bobby Kennedy, Eunice Kennedy Shriver; all the people whom we recognized.

But TED KENNEDY said to us, "These are my family photos."

These were people we recognized in the photos, but I had never seen those photos, none of us had. These were not the photos in *Life* magazine; these were the photos of the Kennedy family.

But what impressed me about that was they were the Kennedys at Hyannis Port, the Kennedys sailing, the Kennedys in the Capitol, the Kennedys at the White House. What impressed me was TED KENNEDY so easily could have given up; he could have gone back to a very easy life, particularly after the assassination of Robert Kennedy in 1968. TED had been in the Senate for 6 years. It would have been so easy for him to walk away from this job, from this kind of life, from the danger he faced.

Instead, he stayed and he fought. He had everything anybody could hope for in life. He had a loving family who cared so much about him. He had all the wealth he needed and the lifestyle so many would have been so tempted by. But, instead, he stayed and served right up until his death.

That says to me everything I love about TED KENNEDY and everything we all should need to know about Senator KENNEDY.

The PRESIDING OFFICER (Mr. Brown.) The Senator from Arizona.

Mr. KYL. I would say to my colleague from Ohio, I commented on the same point. It is pretty obvious Senator KENNEDY could have, because of who he was, done just about anything.

He certainly would not have had to work as hard as he did. But I have never known a harder working Senator than Senator KENNEDY.

Mr. CARDIN. Mr. President, I rise to pay tribute to my friend, our colleague, civil rights icon of the Senate, Senator EDWARD M. KENNEDY, our lion in the Senate. I have lost someone who has been a mentor, a friend, and one of my heroes. The Nation has lost a great leader. To his family, he was a rock. To his wife Vicki, his children, Kara, Edward (Ted, Jr.), and Patrick, my former colleague when I was in the House, and to his sister Jean and the entire Kennedy family, we extend our deepest condolences. To his Senate colleagues and his constituents in Massachusetts, he was a beacon of hope and perseverance for a better day in America.

When I came to the Senate in 2007, I was frequently asked during my first year—I am sure the Presiding Officer has been asked this by people in his State—what is the highlight, what is the difference, what makes this place a special place? What did you find different in the Senate than you did in the House? The example I gave during my first month in the Senate is when I was sitting by myself on the floor of the Senate, Senator KENNEDY came by and sat next to me. He said, "Do you mind if we talk for a moment?" He sat next to me, a new Member of the Senate, and he said, "Ben, can you tell me what you think we should be doing in health care?" He wanted my views. He was looking to find out what this new Senator from Maryland thought was possible in health care reform. That was Senator KENNEDY. Senator KENNEDY engaged each Member of the Senate to find a common denominator to move forward in solving the major problems of America. It was truly a unique experience for me to see one of the most senior Members of the Senate, a person known internationally for his legislative skills, seek out a new Member.

I remember one of my constituents asking me during my first year which Senator I most admire for his or her work ethic. I said immediately: Senator KENNEDY. They were taken aback because they didn't realize that this senior Senator, this person who had served for over 40 years in the Senate, was a person who dedicated every day to doing his very best. Whether it was working with staff or meeting with Members or working his committee or making a speech on the floor of the Senate, his work ethic was one of not wasting a single moment in order to deal with the Nation's problems.

Senator KENNEDY served for 47 years in the Senate and had a tremendous impact on the issues that have shaped our Nation for almost a half century. He authored over 2,500 pieces of legislation. All Americans have been touched by Senator KENNEDY's work. He dedicated his life to the nameless, the poor, and the minority voices in America, and that dedication is legendary. He has touched the lives of all Americans by his work in the Senate, whether it was what he did for voting rights or improving educational opportunities, dealing with the rights of immigrants, minimum wage laws, national service, help for the mentally ill, equality for women, minorities, the disabled, children, the gay and lesbian community. The list goes on and on. He was there fighting for those who otherwise would not have had a voice in our government. He did it whether it was popular or not in the State or Nation. He was true to his principles. The list goes on and on of what he did.

I had the great pleasure of serving with him on the Judiciary Committee for 2 years. What a legacy he has created on that committee. It was a great honor for me to be able to serve those 2 years on the committee with him and to listen to him engage. There has been no greater Senator on the Judiciary Committee to fight on behalf of civil rights than Senator KENNEDY.

He was clearly the conscience of the Senate, to make sure we used every opportunity to advance the rights of all Americans so they could achieve their best. He was a legislator's legislator. He had a gift. He had the ability to work across party lines and get work done.

He believed in progress and doing the right thing. He had a voice that carried through the Halls of the Senate with such passion and yet with such grace.

Senator KENNEDY once said, "We know the future will outlast all of us, but I believe that all of us will live in the future we make." Senator KENNEDY stood for and fought for a better America—even when it was not the popular thing to do. Senator KENNEDY stayed true to his principles throughout his entire life.

With great loss and much sadness, I give much thanks for his service, his friendship, and his dedication. Senator EDWARD KENNEDY will never be forgotten.

I thank my dear friend, Senator KENNEDY, for the contributions he made to this institution, the U.S. Senate, where I now have the great honor of serving the people of Maryland. Senator KENNEDY's legacy will live forever, and we thank him for his service to our Nation.

Mr. President, I yield the floor.

Mr. AKAKA. Mr. President, I rise today to pay tribute to my friend from Massachusetts, Senator EDWARD MOORE KENNEDY, who improved the lives of so many people during his 47 years of service in the Senate. My warm *aloha* and prayers continue to be with Vicki Kennedy, staff members, the Kennedy family, and his many friends.

Senator KENNEDY's extraordinary lifelong commitment to public service produced a proud legacy that has included expanding access to quality of health care and education, protecting and empowering our Nation's workforce, ensuring civil and voting rights, and protecting our Nation's natural and cultural resources.

Before outlining several of Senator KENNEDY's important achievements, I want to share a story that demonstrates our shared commitment to helping working families and his optimistic outlook about the future despite temporary disappointments. A beaming Senator KENNEDY flagged me down on the morning of March 2, 2005. He asked me if I had seen the *Washington Post*. In an editorial criticizing the bankruptcy overhaul under consideration in the Senate, the *Post* indicated the bill could be made more fair by the inclusion of several amendments by Senator KENNEDY intended to protect consumers and my amendment to better inform consumers about the true costs associated with credit card use. After my amendment was defeated, Senator KENNEDY was the first Member to approach me. He complimented me for my work and told me that we would win on the amendment one day. Senator KENNEDY was right. It took me another 4 years, but my credit card minimum payment warning and credit counseling referral legislation was enacted this May as part of the credit card reform law.

As an eternal optimist, Senator KENNEDY never stopped advocating for the causes so important to working families, such as increasing access to quality health care. Senator KENNEDY helped establish community health centers, the Children's Health Insurance Program, and programs that assist individuals suffering from HIV/AIDS. These are just a few of the many health accomplishments that Senator KENNEDY helped bring about that improve the quality of life for millions of people in our country. Despite continuing to battle cancer, Senator KENNEDY's passion to expand access to quality health care never ceased.

Senator KENNEDY had an enormous impact on education policy. He championed early childhood education through his support of Head Start and creation of Early Head Start. His work in reauthorizing the Elementary and Secondary Education Act included improvements such as the Star Schools Program Assistance Act, which improves instruction in critical areas such as mathematics, science, and foreign languages, as well as the No Child Left Behind Act, which requires standards-based assessments for elementary and middle school students among other reforms. With regard to higher education, Senator KENNEDY supported the creation of the Pell Grant Program, the Direct Lending Program, and

the Ensuring Continued Access to Student Loans Act to aid
Americans in paying for college. Throughout his efforts in
education policy, he recognized the needs of underserved
populations, and endeavored to make education more affordable. I also appreciated his working with me on the Excellence in Economics Education authorization and subsequent
funding requests so that more children could be better prepared for the financial decisions they will have to make as
consumers, investors, and heads of households.

I also greatly appreciate all of the work done by Senator
KENNEDY to improve the lives of members of our Nation's
workforce. Senator KENNEDY helped increase the Federal
minimum wage 16 times. He fought for strong workplace
health and safety standards, promoted equal pay for equal
work, and secure retirement benefits. Senator KENNEDY believed the right of workers to unionize and bargain collectively was fundamental, and he was always a tireless advocate for this cause. In addition, Senator KENNEDY was a
champion of our Federal workers and opposed efforts to
outsource Federal jobs and erode workers' rights. I recall his
staunch opposition to weaken the rights of Department of
Defense and Department of Homeland Security employees
and his strong statements in support of granting Transportation Security Administration security officers real rights
and protections.

Senator KENNEDY's career-long dedication to ensuring civil
and voting rights helped bring about numerous changes that
have made our country stronger, more equitable, and just.
He condemned the poll tax, led efforts to lower the voting
age to 18, and removed voting barriers. His fierce and noble
opposition to discrimination by race, ethnicity, gender, age,
disability, sexual orientation, or religion guided much of his
work.

Senator KENNEDY's advocacy for natural and cultural resources helped advance the protection of our environment for
our benefit now and into the future. He was an important
supporter of energy efficiency programs, including those that
aid Americans most in need, and he helped improve fuel
economy standards and energy research and development.
His work led to the enhanced preservation of numerous
treasured resources in Massachusetts, including the Minute
Man National Historic Park, the Taunton River, the New
England Scenic Trail, the Freedom's Way National Heritage
Corridor, the Boston Harbor Islands, the Quinebaug-

Shetucket National Heritage Corridor, the Essex National Heritage Area, and the Lowell National Historical Park.

In addition to his accomplishments and advocacy on behalf of the people of our country, I will remember TED KENNEDY as a true friend, always generous with his assistance and time. For many years, my desk was next to Senator KENNEDY's. He welcomed me to the Senate and always provided sound advice and guidance.

In 1990, despite the long journey, Senator KENNEDY came to Hawaii to help me during my first Senate campaign. I remember the rally that we held in Honolulu at McKinley High School as being one of the largest ever held in Hawaii. We also had a memorable visit to an early childhood development program. Footage of the event was recently replayed on the news in Hawaii, showing Senator KENNEDY and me singing "Itsy Bitsy Spider" with the children.

We toured Kapiolani Children's Hospital where we saw the devastating effect that crystal meth was having on families.

Senator KENNEDY visited the University of Hawaii's John F. Kennedy Theatre, where he received an award for his work on health care. He spoke eloquently about our great country, congressional debates, civil rights, and economic empowerment programs.

I, along with every Member of this body, will very much miss our friend from Massachusetts. Senator KENNEDY's extraordinary work has improved the quality of life for so many people.

We can honor his memory by continuing to work to address the issues Senator KENNEDY was so passionate about such as meaningful health care and immigration reform.

I say *aloha* to my good friend and colleague, Senator KENNEDY.

Mr. President, I yield the floor.

Mr. INOUYE. Mr. President, there are no words to express the sadness of the great loss of our dear friend Senator EDWARD M. KENNEDY. America has lost a great patriot and a great leader. I have lost a good friend.

While it is difficult to say goodbye to a dear friend, I am consoled with the certainty that TED's spirit and message will continue to resonate in the Senate. The solemn but joyful celebration of TED's life reminded one and all that we should remember to help the poor, to heal the sick, to feed the hungry, and to be compassionate with those who are less fortunate than us. I will do my best to keep TED's spirit alive.

I offer my deepest condolences to the Kennedy family.

Mr. President, as America mourns, I ask my colleagues to join me in paying tribute to this magnificent Senator.

Ms. COLLINS. Mr. President, the 1955 football season was not a good one for the Harvard Crimson. With only three victories, it was somewhat surprising that no less a team than the mighty Green Bay Packers reached out to a senior end with a professional job offer. "No thanks," replied young TED KENNEDY, "I have plans to go into another contact sport—politics."

Few have played this rough-and-tumble game with as much energy, determination, and joy as Senator EDWARD KENNEDY. He served the people of his State and our Nation through 5 decades and under 10 Presidents. He authored more than 300 bills that became law and co-sponsored another 550. His remarkable record of legislation has touched the lives of virtually every American, always with a focus on improving lives, bringing justice, and creating opportunity.

As we recall what he gave to our Nation, we also reflect upon what we have lost. It is my sincere hope that the Kennedy family will find comfort in the thoughts and prayers offered by so many around the country and the world. To those who have lost a friend and to his outstanding staff, which has lost an inspiring leader, I extend my deepest condolences. I considered him a dear friend as well as an esteemed colleague.

When I first came to the Senate in 1997, I knew Senator KENNEDY only by reputation. It was a reputation that was not entirely flattering, based upon such labels as "ultra-liberal" and "utterly partisan." That was not the Senator KENNEDY I came to know and admire. He was easy to work with, and his heart was always in the right place. I worked closely with TED on many education issues, particularly by increasing Pell grants which help our neediest students. In our work together on the Armed Services Committee, we teamed up to strengthen our Navy as members of the Seapower Subcommittee.

I found him to be a partner who always sought solutions. I saw in him the same traits that drew the attention of the Green Bay Packers—a tough competitor and a great teammate.

The lion is a symbol of courage. Certainly, Senator KENNEDY possessed great political courage. He fought for his convictions, but he was always willing to reach across party lines. He never, as he often said, let the pursuit of the perfect become the enemy of the good.

But he also possessed courage at the most fundamental level—the willingness to face danger. His historic trip to South Africa in 1985, conducted against the stern warnings of the pro-apartheid government and in defiance of violent demonstrations, helped tear down the wall of racial separatism in that country.

Senator KENNEDY often said that a day never went by that he did not think of his brothers. He did more than merely think of them; he strove always to emulate them. Like Jack, he asked what he could do for his country. Like Bobby, he dreamed things that never were and said why not.

The end of a life so devoted to public service brings to mind the Parable of the Talents. The master, leaving on a journey, entrusts a servant with a portion of his treasure. Upon his return, the master is delighted to find that his wealth has been wisely invested and multiplied.

EDWARD MOORE KENNEDY was entrusted with the great treasure of convictions, energy, and passion. He invested that treasure wisely and multiplied its benefits to all. Like the master in the New Testament, to him we say, "Well done, good and faithful servant."

Mr. ENSIGN. Mr. President, I rise today to honor the memory of one our Nation's most dedicated public servants. For most Americans, TED KENNEDY was an icon—part of an esteemed family that raised strong leaders and committed patriots. Much has been said since his passing of his contributions to our country and his love for his wife, children, grandchildren, and extended family. Those who eulogized him, at his funeral and on main streets across America, have done so with great admiration and respect.

From my position on the opposite side of the aisle in this Chamber, I saw Senator KENNEDY as every bit the legendary and tireless advocate that he was portrayed as. I may have been advocating the opposing view on many issues, but in this country we should always be able to join together to recognize someone who has—with the best intentions—dedicated his life's work to improving opportunities.

I had the privilege of working on a very significant piece of legislation with Senator KENNEDY a few years ago. It was the America COMPETES Act. I was, and continue to be, passionate about making sure that our children remain competitive in this increasingly global economy. Students in Nevada aren't just competing against students in Massachusetts anymore. They are all competing against students in India, China, and around the world. If we don't give our students the tools to compete, the innovative fire and spirit that has always fueled America will be lost.

TED KENNEDY understood this. We put together bipartisan legislation that was signed into law to increase investment in scientific research; strengthen educational opportunities in science, technology, engineering, and mathematics from kindergarten through graduate school; and help develop an innovative infrastructure for the 21st century. I am confident that the impact of this law will be felt for generations to come.

I am also confident that TED KENNEDY's decades of service, his passion for health care and education, and his deep love for this country will inspire a new generation of public servants. When you look at the legacy of TED KENNEDY and at how he dedicated his life to service, you can't help but be moved to do more for this country.

Senator KENNEDY will be missed in this Chamber and in the Halls of Congress. God bless you, Senator TED KENNEDY.

Mr. KAUFMAN. Mr. President, I rise to join the chorus of those celebrating the life of our dear friend and colleague, Senator EDWARD M. KENNEDY.

So much has already been said about him, his life, and his contribution to our Nation, but I would like to take a few minutes to reflect upon the legacy he left as a warm individual and an exemplary statesman.

His life was, to borrow the words of Robert Frost, "a gift outright." TED KENNEDY was ours before we were his.

As a young man and a young Senator, history bequeathed to him weighty expectations. He became the accidental shepherd not only to a flock of nephews and nieces but also to a storied legacy.

An ordinary person would have been daunted by such expectations. But TED KENNEDY was extraordinary. He confounded them and, in the process, defined his life not by what others had left him to complete but by the goals he set for himself.

For all of the rhetoric recently about TED KENNEDY as the Senate's lion, we can never forget that he was also a deeply caring man with a gentle spirit. It was this dual nature of his to fight passionately and to befriend heartily that transformed adversaries into admirers and endeared him forever to his friends.

In February 1988, I was serving as chief of staff to then-Senator Joe Biden when he suffered a serious brain aneurysm. After two precarious surgeries, the doctors said that Senator Biden would need to avoid work completely for a few months while in that first stage of recovery or risk another aneurysm.

When President Reagan called to check up on him, we knew that if he took that call, Senator Biden would be obliged to take all the calls that would follow. It would have been too much for him, so his family made the decision that he would not take any calls, even from the President.

TED KENNEDY kept calling to check on his friend, but our office wouldn't put him through. One Sunday, while Senator Biden was resting at home in Wilmington, Jill heard a knock on their back door. To her surprise, Senator KENNEDY was standing there, holding a framed etching of an Irish stag. He had personally taken it upon himself to bring the gift in order to lift Senator Biden's spirits. He also had with him a bathing suit, ready to relax with his friend and keep him company without discussing Senate business.

We shouldn't have been surprised, though. That was classic TED KENNEDY.

With him there was always a personal touch, especially with those he represented. In the words of one of his constituents, "TEDDY was Massachusetts."

But his constituency was always larger than just the residents of the Bay State. He felt that it was his responsibility to speak for those who could not. TED KENNEDY was, first and foremost, a representative of the poor, the young, the silenced, and the oppressed. He fought tirelessly for the rights of the disabled and those suffering discrimination. Throughout decades of public service, he proved to be their faithful champion at every turn.

For nearly 47 years, TED KENNEDY was the Senate's steady compass through uncertain waters. When others coasted along, satisfied with the status quo or set uneasy by the prospect of change, he trimmed his sails and pushed forward.

He pushed forward by building strong, meaningful relationships with his colleagues on both sides of the aisle. He was committed to civility in politics.

That he so genuinely befriended those who debated vigorously against him on this floor testifies to KENNEDY's greatest gift to his colleagues. As his son Teddy, Jr. said so eloquently at his father's funeral mass, KENNEDY taught us all that all of us who serve in government, regardless of party, love this country dearly—that we share a common bond of responsibility and commitment to public service.

My hope is that the lessons TED KENNEDY taught his colleagues about bipartisanship will guide the Senate today and in the future.

Just outside this Chamber is the Senate Reception Room, ornately decorated by the 19th century immigrant and master painter of the Capitol, Constantino Brumidi. He adorned the ceiling with four allegorical scenes depicting what today we would call Justice, Security, Peace, and Prosperity—four virtues a great Senator should promote.

It was decided that portraits of the greatest Senators ever to serve would cover its walls. In the 1950s, the Senate established a panel to choose the first five to be so honored. Chaired by a young, energetic Senator from Massachusetts, who had authored a Pulitzer Prize winning book on political courage, this "Kennedy Commission" selected five Senators whose portraits now grace those walls.

The commission chose to recognize Henry Clay, Daniel Webster, John C. Calhoun, Robert La Follette, and Robert Taft. A few years ago, the Senate voted to extend this honor as well to Arthur Vandenberg and Robert F. Wagner.

All seven earned their place in this pantheon by placing the good of the Nation above political interest. All but one ran unsuccessfully for President, distinguishing themselves not as Commanders-in-Chief, but as brilliant legislators and versatile statesmen. Each exemplified a commitment to the four virtues depicted by Brumidi on the Reception Room's ceiling.

TED KENNEDY was a champion of all four of these virtues; indeed, he set a new standard by which future Senators will be judged.

Whether it was leading the charge for the Civil Rights Act, enfranchising young people of military age, or promoting human rights around the world, KENNEDY pursued justice without relent.

TED KENNEDY was committed to ensuring our Nation's security by advocating for nuclear disarmament, leading the way on energy conservation, and supporting legislation to punish sponsors of terrorism.

He worked tirelessly to bring peace to troubled regions, including Northern Ireland.

Throughout his career in the Senate, TED KENNEDY did all he could to open the doors of prosperity to millions of Americans seeking fair wages, health insurance, or job opportunities.

Furthermore, he fought to expand education access, fund scholarships, and promote community involvement. KENNEDY's efforts have helped invest America in a bright future in fields such as science, technology, business, and the arts.

Even with the seven distinguished Senators now immortalized, the walls of the Senate Reception Room remain mostly bare. They await future Senate commissions, following in the tradition of John F. Kennedy's panel, to honor those serving from our generation or from generations yet to come.

I am certain that, if I could cast my vote today for the next to be so honored, I would proudly and unhesitatingly choose Senator EDWARD M. KENNEDY.

Mr. KOHL. Mr. President, I rise today with great sadness to pay tribute to my friend, colleague, and great statesman, Senator TED KENNEDY.

As many of my colleagues have noted here today, over his nearly 47 years of public service in the Senate, TED KENNEDY displayed exemplary leadership, a commitment to progress, and the vision that by working together, this body could truly better the lives of Americans.

For many years as a member of the Judiciary Committee, I had the privilege to work with and learn from Senator KENNEDY. Since 1997, I sat just one seat away from him, then-Senator Biden to my right and Senator KENNEDY next to him. Senator KENNEDY was always so encouraging. A simple "good job" or pat on the back might be expected from a busy Senator like him, but from time to time he would take a moment to write a note and offer encouragement for a bill I was trying to move through committee or a concern I was expressing about an issue important to the people of Wisconsin. We have heard so much over the past weeks about what he gave to our country throughout his long Senate career. Just as important, he gave all of us on the committee and in the Senate an example of how to be an effective legislator, a fair negotiator, and a friend to allies and foes alike.

As has been noted by many of those who worked alongside him, Senator KENNEDY masterfully negotiated with others in the long process of shaping policy but refused to retreat from his principles—or from his quest toward equality and social justice for all. His tireless advocacy on behalf of those Americans most in need of an advocate—children, senior citizens, the sick, disabled and mentally ill, students, workers, and families—has changed the course of this Nation and impacted millions of lives. Senator KENNEDY's many legislative battles—for civil rights, voting rights, and workers rights, among others—illustrated that although we may differ in our politics and our ideologies, it is still possible to work with each other, across the aisle and across the political spectrum, toward the common good. Although I am sad today to realize that we will never hear another of his fiery speeches, many of them given just a few desks away from mine in the back row of this Chamber, he leaves a legacy behind that will endure.

I extend my deepest sympathies to his wife Victoria and to the rest of his family during this difficult time. Senator KENNEDY's passion, diligence, good humor, and kindness will be greatly missed, by me and by many others, in this body and across the Nation.

Mr. VOINOVICH. Mr. President, I rise today to speak about the passing of our dear colleague and friend, Senator EDWARD M. KENNEDY.

Our great Nation has lost a true statesman, and the Kennedy family has lost its beloved patriarch. Senator KENNEDY's unparalleled leadership and decades spent in service to his fellow Americans will be missed by all, especially here in the U.S. Senate. No one can deny that TED was a man of convictions, passion, and resolve for doing what he felt was best for the country. While I was not always in agreement with him on policy, I always knew he was my friend.

His willingness to reach across the aisle and find common ground serves as an inspiration to all of us during this pivotal moment in our Nation's history. Senator KENNEDY and I shared a passion for early childhood development, and together with Senator Gregg, we worked on legislation to improve the quality and availability of early education for all children.

On a more personal note, TED was a guiding light for me during my late nephew's treatment for bone cancer. His uplifting spirit and thoughtfulness helped steer my family through a very difficult time, and I will never forget the words he shared with us: "Even when it's sometimes stormy one day, the sun always seems to shine the next."

Janet and I will keep Victoria and the entire Kennedy family in our thoughts and prayers during this trying time, as they mourn the loss of both TED and his sister Eunice. Senator KENNEDY's great shadow of leadership which loomed so large across the U.S. Senate will continue for years to come, and I hope the Kennedy family and my colleagues can find solace in the fact that TED has joined our Heavenly Father.

Mr. ROCKEFELLER. Mr. President, I rise today to remember and celebrate EDWARD MOORE KENNEDY.

Senator KENNEDY passed away, as we know, on August 25. The American people, in more ways than they will ever know—as so often happens in history with historic figures, people don't know what they had when they had it, and then when they no longer have it, they discover how great that person really was if one deserves to be so identified, and surely TED KENNEDY did—the American people lost a touchstone. The cause of justice lost one of its bravest and boldest champions, and I lost a very close friend.

I met TED KENNEDY around 1964, which is quite a long time ago, in Hyannis Port. His family invited me to come there for the weekend. He was still recovering from his back injury. He broke his back in 12 places. He was in one of those old-fashioned circle things where they sort of turned you so you wouldn't get bed sores. We had a nice conversation, and he wrote and thanked me with his hand for coming to see him.

Obviously, I have and will always be thinking about Vicki, his incredible wife, his children, and the entire Kennedy family who operates as one unit.

Because of TED, I think all of us are better. I know I am. I think we are stronger. We are more inclusive as a Nation. He caused us to be that way.

For more than 46 years, he was a legislative lion, as they say, who gave voice to the voiceless. That is not a cliche; that is an extraordinary and powerful deep fact from the junior Senator from the State of West Virginia. The people of West Virginia were given voice, and TED KENNEDY gave them that voice. He fought for working families, civil rights, women's rights, health care for all, and transformed the lives of children, seniors, Americans of all ages, all colors, all backgrounds. Everybody was part of his sphere, part of his responsibility.

In his private life he worked tirelessly to touch so many people with endless human acts of kindness that came naturally to him. He had to do it. I don't think he chose to do these things; he just had to do them and, therefore, did do them. People forget, those who didn't know about what he did, but he never stopped reaching out to help people at every turn, in sometimes very small ways.

TED and his family reached amazing heights, and they inspired a Nation. Each and every day of his life he honored the fallen heroes we always cherish.

This needs to be said: TED traveled to West Virginia often. I was personally very grateful for that. It is a small State, not unlike that of the Presiding Officer. Our State has always had very close communication with the Kennedy family. We are them; they are us. You know, we put them over the top, we feel, in the 1960 election, and we did. When President KENNEDY returned to West Virginia, he, at the State's centennial, said that classic phrase which we have heard so many times in West Virginia: "The Sun does not always shine in West Virginia, but the people always do."

People are still to this day moved by that statement. It is a sentiment I have always held near to my heart, that he and his brothers felt the way they did about West Virginia. I remember a picture of Bobby Kennedy sitting on a slag heap, a sort of pile of coal in southern West Virginia, just sort of thinking. He wasn't shaking hands, he was doing a typical Bobby Kennedy-type thing: thinking, deep in thought; philosophical, wondering about what to do in the world.

Over the last four decades, TED's frequent visits not only strengthened West Virginia's bond with him and the Kennedy family, but he also provided enormous color, interest, and fun. I remember him at political rallies in West Virginia where some politician was going on and on. I have an album of photographs that were taken sequentially of different faces, very long and large speeches, and he is this way, he is wiping his brow. He enjoyed all of it. He just loved it.

Everywhere he went he found common ground. He spoke honestly. People came out to see him. He didn't hesitate to plunge into the crowd or jump on the back of a pickup truck. Indeed, the American worker knew a strong friend in TED KENNEDY. That much was clear in the tireless work he did as an advocate for our miners, for our seniors, for all of our people.

He has been with us in some of our very darkest hours. We had a mining tragedy several years ago. Johnny Isakson, who was speaking not long ago, was there as were several members of the HELP Committee, the Health, Education, Labor, and Pensions Committee. We had a cave-in and a blowup in a mine in Sago in Upshur County. He came down there. He sat with those families and watched them. I watched his hurt resonating against their hurt, and the words he spoke to them had deep comfort to them. As a result, we had the first major overhaul of mine safety laws at the Federal level since 1977. He, obviously, was driving the committee and driving that, as were Senator Johnny Isakson and Mike Enzi.

People liked TED. They were drawn to his energy and his fundamental belief that America's best days were always ahead. I love that attitude because you can always pick it out. I just did a TV appearance and everybody was asking me about the person who spoke out last night, interrupting the President and saying something rather unusual, and the President just went right on ahead. He had bigger things to do. TED was that way.

He had hard parts of his personal life and his own family life. He was the father of endless numbers of nieces and nephews, as well as his own children. Nothing ever stopped him.

People wanted to work with him. He never, ever talked about his own achievements. That is the incredible thing about him. As a result of the plane accident, he broke his back in 12 places. That is a lot of places to break a back. He never spent another day the rest of his life, he once told me fairly recently, without being in pain. You could see him walking across the floor of the Senate. He was always bent, and he walked quickly, sort of subconsciously, to cover up the fact that he was hurting. But he never said anything about it. He never said anything about himself. It was always: What is going on in your life? What is happening with you? What are your thoughts? What do you think we should be doing on such a subject? That was simply the way he was.

He refused to be slowed. He brought that iron will to everything he did. He never quit. He never gave up. He was a happy fighter. He loved life. He loved the battle, driven not out of anger but out of passion for people and the individual parts of their lives he wanted to improve. It just drove him. He didn't do it out of duty; he did it because he had to. It was a natural thing. For TED, every day was new. Everything could be made better through hard work and dedication. Nearly every piece of legislation that has passed in this body bore his imprint or bears his imprint and reflected his commitment to making life better for every American.

It has been my honor to lock arms with him in our efforts, including the Children's Health Program. Interestingly—we just found it—Senator KENNEDY called it the most far-reaching step that Congress has ever taken to help the Nation's children and the most far-reaching advance in health care since the enactment of Medicare and Medicaid a generation ago. Now, in the Finance Committee we are trying to decide whether we are going to cast them into the melting pot along with all the other plans and take away the defined benefits. I am obviously very much against that. Eleven million children's health care is at stake.

TED worked on the Higher Education Act of 1965 and to protect Federal student loans. Again, let me get back to the personal side.

I have a daughter. We only have one daughter and three sons. She is a teacher, and she is trained in special ed. She taught at Jackie Robinson Junior High School in Harlem. TED was in New York. His chief of staff at that time was my daughter's best friend. She said, "You know, Jay Rockefeller's daughter teaches there."

TED said, "Let's go in."

So here is my daughter teaching class in junior high school and in walks TED KENNEDY. Of course, the whole place just falls apart with happiness. He loved doing it. He does it in the District of Columbia; he does it in Massachusetts. He is always interacting with students. He greets them, talks with them, and learns from them.

The principal gave my daughter a very hard time. He said, "Don't you ever bring a U.S. Senator into my school without telling me in advance."

Well, of course, that is the beauty of it. There is no way she could, because it was just a natural act of TED KENNEDY.

It was that commitment to service that we celebrated just this spring when the President signed the Serve America Act which inspires young people to serve their country through public service. There are a lot of ways to remake America, but I think people, as the Presiding Officer has been in a variety of situations—people going abroad, people meeting other people who are unlike them, living with them, eating with them, sharing with them, coming to know them, coming to have very strong feelings about them—it is that kind of thing which makes people want to get into public service.

So he doubled the Peace Corps, he doubled Legal Aid, he doubled Vista, he doubled all of those programs, a lot of which were run by his brother-in-law, Sargent Shriver, who is one of the great men of America who is never discussed. He is a Kennedy, but he doesn't bear that as a last name.

He changed my life—the Kennedy family did. When I went to West Virginia as a Vista volunteer, I was trying to figure out what I was going to do in life, and I kind of wanted to be a Foreign Service officer. Frankly, I wanted to be America's first Ambassador to China. This was back in 1961, so it does really make sense. I had studied Chinese for a year, so I thought I was on my way. But Vista started and Sargent Shriver called me and said, "Come work for me at the Peace Corps." And I did that. Then I went to southern West Virginia as a Vista volunteer, and it told me what I wanted to do in life. This part of your gut knows when you are doing something that is meaningful to you and is something that you want to dedicate your life to. That was the effect of the Kennedys.

TED KENNEDY was a giant. There was not and never will be anyone like him in American history. He shaped this institution for decades by honoring its history and pushing us forward to be a better institution.

Now that he is gone, I know his legacy and inspiration make him a giant greater still, moving us to reach across the aisle, hopefully, and make a difference in people's lives. He was a great friend. We are all forever grateful for his service and his kind heart. We will miss him very dearly. Now he belongs to the ages.

Mr. WHITEHOUSE. Mr. President, this would be a particularly opportune, important time for me to say a word about our friend, Senator KENNEDY. I had not planned on doing so at this particular juncture, but someone very important to him, and in a very different way to me, is now in the gallery. So I will speak very briefly, but I do want to, as I have said before, thank Senator KENNEDY for his kindness to me.

As a very senior and distinguished Senator, a person with a national and, indeed, international reputation, a person whose standing in this body was unmatched, a person whose legislative prowess and capability were unmatched, he did not need to pay any attention to a new Senator of no particular seniority, clout, or renown from Rhode Island. Yet he did, I think in large part due to the friendship the new Senator from Rhode Island had with his son, a very talented and able Member of the House of Representatives, who is senior to me in our Rhode Island delegation and who represents Rhode Island with exceptional distinction over in the House of Representatives. For that reason, and for the reason of a number of other family friendships, he was particularly kind to me. I appreciate that more than he could have imagined.

It is a bit daunting to come here as a new Senator not knowing whether you will find your way, not knowing whether you will evince any ability, not knowing whether you will have any effect, not knowing whether, indeed, you will be very welcome. You have to fight yourself through that stuff as a new Senator.

I can remember when I was presiding, where the distinguished junior Senator from Alaska is now sitting, and a colleague of ours who shall remain nameless was giving a speech of some length. Senator KENNEDY was waiting to speak, and he sent a note up to me inquiring whether I felt that the standards of the speech we were then being treated to met the high standards of our common alma mater, the University of Virginia School of Law. I could not help but smile back and return the note, saying: No, I do not think so, but that is OK because I am waiting for a great speech from you.

There is one particular kindness I wanted to mention. Senator KENNEDY was very important to Rhode Island, not just because of his son Patrick but because Rhode Island pays a lot of attention to Massachusetts. There is a lot of overlap in the constituencies of Massachusetts and Rhode Island, and Rhode Islanders have long admired Senator KENNEDY. When he came on behalf of candidates, on behalf of his son, on behalf of me, on behalf of others, there was always an atmosphere of celebration around him and around the events he attended. Other speakers have spoken of his ability to rev up a crowd and get people fired up and enthusiastic, and he was really remarkable in that respect. We never tired of his visits, and Rhode Island always welcomed him with open arms.

He had a special place for Rhode Island, and in particular he had a special place for somebody who was very dear to both Congressman Kennedy and to myself; that is, a predecessor of mine here in the Senate from Rhode Island, Senator Claiborne Pell. Senator Pell was a political legend in Rhode Island, in many ways an improbable candidate.

Senator KENNEDY's brother, President Kennedy, at one point said, publicly enough that it became a matter of sort of common discussion in Rhode Island, that Claiborne Pell was the least-electable candidate he had ever seen. So when Claiborne Pell ran ahead of President Kennedy in Rhode Island in the election, it was a matter of great pride to Claiborne Pell and one that he was fond of reminding all Kennedys about.

It was, I guess as they would say in "Casablanca," the beginning of a beautiful friendship. The friendship began back then. It continued long after Senator Pell had left the Senate. It continued long after Senator Pell had lost his ability to walk around and became confined to a wheelchair. It continued even long after Senator Pell could barely speak because of the consequences of his illness.

One of the ways it manifested itself is that every year Senator KENNEDY would take the trouble to sail his sailboat, the *Mya*, from wherever it was in New England to Newport, RI, and there take Claiborne Pell out sailing. I had the pleasure to be on that last sail, and you could just imagine the scene, with the heaving dock and the heaving boat and Senator Pell in his wheelchair and a rather hazardous and impromptu loading of Senator Pell into the sailboat. And then, of course, it got under way. Because Senator Pell was having such trouble speaking, he really could not contribute much to a conversation. But Senator KENNEDY had the gift of being able to handle both sides of a conversation and have everybody feel that a wonderful time was being had. So he carried on in a full, roaring dialog with Senator Pell, essentially providing both sides of that dialog, and Senator Pell was smiling from ear to ear.

It said a lot about what I appreciate so much about Senator KENNEDY. First of all, Rhode Island mattered to him, as it matters to Patrick Kennedy, as it matters to me. Second of all, as powerful as he was and as important as he was, friendship mattered more than authority or clout or power. There was nothing any longer that Senator Pell could do for Senator KENNEDY. There was nothing that could be done to advance his legislative interests or his political interests or his fundraising interests or any other aspirations he may have had. But it mattered to him to do this because he was loyal and because friendship counted.

In a body in which opportunism and self-promotion and self-advancement are not unknown, it was remarkable of Senator KENNEDY to give so much of his time to this particular pursuit, to this particular visit, taking his old, now disabled, friend out for a sail and giving him so much pleasure, with no hope or hint of reward or return to Senator KENNEDY himself.

So I will conclude with that. I guess I will conclude with one other thing. He loved Robert Frost. On his desk here right now is a poem from Robert Frost, "The Road Not Taken."

I know he was fond of Frost's work in particular. I keep a little book of poems and things that matter to me, quotations, and one of them is a poem by Robert Frost. It is not "The Road Not Taken," which is the poem on Senator KENNEDY's desk. It is a different one. But I will close by reading it. It is called "Acquainted with the Night."

I have been one acquainted with the night.
I have walked out in rain—and back in rain.
I have outwalked the furthest city light.

I have looked down the saddest city lane.
I have passed by the watchman on his beat.
And dropped my eyes, unwilling to explain.

I have stood still and stopped the sound of feet
When far away an interrupted cry
Came over houses from another street,

But not to call me back or say good-bye;
And further still at an unearthly height,
O luminary clock against the sky

Proclaimed the time was neither wrong nor right.
I have been one acquainted with the night.

Mr. MENENDEZ. Mr. President, once again, we mourn another Kennedy, the last brother, a friend, a colleague, a Senator's Senator, larger than life even in death, certainly the most effective legislator of our time and arguably the most effective Member of this body in the whole of American history.

Across this Nation and across the political divide, we have seen the impact of his life and work in the tearful eyes of millions of Americans. Each faces a challenge to continue his long and lasting legacy of hard-fought, hard-won battles for hard-working families everywhere. His is a legacy of hope for the unemployed, the dispossessed, the downtrodden, the undereducated, the uninsured; a legacy of hope for Hispanic Americans and Asian Americans, all Americans who have come to this country, often with little more than the clothes on their backs and a glorious dream for a better life.

TED KENNEDY will be remembered by my generation as more than the last brother, more than the end of an era. He will be remembered as America's preeminent leader on fair, responsible, humane immigration policy that always put people first. For all of us, he was the standard-bearer of headier days, of Camelot, of intellectual vitality, political energy, and a deep and abiding commitment to public service and to this beloved Senate. He taught us through actions and deeds, in times of great personal pain, the power of the human spirit to endure and prevail. He symbolized the best of an era of progressive, compassionate leadership in this country and a deep belief that we must always ask what we can do for the country, a torch unexpectedly passed to him which he carried with dignity and humility through great tragedy as well as great triumph.

He understood our personal struggles, however profound, "make us stronger in the broken places," as Hemingway said. For every Hispanic American and every American across this Nation whose family came here to find a better life, whatever their ethnicity or political views, TED KENNEDY was a leader. His deep and abiding concern for the struggles of hard-working people was not political. It is simply part of the Kennedy DNA.

I remember the images of his brother, Bobby Kennedy, in 1967, 6,000 people surrounding him on the flatbed truck that held a severely weakened Cesar Chavez. Bobby Kennedy shared a piece of *semita* with Chavez and the crowd cheered. They grabbed at Bobby to shake his hand and thank him. He stood in front of the crowd and said:

The world must know from this time forward that the migrant farmworker, the Mexican-American, is coming into his own rights . . . .

You are winning a special kind of citizenship; no one is doing it for you—you are doing it yourselves—and therefore, no one can ever take it away.

Fast forward to Washington, DC, in 2006, walking in his brother's footsteps, TED KENNEDY stood in front of hundreds of thousands of marchers on the same ground his brothers had stood upon decades earlier. He stood with immigrants and faith leaders and organizers. He called for comprehensive immigration reform. The crowd of hundreds of thousands roared, and he roared back, "*Si se puede. Si se puede.*" Yes, we can.

Now he is gone, having fought his last battle with courage and dignity, as he fought all others. But the memories remain. I remember first coming to the Senate, sitting down with him, his presence as commanding as I thought it would be. I looked at him to learn all I could from him about the Senate and, frankly, there was no more patient or willing teacher. When I first sought to come to the Senate, the one Member of the Senate who gave me the most time and gave me the most encouragement and the greatest opportunity to understand how to be successful in the Senate was a person I could do the least for. It was TED KENNEDY. I will never forget his kindness.

We worked together to protect the Senate restaurant employees when their jobs were privatized. I learned what made him such an effective legislator—because even as he was dealing with the most incredible issues the country was facing and leading on many of them, he had time to remember the importance of that little person, people in the Senate restaurant who might have been unemployed.

We all know no one can belt out an Irish ballad quite like TEDDY could. One of my favorite memories was of him and me in New Jersey in a campaign where we sang Irish ballads together. I learned then what made him the unique person he is. I will never forget the sound of that voice and the warmth of that heart. Each of us has had our own memories of the man. Each of us has had our own deep emotions when we heard of his death.

The editorial cartoonist, Lalo Alcaraz, said when his wife heard that TED KENNEDY had lost his battle with cancer, she pulled out one of her old buttons that her mother had worn during the Presidential campaign in 1960. That day, Lalo Alcaraz drew a cartoon of a much younger TED KENNEDY. It is captioned with two simple words on the campaign button: "Viva Kennedy."

As I sat in the Basilica in Boston with our colleagues last week, I thought of all TED KENNEDY did to better the lives of so many Americans, and I thought of those two words over and over again: Viva Kennedy. He was a man who truly believed in the idea and ideal that is America. Although we may have come from different backgrounds, different places, different cultures, though we may speak different languages, we are one Nation, indivisible, forged from shared values and common principles, each of us united in our differences working for the betterment of all of us, and no one worked harder for the betterment of all of us than TED KENNEDY.

It is my sincere belief that in his passing he has once again worked his magic and given us an opportunity to come together, united in a deep and profound feeling of loss and emptiness as we are even at this day. It would be like him to be looking down upon these tributes today, nodding his head and smiling, but he would be saying: Don't wait for my memorials to be laid. He would say: Don't wait for my words to be chiseled in marble at Arlington. Don't wait for some bronze statue in Washington or a bridge named after me in Boston. Stand up, do what is right for the American people now. Do what is right for hard-working families in your States, for hard-working families in my State—in New Bedford, Brockton, Fall River, or Worcester. I can see him standing over there where he always stood, committed, informed, imposing, pounding on his desk, shouting at the top of his lungs. You could hear it when you were outside of the Chamber when he was in one of those moments.

Those families don't have time to wait for a decent job and wages. They don't have time to wait for a better job. They don't have time to wait for decent, affordable, quality care that is a right and not a privilege. That booming voice would echo through this Chamber, and I think it will echo through this Chamber for eternity.

When it comes down to it, we are his legacy. We in the Senate are his memorial. We are the burning candles, and he would tell us to have them burn brightly: Stand against the wind. Stand against the storm. Stand against the odds. For it is up to us now to light the world, as he did.

In this past week, I think we have all found new meaning in those familiar words of Aeschylus, when he said:

And even in our sleep, pain that cannot forget falls drop by drop upon the heart, and in our own despair, against our will, comes wisdom to us by the awful grace of God.

Today, in our despair, let wisdom come. Let us honor the memory of Senator EDWARD MOORE KENNEDY by not only remembering the man but by continuing the good work he has done.

I yield the floor.

Mrs. SHAHEEN. Mr. President, I am honored to be here to add my voice to so many of those who today have eloquently remembered Senator TED KENNEDY. Like so many who have spoken today, I was the beneficiary of so many personal kindnesses from Senator KENNEDY.

I first met him on the campaign trail. In 1980, I was actually on the other side in New Hampshire when he was running against Jimmy Carter. Despite the fact that was a very hard-fought campaign, and we won and he lost, when I ran a winning campaign 4 years later in the New Hampshire primary, Senator KENNEDY was one of the first people to call and congratulate me.

After that, I had the opportunity to campaign over the years with Senator KENNEDY. There was no one who could fire up a crowd as he could. In 2000, I remember he was there for Al Gore when times were tough in New Hampshire. He was there for John Kerry in 2004. And I had the opportunity to travel around the country with him in support of John Kerry, his very good friend.

But I really got to see the difference he made in so many lives when I worked with him at the Institute of Politics at the Kennedy School of Government at Harvard. I had the opportunity to be chosen to be the director there, and Senator KENNEDY was one of those people who helped make that decision and make that happen for me. What was so impressive was that it did not matter how busy he was with the work in Washington or with what he was doing in Massachusetts; he never missed a meeting. His first concern was always: What are the students doing? What is going to excite them? What is going to get them involved in politics and public service, because that was the mission of the Institute of Politics. It was one of two memorials that were established by the Kennedy family to remember his brother, President John Kennedy. It was always amazing to me to see someone who was so busy, so prominent in national life, who never missed an opportunity to talk with the freshman student who was there who wasn't quite sure what they wanted to do, to talk with and encourage the young people who were involved at the institute to get involved in politics, in government, in public service.

I know Senator KENNEDY will be remembered for so many of the kindnesses he provided to people. He will be remembered by the tens of thousands of people whose lives he touched. But I think one of his most significant legacies will be those young people who are encouraged to get involved in politics, who appreciate that public service in government is an honorable profession because of his leadership and the work he did.

I feel very honored and privileged to have worked with him and to have had the opportunity to serve with him, however briefly, in the Senate. I know we will all remember for future generations what Senator KENNEDY has done.

PRINTING TRIBUTES FOR SENATORS KENNEDY AND MARTINEZ

Mr. WHITEHOUSE. Mr. President, I ask unanimous consent that the tributes to Senators KENNEDY and Martinez in the *Congressional Record* be printed as separate Senate documents and that Senators be permitted to submit statements for inclusion until Friday, October 9, 2009.

The PRESIDING OFFICER. Without objection, it is so ordered.

Mr. NELSON of Florida. Mr. President, it is equally a solemn subject on which I rise to remember our friend and colleague TED KENNEDY who died at the young age of 77. I say "young age" because it was another one of our colleagues, Senator John Glenn, who flew on a 10-day space flight at age 77. Today, 11 years later, he still looks as young as he looked back then. So 77 is way too young an age for cancer to take our friend TED KENNEDY.

From the funeral and the remembrances, we know that he was the youngest of nine children. He had three brothers. He was born in 1932 and elected to the Senate in 1962. He spent more than 46 years in the Senate, longer than all but two of our colleagues. He loved this institution, and he loved his fellow Senators. Of course, there are so many pieces of major legislation affecting the well-being of the American people, if they don't have his name on it, they certainly bear his fingerprints. Many of those pieces of legislation reflect the work of his pen.

He fought tirelessly for the sick, the poor, the disabled, the children, the old. He was the driving force behind efforts to guarantee rights to the disabled, to provide family and medical leave, and to ensure a fair minimum wage. He also remembered individuals, both his colleagues, his staff, and his constituents. He was the first person to call during hard times. Why do you think that yesterday, our most esteemed colleague, Senator Byrd, in his bent-over, physically disabled condition now, was wheeled to this floor in his wheelchair, and his voice rose to the occasion in memorializing his friend. I remember Senator Byrd telling me how thoughtful Senator KENNEDY was on a major birthday in his eighties, when Senator KENNEDY had sent him the requisite number of roses.

Of course, no matter what your political persuasion, you could see TED KENNEDY as an example of public service. He devoted his entire life to public service. He did so despite his easy financial condition. He did so despite numerous opportunities elsewhere. He did so despite seeing his three brothers sacrifice their lives in service to their country.

I want to quote from our colleague TED KENNEDY, from April 2006. He said:

The defining aspect of our country is opportunity—the hope that you can do better, that your children can do better. But you need an even playing field. To do that, you can't be sick and in school. You've got to have health care. You've got to have an economy working to give people a chance to get ahead. It is not guaranteed. But you do have to have an opportunity. Our country is big enough and strong enough and wealthy enough to give that kind of opportunity to everybody. That's what I work on every day.

What an example for all of us. There is something else I wish to say about our colleague, because much has been made of his flaws. But who among us does not have flaws? Maybe Senator KENNEDY realized so much his flaws that he decided despite those, he was going to do the best he could do for his fellow humankind. So he dedicated his life to the poor, the sick, the young and old, and the disabled. He fought against discrimination of all types. Indeed, he stood up for the least among us. Who cannot admire that, in being a champion for the least among us.

Godspeed, TED KENNEDY.

Ms. KLOBUCHAR. Mr. President, I join my colleagues today in remembering the amazing life of Senator EDWARD KENNEDY, a man beloved in the Senate and beloved in America.

My thoughts and prayers are with his wife Vicki, his children, and his whole family.

Like so many others, I consider myself lucky to have worked with him. He was more than a colleague, he was a mentor and a friend.

I remember that he used to send me a message, "The lantern is lit," when we would have late night votes. It was his way of beckoning me and a small group of Senators—Senator Schumer, Senator Cantwell and maybe one or two others—to his office in the Capitol where he would regale us with stories as only an Irishman would.

TED KENNEDY's wit and stories, his passion for a cause and his country and his love for the Senate made me want to go to work every day. He never gave up and he had a fiery zest for the legislative battles that was always tempered by a bipartisan pragmatism.

I remember last year when we were working on the Medicare improvements bill, which was absolutely critical to Medicare recipients across the country.

Seniors were counting on us to pass this bill, but we were just one vote short of the 60 we needed. But Harry Reid knew how to find that last vote. The afternoon of the vote, the doors of the Senate swung open and in walked Senator KENNEDY.

I will always remember watching him walk onto the Senate floor with then-Senator Obama and his son Patrick on either side of him. Every single Senator had made their way to the floor, and the gallery was full. Applause erupted as he walked in, even though it is against the Senate rules. Each of us gave him a tearful hug and kiss as he made his way to cast his vote.

His very presence seemed to open the floodgates. Suddenly, a bill that was about to fail by one vote passed by nine as Republicans who had spent weeks blocking the bill suddenly switched their votes after Senator KENNEDY voted.

His presence was so persuasive that day because his colleagues knew these were issues he believed in deeply, and had spent his life fighting for. He never gave up on the good fight.

TED KENNEDY, with his booming voice, gave a voice to the voiceless and stood up for those who had no one standing with them. As he said, "We are all part of the American family and we have a responsibility to help members of that family when they are in need."

TED KENNEDY did more than just speak these words; he lived them. Day in and day out on the Senate floor, he fought for justice and equality and opportunity for all Americans.

I will give you just one example: After we tragically lost our friend and colleague Paul Wellstone, Senator KENNEDY picked up his torch and helped get the Mental Health Parity Act through the Senate.

His many achievements will be etched in the history books and his legacy will live on in the hundreds of laws that bear his name.

But TED KENNEDY will be remembered for more than just his legislation; he will remembered for his heart and his humor and his zest for life.

On a snowy winter day in Washington, DC, one year, one of my friends took his family to go sledding and who should he see? Senator KENNEDY and Senator Dodd across the way, sledding down by the National Cathedral.

This is the TED KENNEDY I will remember: a man who made the most of life, a man who loved his friends and his family and a man who worked each and every day to make this country stronger.

While he will no longer walk onto the Senate floor, he will remain with us through the lessons he taught us and the memories he blessed us with.

Today, let us honor his life by picking up his torch and continuing to fight the good fights, while also respecting those on the other side of us.

Let us fulfill his dream of "an America where we can all contend freely and vigorously, but where we will treasure and guard those standards of civility which alone make this Nation safe for both democracy and diversity."

TED KENNEDY loved this country and was willing to work with anyone and find common ground in order to open the doors of opportunity for all Americans.

He carried the weight of history on his shoulders, but rose up to become the lion of the Senate and one of the greatest legislators in our country's history.

Although he is no longer with us, he will continue to inspire us.

Mrs. MURRAY. Mr. President, like all Americans, I will never forget where I was on September 11, 2001, and I will never forget the way our country responded. In the face of great tragedy, Americans came together with courage and unity.

Eight years later, we continue to face great challenges. As a government—and as a Nation—we are working to improve our safety and tackle the many difficulties facing us today. The safety of all Americans remains priority No. 1 for everyone in government. We still have troops working hard to protect and defend our Nation. At the same time, we continue to recognize that our diversity is also America's greatest strength. Despite our many differences, in times of need we are always one Nation united.

This year, for the first time, 9/11 has been designated a National Day of Service and Remembrance. It is with a heavy heart that I stand on the floor of the Senate today, marking this day with a cloak and white roses on the desk of our departed colleague, Senator TED KENNEDY.

TED worked to designate this day as one of service, and in April the President signed the Edward M. Kennedy Serve America Act making that goal a reality. TED would be proud of each and every American who took up that call.

The mission of this new designation is:

[T]o honor the victims of 9/11 and those who rose to service in response to the attacks by encouraging all Americans and others throughout the world to pledge to voluntarily perform at least one good deed, or another service activity, on 9/11 each year. In this way we hope to create a lasting and forward-looking legacy—annually rekindling the spirit of service, tolerance, and compassion that unified America and the world in the immediate aftermath of the 9/11 attacks.

I cannot think of a better way to honor the memory of those who were lost than by taking a moment today to remember, and then performing a good deed or act of service.

September 11 is not just a day of national loss but of personal loss. My thoughts and prayers go out to everyone who lost a friend or loved one. Your loss is our loss, and you are forever in our hearts.

MONDAY, *September 14, 2009*

Mr. DODD. Madam President, I ask unanimous consent that the Senate proceed to the immediate consideration of S. Res. 264, submitted earlier today.

The PRESIDING OFFICER. The clerk will report the resolution by title.

The assistant legislative clerk read as follows:

A resolution (S. Res. 264) designating the Caucus Room of the Russell Senate Office Building as the "Kennedy Caucus Room."

S. RES. 264

Whereas, during the last century, few rooms have borne witness to as much history as the Caucus Room of the Russell Senate Office Building;

Whereas, during the last century, few families have played as integral a role in the history of the United States as has the Kennedy family;

Whereas the Senate mourns the passing of Senator EDWARD MOORE KENNEDY, one of the most accomplished, effective, and beloved Senators of all time;

Whereas Senator EDWARD MOORE KENNEDY played a role in every major national debate during the last 50 years, serving as a constant champion of the disadvantaged and overlooked;

Whereas the legacy of Senator EDWARD MOORE KENNEDY includes not only his prolific achievements on behalf of the people of the United States, but the enduring friendships he formed with colleagues on both sides of the aisle;

Whereas the wit and passion of Senator EDWARD MOORE KENNEDY and his perseverance in the face of adversity will be remembered in equal measure to his impressive legislative and rhetorical skills;

Whereas Senator EDWARD MOORE KENNEDY was part of a proud family tradition of public service, which included 2 other distinguished Senators;

Whereas never before have 3 brothers served in the Senate, and rarely have any 3 brothers served the United States so well;

Whereas John Fitzgerald Kennedy served the people of Massachusetts with distinction in the Senate, before being elected the 35th President of the United States;

Whereas Robert Francis Kennedy served the people of New York with distinction in the Senate, after serving as the 64th Attorney General;

[137]

Whereas EDWARD MOORE KENNEDY served the people of Massachusetts with distinction in the Senate for nearly half a century, acting as a tireless advocate for those who might otherwise have been without an advocate;

Whereas the Senate has been greatly enriched by the dedication, compassion, and talent of the 3 Kennedy brothers who served as Senators;

Whereas, in the Caucus Room of the Russell Senate Office Building, the people of the United States have commemorated tragedy, celebrated triumph, and held hearings of great importance on the most important issues facing the Nation;

Whereas it was in the Caucus Room of the Russell Senate Office Building that both Senator John Fitzgerald Kennedy and Senator Robert Francis Kennedy announced their intention to run for the office of the President of the United States;

Whereas a spirit of passionate advocacy and deep respect for the institution of the Senate should govern the deliberations that take place in the Caucus Room of the Russell Senate Office Building; and

Whereas the Senate wishes to honor the life and work of Senator EDWARD MOORE KENNEDY, to recognize the contributions of the 3 Kennedy brothers who served as Senators, and to celebrate the spirit of public service exemplified by the Kennedy family: Now, therefore, be it

Resolved, That the Senate designates room 325 of the Russell Senate Office Building, commonly referred to as the "Caucus Room", as the "Kennedy Caucus Room", in recognition of the service to the Senate and the people of the United States of Senators EDWARD MOORE KENNEDY, Robert Francis Kennedy, and John Fitzgerald Kennedy.

There being no objection, the Senate proceeded to consider the resolution.

Mr. DODD. Madam President, I wish to take a second and thank, first of all, the majority leader, Senator Reid, for his support in this effort. I recognize as well our colleague from Massachusetts, Senator Kerry, who is my lead co-sponsor in this effort and a very close and dear personal friend of TED KENNEDY for many years. And I thank our colleagues.

We are joined by the presence of our colleague from the other body, Senator TED KENNEDY's son Patrick, who serves with great distinction in the other body. I am pleased he is here with us at this moment to watch this resolution be adopted.

I ask unanimous consent that the resolution be agreed to, the preamble be agreed to, the motions to reconsider be laid upon the table, en bloc, and that any statements relating to the resolution be printed in the *Record*.

The PRESIDING OFFICER. Without objection, it is so ordered.

The resolution (S. Res. 264) was agreed to.

The preamble was agreed to.

The PRESIDING OFFICER. The Senator from Massachusetts.

Mr. KERRY. Madam President, I thank the distinguished Senator from Connecticut. There was no closer or better friend to TED KENNEDY than Chris Dodd. I admire and respect his many efforts in the Senate to fight the fights in the spirit of TED KENNEDY.

This could not be more appropriate, and I do not think anything more needs to be said. I thank him, and I thank the majority leader. It is wonderful to have Patrick, Congressman Kennedy, on the floor of the Senate to share in this moment.

The PRESIDING OFFICER. The Senator from Ohio.

Mr. BROWN. Madam President, I join, of course, Senator Kerry, Senator Dodd, and Congressman Kennedy in honoring Patrick's father and the Kennedy family in what used to be the Russell Caucus Chamber. There is no more appropriate place, I believe, to honor Senator KENNEDY than right there.

TUESDAY, *September 15, 2009*

Ms. SNOWE. Mr. President, I join with my colleagues today to express my profound and heartfelt sadness on the passing of Senator EDWARD M. KENNEDY, a universally acknowledged "lion of this institution"—an unsurpassed colleague, a legislator's legislator, and political icon of incalculable, landmark significance to the U.S. Senate and the Nation and a good friend to me and to so many others in this body through the years.

Like all of my colleagues here today, I want to first and foremost offer my most sincere condolences to TED's extraordinary wife Vicki, who has been such a tower of strength, courage, and faith; as well as to TED's three children, Kara, Ted, Jr., and Patrick Kennedy and two stepchildren, Curran and Caroline Raclin; TED's sister, Jean Kennedy Smith, and to his entire family who have done so much to shape the course of our Nation. My heart goes out to Senator KENNEDY's numerous grandchildren, nieces, and nephews whose participation in his funeral mass could not have been more moving. I also extend my deepest sympathies to the people of Massachusetts. They have lost a legendary champion and fierce advocate who served for nearly half a century.

And how powerful and poignant was the remarkable out-pouring of respect and affection for Senator KENNEDY by the American people—from the streets of Boston, outside the John F. Kennedy Presidential Library and Museum, and near the Basilica of Our Lady of Perpetual Help, to congressional staff assembled on the Senate steps and mourners and well-wishers on the Capitol grounds or along the route to his final resting place at Arlington National Cemetery.

On an occasion of such a large and historic loss, summoning the appropriate words to capture the immense depth and breadth of this moment as well as the magnitude of its meaning represents the most daunting of challenges. Like every Senator fortunate enough to serve in this esteemed Chamber during the span of the last 46 years, I have never known a Senate without TED KENNEDY, and it is difficult to comprehend that this hallowed Chamber will never again resound with Senator KENNEDY's booming voice that would literally shake these walls.

As I look around this Chamber, I know I am far from alone in saying I will miss TED's oratorical command of rhetoric and argumentation as well as his passion-filled gestures that punctuated his statements, and of course I will never forget those occasions when TED would really get wound up as only TED could, and his glasses would come off, and he would swing them around and around, faster and faster as his polemic reached a crescendo. And so, there is a highly personal and inescapable void among all of us that is at once acutely palpable, indescribable, and unforgettable.

I can still remember entering the Senate in 1995 having served in the U.S. House of Representatives and looking to my fellow New Englander, Senator KENNEDY, as a model legislator, the best of his generation even then, for what can be achieved in the Senate with passion and devotion and an almost peerless ability to simply "get things done."

I always profoundly admired TED for his commitment to this country and the steadfast, immutable determination he exhibited each and every day as he sought to better our Nation to benefit not just his constituents in Massachusetts but all Americans. And he did so with uncommon civility and candor, facility and efficacy, partisanship and bipartisanship, as well as the most seriousness of purpose and irrepressible good humor. In short, TED KENNEDY combined legislative craftsmanship and legendary statesmanship that were the marvel of his time and that represented a pinnacle of leadership.

And part and parcel of his historic and overarching legacy is not just the results produced by his hard-fought labors, which have reached every corner of our country, but how he legislated and conducted the demanding task of advancing the public policy process. Where there was a divide, he saw an opportunity to repair the breach. Where there were opposing forces, he resolved to find a point of alliance.

As my colleagues here can attest, Senator KENNEDY was ever-cognizant that your adversary today could, and frankly often would be, your ally tomorrow—the staunch opponent you encounter on one occasion may well support you on another down the road. Because, for TED, common ground was not simply a plot of earth he tilled, cultivated, or nourished; it was soil he intuitively knew was meant to be shared and that would be improved through collaboration. And he understood keenly that the most powerful light was not the spotlight, but reflected light that shone first on someone else.

And if TED KENNEDY put into practice the idea that politics in the often-cited words of German Chancellor Bismarck was indeed "the art of the possible," he was also equally adept at implementing the notion that leadership was the catalyst for accomplishing the impossible. Not, however, by going it alone but rather by enlisting the active support of others.

The fact is, like so many of my colleagues in this Chamber, I was privileged to work with Senator KENNEDY on several memorable measures, and one recent endeavor in particular exemplifies his collaborative spirit—the Genetic Information Nondiscrimination Act. That experience for me represented a microcosm of TED's unrivaled political and public policy acumen.

To begin with, Senator KENNEDY, as chairman of the Senate Committee on Health, Education, Labor, and Pensions, or HELP, ordinarily would have been the lead sponsor on legislation being reported out of his committee. But, as all of us in this Chamber know, there was nothing "ordinary" about TED KENNEDY, and he graciously deferred the lead sponsorship to me and instead joined as lead Democratic sponsor of our measure, a gesture of incredible generosity and good will that I will never forget. And so, after already twice garnering Senate passage, we began a third attempt to achieve Senate enactment of vital reforms to protect Americans from both health insurance and workplace discrimination based on their genetic makeup. Beginning in November 2006, we embarked on what was to be a second 18-month-long effort to systematically address every issue which opponents raised. Senator KENNEDY's remarkable capacity to build consensus with both his colleagues and stakeholders spoke to his consummate skills as a legislator and negotiator.

TED never tired in this undertaking, and his knowledge and skills and those of his superb and dedicated staff helped ensure our success when, on May 21 of last year, we at last witnessed the enactment into law of this landmark civil rights protection. Our victory was tempered, however, by the fact that due to his illness, even then, TED could not join us at the White House that day for the signing. And yet it speaks enormous volumes that Senator KENNEDY chose to devote his remaining energies in the past 15 months prior to his passing to ensuring that health reform advance ever forward.

As anyone who has come into contact with TED KENNEDY can tell you, he possessed and exuded a contagious joy and exuberance that permeated all he did. I well recall a few years ago being in Boston for a Base Closure and Realignment Commission (BRAC) hearing, and we were waiting for an elevator. As many in this Chamber will recall, this was a very anxious and uncertain period for a number of us. But I will always remember seeing the elevator doors open and who should appear but TED KENNEDY, alongside a large group of his constituents, fighting the closure of a facility in Massachusetts. And without missing a beat, he roared with his sonorous voice: "You go fight them Olympia with everything you've got!" The whole crowd with him cheered.

That moment reflected so much of what TED exemplified, encompassed, and meant to so many, and he approached his causes with a ferocity of spirit and feeling that was unmatched. It is true, as all of us in this institution know all too well, if TED KENNEDY were opposite you in a debate, and sometimes I was, it could be rough going, and you had better be prepared! But if he were with you, let's just say your chances for victory increased exponentially!

TED never lost that gusto—not in legislating and not in life. Who could forget witnessing TED throwing out the first pitch for New England's beloved Boston Red Sox at this year's home opener at Fenway Park? Or his zeal for his beloved Massachusetts or, for that matter, the Maine coast which he loved so much where he sailed every summer. Indeed, one year he and Vicki visited an inn near our family place at Hancock Point. And I will always remember the excitement and anticipation he exhibited as he showed me his map of the journey he and Vicki were preparing to undertake, sailing along the beautiful Maine coastline.

As my colleagues know above all, this greatest of deliberative bodies has lost a giant and a legislative standard-bearer who was tirelessly devoted to its history, its stewardship, and its purpose, and his ardor and love for this most august institution and the Nation it serves will never be extinguished. Senator KENNEDY now ranks among a rarefied pantheon of legendary Senators such as Daniel Webster and Henry Clay. He was, to evoke the title of the Pulitzer Prize-winning book by his brother, John, truly a "profile in courage."

The great American poet, Carl Sandburg, once wrote:

I see America not in the setting sun of night ... I see America in the crimson light of a rising sun. I see great days ahead, great days possible to men and women of will and vision.

Those days are indeed possible for this Senate, this Congress, and our country precisely because of the indefatigable will and limitless vision of public servants such as Senator TED KENNEDY. We honor his memory and his legacy best by striving every day to make this process work for the U.S. Senate and for the American people.

And what Maine's own Henry Wadsworth Longfellow penned about another Senator from Massachusetts, Charles Sumner, we say today about Senator KENNEDY:

So when a great man dies,
For years beyond our ken,
The light he leaves behind him lies
Upon the paths of men.

So it will forever be with Senator EDWARD M. KENNEDY. We will not see his like again. He will be sorely missed.

THURSDAY, *September 17, 2009*

Mr. DORGAN. Madam President, the other day when our colleagues were talking about our departed colleague, Senator TED KENNEDY, I was not able to be on the Senate floor, and I did want to say just a few words about my friend TED KENNEDY.

I had the pleasure of serving in this Chamber with him for 16 years. He sat back at that desk in the row behind me, and I had many opportunities to spend time and swap stories and talk about public policy with him. I knew him before I came to the Senate. As a very young man, I worked on his brother Robert Kennedy's campaign for the Presidency, and I met TED KENNEDY then. And I supported TED KENNEDY in his 1980 Presidential campaign and met him again.

When I came to the Senate, from time to time I was invited to go to Hyannis Port to the Kennedy compound and visited there with Senator KENNEDY and his family and went sailing with him. To sail with Senator TED KENNEDY was an extraordinary experience. He was a wonderful sailor.

Many things have been said and written about TED KENNEDY over the years, and especially in recent weeks since his death. I don't need to repeat his many accomplishments here in the Senate; my colleagues have done a great job doing that. Those accomplishments spanned almost 47 years and would take far too long and too much time to detail, and many have done it, as I said.

I will not repeat his love of all things Irish. Everyone understood that. He was a great Irish storyteller. No prouder Irishman in the world, I daresay, than TED KENNEDY.

I don't need to tell of his many acts of thoughtfulness and kindness, large and small, for the powerful and the powerless. They are well known already as well and, already, much missed.

Many have talked about his wit and his love of story telling and a good joke. That, too, was TED KENNEDY. Laughing and making people laugh were part of the hallmark of his character. Often, when I think of him, I think of a booming laughter that filled the entire room when he was full of joy.

I need not talk about his doggedness or his tireless work ethic or his determination, for they, too, were well known to all of us who worked with him. Those were the pillars upon which he built success after success, often small, but then building and building, step by step, until it was consequential and often big.

Those were also the pillars on which he built decades of relationships. I think those relationships were the keys to understanding the man with whom we served—TED KENNEDY.

It didn't matter whether you were a Republican or a Democrat or an Independent. It didn't matter if you were a businessman or a janitor, young or old, White or Black, rich or poor, powerful or powerless. TED KENNEDY wanted to work with you to try to reach a compromise and see what could be achieved together. He just never, ever stopped; never gave up.

The great American essayist and author, Ralph Waldo Emerson, once said:

The characteristic of heroism is in its persistency. All men have wandering impulses, fits and starts of generosity. But when you have chosen your part, abide by it, and do not weakly try to reconcile yourself with the world.

No one I know in this Chamber was more persistent than TED KENNEDY. He chose his part; he abided by it; he didn't try to reconcile his principles to the moment or to the world; and, he fought and fought for what he believed in and what he thought was right. Sometimes it was very controversial, but he was persistent and fought long and hard until the end.

Even when he was sick and tired and worn out, he fought on because he loved his country, and he knew his colleagues and others loved this country as much as he did. He knew there was always that common ground, love of country, and he knew that people of good faith, regardless of party and regardless of position, could achieve great things for the country they all loved.

When he was done, he had cast more than 16,000 votes. More than 300 laws bear the name of Senator TED KENNEDY, and he co-sponsored more than 2,000 others. That doesn't include the thousands of laws he merely influenced. Much of that work was done on the Senate floor. It was his life's work.

If the Senate was his home, this Senate floor surely was his front porch, where he would let everyone know what was on his mind. When Senator TED KENNEDY, at that desk, was on the Senate floor, you may not have agreed with him, you might not have even cared about the subject before he began to speak, but you had to listen, you had to respond, and you had to take sides.

He was called the lion of the Senate by many. When he was on the floor roaring, it was quite a sight and sound to behold, a sound that moved hearts. It moved minds. It moved this very institution and, indeed, the country itself. He could be quietly persuasive, but on the Senate floor his passion literally poured out of him.

It was said long ago of Daniel Webster, another famous Senator from Massachusetts, that he was "a great cannon loaded to the lips." Well, Senator KENNEDY was a great cannon loaded to the lips, and this institution will long miss that passion, those words, his spirit, his love of life, and his love of this institution and our country.

There is an old saying that all men die, but not all men live. Well, surely TED KENNEDY lived. Senator TED KENNEDY lives in our hearts and in his good works and in his life's work, and I just wanted today to join my colleagues in saying: TED, Godspeed, rest in peace, and all Members of this Senate miss you dearly.

Mr. SPECTER. Mr. President, I have sought recognition to pay respect to the life and character of our dear friend TED KENNEDY. A man as much a part of this institution as the very walls of the Capitol, TED has earned his place in the world's history books and will never be forgotten.

I consider myself privileged to have worked with TED on several important issues, ranging from hate crimes legislation to our time together on the Judiciary Committee. TED was responsible for the Matthew Shepard Hate Crimes Act, an important piece of legislation providing protection for vulnerable Americans that I was proud to co-sponsor. He was instrumental in the passage of SCHIP, a program that now insures the health of millions of children across the country. The impact TED KENNEDY had on civil rights legislation throughout his career is simply immeasurable. Countless programs now serving the American people could not exist today if not for the hard work and determination of TED KENNEDY.

One of my most vivid memories working with Senator KENNEDY was during the now well-known confirmation hearings of Robert Bork for the Supreme Court. TED spoke eloquently and with conviction against Judge Bork's nomination, fearing the erosion of civil rights that would occur were he confirmed. TED refused to let this erosion of rights take place, and I am proud to have joined him in his fight against the nomination of Robert Bork.

TED proved through his actions, both on and off the Senate floor, that he was, above all, a man of compassion. The single unifying theme of TED's distinguished body of work was his clear commitment to the people of this great country. His love for the American people was clear through the legislation he so strongly supported. TED's greatest concern was for the well-being of every American, and he made it his mission to ensure the underprivileged received the fair treatment they deserved.

In his lifetime, TED KENNEDY was able to accomplish more than most men could ever dream of accomplishing. I have no doubt that if we were lucky enough to have him with us today, he would continue to add even greater accomplishments to his already impressive resume. TED will be deeply missed.

TUESDAY, *September 22, 2009*

Mr. UDALL of Colorado. Mr. President, I rise today to give tribute to Senator EDWARD KENNEDY.

It is impossible to sum up Senator TED KENNEDY in words or a speech. His life and work touched so many diverse interests and issues. Senator KENNEDY was larger than life. He was a champion for the underdog—those in our society who just needed a hand up. For close to five decades, Senator KENNEDY championed policies for American workers, minorities, parents, immigrants, gays and lesbians, people with disabilities and illnesses, among others. And I think I can safely say he was the greatest legislator in the history of the Senate.

In the words of Senator John McCain during his Presidential bid, "I have described TED KENNEDY as the last lion in the Senate ... because he remains the single most effective Member ... if you want to get results."

While he was known as a champion for liberal causes, Senator KENNEDY's hallmark was to reach across the aisle, passing legislation with his Republican friends, such as Orrin Hatch and John McCain. He never let partisanship stop him from doing what was right for the American people.

But his most important role was that of the patriarch of the Kennedy family—a family that faced tragedy that most of us never will experience and can never fathom. Despite the loss of three brothers taken long before their time, and the loss of a nephew, a rising star, TED KENNEDY rose above the burdens of life and became the rudder of the Kennedy ship, the driving force of the family—a family dedicated to public service. Fortunately for all of us, that dedication has been passed on to the next generation, and it has influenced families across our Nation, including mine.

The Kennedy family and my own family first crossed paths decades ago, and our family stories continue to be intertwined. My dad, Mo Udall, and uncle, Stewart Udall, supported John Kennedy in his race for President. TED KENNEDY was JFK's man on the ground in the Southwest States.

[147]

In fact, the Udalls have been called the "Kennedys of the West." And as my Aunt Elma says, "we are flattered" by that comparison.

In many ways we are as different as they come. Kennedys are the East. Kennedys are the ocean. Kennedys are Catholic immigrants. Udalls are the West. Udalls are the desert. Udalls are Mormon dirt farmers.

But it is true that my family was drawn to the Kennedys' deep commitment to religious freedom and dedication to public service. My family also shares a commitment to public service. My Uncle Stewart served as President Kennedy's Secretary of the Interior. And my father ran for and won in a special election in 1960 for Uncle Stewart's congressional seat. Some claim that his race was a referendum on the fledgling Kennedy administration, and that his victory was an affirmation of America's support for the goals of his Presidency.

Whether that is true, it has proved to be a connection that would keep our families close for decades. And what binds the two families are the friendships that have been fostered over decades, since friendships that cross generations hopefully will continue into the next.

In 1971, my father ran for majority leader of the House of Representatives and lost. The same year, Senator KENNEDY lost his bid for Senate whip. Soon after came a note to my father from Senator KENNEDY which said, "Mo, as soon as I pull the liberal knives out of my back, I'll help you dig out the liberal buckshot from your backside."

My dad supported TED KENNEDY in his primary bid to become President in 1980.

He and TED were friends for many decades, and in many ways they were kindred spirits. They loved the outdoors, national parks, skiing in Colorado, and family touch football. We all will remember the photographs of TED on his sailboat with his family, his love of the ocean and boating, and sharing it with generations of Kennedy children.

A few years after my dad lost his battle with Parkinson's disease, Senator Dennis DeConcini of Arizona sponsored legislation to establish the Morris K. Udall Foundation. Senator KENNEDY joined in sponsoring the measure. In speaking about my dad, he noted:

He will rank as one of the greatest Members of the House of Representatives of all time, and also as one of the most beloved. ... Somehow, for 30 years, whenever you probed to the heart of the great concerns of the day, you found Mo Udall in the thick of the battle, championing the rights of average citizens against special interest pressures, defending the highest ideals of America, and always doing it with the special grace and wit that were his trademark and that endeared him to Democrats and Republicans alike.

If my dad were alive today, I think he would use the same words to describe Senator KENNEDY. They both brought people together to do what is right for our country.

Recently, as I have thought about Senator KENNEDY's legacy, I have remembered my dad's 1980 speech at the Democratic National Convention. After a tough primary battle, the Democrats were digging in and fighting among themselves. They needed to set aside their differences and join together to win the election. My dad rose to give the keynote address to remind Democrats that they were in this fight together. "We do fight, and we kick and yell and scream and maybe even scratch a bit, but we fight because we are a diverse party and because we've always tried to listen up to new ideas."

He concluded the speech with these comments:

This Nation that we love will only survive if each generation of caring Americans can blend two elements: change and the ability to adjust things to the special needs of our times; and second, stability, the good sense to carry forward the old values which are just as good now as they were 200 years ago.

These elements epitomize TED KENNEDY's legacy. He knew when a person or group of people needed a change in their circumstances.

His strong Catholic faith was the compass that guided his life. It was the driving force that led him to fight to make a difference in other people's lives, particularly those who were less fortunate.

TED KENNEDY's legislative successes are numerous and unquestionably have changed lives for the better. He fought to pass the Civil Rights Act of 1964 and the Voting Rights Act of 1965. In the 1990s, he labored to pass the Family and Medical Leave Act. And he and Senator Hatch worked across the aisle to pass the Ryan White CARE Act. And it is his lifelong battle for universal health care coverage for Americans that he is best known for today.

The Kennedy and Udall ideals can live on through the younger generation. My cousin Tom and I served in the House of Representatives with Patrick Kennedy. Not only were we colleagues, but we are friends. We grew up in political families and, from an early age, public service was a way of life. I was a proud supporter of Patrick's crusade to pass mental health parity legislation in the House. Fortunately,

Senator KENNEDY lived to see his son's work come to fruition, keeping faith with the special Kennedy credo: aid those who need a helping hand.

Tom, Patrick, and I, as well as the rest of the Kennedy and Udall family members, have big shoes to fill. Whether we can actually fill them remains to be seen, but we must certainly push the trail blazed by our aunts and uncles, fathers and mothers as far as our endurance allows.

Senator TED KENNEDY surely will be missed not only on the Senate floor, but in our lives. I deeply regret I will not serve with him in the Senate in the years ahead. He was a champion, a fighter, and a friend. I want to say "goodbye" not only for me, but for my dad, his friend. And I send my thoughts and prayers to Vicki, Patrick, and the rest of the Kennedy family.

TUESDAY, *September 29, 2009*

Mr. BUNNING. Mr. President, I am saddened by the death of my colleague from Massachusetts, Senator EDWARD KENNEDY.

Born and raised in Massachusetts, Senator KENNEDY dedicated his life to serving his country and the Commonwealth. He enlisted in the U.S. Army in 1951, beginning his long career of public service. Elected in 1962, Senator KENNEDY is the third longest serving Senator in the history of the Senate. He served the people of Massachusetts well for more than 46 years, and I know his family and the people of Massachusetts are proud to call him one of their own.

Senator KENNEDY had a long list of accomplishments to show for the people of Massachusetts and the Nation. He was a political icon who served with great distinction and passion for nearly a half century in the U.S. Senate, and whether I agreed with him or not, I always admired the way he fought for the issues he believed in. His leadership in the Senate will be missed and it has truly been an honor serving with him.

Mr. President, Senator KENNEDY will be greatly missed. Mary and I give our heartfelt condolences to his wife, Vicki, and the entire Kennedy family.

Mr. REID. ... He [Orrin Hatch] excelled in his younger days as a basketball player, has fought in the ring, and as we have heard from the Republican leader, he is an accomplished musician, and he really is. He recently wrote a song in honor of Senator KENNEDY. It is not the first song he has written about his friend. ...

Mr. HATCH. ... This body means a great deal to me. We all saw what it meant to TED KENNEDY and the great accolades he received throughout his lifetime. It was a real privilege to be close to him, as I am to almost all of you and will be to all of you. ...

Mr. LIEBERMAN. Mr. President, I ask to have printed in the *Record* a poem written by Mr. Albert Carey Caswell. Mr. Caswell is a valued tour guide of the U.S. Capitol whose great enthusiasm and love of our country has inspired him to compose over 500 poems. Mr. Caswell wrote this poem in tribute to the remarkable life and work of our beloved late colleague Senator TED KENNEDY.

The information follows.

UPON THIS FLOOR

(In honor of and in memory of Senator EDWARD M. KENNEDY)

(By Albert Carey Caswell)

Upon this floor ...
From our forefathers so bore ...
A dream, for all our futures to ensure ...
Now in history, the world's greatest of all democracies ...

Upon this floor ...
For as the years have played out ...
The United States Senate, would so tout!
Some of the greatest, from Clay, Calhoun to Webster no doubt ...
Men of conscience and of faith, who would so debate ...
Who but in their hands, were but put our nation's future fate.

Upon this floor!
Who all but for the greater good, did but all they could ...
Giants one and all, who but heard our nation's call ...
Her call to public service, upon this floor ...

And now as the years have gone by ...
A new great, a new giant has so arrived ...
A name we now so utter with tear in eye ...
EDWARD M. KENNEDY, who upon this floor spoke so eloquently!

Whose word was one to be cherished and respected!
The most effective Senator, as John McCain expressed this!
For legislation can be a blood sport ...

For only those of great heart and courage, will like lions roar!

And yet, in all that heat ... it takes a leader who can make minds meet!
As was this man, so charming and sweet!
And leave their most hallowed marks upon this floor ...
With TEDDY's passing, I rise to state ...

Without objection, we have lost one of the truly greats!
There will be no quorum call, or voice vote expected!
Or a bill, for The President to sign ... stating of such perfection!
For he, was A Man For All Seasons ...

Who knew how to debate, and more importantly how to reason!
A giant among mere men, who with his principles would so splendidly and
steadfastly defend!
Motivating women and men, with but his heart of a champion ...
Time and time again, upon this floor ...

TED, you are gone, but not forgotten ...
For history and heaven so holds a place, for the champions of the down-
trodden!
For artists, who know how to so create ... and legislate!
Whether, with a voice of a lion making the Senate quake!

Or like a fine surgeon, so delicately legislation you'd manipulate ...
Yea, TEDDY ... Daniel Webster ain't got nothing on you!
And in the Senate reception room ...
And upon this floor my son ... history will you so view!

One of the greatest who's who!
Now, up in Heaven ... it's the greatest of debates between Daniel and you!

TUESDAY, *October 6, 2009*

Mr. CARDIN. ... He [Tom Perez] then later took a very important assignment in the Senate. He became special counsel to Senator TED KENNEDY. What a mentor for him. He has commented frequently about his year in the Senate and what a great learning experience it was to understand the importance of the Civil Rights Division from the champion of civil rights in the Senate, Senator KENNEDY. ...

WEDNESDAY, *October 7, 2009*

Mr. INHOFE. Madam President, it was called to my attention a few minutes ago that our deadline for comments about TED KENNEDY is coming up tomorrow. I wanted to beat the deadline. I always wait until the last minute, it seems. One of the reasons I did is because there are so many things people are not aware of, so I took the time to send to places such as Western Sahara and elsewhere to get documents that better explained a little bit more about who TED KENNEDY was than has already been stated on the floor of the Senate.

I have a good friend whose name is Mouloud Said. He is the Ambassador at Large of Western Sahara. He and I worked together for many years trying to bring some sanity into what has happened over the last 35 years in Western Sahara.

For the record, since people are not aware of this conflict that took place, back in 1975, the Moroccans invaded what was then called Spanish Sahara, later called Western Sahara. There were a lot of people chased out at that time. They fled. War ensued between 1975 and 1991. It continued during that time. When Morocco invaded that area that was later called Western Sahara, the refugees, the people who were living there who rightfully should be in that area, who should be living there today, were chased into Algeria. Tindouf is an area I have been to a couple times. The refugee camps there are so large. There are actually 175,000 refugees who were chased out of Western Sahara and have been wanting to be repatriated since then.

One of the former Secretaries of State, James Baker, was a hero in this area. He did the best he could to see that repatriation would take place. It seemed like every time they got close to working out something with Morocco, they would get right up to the altar, and then they would cut it off. They would agree something should be done, but as they would come to agreement and get together, Morocco would back down. That took place for a long period of time.

You cannot be empathetic with the people who are there until you have walked through the little alleys and the stucco houses in Tindouf and see how these people are living, hearing their chants, their cries for freedom. Three generations now have been trying to escape, to be repatriated, and it hasn't worked.

I have a letter—I will read part of it—that ties Senator KENNEDY and me to this issue. This is from Mouloud Said, who is Ambassador at Large of Western Sahara:

Indeed, this was precisely the case when Senator James Inhofe and the late Senator EDWARD KENNEDY reached across the political aisle to jointly promote the cause of justice and freedom in the Western Sahara, and respect for human rights of the Saharawi people. As recognized by the United Nations Charter, the African Union, and the American Constitution, all people have the inalienable right to freedom and self-determination, and the Saharawi people will be forever indebted to these great Senators for their principled and bipartisan stand on behalf of the Saharawi's fundamental rights.

That is what it is all about. We would see these people out there, and they had no one to take care of them. The Moroccans, they have friends. I have to say this: I testified probably 2 or 3 years ago at a House committee hearing. At that time, we made a list of all the lobbyists Morocco had hired. They had everybody. The money was all on one side, and only the Lord and a few people who were sympathetic to them were on the side of those people who have been living on the Algerian border for the last 35 years. That is what they are going through at this time. It is very sad.

I want to mention, talking about TED KENNEDY, how persistent he was. This goes all the way back to his involvement, back to the time when the war was still taking place. I have statements I am going to enter into the *Record*. They are not long. One goes back to October 1, 1992, a "Statement by Senator EDWARD M. KENNEDY at Senate Foreign Relations Africa Subcommittee Hearing on the Western Sahara." He goes through and tells the story of what he has attempted to do, and he had not been able to successfully get it done. The same as with James Baker and myself.

January 1994, "Statement by EDWARD M. KENNEDY in Support of Amendment Promoting Implementation of Peace Plan in the Western Sahara." January 1994, we thought at that time we had it done. Again, an arrangement was made. It was agreed to by all parties until they got together.

June 23, 1999, "Senator KENNEDY Calls for Greater Progress on Western Sahara Referendum." A referendum is all they want. They want self-determination. They want to be able to vote as to whether they want to be repatriated, which is something we in America would assume everybody has that right. But that is not the situation.

Senator KENNEDY, again, went to battle to help them in June 23, 1999, and was not able to get it done.

Then, again, in 2000, he actually offered amendments for holding referendums in Western Sahara.

Later in that same year, he appealed to King Mohammed VI of Morocco to give these people a chance, at least, of self-determination. He was unable to get that done.

I ask unanimous consent to have printed in the *Record* these documents.

There being no objection, the material was ordered to be printed in the *Record*, as follows:

I want to thank Senator Simon, the subcommittee chairman, for holding
this important hearing today.

The ongoing crisis in the Western Sahara raises serious questions regarding the Government of Morocco's willingness to honor its international commitment to a free and fair referendum in that territory. It also brings into
question the credibility of the United Nations in administering the Western
Saharan peace plan, and our own government's commitment to the principles of sovereignty and self-determination.

Barring immediate and dramatic progress, the peace plan for the Western
Sahara is destined to fail. If the peace plan is to succeed, the United States
must do more to make clear—through deed as well as word—its commitment to a free and fair referendum for the indigenous Saharawi people.

The Western Sahara is the last vestige of colonialism in Africa. The U.N.
Decolonization Committee called for decolonization in 1966, while it was
still under Spanish rule. In 1973, the General Assembly called for a referendum on self-determination by the Saharawi. Spain agreed to hold a referendum and took a census to provide a voting list.

Shortly thereafter, Morocco and Mauritania, seeking access to the territory's valuable natural resources, laid claim to the Western Sahara. In an
effort to strengthen its claim to the territory, Morocco requested an advisory
opinion from the International Court of Justice on its legal status. The
Court found that neither Morocco nor Mauritania had ties to the Western
Sahara sufficient for claims of territorial sovereignty. Like the United Nations, the Court supported "self-determination and genuine expression of the
will of the peoples" to determine the territory's legal status.

Rather than accept that decision, King Hassan II sent Moroccan troops
into the Western Sahara. Clashes ensued between Moroccan forces and the
Polisario, the armed resistance of the Saharawi. Invading troops "disappeared" thousands of Saharawi civilians, most of whom were killed. Hundreds of others were detained without charge—and remain imprisoned
today.

The Moroccan invasion touched off an exodus of refugees from the Western Sahara into Algeria. Seventeen years later, tens of thousands of these
refugees continue to subsist in emergency relief tents with minimal food and
water under extremely oppressive desert conditions including violent sand-
storms and blistering heat exceeding 160 degrees.

In what became known as the "Green March," King Hassan then sent
350,000 Moroccan civilians into the territory to strengthen his claim. Within
months of the Moroccan influx Spain withdrew, granting Morocco and Mauritania "temporary authority" to administer the territory until a referendum
could be held.

Neither Morocco nor Mauritania granted the Saharawi the right to self-
determination, and their war against the Polisario steadily escalated. The
Polisario's use of land rovers and quick strike tactics, however, achieved surprising successes against Moroccan and Mauritanian forces, and in 1979
Mauritania renounced its claims to the territory.

Finally, after over a decade of war, the Government of Morocco agreed to
a U.N.-sponsored peace plan leading to a referendum, under which the
Saharawi would vote for independence or integration with Morocco. In 1990,
the Security Council adopted resolutions approving the plan and estab-

lishing the United Nations Mission for the Referendum in Western Sahara (MINURSO).

Under the plan, a cease-fire was to go into effect on September 6, 1991, and the referendum was to be held in early 1992. The parties agreed to use the 1974 Spanish census, which recorded approximately 74,000 Saharawis, to establish a voting list for the referendum.

Yet, only days before the cease-fire was to go into effect, Morocco bombed a compound that the Saharawi had constructed to house MINURSO personnel.

Inexplicably, the United States was the sole country on the U.N. Security Council which failed to condemn this outrageous action.

After the cease-fire went into effect, King Hassan changed his position on the voting list. After he agreed to base the list upon the 1974 census, he presented the U.N. with a list of 120,000 additional voters from Morocco whom he claimed were Saharawi and should also be permitted to vote. These individuals were transported into the Western Sahara in violation of the peace plan, which forbids the unilateral transfer of populations into the territory without identification at the border by U.N. personnel.

Under the peace plan, MINURSO observers are to implement and monitor the cease-fire, oversee the release of POWs, identify and register voters, and organize the referendum. Fully employed, MINURSO was to consist of 1,695 military and civilian personnel.

Yet as of today, 9 months after the referendum was to have been held, fewer than 400 MINURSO personnel are in Western Sahara. With severely limited equipment and personnel, these observers have been forced to restrict their focus to monitoring the cease-fire. Due to serious violations of the peace plan by the Government of Morocco, the observers have been prevented from fostering an atmosphere of confidence and stability conducive to holding a free and fair referendum.

These violations include preventing critical supplies for U.N. personnel from reaching the field; denying U.N. observers access to military areas; threatening to shoot U.N. personnel; intercepting and blocking U.N. patrols and sideswiping U.N. vehicles; refusing to identify land mines to U.N. observers, resulting in the loss of three U.N. vehicles and serious injury to U.N. personnel; banning access to the territory by international observers, reporters, and human rights organizations; refusing to withdraw any of its 130,000 troops; and declining to provide figures on the strength and deployment of its armed forces, despite written instructions to do so from the U.N. Secretary General.

Last month, in the most serious violation of the peace process, King Hassan announced his intention to hold his own elections in the territory, independently of the United Nations—thereby wholly undermining the U.N. effort.

Ironically, U.N. observers have also been severely hampered by lack of material and political support from the United Nations in New York, which has routinely ignored Moroccan violations of the peace plan. The Secretary General has failed to respond politically to MINURSO's reports of cease-fire violations—including 178 confirmed violations of the cease-fire, the transfer of thousands of Moroccan citizens to the territory prior to their identification by the United Nations, and continuous misbehavior with respect to MINURSO.

Accordingly, MINURSO personnel in the field today are attempting to carry out their duties without the cooperation of the Government of Morocco and without the political backing of the United Nations.

Despite Morocco's flagrant violations of the peace plan, the Bush administration has failed to press King Hassan in any significant manner with respect to the Western Sahara. To the contrary, the administration has requested that $40 million in military aid and $12 million in economic support funds be earmarked for Morocco for FY 1993. This is particularly perplexing, inasmuch as no funds were earmarked for Morocco during FY 1992.

I hope that the witnesses for the administration will make clear today why the United States is not condemning Morocco for its violations of the peace plan. The administration should also explain why it is unwilling to urge the United Nations to do more to defend this important peace initiative.

Failure of the U.N. peace plan will have serious consequences for the stability of North Africa. Unless the administration makes clear to the Government of Morocco its commitment to a free and fair referendum for the Saharawi, fighting in the Western Sahara may soon be renewed. That is a result none of us wants, and now is the time to prevent it from happening.

✖

STATEMENT BY SENATOR EDWARD M. KENNEDY IN SUPPORT OF AMENDMENT
PROMOTING IMPLEMENTATION OF PEACE PLAN IN THE WESTERN SAHARA

(January 1994)

I am introducing today, on behalf of myself and Senators Pell, Kassebaum, and Simon an amendment to support the indigenous people of the Western Sahara in their long and arduous struggle for self-determination.

As U.S. citizens, we are fortunate to live in a country founded on human rights principles and the right to a government of our own choosing. Our democratic ideals have inspired peoples in all hemispheres around the world. Elections during the past 12 months in Russia, Burundi, Cambodia, Paraguay, and Yemen are examples of the world-wide trend away from authoritarianism and toward representative government.

Sadly, this trend has not yet reached all regions of the world. The indigenous Saharawi people in the Western Sahara have waited more than 18 years to regain their right to self-determination. Hopefully, that right will soon be restored to them.

Since Morocco's invasion of the Western Sahara in 1975, King Hassan II has staged a long and costly war against the Saharawi people to obtain permanent access to that territory's valuable natural resources.

For years, Morocco ignored proposals by the U.N. General Assembly calling for a referendum on self-determination by the Saharawi. When Morocco took its claim over the territory before the International Court of Justice, the Court found that Morocco did not have ties sufficient for claims of territorial sovereignty. Like the United Nations, the Court supported "self-determination and genuine expression of the will of the peoples" to determine the territory's legal status.

Rather than accept that decision, King Hassan sent Moroccan troops into the territory who killed and "disappeared" thousands of Saharawi who were unwilling to recognize Moroccan sovereignty. Then, in what became known as the "Green March," King Hassan sent 350,000 Moroccan citizens into the Western Sahara to strengthen his claim to it.

Finally, after over a decade of war, the Government of Morocco agreed to a U.N.-sponsored peace plan leading up to a referendum under which the Saharawi would vote for independence or integration with Morocco. Under

[157]

this plan, a cease-fire was to go into effect on September 6, 1991, and the referendum was to be held in early 1992. The parties agreed to use a 1974 census, which recorded approximately 74,000 Saharawis, to establish a voting list for the referendum.

Yet, only days before the cease-fire was to go into effect, Morocco bombed a compound the Saharawi had constructed to house U.N. personnel. In addition, King Hassan changed his position on the voter list.

After having previously agreed to base the list upon the 1974 census, he presented the United Nations with a list of 170,000 Moroccans whom he claimed should also be permitted to vote. These individuals were moved into the Western Sahara in violation of the peace plan, which forbids the unilateral transfer of population into the territory without prior identification by U.N. personnel.

U.N. observers have also expressed concern regarding other violations of the peace plan by the Government of Morocco. These violations have prevented the observers from fostering an atmosphere of confidence and stability conducive to holding a free and fair referendum.

The violations include preventing critical supplies for U.N. personnel from reaching the field; denying U.N. observers access to military areas; threatening to shoot U.N. personnel; intercepting and blocking U.N. patrols and sideswiping U.N. vehicles; refusing to identify land mines to U.N. observers, resulting in the loss of three U.N. vehicles and serious injury to U.N. personnel; banning access to the territory by international observers, reporters, and human rights organizations; refusing to withdraw its troops; and declining to provide figures on the strength and deployment of its armed forces, despite written instructions to do so from the U.N. Secretary General.

In one of the most serious violations of the peace process, King Hassan held his own elections in the territory in June—thereby directly undermining the U.N. effort.

U.N. officials nonetheless remain hopeful of holding the referendum this year. For the referendum to be free and fair, the United Nations must disqualify Moroccan settlers from eligibility to vote in the referendum.

Failure of the U.N. peace plan is likely to have serious consequences for the stability of North Africa. If the Government of Morocco continues to obstruct the peace process, fighting in the Western Sahara may well be renewed.

At this critical stage in the peace process the United States must do more to make clear—through deed as well as word—our commitment to a free and fair referendum for the Saharawi people.

The amendment we are introducing today:

(1) Commends the President for his commitment within the United Nations and in bilateral relations to a free and fair referendum on self-determination in the Western Sahara;

(2) Supports the United Nations' commitment to holding a free and fair referendum, and commends the Secretary General for intensifying his efforts toward that end;

(3) Commends the administration for undertaking new policy initiatives with regard to the Western Sahara, including the opening of contacts with the Polisario Front at the Saharawi refugee camp in Tindouf, Algeria;

(4) Calls upon Morocco and the Polisario Front to comply strictly with the terms of the peace plan as accepted by the parties and approved by the U.N. Security Council;

(5) Calls upon Morocco to put an end to the transfer of population not properly identified by the United Nations as eligible voters in the ref-

erendum from Morocco into the Western Sahara, and to return to Morocco all such individuals currently in the Western Sahara;

(6) Calls upon Morocco and the Polisario Front to continue the direct dialog they began under the auspices of the United Nations in July 1993 with the goal of furthering the peace process;

(7) Calls upon Morocco and the Polisario Front to allow international human rights organizations to enter Morocco, the Western Sahara, and refugee camps under their control to assess the human rights situation; and

(8) Calls upon the President to:

Strongly advocate within the United Nations and in bilateral relations the implementation of the peace plan as accepted by the Polisario Front and Morocco and approved by the U.N. Security Council;

Urge all parties concerned to take all steps necessary to begin voter registration, starting with the updated lists of the 1974 Spanish census, and to overcome their differences regarding the interpretation and application of the criteria for voter eligibility;

Institute regular contact at all levels in Washington with representatives of the Polisario Front, in order to strengthen the United States' evenhanded position with respect to the Western Sahara; and

Encourage the parties to allow independent international observers, including human rights organizations, to monitor the situation in the territory and observe the referendum process.

The ongoing crisis in the Western Sahara raises serious questions regarding the Government of Morocco's willingness to honor its international commitment to a free and fair referendum in the Western Sahara. This amendment would make clear our government's support for the U.N. peace process and America's commitment to the principles of sovereignty and self-determination.

I urge my colleagues to join us in enacting this timely and important measure.

❧

SENATOR KENNEDY CALLS FOR GREATER PROGRESS ON WESTERN SAHARA
REFERENDUM

(June 23, 1999)

Senator EDWARD M. KENNEDY today praised the Senate for calling for greater progress on a long-stalled referendum on self-determination for the people of the Western Sahara.

Since 1988, the United Nations has sought to organize a free, fair, and open referendum in the Western Sahara, the former Spanish colony that Morocco has illegally occupied since 1975.

KENNEDY said, "A solution to the conflict over the Western Sahara will enhance security and stability in Northern Africa. After more than ten years of delay, the people of the Western Sahara should be permitted to determine for themselves who will govern them."

KENNEDY, Republican Senator Gordon Smith, and Democratic Senator Patrick Leahy sponsored an amendment accepted by the Senate on the State Department Reauthorization Bill to require the State Department to report on progress on the referendum. The bill, including the Western Sahara amendment, was passed by the Senate yesterday.

The International Court of Justice, the Organization of African Unity, the United States, and many other nations throughout the world have not rec-

[159]

ognized Morocco's claim to the Western Sahara, but Morocco's occupation continues. Tens of thousands of the Saharawi people languish in refugee camps in Southern Algeria and have been denied the opportunity to determine their own future.

A UN referendum was originally scheduled for 1992. It has since been delayed many times, primarily due to the resistance of the Government of Morocco. The referendum is now scheduled for July 2000.

In the 1997 Houston Accords, achieved under the leadership of former Secretary of State James Baker, and in a UN plan last December, the international community called for the conclusion of the voter registration process and a referendum. Morocco subsequently agreed to allow the referendum to occur by July 2000.

Senator KENNEDY praised the Administration's efforts to resolve this long-standing dispute. He urged the State Department to make it clear to both parties to this dispute that the United States expects the people of the Western Sahara to be allowed to exercise their right to self-determination in a free, fair, and open referendum by July 2000.

"Morocco has been a faithful ally of the United States for more than 200 years," said KENNEDY, "but its refusal to allow the people of the Western Sahara to determine their own political future undercuts America's efforts to promote democracy worldwide."

The Kennedy-Smith-Leahy amendment requires the State Department to report on January 1, 2000 and again on June 1, 2000 on specific steps being taken by the Government of Morocco and by the Popular Front for the Liberation of Saguia el-Hamra and Rio de Oro (Polisario) to ensure a free, fair, and open referendum by July 2000 for the people of the Western Sahara to choose between independence and integration with Morocco.

The State Department reports will include a description of preparations for the referendum and the extent to which free access to the territory will be guaranteed for independent and international organizations, including election observers and international media. Human rights organizations and other international organizations must also be permitted to observe the referendum.

In addition, the reports will include a description of current efforts by the Department of State to ensure that the referendum will be held, and an assessment of the likelihood that the July 2000 date will be met.

The reports will also include a description of obstacles, if any, to the voter registration process and other preparations for the referendum and efforts being made by the parties and the United States Government to overcome those obstacles. Finally, the reports will include an assessment of progress being made in the repatriation process.

~∞~

(Purpose: To require reports with respect to the holding of a referendum on Western Sahara)

On page 115; after line 18, add the following new section:

SEC. _____. REPORTS WITH RESPECT TO A REFERENDUM ON WESTERN SAHARA.

(a) REPORTS REQUIRED.—

(1) IN GENERAL.—Not later than each of the dates specified in paragraph (2)1 the Secretary of State shall submit a report to the appropriate Congressional committees describing specific steps being taken by the Government of Morocco and by the Popular Front for the Liberation of Saguia el-Hamra and Rio de Oro (POLIS–RIO)[1] to ensure that a referendum in which the people of the Western Sahara will choose between independence and integration with Morocco will be held by March 2000.

(2) DEADLINES FOR SUBMISSION OF REPORT.—The dates referred to in paragraph (1) are November 1, 1999, and February 1, 2000.

(b) REPORT ELEMENTS.—The report shall include—

(1) a description of preparations for the referendum,

(2) a description of current efforts by the Department of State to ensure that a referendum will be held by March 2000;

(3) an assessment of the likelihood that the March 2000 date will be met,

(4) a description of obstacles, if any, to the voter-registration process and other preparations for the referendum, and efforts being made by the parties and the United States Government to overcome those obstacles;

(5) an assessment of progress being made in the repatriation process; and

*

STATEMENT OF SENATOR EDWARD M. KENNEDY ON IDS MEETING WITH KING MOHAMMED VI OF MOROCCO

I welcome this opportunity to meet with the King. I have great respect for his leadership, and I wished him well in his important responsibilities, and in maintaining close ties between our nations.

A particular issue I discussed with the King was the United Nations referendum on the Western Sahara.

Morocco gained the respect of the international community when it agreed in 1991 and again in 1997 to allow a referendum on the future of the Western Sahara. These actions demonstrated an impressive commitment to the right of self-determination for the people of the Western Sahara.

The referendum is an important part of the peace process, and I hope that it will take place as soon as possible.

Mr. INHOFE. Madam President, let me conclude by saying that other things were happening too. When you think about countries, I often said Africa is the forgotten continent. I can remember so well, back when they were talking about taking our troops into Bosnia and then later Kosovo, the excuse they were using—this is back in the Clinton administration—they were saying it was ethnic cleansing taking place there. I said on the Senate floor standing at this podium— this is way back in the late 1990s—I said for every person who has been ethnically cleansed in Bosnia, there are hun-

---

[1] Should probably read (Polisario).

dreds on any given day in any Western Africa country. But people did not care about it. Senator KENNEDY did.

I know this subject is a little bit sensitive, but even to this day, right now, every other week, there is a group of people, staff people, who get together. They have nothing in common except a heart for Africa. There are liberal Democrats and conservative Republicans. They meet every other week, in Senator KENNEDY's office and then in my office, and they pray for Africa. This is something about Senator KENNEDY people did not know. That is something that takes place even to this date.

I have a letter written recently by Lindsay Gilchrist of Senator KENNEDY's office:

I know Senator KENNEDY and Senator Inhofe had always been thought of as the bipartisan leaders on this issue. The Africa prayer group was not something Senator KENNEDY was directly involved in [or Senator Inhofe]— but they have stimulated and motivated us to do this very thing. That was one of the things that occupied 20 years of Senator KENNEDY's time. I feel committed to continuing to work with the people of Western Sahara to try to make that a reality. When that happens, we are going to be able to say— he will be watching down—All right, we finally did it.

Let me share a couple personal experiences I had with Senator KENNEDY. One is a little bit humorous. In 2005, the Republicans were in the majority. I was chairman of the Environment and Public Works Committee. We did the 2005 transportation reauthorization bill. It was a huge thing. I am a conservative, but this is something we need to be doing in this country, something about infrastructure.

As is always the custom of the Senate, as the Chair is well aware, when we pass a big bill, we stand on the floor and thank all the staff people and talk about the significance of it and how important it is.

We had just passed the bill when I was getting ready to make my speech about what a great job we did when the bells went off. They said: "Bomb threat, bomb threat; evacuate, evacuate." Everybody started running. I had not made my speech yet, so I stood up. It is kind of eerie when you are the only person in the Capitol and giving a speech. Of course, there was nobody here, and the cameras were still going.

I remember, after finishing my speech, I looked down at the bottom of the stairs and saw a very large man walking out. I went down and I said, "TED, we better get out; this place might blow up."

He said, "Well, Jim, these old legs don't work like they used to."

I said, "Let me help you." It happened, by the way, this was right after the American Conservative Union came out with the ratings where I was the No. 1 Most Conservative Member of the Senate and he was the second from the Most Liberal Member of the Senate. I said, "Let me help you." I put my arm around his waist and he put his arm around my arm. Someone took a picture. It ended up on the front page of a magazine. The caption was: "Who Says Conservatives Are Not Compassionate?" That is the kind of relationship we had. I will always remember this.

He did things that people are not expected to do. There was a show—they don't have it on television anymore—called "Crossfire." Some might remember that. It was an aggressive program, where you get two people debating each other on an issue. The issue that particular day—this was back in 2000—was Vieques. Vieques is an island off Puerto Rico. They were trying to shut it down. They were successful. I don't blame it on the Democrats or Republicans. President Bush went along with Al Gore and closed down the live range at Vieques, which was the only place the Navy and Marines could do integrated training.

I was actually debating Bobby Kennedy, Jr.—he was Senator KENNEDY's nephew—on the "Crossfire" show. It was one of these things where I really knew the issue. I knew I had him on this debate. It came down to the end, and I could have put the knife in at that time. I didn't have the heart to do it.

I was sitting, Madam President, where you are sitting the next day, presiding over the Senate, and TED KENNEDY came up. He said, "Well, Jim, I came up to say thank you."

"Thank you for what?," I said.

He said, "I was watching this debate you had last night, and I knew what you were thinking, and I knew that you had won this thing, and right at the last you could have inflicted great harm to Bobby. You elected not to do it. I want to tell you I appreciate it very much."

That was Senator KENNEDY.

There are things still going on today to which he committed his life. We are going to win some of those, and we are going to rejoice when that happens. He will be right here with us.

I yield the floor and suggest the absence of a quorum.

Mr. CASEY. Mr. President, today we remember our colleague and our friend Senator TED KENNEDY. There are few people alive today whose lives have not been impacted by the work of Senator KENNEDY.

A brilliant legislator, Senator KENNEDY championed bipartisanship and compromise to leave behind an incomparable record. In his 46-plus years in the U.S. Senate, he authored over 2,500 bills and several hundred became law. Today, people with disabilities cannot be discriminated against in the workplace because of Senator KENNEDY. Women must be paid the same as men for the same work because of Senator KENNEDY. And low-income children have access to health care because of Senator KENNEDY.

Like his brothers before him, Senator KENNEDY challenged young people across America and around the world to devote their lives to something more than just themselves and lead by example. Whether it was championing civil rights legislation in the 1960s, condemning apartheid in South Africa before it became politically popular to do so, promoting the need for early childhood education, or advocating for health care, Senator KENNEDY led the charge.

Senator Hubert Humphrey once said that the moral test of government is how it treats those in the dawn of life, our children; those in the twilight of life, our older citizens; and those in the shadows of life, people with disabilities, the homeless, the dispossessed. Senator KENNEDY took up the causes of these Americans as his own. The poor, the powerless, and the forgotten lost an ever-faithful protector and their tireless advocate.

On a personal note, I recall in early 2007, during my first weeks in the Senate, Senator KENNEDY gave me and other freshman Senators floor time to speak about increasing the minimum wage. In early 2009, when I was named to the HELP Committee, Senator KENNEDY called to welcome me to the committee and invited me to hold field hearings in Pennsylvania on issues like health care and education. I will never forget his courtesy and the respect he showed to fellow Senators.

In closing, I am reminded of the words Senator KENNEDY spoke about Mike Mansfield when the majority leader retired:

No one in this body personifies more nearly than Mike Mansfield the ideal of the Senate. Wisdom, integrity, compassion, fairness, humanity—these virtues are his daily life. He inspired all of us, Democrat and Republican, by his unequaled example. He could stretch this institution beyond its ordinary ability, as easily as he could shame it for failing to meet its responsibility.

The same can be said about Senator KENNEDY. We will miss him in this Chamber, but we will never forget the lessons he taught us or the legacy he leaves behind.

THURSDAY, *October 8, 2009*

Mr. BARRASSO. Mr. President, in this Chamber we have witnessed incredibly moving eulogies and remembrances of our departed colleague Senator EDWARD KENNEDY. Obituaries in national and international newspapers convey the historic milestones of his life that none could forget, as well as more personal stories of the man that fewer knew.

So much has been said and written since Senator KENNEDY's death August 25, 2009. Many of these stories paint the picture of his family, his life, his accomplishments, his legacy—all of it extraordinary. Many of us are students of history. Indeed Senator KENNEDY lived history.

I am reminded of the recollections of one of my predecessors as U.S. Senator for Wyoming, and a dear friend of Senator KENNEDY, Senator Al Simpson. In an interview from 1997 given to the Institute of International Studies at the University of California as part of their "Conversation of History Project," Senator Simpson was asked who was the finest legislator he had ever worked with? Senator Simpson replied:

The finest legislator I ever worked with was TED KENNEDY. He had a magnificent staff, he even had a parliamentarian on that staff of his. So when you were in the legislative arena and you were bringing your lunch and staying late, you wanted to get TED on your side or at least use some of his expertise. I would go to him sometimes early on and say, "Look, you'll have to trust me, what the hell do I do right now to move this bill?" Boy I'll tell you he had ways to do it and as you can see he uses those skills on issues in which I was totally on the other side. I can't remember them all there were so many. We were never on the same side. But he is a legislator.

And so he was. He was a quintessential legislator. There is no question about that.

Most of those who have so eloquently written and spoken since his death knew the Senator much better than I. Presidents, Senators, world leaders, and other dignitaries, members of his family and friends back in New England. They recall the Senator all of us in the Senate knew, even if only briefly, a kind, caring, passionate, and deliberate figure.

Others have detailed his accomplishments. They are legendary and lasting. What can I add to these recollections?

[165]

I was neither a close friend, confidant, nor legislative partner to Senator KENNEDY. I was a new Senator from Wyoming when I first met him. But the story I have, I would like to share, as it is meaningful and illustrates his larger than life personality in the U.S. Senate.

On June 25, 2007, I was sworn in to the U.S. Senate. Senator KENNEDY was one of a handful of Democrats in the Chamber. As you would expect, I had a lot of family members in the gallery. Later, they joined me along with Malcolm Wallop, former U.S. Senator for Wyoming, and Senator Mike Enzi in a reception off this floor.

As I was walking up the center aisle to leave the Chamber, there was a booming voice that reverberated through the Chamber. "Senator, Senator!" I was new. I had been a U.S. Senator at that point for all of 60 seconds, so I ignored the calls. At that moment a hand grabbed my shoulder, I turned and heard this booming voice again. "Hi, I'm TED KENNEDY." Senator KENNEDY through his voice and his presence knew how to get your attention.

All of those who came to see me sworn in—family, friends from Wyoming—they heard it too, and we all broke out laughing. "Senator KENNEDY, we know who you are."

Senator KENNEDY began to tell me stories of his life and about his visits to Wyoming. He spoke about a trip to Rock Springs, WY, when his brother John was running for President. He spoke of Wyoming casting the votes to secure the nomination for John.

He told me about the people he had met—members of the Wyoming Democratic Party at the time—relationships he had built nearly 50 years ago. He named one after another as if he was reading from text. It was a stunning moment to watch Senator KENNEDY recall places, events, and people in my home State from 1960.

At my welcoming reception he took personal time with my son Peter and my daughter Emma, both in college. He said to them, "So you're the brother and you're the sister—you know I had some brothers." He talked about John and Robert and Joe. A living history lesson. He invited them up to his office to show them pictures and other memorabilia.

In his office in the Russell Building he must have spent half an hour with Peter and Emma going over pictures of his father Joe, mother Rose, and the Kennedy kids. He shared letters, notes from history.

I think he enjoyed it nearly as much as we did. He beamed when he spoke about his family.

Senator KENNEDY leaves behind an astonishing legislative record of accomplishment. He achieved his goals to a degree that perhaps no other Senator in history has. As a public servant, he has few equals.

But he was so much more. TED also leaves us with the memory of the man—the memory of his kindness and grace, his humility.

Books will detail TED KENNEDY's legislative victories. His moments in history. I will remember the moments he took to warmly and unexpectedly welcome this new Senator and touch the lives of my family that day as well.

To Vicki, we extend our family's sympathy and hope the coming days are filled with more love, God's grace, and strength to go on. Bobbi and I wish the Kennedy family our best and our prayers are with you.

Ms. MURKOWSKI. Mr. President, I was deeply saddened by the passing of Senator EDWARD M. KENNEDY in August, my colleague on the Health, Education, and Labor Committee, a statesman in every sense of the word, and a Senator not just for the people of Massachusetts but for every corner of the Nation. I am grateful for the time I shared with him as a colleague and as a friend.

Senator KENNEDY may be best known in this body for his consistent leadership on the big national issues. Whether you agreed with him or not, Senator KENNEDY was "all in" on the issues he cared about, like health care and education, and a formidable force to be reckoned with.

While Senator KENNEDY was firm in his convictions, he was open to the ideas of other Senators, regardless of party affiliation. As most Senators who worked with him know, Senator KENNEDY had an unequaled reputation for compromise and negotiation. As legislation was being written and developed, he recognized the importance of other Senators' perspectives on an issue, including mine, and was therefore willing to alter legislative proposals for the sake of cooperation and finding middle ground with Senators from any political party. The 2 years I spent on the HELP Committee with him as my chairman were truly a blessing.

There was so much to admire about Senator KENNEDY's career. But the thing I really admired about Senator KENNEDY was his ability to look beyond the beltway to take up causes that might seem obscure to many in this body— causes that offended Senator KENNEDY's sense of justice. Let me offer a few examples from my State of Alaska.

[167]

Federal law requires agencies to reinstate civil servants who go on active duty in the National Guard and Reserves when their service is complete. The law goes by the acronym USERRA. When Bob Traut of Palmer, AK, completed his active duty service with the Alaska National Guard, he was not reinstated to his position in the Indian Health Service. His position had been eliminated, and he was not offered another. He filed a USERRA complaint with the Department of Labor, which was passed around among investigators and ultimately lost. Several years after he started this process he was offered a Federal position at a U.S. Coast Guard base hundreds of miles from his home. He couldn't drive to his new workplace—he had to fly there because Kodiak is an island not connected by road to the rest of Alaska. Even then his back pay claims were lost in a morass of bureaucracy, in spite of repeated inquiries from my office. Bob Traut's fortunes changed when Senator KENNEDY decided to hold an oversight hearing about USERRA focused on Bob Traut's case.

The Alaska Native Claims Settlement Act, the 1971 law which resolved the aboriginal land claims of Alaska's first peoples, is truly one of the landmark pieces of Federal Indian legislation. The administration offered Alaska's Native people 10 million acres of land. Senator KENNEDY came to the floor on several occasions to argue that the number of acres should be no less than 40 million. The ultimate settlement was 44 million acres—a settlement that might not have been possible without Senator KENNEDY's leadership.

As the chairman of the Subcommittee on Indian Education, KENNEDY joined a few other Senate colleagues on a trip to several Alaska Native villages in April 1969. KENNEDY recalls being stunned by the poverty and despair in the villages, many of which still lack basic sanitation and are plagued by high rates of sexual assault, domestic violence, and suicide. It affected Senator KENNEDY so deeply that he found it difficult to "numb the pain."

The course of Senator KENNEDY's life brought him many blessings and accomplishments. He was a father of three beautiful children and two stepchildren, a Harvard graduate, a nine-term Senator with the third longest time serving in the U.S. Senate in American history, a veteran of the Army, a talented football player who almost went pro but opted instead for a life of public service ... the list goes on.

My condolences and blessings go out to his family, especially his wife and children. Despite TED's passing, his spirit lives on. There is little doubt in my mind that this spirit will inspire generations of our colleagues in the years ahead to take up his causes and ensure that the vulnerable in America, the often forgotten Americans who live in remote places like rural Alaska, are never forgotten.

TED, thank you for your service.

EXTENSION FOR TRIBUTES TO SENATORS KENNEDY AND MARTINEZ

Mr. BEGICH. I ask unanimous consent that the deadline for tributes to Senators KENNEDY and Martinez to be submitted to the *Congressional Record* be extended until Wednesday, October 14, 2009.

The PRESIDING OFFICER. Without objection, it is so ordered.

TUESDAY, *October 13, 2009*

Mr. UDALL of New Mexico. Mr. President, with the passing of Senator TEDDY KENNEDY, Americans lost a champion, the Senate lost a living legend, and those of us who were fortunate to know him personally lost a friend and mentor.

My memories of TEDDY KENNEDY reach beyond our short time together in the Senate all the way back to my days as a kid when his brother Jack was running for President of the United States. My father was an early supporter of Jack's campaign, and TEDDY stayed at our house in Arizona while he was campaigning for his brother in the West. In those days, the West was not considered a plum campaign assignment so, naturally, as the youngest of his clan, it fell to him. We had a full house at the time, with all of my brothers and sisters at home, so there wasn't even a bed for him to sleep on. So he slept on the floor and never uttered a word of complaint. My memories of him from that time reflect the same TEDDY KENNEDY everyone describes today. He was a kind man, dedicated to his brother and his family, and always patient with all of us kids and our questions.

In later years, TEDDY continued to be a frequent visitor to New Mexico. When our family was in the midst of a campaign and needed that extra bit of star power, TEDDY was there, the one person who could ignite a crowd like no other. As Democrats, we loved having him in our State because he could always get a turnout. He had rallies with 10,000–12,000 people—huge crowds for New Mexico.

TEDDY KENNEDY loved New Mexico and New Mexicans. And New Mexicans loved TEDDY right back. In most family living rooms, you can find two prominently displayed photographs. They include at least one of the Kennedys, be it Jack, Bobby, or TEDDY and at least one of the Pope. New Mexicans just have a very deep affection for the entire Kennedy family.

My father eventually served in Jack Kennedy's Cabinet as Interior Secretary. These days, he talks a lot about his time in JFK's administration. He says he is now the last of the generation. The last leaf on the tree from the Kennedy Cabinet. My father was greatly saddened by Senator KENNEDY's passing.

Just about every piece of monumental legislation that has come out of this Senate over the past 50 years has had TEDDY KENNEDY's stamp on it somehow. Whether it was voting rights or education improvements or health care reform—the cause of TEDDY's life—America owes a debt of gratitude to the senior Senator from Massachusetts for his leadership and unwavering dedication to making our country a better place for all who call it home.

But the last chapter in TEDDY's legacy remains incomplete. That chapter is health care reform, and it is our job as TEDDY's colleagues and friends to pick up where he left off and pass legislation that helps all Americans obtain affordable, quality health coverage. TEDDY KENNEDY dreamed of a day when decent, quality health care is a fundamental right and not just a privilege. We are once again at the edge of transformative change in our country. We have TEDDY KENNEDY to thank for getting us to this point. I look forward to joining my colleagues as we make TEDDY's final dream a reality.

Mr. BEGICH. Mr. President, I rise to speak of the enormous contributions to this body and to our Nation of our former colleague, the late senior Senator from Massachusetts, TED KENNEDY.

When I took the oath as a U.S. Senator on January 3, 2009, I have to confess to a fair amount of trepidation. Many great statesmen have served before me in this esteemed body. For a former mayor from a State so distant from Washington, DC, taking a seat among these American leaders was a little intimidating.

No sitting Senator was a larger giant than TED KENNEDY, and he impacted my life long before I arrived here. As a boy born and raised in Anchorage, I recall my parents spoke of the great pride in public service the Kennedy family inspired in our family and in our Nation. My father, the late Nick Begich, served for 2 years in the Congress with Senator KENNEDY, before my dad's death in 1972.

In many ways, Alaska and Massachusetts can't be further apart. Alaska is just celebrating its 50th year of admission to the United States and is a vast land rich in natural resources and of conservative, independent-minded people. The Bay State was the site of one of America's first settlements more than four centuries ago, is well developed, and its residents decidedly more liberal.

Yet in the first week of April 1968, those differences faded when Senator KENNEDY traveled to Sitka to deliver a speech to the Alaska Democratic State Convention. The days-old assassination of Dr. Martin Luther King, Jr., still ached in the hearts of Americans. In a scratchy tape recording of his speech, Senator KENNEDY calls on Americans to rise above the frustration and fury they felt and to rededicate ourselves to "wipe away cynicism and to introduce the understanding that we wish to see future generations exercise so they will not suffer as their mothers and fathers have suffered."

The transcript of that speech shows that Alaska U.S. Senator Ernest Gruening and the gathered Alaskans rose to a standing ovation as Senator KENNEDY concluded his inspirational remarks. Today, 41 years later, those words continue to serve as an inspiration to me.

Mr. President, I had the opportunity to meet Senator KENNEDY only once, when he welcomed me as a Member of this body just a few months ago. The intimidation I felt as a new Senator melted in his warmth and graciousness. It will be a moment I will remember for the rest of my life.

WEDNESDAY, *October 14, 2009*

Mrs. McCASKILL. Mr. President, I rise today to recognize a great leader, inspiring public servant and American icon, Senator EDWARD MOORE KENNEDY.

I do not need to stand here and talk about what the Kennedy legacy has meant and continues to mean to this country. It is, at this point, simply a part of the fabric of our country.

I do not need to recite the resume of EDWARD KENNEDY or extol his many accomplishments. His life's work speaks for itself. It will stand the test of time and, no doubt, become even more remarkable when viewed in hindsight.

I do not need to reiterate each of the noble causes Senator KENNEDY fought for with passion and vigor. We know that his pursuit of dignity, opportunity, and respect for every man and woman will benefit generations to come, and inspire so many more to carry on in the cause.

Yes, there is no doubt that Senator EDWARD KENNEDY will be remembered far into the future and that history will treat him well, but I want to take some time today to talk about the people here and now that he leaves behind that may be the most telling about TED KENNEDY. In those moments and for those people, we got a chance to see something very special.

For some people it was very personal moments shared between family and friends—the opportunity to know him in a way others could only hope to glimpse.

And some were his archenemies at the podium while also his dearest, most respected partners on causes behind closed doors.

Some became believers based on passion-filled political speeches delivered from his earliest of days in the spotlight to some of his last, spectacular moments right here on the Senate floor.

While others had their lives changed because he was brave enough to stand up for them when the cameras were not rolling and the majority was not on his side.

TED KENNEDY, the lion of the Senate, would roar about the need for better health care, improved public schools, and providing help to working families. He knew how to channel the emotion, the urgency, and the helplessness he saw in the eyes and heard in the voices of those he was fighting for. And he didn't just beam it from the mountaintops—he worked on the solutions to these needs day in and day out with astute skill.

There is a TED KENNEDY who will be remembered in the history books, and he will be great and strong and smart and good, but there is also a unique part of TED KENNEDY that will stay with many of us in our own special ways.

A politician. A public servant. A patriot. A prince of Camelot. A fighter. A negotiator. A liberal. A brother, husband, father, and friend.

The lion sleeps ...

Mr. CORNYN. Mr. President, I join my colleagues in appreciation and admiration of Senator TED KENNEDY.

By the time I took my seat in the Senate, TED had already held his for nearly four decades. He had already established himself as one of the most influential Members in this body's history. He had already introduced hundreds of bills that became laws and shaped thousands of others. He had already grown from youngest son to elder statesman and become an icon for millions of Americans.

Before I was ever elected, I respected TED KENNEDY. And after becoming his colleague, my respect grew. I was privileged to serve with him on the Judiciary Committee and to be a ranking member when he chaired our Subcommittee on Immigration, Refugees, and Border Security. We worked together closely, and that experience has made me a more effective Senator.

TED KENNEDY and I often held different principles, but we shared key convictions too. We agreed that our immigration laws needed reform. We recognized that judicial philosophy mattered. We believed that providing advice and consent on appointments to the Federal bench was not merely a right of Senators but one of our most solemn responsibilities.

TED KENNEDY understood the power of language. On the Senate floor, he used words of passion, calling his colleagues to embrace grand visions with great urgency. In bill negotiations, he used words with precision, understanding better than anyone how legislative language governs, and how to codify his convictions into the law of the land.

Senator KENNEDY and I shared an interest in the history of this body, and a special pride in those who held our seats before us. In my case, I have long admired Sam Houston, who liberated the people of Texas, served as one of our first Senators, and raised his voice against secession. In TED's case, he looked to the great Daniel Webster, who also stood for union, and for liberty.

TED was drawn in particular to this quote by Webster:

Let us develop the resources of our land, call forth its powers, build up its institutions, promote all its great interests, and see whether we also in our day and generation may not perform something worthy to be remembered.

All Americans can agree that TED KENNEDY's service in the U.S. Senate is something worthy to be remembered. Sandy and I continue to keep his wife Vicki in our prayers. And we offer our condolences to all who miss him most.

Mr. KIRK. Mr. President, yesterday evening, President Obama delivered another eloquent tribute to Senator ED-WARD M. KENNEDY. I am sure my colleagues will be pleased and touched to see it, and I ask unanimous consent that excerpts from the tribute may be printed at this point in the *Record*. I also ask unanimous consent that a series of tributes to Senator KENNEDY from the *Hill* newspaper on August 29, 2009, may be printed in the *Record*.

There being no objection, the material was ordered to be printed in the *Record*, as follows:

EXCERPTS FROM REMARKS BY THE PRESIDENT AT AN EVENT CELEBRATING THE EDWARD M. KENNEDY INSTITUTE FOR THE UNITED STATES SENATE

(Ritz Carlton Hotel, Washington, DC, October 14, 2009)

Thank you so much. Thank you, Patrick, for that generous introduction, and for ensuring that the Kennedy family spirit of public service lives on as strong as ever ...

And to Vicki and all the members of the Kennedy family—to Ted and Kara, obviously Patrick—there are few who are not inspired by the grace and love that all of you have shown throughout a difficult time.

Our friend TED left us less than 2 months ago. In the days that followed, we gathered in Boston to celebrate his life—with a joyous Irish wake of sorts at the John F. Kennedy Library, and with heavy hearts on Mission Hill. We watched as mourners lined the streets of Massachusetts and Washington in the rain to say a final thank you; and as decades' worth of his colleagues and staff lined the steps of the Capitol to say a final goodbye. We smiled as the Caucus Room in the Russell Building, a room where so much American history was made, was renamed for the three Kennedy brothers who served there.

And over those days, there was some small measure of comfort in the fact that millions of Americans were reminded of TED KENNEDY's legacy, and a new generation came to know it. His legacy as a man, who loved his family and loved his country. His legacy as a Senator, who crafted hundreds of pieces of legislation and helped pass thousands more, all with an incalculable impact on the lives of millions.

His legacy as a mentor, who not only taught so many young Senators, including myself, but inspired so many young people and young staffers, some who entered public service because of TEDDY, others who—because of him—just plain refused to leave ....

When TEDDY first arrived in the U.S. Senate, he immersed himself in the issues of the day and the concerns of folks back home. But he also threw himself into the history of the Chamber. He studied its philosophical underpinnings; he studied its giants and their careers; the times that influenced its Members, and how its Members influenced the times. He became fluent in procedure and protocol, no matter how obscure, until he could master the Senate as easily as he mastered the oceans.

No one made the Senate come alive like he did. He loved its history and its place in our American story. Rarely was he more animated than when he'd lead you through the living museums that were his office and his hide-

[174]

away office in the Capitol. They held memories that stood still, even as he refused to. And he could—and he would—tell you everything there was to know about each artifact, each object that you were seeing.

Any of us who've had the privilege to serve in that institution know that it's impossible not to share TEDDY's feeling for the history that swirls around us. It's a place where you instinctively pull yourself a little straighter and commit yourself to acting a little nobler.

I still remember the first time I pulled open the drawer of my desk and saw the names like Taft and Baker; Simon and Wellstone—and Robert F. Kennedy. I thought of the great battles they'd waged and how they still echoed through the Senate Chambers. And one can't enter the Chamber without thinking of the momentous debates that have occurred within its walls—questions of war and peace; of tangled bargain between North and South; Federal and State; of the origins of slavery and prejudice; of the unfinished battles for civil rights, and equality, and opportunity.

It was where Americans of great eloquence deliberated and discussed the great issues of the age; where Webster and Clay and Calhoun fought and forged compromise; where LBJ stalked the aisles, imposing his will and collecting votes; and where TED KENNEDY raged at injustice like a force of nature, even after a staffer would hand him a note saying, "Sir, you're shouting."

At its worst, it could be a place where progress was stymied. There was a time, of course, when there were no desks for women, or African Americans, or Latino Americans, or Asian Americans. There was a time when a Senator might have referred to another as a—I like this—"noisome, squat and nameless animal," just to name one instance of the occasional lack of decorum. And we should all view it as a positive sign that there hasn't been a caning on the Senate floor in more than 150 years. That's good.

But at its best, it was what TED KENNEDY loved; a place of community and camaraderie where Senators inspired their colleagues to seek out those better angels and work collectively to perfect our union, bit by bit. And in my time in the Senate, I never met a colleague, not even one with whom I most deeply disagreed, who didn't have a deep sincerity in his or her beliefs, an abiding love for this country, and a genuine desire to leave it stronger and better.

Still, I know that many of us, from both parties, shared TED's sentiment that something vital about the Senate has been lost. Where it once was a more personal and more collegial place, it's become more polarized and more confrontational. And gone, sometimes, is that deeper understanding of one another; that idea that there are great battles to be won and great battles to be waged—but not against the person on the other side of the aisle, rather to be waged on behalf of the country.

What TED wanted to save, above anything else, is that sense of community and collegiality and mutual responsibility—to our constituents, to the institution, and to one another. "As Senators," he wrote, "we need to be vigilant that we don't lose track of the whole essence of what the Senate is; of what our involvement in it signifies; of our relationship with people; and of what all of that should lead to, which is the unfettered and vital exchange of ideas."

That's why whenever heartbreak struck a colleague, he was always the first to call. That's why whenever a stalemate needed to be broken, he was the first to visit another Senator's office. That's why whenever debate got fierce he never got personal—because that was the fastest way to ensure nothing got done. Once, after he and Strom Thurmond went at each other for a few rounds—as you'd imagine TED and Strom might do—TED put his arm around him and said, "C'mon, Strom. Let's go upstairs and I'll give you a few judges."

The thing is, even though he never technically ran the Senate, it often felt like TEDDY did. It was his arena. That's why, if you came to the Senate hoping to be a great Senator some day, he was who you went to see first. I know that's who I went to see first. Because rather than lord over it, TEDDY sought to mentor others to better navigate it. Rather than to go it alone, he sought cooperation. He never hesitated to cede credit. Rather than abandon course when political winds got rough, he always followed his North Star—the cause of a society that is more fair, more decent, and more just. And through all of it, his seriousness of purpose was rivaled only by his humility, his warmth, his good cheer, his sense of humor.

That is who TED KENNEDY was. That's what he did. And that's why he's so missed . . . .

For it is now—especially now—that we need to get people interested in our public problems, and reignite their faith in our public institutions, bring Americans together to forge consensus and understand not just the U.S. Senate's role in our government—but their role in it as well.

Today, the Senate is engaged in another important battle on one of the great causes of our time, and the cause of TED KENNEDY's life—the battle to make health care not a privilege for some, but a right for all. He has been so sorely missed in this debate; especially now that we're closer than we've ever been to passing real health reform. But even though we took a critical step forward this week, we've got more work to do. And I hope and believe that we will continue to engage each other with the spirit of civility and seriousness that has brought us this far—a spirit that I think TEDDY would have liked to see.

More than a half century ago, a Senate committee was set up to choose the five greatest Senators of all time. No, it wasn't an exercise in the Senate's own vanity—it was because there were five empty spaces designated for portraits in the Senate Reception Room.

"There are no standard tests to apply to a Senator," the chairman of that committee wrote. "No Dun & Bradstreet rating, no scouting reports. His talents may vary with his time; his contribution may be limited by his politics. To judge his own true greatness, particularly in comparison with his fellow senators long after they are all dead, is nearly an impossible task."

When John F. Kennedy wrote those words, I doubt that he imagined his 25-year-old brother would one day stand as indisputably one of the finest Senators of this or any age. But here's the thing: TEDDY didn't earn that distinction just because he served in the U.S. Senate for nearly 1 out of every 5 days of its existence. He earned it because each of those days was full, and passionate, and productive, and advanced the life of this Nation in a way that few Americans ever have. And he did it all by bridging the partisan divide again and again in an era that someday may be recalled as one where bipartisanship was too rare an achievement.

There will never be another like TED KENNEDY. But there will be other great Senators who follow in his footsteps. That's not an insult to his legacy—it is, rather, the legacy he sought to leave, both with this institute and with his example.

"Being a senator changes a person," he wrote in his memoirs. "Something fundamental and profound happens to you when you arrive there, and it stays with you all the time that you are privileged to serve. I have seen the changes in people who have come into the Senate. It may take a year, or two years, or three years, but it always happens: it fills you with a heightened sense of purpose."

In all our debates, through all our tests, over all the years that are left to come—may we all be blessed with a sense of purpose like EDWARD M. KENNEDY'S. Thank you, Vicki, thanks to all of you. Thanks for making this such a success. God bless you, God bless America.

⚘

TED KENNEDY: A Life of Service

(By Speaker Nancy Pelosi (D–Calif.))

With the passing of Sen. EDWARD M. KENNEDY (D–Mass.), this nation lost a great patriot, a force for justice and equality and a passionate voice for a brighter future.

Sen. KENNEDY was the beloved patriarch of a beautiful family. At this moment of mourning, our thoughts and prayers are with his loving, caring and devoted wife, Vicki; and with his children, Kara, Teddy Jr. and our colleague Patrick. Surely it was a highlight for both father and son to see the Kennedy-Kennedy Mental Health Parity bill become law last year—ending discriminatory treatment toward mental health coverage—and a true tribute to the Kennedy family's unyielding commitment to the common good.

Above all else, Sen. KENNEDY was a champion—of the poor and the oppressed, of the forgotten and the voiceless, of young and old. Over a lifetime of leadership, Sen. KENNEDY's statesmanship, passionate arguments and political prowess produced a wealth of accomplishment that expanded opportunity for every American and extended the blessings of prosperity to millions of his fellow citizens.

He had a grand vision for America and an unparalleled ability to effect change and inspire others to devote themselves to that change. And no one did more to educate our children, care for our seniors and ensure equality for all Americans.

The reach of Sen. KENNEDY's achievements extends far beyond any one state, issue or group. And the light of his example shone bright across lines of party or philosophy. Because of his work, countless students can afford to reach for a college diploma.

Because he returned to the Senate floor for one day last July, once-fierce opponents of Medicare understood their responsibility not to politics, but to the people they serve—and today, America's seniors have a stronger and more enduring safety net to keep them healthy.

Because he believed in the need for bold action to rescue our economy, from his hospital bed he played a pivotal role in ensuring the passage of the American Recovery and Reinvestment Act, putting people back to work and setting our nation on the road to recovery. And because of his stirring words of optimism, vitality and courage at the Democratic convention exactly one year before he passed away, he laid a foundation for the election of a president who shared his ideals and intellect—and personified his vision of an America where race was no longer a barrier or qualification.

Sen. KENNEDY's deep faith remained a palpable force in his life. It inspired his belief in social justice. It demanded action on behalf of the least among us. It sustained him, and offered a refuge from the spotlight of elected office. When his daughter, Kara, was diagnosed with lung cancer, Sen. KENNEDY turned to his faith for solace, going to Mass each morning in the

[177]

same house of worship where his funeral service will be conducted—a basilica that became a source of hope and optimism for him in recent years.

Throughout his career, TED KENNEDY spoke of a new hope; of holding fast to our ideals and fulfilling the promise of our country. He carried on the legacy of an extraordinary family—a family defined by service and a family that inspired an entire generation, including myself, to take action and to serve a cause greater than our individual interests. And with the Edward M. Kennedy Serve America Act now the law of the land, another generation of teachers and volunteers, students and community organizers will put those values into action.

Perhaps more than any other issue, Sen. KENNEDY never stopped fighting for what he called "the cause of my life"—ensuring quality, affordable healthcare for every American. He believed it was a moral imperative. He viewed it "as a fundamental right, not a privilege." It is a tribute to him—but really to the Americans for whom he fought every day—that this dream will become reality this year.

⚶

ONE OF A KIND

(By Rep. Dale E. Kildee (D–Mich.), Chairman of the Subcommittee on Early Childhood, Elementary and Secondary Education)

I have a lot of acquaintances in Congress and many friends, but one who stood out above the rest and to whom I always felt close was TED KENNEDY. It was a privilege to know him as a friend, and it was an honor to work with one of the most dedicated and knowledgeable senators I ever met. His passing is truly a great loss for our country. I am hopeful, however, that in mourning his death, we will be inspired to continue to fight for the causes to which he dedicated himself so tirelessly and work together to pass the comprehensive healthcare reform that he called "the cause of my life."

My relationship with the Kennedys started back in 1960 when I was a volunteer on John F. Kennedy's campaign for president and had the privilege of meeting his mother Rose, who was nothing but gracious and kind. When Rose came to my hometown of Flint, Mich., to campaign for her son, it was my responsibility to get her to Mass at St. Michael's. It wasn't even Sunday, but Rose went to Mass every day. I met John later that year when he was campaigning for the presidency and again in October of 1962 when he came to campaign for the midterm congressional elections. Shortly thereafter he went back to Washington claiming he had a "bad cold," even though he appeared to be the picture of health. We learned later that we weren't completely misled, but that it was a different kind of cold flaring up—the Cuban Missile Crisis, one of the most heated moments of the Cold War.

TED was the last member of the Kennedy family whom I actually met, but my relationship with him lasted the longest. Like his brothers, TED was born into a life of privilege, but instead of choosing a comfortable life of leisure, he chose to work hard in the U.S. Senate, fighting to improve the lives of American families. TED successfully fought to raise the minimum wage, protect Americans with disabilities, expand health insurance for low-income children and improve educational opportunities for all students, regardless of family income. His legislative accomplishments were so wide in scope that his work has changed the life of nearly every American for the better.

TED and I shared a passion to improve education and we worked together often, particularly during the Head Start Reauthorization of 2007, which he and I authored. During many of the other conferences we worked on together, when differences arose that were slowing down the passage of legislation, TED was a skilled and fair negotiator who would keep the conversation going until late into the night to make sure things were resolved. From TED, I learned that compromise is often necessary to achieve the greater good. But above all, he taught me that we must never stop fighting for what we believe in.

While TED achieved greatness in his political life, he was no stranger to personal tragedy and suffering. The country mourned with him as first John and then Bobby were taken from us in acts of violence, leaving TED as the only remaining Kennedy brother. A 1964 plane crash broke his back and left him with terrible pain that plagued him for the rest of his life, but he never let his condition get in the way of his goals for the country. His discomfort was evident on the trips he often took with me to Flint, where he always enjoyed visiting Buick UAW Local 599. It was difficult for him to stand for long, but he would patiently pose for pictures and sign autographs for the workers there, who greeted him as a hero. He would stay until his back became too painful and then he would turn to me and say, "Dale, you have to get me out of here, now," and we would make a quick exit so he could rest in my campaign van, which he referred to as the "Kildee Express." Even while in pain, he always had a smile on his face and was an inspiration to those around him.

I have never known another senator like TED KENNEDY, and we may never see another like him again. He carried on the torch of his family's political legacy, masterfully reaching across the aisle to shepherd important and often difficult pieces of legislation through Congress. As we mourn the passing of our friend TED, let us celebrate his numerous achievements and remember him for the great humanitarian and leader that he was. Let us honor his memory by never giving up the fight for social justice, never resting until every child has an equal chance to learn, and never backing down until every American has access to quality affordable healthcare. He often called universal healthcare "the cause of my life" and it is a tragedy that he will not be around to vote for the legislation for which he fought so tirelessly. So let's continue the fight in his honor and pass healthcare reform so that all Americans, regardless of income, age or pre-existing condition, will have access to quality, affordable healthcare. Let's realize this dream for TED and for America.

❧

A DEDICATED SERVANT AND A DEAR FRIEND

(By Secretary Dirk Kempthorne, former Secretary of the Interior)

As a very junior senator from Idaho, I selected an office on the third floor of the Russell Building, which happened to be next door to Sen. TED KENNEDY's office. The first day that we were allowed to officially occupy the space, in came Sen. KENNEDY, walking through each of the offices and introducing himself to all of my staff and welcoming each of them to the Russell. Later that day, a beautiful bouquet of flowers showed up for my wife, Patricia, with a note saying, "Welcome to the neighborhood—TED." With that, Patricia and I began a wonderful and enduring relationship with TED and Vicki Kennedy.

Our offices shared a common balcony, and I had a friend from the Kennedy offices who used that route to come see me every day ... Blarney, his Jack Russell Terrier. I began keeping a box of Milk Bones for Blarney's morning visits—and he gladly accepted these treats. In his classical Boston accent, TED would pretend frustration with Blarney's habit of taking the treats back down the balcony and eating them in his office while leaving all the crumbs on his floor!

When I decided to come home to Idaho and run for governor, Sen. KENNEDY said he completely understood my decision. There was no second-guessing why I would want to return to a beautiful state like Idaho and be closer to the people there. He wished me well and said that he would miss me. Little did we both know that in 2006 President George W. Bush would nominate me to become the 49th Secretary of the Interior. One of the very first calls I received after the announcement was from TED KENNEDY, who said he was so glad I was coming back and he asked what he could do to help with my confirmation. That was the kind of man he was and the kind of friend he was. It didn't matter that I was a conservative Republican or he was a liberal Democrat. We were friends, and he wanted to help. And he did.

Several months later, I got another call from TED KENNEDY telling me he had been invited to speak at the Ronald Reagan Library. Nancy Reagan was going to host an intimate dinner for him in her residence at the library and she said he could invite a few friends. He was calling to see if I would go. After extending the invitation, he started laughing and said, "What a pal I am, right? Inviting you to dinner 2,500 miles from here!" We both laughed, and I said I wouldn't miss it for anything.

The night of the speech, I was seated in the front row along with Nancy Reagan and California Gov. Arnold Schwarzenegger. Sen. KENNEDY commented on how three of his favorite Republicans were there for him. I don't think many people realize how much Ronald Reagan and TED KENNEDY liked each other, but it was very apparent that night at the dinner that Nancy gave for her friend, TED, and his great wife Vicki, and a few of their friends.

After Sen. KENNEDY was diagnosed with his illness and it was made public, I wrote him a two-page letter recapping some of the positive and enjoyable things we had done together. I received an immediate call from Vicki saying how it had brightened his day. That was followed by a handwritten note from TED, and that was followed by a phone call from him. It was a good visit on the phone, but, as usual, he also had some business he wanted to discuss. He always worked so diligently for his constituents. I last spoke to him in January of this year. It was that same jovial voice of a friend with no hint of the personal health battle he was fighting.

It is universally noted how hard he worked as a senator. He also worked hard at affirming and maintaining friendships. Wouldn't this be a better place if we all worked a little harder at affirming and maintaining friendships? Perhaps this, too, was one of TED KENNEDY's lasting legacies.

I will miss my friend.

❧

IN MEMORY OF TED KENNEDY

(By Nancy Reagan)

Sometimes the best friendships are made under unlikely circumstances. Such was the case with the Kennedys and the Reagans.

Of course there were differences in our political beliefs, and some believed that those differences would make it impossible for us to get along. Most people are very surprised to learn that our families are actually quite close.

TED and I have corresponded regularly for years. He always wrote lovely letters of support, encouragement and appreciation. He phoned often—I'll never forget that he managed to track me down in the middle of the Pacific Ocean to wish me a happy birthday one year. I enjoyed working together with him over the past few years on behalf of a cause that was important to both of us, stem cell research.

As a Republican president and a Democratic senator, Ronnie and TED certainly had their battles. There were conflicts to overcome, disagreements to settle and compromises to be made, but in doing so, the mutual respect that came from struggling to work together led to a deeper understanding and friendship. Both were men of strong convictions, but they understood an important principle: Politicians can disagree without being disagreeable.

When Ronnie and I were presented with the Congressional Gold Medal in 2002, TED gave a beautiful tribute to Ronnie. As I reread that speech today, I was struck by how some of the wonderful things he said about Ronnie also describe TED: "He was a fierce competitor who wanted to win—not just for himself, but for his beliefs. He sought to defeat his opponents, not destroy them. He taught us that while the battle would inevitably resume the next morning, at the end of each day we could put aside the divisions and the debates. We could sit down together side by side ... And above all, whatever our differences, we were bound together by our love of our country and its ideals." That was Ronnie, all right—and that was TED, too.

TED and Ronnie were the kind of old-fashioned politicians who could see beyond their own partisan convictions and work together for the good of the country. I wish there were more of that spirit in Washington today. I am encouraged to see how many politicians "from across the aisle" spoke of their admiration for TED after his passing, so maybe it isn't really lost. Maybe we can all be inspired by TED and Ronnie to renew that spirit of bipartisan cooperation.

TED KENNEDY was a kind man, a great ally and dear friend. I will miss him.

❧

KENNEDY AND THE GOP: A MARRIAGE OF MUTUAL RESPECT

(By J. Taylor Rushing)

Despite his affinity for liberal policymaking, Republicans on Capitol Hill greatly admired Sen. EDWARD KENNEDY (D–Mass.).

"He's a legislator's legislator," Sen. Jon Kyl (R–Ariz.) told The Hill last May, immediately after KENNEDY's diagnosis of brain cancer. "At the end of the day, he wants to legislate, he understands how, and he understands compromise. And it's worth talking about because it shows how people with drastically different points of view can come together."

In April, The Hill conducted a survey of all sitting senators to ask which member of the opposing party they most enjoyed working with. The most common answer among Republicans was KENNEDY, being specifically mentioned by Kyl, Orrin Hatch of Utah, Kit Bond of Missouri, Richard Burr of North Carolina, Sam Brownback of Kansas, Mike Enzi of Wyoming, Johnny Isakson of Georgia and Jeff Sessions of Alabama.

"I'd love to co-sponsor every piece of legislation with TED KENNEDY," Burr said at the time. "When TED says he's going to do something, he's committed to it."

KENNEDY's 47 years in the Senate began as his brother, Democrat John F. Kennedy, was president and were marked by a legislative record of liberalism long and prominent enough to earn him his liberal lion moniker. Republican Party leaders even used him as a fundraising tool for years in races across the country.

In the Senate itself, though, the Massachusetts senator was mostly known by Republicans for his bipartisanship—for diligent, patient and consistent reaching across the aisle to find common ground on the country's most pressing concerns. Eventually, some of the chamber's most conservative Republicans, from Alan Simpson of Wyoming to Hatch to Kyl, came to discover that while KENNEDY may have had the heart of a liberal, he possessed the mind of a pragmatist.

Republican leaders such as Conference Chairman Lamar Alexander of Tennessee recalled that KENNEDY was known for reaching out since his earliest days in Congress. Alexander came to Congress in 1967 as an aide to then-Sen. Howard Baker of Tennessee and worked with KENNEDY near the end of his first term.

"I've known and worked with him for 40 years. He's results-oriented. He takes his positions, but he sits down and gets results," Alexander said last May.

In recent years, examples of KENNEDY's bipartisan efforts included teaming up with Kansas Republican Nancy Kassebaum on healthcare in 1996, with President George W. Bush on education reform in 2001, and on unsuccessful attempts with Sen. John McCain (R–Ariz.) and other Republicans to pass immigration reform in the 110th and 111th Congresses.

⚜

KENNEDY BROUGHT INTENSITY, PASSION TO THE SENATE

(By Jim Manley)

Coming from a wealthy, famous family, Sen. KENNEDY could have taken shortcuts. But he never did that—he brought a passion and intensity to his work the likes of which I will never forget.

His staff accepted the long hours and dedication he demanded from us because he stood with us working twice as hard.

Former Senate Majority Leader George Mitchell (D–Maine) once accurately remarked that Sen. KENNEDY was better-prepared than any other senator. His No Child Left Behind briefing book was legendary—a huge binder full of studies and analyses. It seemed every page was dog-eared, heavily underlined and carefully tabbed.

One Friday, there was a lull in a debate over a minimum-wage increase. On pure impulse, he went to the Senate floor and delivered one of the most impassioned speeches I had ever heard from him. At one point, his voice echoed through the chamber so loud that I had to leave the floor because my ears were ringing.

As Sen. KENNEDY said of his brother Robert, the same can be said of him. He "need not be idealized, or enlarged in death beyond what he was in life, to be remembered simply as a good and decent man, who saw wrong and tried to right it, saw suffering and tried to heal it, saw war and tried to stop it."

⚜

BAYH REMEMBERS 1964 PLANE CRASH

(By J. Taylor Rushing)

If not for former Sen. Birch Bayh of Indiana, Sen. EDWARD KENNEDY very well may have died on the night of June 19, 1964.

Both nearly died in a plane crash the night the Senate passed the 1964 Civil Rights Act. Delayed by the vote, the two men were flying through a thunderstorm to get to the Massachusetts state Democratic convention.

"We were bounced around so much we couldn't see the moon in any steady way," said Bayh, who served in the Senate from 1963 to 1981 and is now a partner in the D.C. law firm Venable LLP. "Then I looked out and saw this black line coming. I thought it was another storm, but it was the tops of trees."

Pilot Ed Zimy pulled out of the trees but quickly lost control again, crashing into an apple orchard just short of the Springfield airport. Bayh said he thought the plane had been hit by lightning, and was convinced he was dead. When he woke up, Bayh said, his wife Marvella was screaming, the pilot and KENNEDY aide Ed Moss were both mortally wounded and KENNEDY was barely responsive.

Bayh said he resisted initial thoughts of leaving KENNEDY in the wreckage, but was later amazed at how he carried the hefty senator.

"We've all heard adrenaline stories about how a mother can lift a car off a trapped infant. Well, KENNEDY was no small guy, and I was able to lug him out of there like a sack of corn under my arm," Bayh said.

KENNEDY spent five months in the hospital, re-emerging barely in time to win reelection in November 1964.

"A lot of the older senators were wondering if they were going to have to kiss his ring. I mean, he could have been a pariah," Bayh said. "But he had no airs, and just did a remarkable job of ingratiating himself not only to his new colleagues but the older members."

"He was a Kennedy, and you could say he was born with a silver spoon in his mouth, but he was determined to spend his life helping the little people. That tells you what he was made of."

$\sim$

BOEHNER FOUND KENNEDY A GENEROUS PARTNER IN FAITH

(By Christina Wilkie)

Rep. John Boehner (R–Ohio) needed a favor.

In 2003, Boehner wanted to support Washington's Catholic schools, which were suffering severe budget shortfalls. He needed an A-list Democrat willing to lend his name to the effort.

What he got instead was access to one of the most powerful Democratic fundraising machines in politics.

The GOP congressman was setting up a gala dinner complete with celebrities, politicos and media personalities. He went for the most powerful Catholic in Congress, Sen. EDWARD KENNEDY (D–Mass.), to be his partner at the event and balance the politics.

Presented with Boehner's request to co-chair the inaugural gala dinner, KENNEDY "didn't blink" before signing on; and true to his reputation for generosity, KENNEDY's response went well beyond that.

KENNEDY threw himself into the project, offering Boehner the use of his entire fundraising staff to assist with the event. He wrote letters and made personal appeals on behalf of the struggling schools. And perhaps most importantly, KENNEDY pulled in real talent: NBC's Tim Russert to emcee the inaugural evening and comedian Bill Cosby to keep the guests laughing.

Boehner and KENNEDY were both lifelong Catholics and graduates of Catholic schools. They had recently worked together on the House and Senate versions, respectively, of the 2002 education law known as the No Child Left Behind Act.

As colleagues, they enjoyed a comfortable rapport, which, according to a staff member, was strengthened by the fact that "Boehner and KENNEDY always knew what the other had to do to get legislation passed."

This dinner was no exception. It marked the start of a five-year collaboration between two men who served radically different constituencies, but who found common ground in their shared commitment to education, service and their faith.

Both lawmakers also believed they had an obligation to give back to the citizens of Washington, their "adopted city." To help illustrate this point, each year at a pre-gala breakfast KENNEDY would share the example of his brother, former President John F. Kennedy, who instructed his entire Cabinet to visit Washington's public schools and read books to the students.

Dubbed the Boehner-Kennedy Dinner, the annual event takes place each September, and since its inception has raised more than $5 million for the District's Catholic schools.

Much of the credit for this success belongs to KENNEDY. As one Boehner staff member told The Hill, "This event may have been John Boehner's idea, but it was Sen. KENNEDY who really got it off the ground."

During the last year of his life, KENNEDY's illness forced him to scale back his commitments. As a result, former Washington Mayor Anthony Williams assumed the co-chairman's role alongside Boehner in 2008.

This year's Boehner-Williams Dinner will be held on Sept. 23 at the Washington Hilton. Discussions are under way about how best to honor KENNEDY at the event.

⌇

TRIBUTES TO EDWARD M. KENNEDY

We've lost the irreplaceable center of our family and joyous light in our lives, but the inspiration of his faith, optimism, and perseverance will live on in our hearts forever. He loved this country and devoted his life to serving it. He always believed that our best days were still ahead, but it's hard to imagine any of them without him.

—THE KENNEDY FAMILY

Michelle and I were heartbroken to learn this morning of the death of our dear friend, Sen. TED KENNEDY.

For five decades, virtually every major piece of legislation to advance the civil rights, health and economic well being of the American people bore his name and resulted from his efforts.

I valued his wise counsel in the Senate, where, regardless of the swirl of events, he always had time for a new colleague. I cherished his confidence and momentous support in my race for the Presidency. And even as he waged a valiant struggle with a mortal illness, I've profited as President from his encouragement and wisdom.

An important chapter in our history has come to an end. Our country has lost a great leader, who picked up the torch of his fallen brothers and became the greatest United States Sen. of our time.

And the Kennedy family has lost their patriarch, a tower of strength and support through good times and bad.

Our hearts and prayers go out to them today—to his wonderful wife, Vicki, his children Ted Jr., Patrick and Kara, his grandchildren and his extended family.

—PRESIDENT BARACK OBAMA

TEDDY spent a lifetime working for a fair and more just America. And for 36 years, I had the privilege of going to work every day and literally, not figuratively sitting next to him, and being witness to history.

In 1972 [when] I was a 29 year old kid with three weeks left to go in a campaign, [he showed up] at the Delaware Armory in the middle of what we called Little Italy .... I won by 3,100 votes and got 85 percent of the vote in that district, or something to that effect. I literally would not be standing here were it not for TEDDY KENNEDY—not figuratively, this is not hyperbole—literally.

He was there—he stood with me when my wife and daughter were killed in an accident. He was on the phone with me literally every day in the hospital, my two children were attempting, and, God willing, thankfully survived very serious injuries. I'd turn around and there would be some specialist from Massachusetts, a doc I never even asked for, literally sitting in the room with me.

He's left a great void in our public life and a hole in the hearts of millions of Americans and hundreds of us who were affected by his personal touch throughout our lives.

—VICE PRESIDENT JOE BIDEN,
IN REMARKS AT AN EVENT WEDNESDAY
AT THE DEPARTMENT OF ENERGY

Laura and I are saddened by the death of Sen. TED KENNEDY. TED KENNEDY spent more than half his life in the United States Senate. He was a man of passion who advocated fiercely for his convictions. I was pleased to work with Sen. KENNEDY on legislation to raise standards in public schools, reform immigration and ensure dignity and fair treatment for Americans suffering from mental illness.

In a life filled with trials, TED KENNEDY never gave in to self-pity or despair. He maintained his optimistic spirit, his sense of humor, and his faith in his fellow citizens. He loved his family and his country—and he served them until the end. He will be deeply missed.

—FORMER PRESIDENT GEORGE W. BUSH

Sen. TED KENNEDY was one of the most influential leaders of our time, and one of the greatest senators in American history. His big heart, sharp mind, and boundless energy were gifts he gave to make our democracy a more perfect union.

As president, I was thankful for his fierce advocacy for universal health care and his leadership in providing health coverage to millions of children. His tireless efforts have brought us to the threshold of real health care reform. I was also grateful for his efforts, often in partnership with Republicans as well as Democrats, to advance civil rights, promote religious freedom, make college more affordable, and give young Americans the opportunity to serve at home in Americorp[s]. I am glad the bill President Obama signed to expand Americorp[s] and other youth service opportunities is named the Edward M. Kennedy Serve America Act. Through it, his commitment to public service will live on in millions of young people across our nation.

Hillary and I will always be grateful for the many gestures of kindness and generosity he extended to us, for the concern he showed for all the children and grandchildren of the Kennedy clan, and for his devotion to all those in need whose lives were better because he stood up for them.

—FORMER PRESIDENT BILL CLINTON

Barbara and I were deeply saddened to learn TED KENNEDY lost his valiant battle with cancer. While we didn't see eye-to-eye on many political issues through the years, I always respected his steadfast public service—so much so, in fact, that I invited him to my library in 2003 to receive the Bush Award for Excellence in Public Service. TED KENNEDY was a seminal figure in the United States Senate—a leader who answered the call to duty for some 47 years, and whose death closes a remarkable chapter in that body's history.

—FORMER PRESIDENT GEORGE H.W. BUSH

Rosalynn and I extend our condolences to the Kennedy family. Sen. KENNEDY was a passionate voice for the citizens of Massachusetts and an unwavering advocate for the millions of less fortunate in our country. The courage and dignity he exhibited in his fight with cancer was surpassed only by his lifelong commitment and service to his country.

—FORMER PRESIDENT JIMMY CARTER

It was the thrill of my lifetime to work with TED KENNEDY. He was a friend, the model of public service and an American icon.

As we mourn his loss, we rededicate ourselves to the causes for which he so dutifully dedicated his life. Sen. KENNEDY's legacy stands with the greatest, the most devoted, the most patriotic men and women to ever serve in these halls.

Because of TED KENNEDY, more young children could afford to become healthy. More young adults could afford to become students. More of our oldest citizens and our poorest citizens could get the care they need to live longer, fuller lives. More minorities, women and immigrants could realize the rights our founding documents promised them. And more Americans could be proud of their country.

TED KENNEDY's America was one in which all could pursue justice, enjoy equality and know freedom. TED KENNEDY's life was driven by his love of a family that loved him, and his belief in a country that believed in him. TED KENNEDY's dream was the one for which the founding fathers fought and his brothers sought to realize.

The liberal lion's mighty roar may now fall silent, but his dream shall never die.

—SENATE MAJORITY LEADER HARRY REID (D–NEV.)

It is with great sadness that Elaine and I note the passing of Sen. TED KENNEDY, one of the giants of American political life, a longtime Senate colleague, and a friend.

[186]

No one could have known the man without admiring the passion and vigor he poured into a truly momentous life.

—SENATE MINORITY LEADER MITCH MCCONNELL (R–KY.)

Today, with the passing of Sen. EDWARD M. KENNEDY, the American people have lost a great patriot, and the Kennedy family has lost a beloved patriarch. Over a lifetime of leadership, Sen. KENNEDY's statesmanship and political prowess produced a wealth of accomplishment that has improved opportunity for every American.

Sen. KENNEDY had a grand vision for America, and an unparalleled ability to effect change. Rooted in his deep patriotism, his abiding faith, and his deep concern for the least among us, no one has done more than Sen. KENNEDY to educate our children, care for our seniors, and ensure equality for all Americans.

—HOUSE SPEAKER NANCY PELOSI (D)

Sen. KENNEDY devoted his entire life to public policy. At any point he could have accepted a life of leisure. Instead he carried on his family's commitment to public service.

The Senate will be a smaller and sadder place without his enthusiasm, his energy, and his persistent courage.

—FORMER HOUSE SPEAKER NEWT GINGRICH (R–GA.)

Today, America mourns the death of Sen. TED KENNEDY. He was one of the most dynamic and influential legislators in our Nation's history, and his legacy will live on in the work of the colleagues he inspired, and in the lives of the millions of Americans for whom his passion for social justice made a difference. My thoughts and prayers are with his family and friends; even though this day was anticipated, I am sure that little can soften the blow. Throughout his final illness, Sen. KENNEDY was privileged to have the best doctors and the best treatment. But he never forgot, in this as in all cases, those who were not similarly privileged: those waiting hours in emergency rooms this morning for a doctor's care; those who went to sleep last night unsure that they were covered, uncertain that their families could cope with the financial burden of an illness. For their sake, health care reform was the cause of TED KENNEDY's life. For their sake, and his, it must be the cause of ours.

—HOUSE MAJORITY LEADER STENY HOYER (D–MD.)

TED KENNEDY was my friend. While there were few political issues on which he and I agreed, our relationship was never disagreeable, and was always marked by good humor, hard work, and a desire to find common ground. TED KENNEDY was also a friend to inner-city children and teachers. For the better part of the last decade, TED and I worked together to support struggling Catholic grade schools in inner-city Washington. By helping these schools keep their doors open and helping them retain their committed teachers and faculty, this joint effort made a positive difference in the lives of thousands of inner-city children, who otherwise would have been denied the opportunity for a quality education. It wouldn't have been possible without Sen. KENNEDY and his genuine desire to give something back to help inner-city students in the city in which he'd served for many years. I'm

[187]

proud to have worked with Sen. KENNEDY on this project, and I will dearly miss his friendship and his partnership in this cause.

—HOUSE MINORITY LEADER JOHN BOEHNER (R–OHIO)

I'm not sure America has ever had a greater senator, but I know for certain that no one has had a greater friend than I and so many others did in TED KENNEDY.

I will always remember TEDDY as the ultimate example for all of us who seek to serve, a hero for those Americans in the shadow of life who so desperately needed one.

He worked tirelessly to lift Americans out of poverty, advance the cause of civil rights, and provide opportunity to all. He fought to the very end for the cause of his life—ensuring that all Americans have the health care they need.

The commitment to build a stronger and fairer America, a more perfect union, was deeply ingrained in the fiber of who he was, and what he believed in, and why he served.

That's why he stands among the most respected senators in history. But it was his sympathetic ear, his razor wit, and his booming, raucous laugh that made him among the most beloved.

Whatever tragedy befell TEDDY's family, he would always be there for them. Whatever tragedy befell the family of one of his friends, he would always be there for us.

—SEN. CHRIS DODD (D–CONN.),
A CLOSE FRIEND WHO IN KENNEDY'S ABSENCE
TOOK OVER THE SENATE HEALTH, EDUCATION,
LABOR, AND PENSIONS (HELP) COMMITTEE

I had hoped and prayed that this day would never come. My heart and soul weep at the loss of my best friend in the Senate, my beloved friend, TED KENNEDY.

Sen. KENNEDY and I both witnessed too many wars in our lives, and believed too strongly in the Constitution of the United States to allow us to go blindly into war. That is why we stood side by side in the Senate against the war in Iraq.

Neither years of age nor years of political combat, nor his illness, diminished the idealism and energy of this talented, imaginative, and intelligent man. And that is the kind of Senator TED KENNEDY was. Throughout his career, Sen. KENNEDY believed in a simple premise: that our society's greatness lies in its ability and willingness to provide for its less fortunate members. Whether striving to increase the minimum wage, ensuring that all children have medical insurance, or securing better access to higher education, Sen. KENNEDY always showed that he cares deeply for those whose needs exceed their political clout. Unbowed by personal setbacks or by the terrible sorrows that have fallen upon his family, his spirit continued to soar, and he continued to work as hard as ever to make his dreams a reality.

In his honor and as a tribute to his commitment to his ideals, let us stop the shouting and name calling and have a civilized debate on health care reform which I hope, when legislation has been signed into law, will bear his name for his commitment to insuring the health of every American.

God bless his wife Vicki, his family, and the institution that he served so ably, which will never be the same without his voice of eloquence and reason. And God bless you TED. I love you and will miss you terribly. In my autobiography I wrote that during a visit to West Virginia in 1968 to help dedicate the "Robert F. Kennedy Youth Center" in Morgantown, "Sen. KENNEDY's voice quivered with emotion as he talked of his late brothers and their love for West Virginia. 'These hills, these people, and this state have had a very special meaning for my family. Our lives have been tightly intertwined with yours.'"

I am sure the people of the great state of West Virginia join me in expressing our heartfelt condolences to the Kennedy family at this moment of deep sorrow.

—SEN. ROBERT BYRD (D–W.VA.)

He had a gregarious personality. He had a keen sense of how to position himself with people. He had an old Irish wit and was a great storyteller. But all of those things probably pale in—in comparison to the fact that once he was on an issue, he was relentless. And he—once he gave his word, then there was never any—any variance from that, to the point where he would cast votes on amendments that really were against his own position in order to keep a carefully crafted compromise intact. And when others from his own party and our party didn't do that, I've seen him chastise them rather severely.

History judges all of us. And after a period of time, I think history will make a judgment about TED KENNEDY. All of us had our failings and weaknesses. But the fact is that TED KENNEDY was an institution within the institution of the Senate. And all of my colleagues, no matter how they felt about his causes or his positions, I think, would agree with that.

—SEN. JOHN MCCAIN (R–ARIZ.),
WHO OFTEN REFERRED TO KENNEDY AS A "GOOD FRIEND,"
TALKED ABOUT WHAT MADE THE LIBERAL SENATOR
LIKABLE TO HIS GOP ADVERSARIES,
ABOUT THEIR TIME WORKING TOGETHER
ON IMMIGRATION LEGISLATION
AND ABOUT HIS SPIRIT IN THE END,
IN AN INTERVIEW WITH CNN'S
"LARRY KING LIVE" ON THURSDAY

We have known for some time that this day was coming, but nothing makes it easier. We have lost a great light in our lives and our politics, and it will never be the same again. TED KENNEDY was such an extraordinary force, yes for the issues he cared about, but more importantly for the humanity and caring in our politics that is at the center of faith and true public service. No words can ever do justice to this irrepressible, larger than life presence who was simply the best—the best senator, the best advocate you could ever hope for, the best colleague, and the best person to stand by your side in the toughest of times. He faced the last challenge of his life with the same grace, courage, and determination with which he fought for the causes and principles he held so dear. He taught us how to fight, how to laugh, how to treat each other, and how to turn idealism into action, and in these last fourteen months he taught us much more about how to live life, sailing into the wind one last time. For almost 25 years, I was privileged to serve as his colleague and share his friendship for which I will always be grateful.

—SEN. JOHN KERRY (D–MASS.)

Many have come before, and many will come after, but TED KENNEDY's name will always be remembered as someone who lived and breathed the United States Senate and the work completed within its chamber. When I first came to the United States Senate I was filled with conservative fire in my belly and an itch to take on any and everyone who stood in my way, including TED KENNEDY. As I began working within the confines of my office I soon found out that while we almost always disagreed on most issues, once in a while we could actually get together and find the common ground, which is essential in passing legislation.

—SEN. ORRIN HATCH (R–UTAH),
ONE OF KENNEDY'S CLOSEST REPUBLICAN
FRIENDS IN THE SENATE

TED KENNEDY was a mentor, a guiding light, and a close friend—we all loved the man. In the Senate, TED KENNEDY was our sun—the center of our universe. To be pulled by his strong gravitational field, to bask in his warmth was a privilege, an honor, and, for many of us, even a life changing experience. His death leaves our world dark but, as he said in his own words, "the work goes on, the cause endures, the hope still lives, and the dream shall never die." TED, we will not let your flag fall.

—SEN. CHARLES SCHUMER (D–N.Y.)

TED KENNEDY was at once the most partisan and the most constructive United States senator. He could preach the party line as well as bridge differences better than any Democrat. I will especially miss his cheery disposition and his devotion to United States history of which he was such a consequential part.

—SENATE REPUBLICAN CONFERENCE CHAIRMAN
LAMAR ALEXANDER (R–TENN.)

With the passing of Sen. KENNEDY the United States Senate has lost one of its most effective and respected voices.

Sen. KENNEDY's colleagues—Republicans and Democrats—greatly enjoyed working with him and respected his views.

A handshake from Sen. KENNEDY was all that was ever needed. His word was his bond.

When the history of the United States Senate is written, his name will be toward the top of the list of senators who made a tremendous impact on the institution. Sen. KENNEDY was never afraid to work across the aisle to get things done. We can all learn from the example he set and work together to build a stronger nation.

—SEN. LINDSEY GRAHAM (R–S.C.)

I have known TED KENNEDY for more than 47 years. In that time, it has been my greatest pleasure to work with him in the Congress to try to tackle many human problems, but I am especially gratified by his contributions to the cause of civil rights and voting rights.

At some of the most tragic and difficult moments in this nation's history, TED KENNEDY gathered his strength and led us toward a more hopeful future. As a nation and as a people, he encouraged us to build upon the inspirational leadership of his two brothers and use it to leave a legacy of social transformation that has left its mark on history.

—REP. JOHN LEWIS (D–GA.)

Maria and I are immensely saddened by the passing of Uncle TEDDY. He was known to the world as the Lion of the Senate, a champion of social justice, and a political icon.

Most importantly, he was the rock of our family: a loving husband, father, brother and uncle. He was a man of great faith and character.

—CALIFORNIA GOV. ARNOLD SCHWARZENEGGER (R)
AND WIFE MARIA SHRIVER, A NIECE OF KENNEDY

The loss of Sen. TED KENNEDY is a sad event for America, and especially for Massachusetts. The last son of Rose Fitzgerald and Joseph Kennedy was granted a much longer life than his brothers, and he filled those years with endeavor and achievement that would have made them proud. In 1994, I joined the long list of those who ran against TED and came up short. But he was the kind of man you could like even if he was your adversary. I came to admire TED enormously for his charm and sense of humor—qualities all the more impressive in a man who had known so much loss and sorrow. I will always remember his great personal kindness, and the fighting spirit he brought to every cause he served and every challenge he faced. I was proud to know TED KENNEDY as a friend, and today my family and I mourn the passing of this big-hearted, unforgettable man.

—FORMER MASSACHUSETTS GOV. MITT ROMNEY (R),
WHO RAN AGAINST KENNEDY IN 1994

I would like to extend our sympathies to the Kennedy family as we hear word about the passing of Sen. TED KENNEDY. He believed in our country and fought passionately for his convictions.

—FORMER ALASKA GOV. SARAH PALIN (R)

I am very saddened to learn of the passing of Sen. TED KENNEDY last night. TED KENNEDY will be remembered with great affection and enduring respect here in Ireland. TED KENNEDY was a great friend of Ireland.

In good days and bad, TED KENNEDY worked valiantly for the cause of peace on this island. He played a particularly important role in the formative days of the Northern Ireland Peace Process. He maintained a strong and genuine interest in its progress. He used his political influence wisely. He was the voice of moderation and common sense. He was unequivocal in his rejection of violence at all times and from all quarters. He believed that only politics would provide a sustainable and enduring way forward. His belief that the United States could play a strong role in solving our problems has been vindicated by the success of the Peace Process.

Today, America has lost a great and respected statesman and Ireland has lost a long-standing and true friend.

Ar dheis Dé go raibh a anam.

—BRIAN COWEN, PRIME MINISTER OF IRELAND

Sen. EDWARD KENNEDY will be mourned not just in America but in every continent. He is admired around the world as the Senator of Senators. He led the world in championing children's education and health care, and believed that every single child should have the chance to realise their potential to the full. Even facing illness and death he never stopped fighting for the causes which were his life's work.

I am proud to have counted him as a friend and proud that the United Kingdom recognised his service earlier this year with the award of an honorary knighthood.

—GORDON BROWN, PRIME MINISTER
OF THE UNITED KINGDOM

TUESDAY, *October 20, 2009*

Ms. MIKULSKI. Mr. President, I want to talk today about the Ryan White authorization. The Ryan White authorization passed last night by, really, unanimous approval. As many people know, the Ryan White legislation is one of the most important pieces of legislation to fund help for those people living with HIV and AIDS.

I want to comment on the importance of the bill, but essentially, in today's world, remind people of where we were and how far we have come. I want to talk about the importance of the bill. I could cite statistics from my own State. I have a State with one of the largest numbers of surviving AIDS patients, for which we are so happy and grateful. I have over 34,000 Marylanders living today with HIV and AIDS.

As I said, the passage was almost unanimous. The debate was noncontroversial. It was the same way in our Health, Education Committee. We were focusing on the details of funding, how to include more assistance for rural communities where there is a spike in the number of AIDS cases. It was actually quite civil and collegial—robust as it always is in the HELP Committee. But as I sat there and listened to my colleagues—and it was somewhat dull, the usual—I thought back to 1990 when it was not like that at all.

I say that today as we take up health reform. We are gripped by fear, we are gripped by frenzy where all kinds of myths and misconceptions are out there. The debate is prickly. It is tense. We don't listen to each other. We are out there, hurling, hurling accusations.

I want to go back to a day in 1990, a day in the HELP Committee chaired by Senator KENNEDY, when this young boy, Ryan White, came to testify. Ryan White was diagnosed with AIDS at age 13. He came to testify at the committee when we were trying to figure out what to do with this new disease that was gripping the land, where people in our urban communities were dying, adults who contracted it. Here was this little boy who came, who was so frail, who was so sick, and he wrenched our hearts that day as he talked

[192]

about this new disease that he had gotten. He had gotten it through a blood transfusion.

But what he also told us about was what he was going through. He testified that day, mustering every bit of energy he had, speaking with verve and pluck about his plight; he told us about what had happened to him—how he was shunned in the class, how he was locked in a room, how children were forbidden to play with him. He lived a life of isolation and a life of desolation. He was treated like a pariah.

He wasn't the only one. Anyone who had AIDS in those days was greeted as if they were the untouchables. I remember it well. If you had AIDS, you were hated, you were vilified, you were viewed as a pariah. People were afraid to get near you, afraid to use the water fountain. If you heard someone in our office had AIDS, you didn't want to use the same bathroom.

Firefighters and emergency people were afraid to touch people bleeding at the site because they were concerned they could get it. Funeral homes would not bury people who had AIDS. I remember a little girl who died in my State who had AIDS, and only one funeral home in the Baltimore area would bury her. This is the way it was then.

As that little boy spoke, we were gripped by tears and we were gripped by shame. We were so embarrassed at what was happening in our country. Both sides of the aisle were touched. The Senate stepped up and they did it on a bipartisan basis. I was so proud that day when Senator TED KENNEDY, whom we miss dearly, said, "Tell me, young man, what can we do for you?"

And he said, "Help the other kids. Help the other people who have AIDS."

TED said, "I certainly will."

And Senator Orrin Hatch immediately stepped up—sitting next to KENNEDY—and said, "I want to be involved. I want to work on that legislation."

TED KENNEDY, Orrin Hatch, Chris Dodd, Tom Harkin, Barbara Mikulski, Nancy Kassebaum—we all came together. We worked on a bipartisan basis and we did move the Ryan White bill against the grain of many people in this country and in the face of the fear and frenzy.

As Ryan White left with his mother that day, as he walked out in a very halting way, he was gripped by a media frenzy. The noise went on. They were pushing and shoving to try to get a picture of this poignant little lad. Senator KENNEDY jumped up, built like the linebacker he once was in Harvard, and ran out and he said, "Barb, come with me; Chris, get over there; Orrin, grab that chair." We all ran out and TED KENNEDY literally threw himself in front of Ryan White to protect him from being run over by TV cameras.

Again, both sides of the aisle, we were there—TED, calling this out—Chris, you go there; Barb, open the door; Orrin, stick with me, and Orrin stuck with him. They put their arms around him and got him into a safe haven in one of our offices.

TED KENNEDY literally put himself on the line that day of fear and frenzy, and Republicans were right there with him, helping him out to get that young man to a safe room. TED KENNEDY protected that little boy that day, literally and figuratively, and he had the support of the committee.

So as we move ahead today, as we reauthorize the Ryan White Program for 4 more years, remembering that it is the largest source of Federal funding for HIV/AIDS programs, I want us to remember how we worked together, what it is like when we literally stand up for each other. TED KENNEDY literally protected that child 19 years ago. He stood up and protected the people who count on us to protect them every day. It was a moving day. It was a lesson to be learned today—TED KENNEDY leading the way, the ranking member by his side, all of us coming together. . . .

WEDNESDAY, *October 21, 2009*

Mr. LEAHY. . . . If I might, as I look over where my dear friend and colleague, Senator KENNEDY, sat for decades on this floor, I wish to take the opportunity to remember Senator TED KENNEDY, who provided steadfast leadership on this issue [hate crimes] for more than a decade. I wish he could have been here to see this bill [Matthew Shepard and James Byrd, Jr. Hate Crimes Prevention Act of 2009], about which he was so passionate, finally get enacted. I wish he was here in any event, but I am honored to be able to see it through to the finish line for him. I know it meant a lot to him. I miss him, but I think this is a way we can say to Senator KENNEDY his good work goes on. . . .

Mr. DURBIN. . . . This bill [Matthew Shepard and James Byrd, Jr. Hate Crimes Prevention Act of 2009] has another important champion who sadly is no longer with us. Senator TED KENNEDY of Massachusetts was our leader on this issue [hate crimes] for over a decade. I only wish he were here to vote and join us on the passage of this important legislation. Nobody spoke to this issue with more authority and clarity than Senator TED KENNEDY. He was the heart and soul of the Senate, and passing this bill will honor the great work he gave in his public career to the cause of civil rights. ...

In closing, I wish to quote the words of Senator KENNEDY when he introduced the hate crimes bill in April. This is what he said:

It has been over 10 years since Matthew Shepard was left to die on a fence in Wyoming because of who he was. It has also been 10 years since this bill was initially considered by Congress. In those 10 years, we have gained the political and public support that is needed to make this bill into law. Today, we have a President who is prepared to sign hate crimes legislation into law, and a Justice Department that is willing to enforce it. We must not delay the passage of this bill. Now is the time to stand up against hate-motivated violence and recognize the shameful damage it has done to our Nation.

We will honor the memory and legacy of Senator EDWARD KENNEDY by passing this defense authorization conference report, which includes the hate crimes law language. We need to send this to President Obama, who has promised he will sign it into law. I urge my colleagues to join me in support of this important legislation.

I yield the floor and suggest the absence of a quorum.

THURSDAY, *October 22, 2009*

Mr. BENNET. ... I thank all of those who worked so hard over the past 10 years to update our hate crimes laws, particularly the late Senator TED KENNEDY, who long championed this cause. In a speech he gave back in 2007 on this very subject, Senator KENNEDY asked how long those living in fear of attack or reprisal would have to wait until Congress did the right thing. How long, he asked, would it take for Washington to show that violence on account of gender, sexual orientation, or gender identity is absolutely inconsistent with our values and as such will not be tolerated in the United States of America.

Today, is Senator KENNEDY's answer. Today we send a bill [Hate Crimes Prevention Act] to the President that ensures America's enduring principles apply to all Americans. Today we approve a bill that, as Senator KENNEDY predicted, "sends a message about freedom and equality that will resonate around the world." It is a proud amendment. I urge my colleagues to set the right example and pass this important legislation.

Mr. KIRK. Madam President, Congress will pass an exceptional bill today. I know that Senator KENNEDY would have been proud of this responsible legislation and the ways in which it benefits our Armed Forces and our country.

The bill specifically honors the sacrifice of our men and women in uniform, and it includes provisions to put mechanisms in place to strengthen our current defense operations and our national security. I commend my colleagues on the Armed Services Committee for their leadership on these issues, and I am honored to serve on the committee in Senator KENNEDY's place.

I wanted to spend a moment praising our colleagues for agreeing to include another important provision in the bill, the Matthew Shepard Hate Crimes Prevention Act. I know Senator KENNEDY would have been especially pleased by its inclusion. It is an extremely important bill and was especially important to Senator KENNEDY.

He worked on it for years to close the loopholes that have prevented effective prosecution of these flagrant crimes that terrorize entire groups of communities across America.

As Senator KENNEDY said so well:

> We want to be able to have a value system that is worthy for our brave men and women to defend. They are fighting overseas for our values. One of the values is that we should not, in this country, in this democracy, permit the kind of hatred and bigotry that has stained the history of this nation over a considerable period of time.

The statistics about hate crimes are shocking and shameful. For far too long, law enforcement has been forced to investigate these vicious crimes with one hand tied behind its back. The Matthew Shepard Hate Crimes Prevention Act gives Federal, State, and local law enforcement agencies the real power and authority they need to combat these brutal acts of domestic terrorism.

The bill makes it clear that the time is now to stand up for all victims of hate crimes across America. It would not have advanced this far without the dedication of Senator KENNEDY and other key colleagues, especially Senator Reid, Senator Leahy and Senator Levin. I also praise the incredible and tireless advocacy of Matthew Shepard's mother, Judy. She educated all of us about the immense impact of such crimes, and I know how much Senator KENNEDY admired her for all she's done to make sure that no other families have to endure the horror she faced in the loss of her son.

I know that it is unusual to include such a measure in the defense bill, but the rule of law will be stronger in America because of the inclusion of the Matthew Shepard Hate Crimes Prevention Act in this year's National Defense Authorization Act. I look forward to it becoming law as soon as possible.

TUESDAY, *October 27, 2009*

Mr. KIRK. Madam President, as the Senate prepares to debate the critical reform of our Nation's health care system, I am privileged to stand at the Massachusetts desk from which the voice—that unmistakable, booming voice—of the most effective legislator of our time was heard throughout this Chamber that he loved for nearly a half century.

The voice of Senator EDWARD M. KENNEDY called out against injustice, denial of opportunity, and needless suffering of every kind. Sometimes with humor, sometimes with indignation, he spoke skillfully and tirelessly as a champion of working families, the poor, the disabled, and those engaged in a constant struggle for economic and social justice.

Of all the issues on which he led the Senate and our Nation, the one TED KENNEDY called the cause of his life was the battle for affordable, quality health care. He saw the need as universal—made real by experiences deeply personal. He was the father of three children who faced serious illnesses and received the finest health care in the world.

He understood first hand the anguish of a parent who learns that a child is gravely ill. He found it unacceptable that some Americans receive quality health care while millions of others do not.

For almost 50 years, his voice thundered in this Chamber and across the Nation with a clear and compelling message: affordable, quality health care must be a basic right for all, not a privilege for the few.

In Senator KENNEDY's own maiden speech in this Chamber, he noted the conventional wisdom that freshman Senators should be seen and not heard. But he felt compelled to speak out on the Civil Rights Act of 1964 because it was the defining moral issue of that time.

As the newest of freshman Senators, who is honored to stand briefly in his place, I have no doubt about my obligation to Senator KENNEDY, to the values and friendship we shared, to the citizens of Massachusetts, and to the country we love. So I am grateful for this opportunity to speak out at another defining moment for our Nation, on what I and Senator KENNEDY believe to be the moral issue of this time. . . .

Mr. DURBIN. Madam President, next to the door of Senator KENNEDY's old office—now Senator Kirk's office—is a small brass plaque that Senator KENNEDY had mounted near the door with an old Gaelic greeting: *Cead Mile Failte*—100,000 welcomes. With his first maiden speech on the floor of the Senate, I extend to Senator Kirk, my colleague, officially, *Cead Mile Failte*, 100,000 welcomes to this great body. The fact the Senator would stand and speak to an issue of such enduring significance, not only to the Nation but to Senator TED KENNEDY, is entirely fitting.

Forty-five years ago, TED KENNEDY gave his maiden speech on the floor of the Senate, addressing the moral issue of his time—the issue of civil rights. Over the years, he came to understand the issue of health care is an issue of civil rights. His son, Congressman Patrick Kennedy, tells the story when his dad was in the hospital recently recuperating from cancer, he would walk the wards. We can see him plodding along, going from room to room, talking to people about how they were doing and, more specifically, how they were paying for their medical care.

TED never stopped caring about not only the many people he represented in Massachusetts and around the Nation but around the world. During the time he served in the Senate, he extended the reach of civil rights and opportunity through health care, with Medicaid and Medicare and COBRA and children's health insurance and so many other things that he was a part of. I am honored the Senator is here today, as he has said, to be the voice and the vote of Senator EDWARD M. KENNEDY. The question asked is: Will the circle go unbroken? With the Senator's speech today, it is clear it is unbroken; that the Senator is carrying on the fine tradition not only of Senator KENNEDY but of so many people who were inspired by his words over the years.

I congratulate my colleague on his maiden speech on the floor of the Senate.

Mr. LEAHY. . . . I also want to take this opportunity to remember Senator TED KENNEDY who provided steadfast leadership on this issue [hate crimes] for more than a decade. I wish he could have been here to see this bill [Matthew Shepard and James Byrd, Jr. Hate Crimes Prevention Act], about which he was so passionate, finally enacted. I am honored to be able to see it through to the finish for him. I know it meant a lot to him. We miss him but his good work goes on. ...

WEDNESDAY, *October 28, 2009*

Mr. KIRK. ... Today in the United States, there are approximately 200 million people who are elderly or disabled. These individuals are some of our most vulnerable and often they are forgotten. But they always had a friend and advocate in Senator TED KENNEDY. He was the premier legislative innovator.

Senator KENNEDY understood the current system is not working; that it cried out for innovation. He knew it was wrong that in order for individuals with disabilities and the elderly to receive the services and support they needed, they had to stop working, spend down their savings, abandon their dreams, abandon their homes, and possibly go into a permanent facility—all the wrong incentives for individuals who deserve dignity in those fragile years. All this, he felt, was directly contrary to our idea of living the American dream.

Senator KENNEDY was not one to sit idly by. He acted. He acted to try to help as many of these men and women as possible. The Community Living Assistance Services and Supports Act—known as the CLASS Act—was at the heart of his efforts to help people with functional limitations and their families obtain the services and support they needed in order to keep their independence and continue as active members of their communities. I am honored to take up that worthy cause. ...

Mr. BEGICH. Mr. President, I thank Senator Kirk for describing the CLASS Act, an important program for long-term care, and the legacy of Senator KENNEDY and his work regarding that innovation. ...

Mr. KERRY. Mr. President, during his long illness, the Senate missed TED KENNEDY, and TED KENNEDY missed the Senate. But TED was especially missed by a young Senate page with whom he had a special connection—his nephew, Jack Schlossberg, Caroline Kennedy's son.

Jack worked as a page over the summer months, and I got to know him. When he wasn't busy with his page duties in the Cloakroom and on the Senate floor, we talked about the lessons he had learned from his uncle.

Ted was thrilled that Jack was walking the same corridors where his Uncle Bobby and his grandfather, John F. Kennedy, had once served. When young Jack returned to school this fall, he had a chance to reflect on all that had happened during his summer in Washington, but mostly he thought about his Uncle TEDDY. He wrote about it in an essay he titled "EMK."

Jack shared his essay with me, and I would like to share it with the Congress, because it reflects not only what a tower of strength TEDDY was to his family, but also the extraordinary qualities of TED's loving nephew, Jack Schlossberg.

Mr. President, I ask unanimous consent that Jack's essay be printed in the *Record*, and I recommend that it be read by all who knew TED, all who called him their friend, all who benefited from his extraordinary career in the U.S. Senate:

There being no objection, the material was ordered to be printed in the *Record* as follows:

EMK

(By Jack Schlossberg)

When I was little, I could only remember general things about him, like the way his voice sounded, or the feeling I got when we went sailing on his boat. As I grew up I started to understand what Uncle TEDDY was saying to me and what he meant. As TEDDY became sick, I understood him differently. He was still at times the same person I knew and loved, but his imperfections startled me. During his last few months I began to study every word he said. I idolized him in a way I never had before. No longer was my Uncle TEDDY a summer memory or someone I heard about from my mother; he meant something to me. As I watched him go through Boston for the last time in August, I realized that I was not the only person who grew up with him this way, and that multiple generations had. Hundreds of thousands of people knew TEDDY as the loving man who had always been there, and who never disappointed them.

It was my first year playing basketball, and my team had made it to the championships. I was 10 years old and I had never been more excited in my life. It was a tie game well into the fourth quarter when TEDDY showed up.

He came barreling into the gloomy PS 188 gym and sat down with my mother and father on the sidelines. He did not cheer too loud or even make himself heard, he just sat there and watched me. After my team's victory, he got up and gave me a great big hug. Soon after, he left and went home, as did I. I did not think twice about him coming to my game. I had not told him about it—he probably asked my mother what time and where it was, and moved everything that he was doing that day around my 11 am basketball game. That night I got a call from him: "The game of all games," he shouted into the phone. "And you scored the winning shot. I can't believe it. I just can't believe it," he said. Of course, I had not actually scored the winning shot, but all of a sudden I believed I had. TEDDY was always there to make your story a little more dramatic and entirely more fun. After he told a story about something you both had done, you started telling the story exactly as he had. At the time, I never understood how much effort he put into our relationship. Not only was he the senior Senator from Massachusetts, but he was also quite busy, unlike many Senators. It was not as if he called me every day, every week, or even every month, but without fail, when you needed TEDDY, he was there.

A year ago TEDDY was diagnosed with brain cancer. A person who never made me sad, and never seemed weak, was said to have months to live. At first I was more baffled than I was upset. We were not talking about your average person, this was TEDDY. He was not someone who came and went, he simply was always there. This was the first time I saw him affected by anything, and I was so confused by his vulnerability. My view of TEDDY changed completely without any interaction with him. I suddenly became endlessly interested in his life. I read about him. I followed his policy and studied his speeches. Soon after his diagnosis, my family and I went to visit TEDDY in Florida. For the first time, I was aware of who TEDDY was when he was not with me. In Florida, I asked him about his life and his politics, something I had never done before. He explained how he was 7 years old (in the eighth grade because he was sent to school with his older brother) and his classmates stole his turtle and buried it: "I cried for hours and ran outside to dig him up," he said with a grin. "They were so mean over there at Riverdale." Although he could not express himself the way he wanted to at all times, he still stunned me with stories about civil rights and Lyndon Johnson. He also triggered the same emotions he always had. As he and his wife, Vicki, sat down to watch "24" one night, I saw TEDDY as himself. I sat next to him as he commented on the show: "She's always cross," he said about one character. He made joke after joke about every possible thing he could and had everyone in the room laughing. This was TEDDY's way. It was not as if every word he said was brilliant, but his way as a person was truly unique. He could make a very depressing evening hilarious just by cracking a few jokes.

My final memories of TEDDY are not really of him, but of what I learned about him. His death was both upsetting and uplifting. At first I only thought of how I would miss him and how unfair it was that he was gone. But, as I went through Boston with him for the last time, I realized that many others loved him too. The drive started slowly as we went through Hyannis and waved to the people we passed on the street. The crowds got bigger as we approached Boston, and as we passed TEDDY's famed "Rose Fitzgerald Kennedy Greenway," the crowd was enormous. The signs people held that said "We love you, TEDDY" struck deep in my heart. We drove through all of Boston as people lined the streets everywhere. There was no animosity, no hatred, just appreciation and love for TEDDY. This made me realize that I was not the only person who loved him, and that the same effort he had made for me, he had made for everyone. He is the only person I know who was capable of making the type of effort he made. Whether it was my basketball game or grandparents day, TEDDY showed up and made you laugh.

The drive continued as we pulled into the JFK Library and saw news cameras, photographers, and another gigantic crowd. It became clear to me then that in both political and personal life, he had something only few have: people trusted him. Everyone who came out to see TEDDY trusted that he was going to take care of them, because he always had. I never knew any of this to be true until that day. TEDDY was my uncle, so naturally I figured only those who really knew him would feel like I did. But TEDDY's charm was universal, although he brought it up a notch in Massachusetts. The final way in which I remember TEDDY, is as someone who always was truly who they appear to be. It would have been possible for his trust to apply only to his family and friends, and for it to have been somewhat artificial, the way most people behave. However, TEDDY acted toward everyone the way he did with me, and this is the highest praise any public figure can attain.

TEDDY's relationship with me during his life was spectacular. Not once did he disappoint me, and he provided continuous support and much-needed laughs. TEDDY's legacy lies in many places. It lies in his legislative and political accomplishments. It lies in changes in the lives of his friends and constituents. It lies in his family bonds, and his love for the sea. However, it also lies in the way he left us. TEDDY's illness at first seemed unfair and depressing. This is not the case at all. TEDDY was able to teach everyone who watched him how to fight and how to succeed. Many people do not realize that he outlived everyone's initial predictions, and lived seven times as long as anyone thought possible. This was not because his doctors were wrong about the severity of his cancer, but because this prediction did not consider that they were dealing with TEDDY. Not once did he stop fighting. In fact, he took the most aggressive and strenuous approach to fighting his cancer, and always remained hopeful. TEDDY's death taught me that no cause is lost, and that every day is worth living.

SATURDAY, *November 21, 2009*

Mr. CARDIN. I was going to comment, listening to the Senator [Mr. Kirk], at the desk that was Senator KENNEDY's desk, how proud he would be of the statements the Senator is making here this evening. Senator KENNEDY was our champion for middle-income families in America. He understood they needed a voice in the Senate, and he was their strong, passionate voice.

This [health care reform] bill speaks to middle-income families. It is what Senator KENNEDY fought his whole career for here in the Senate, to do something that would help middle-income families. ...

I thank the Senator because those of us who have heard Senator KENNEDY speak on the floor of the Senate know how sorely missed he is here, and we are proud you are representing that vote here on the floor of the Senate tonight.

Mr. REED. Mr. President, I thank the Senator from Minnesota. I want to add my comments to that of the Senator from Maryland and the Senator from Delaware to commend the new Senator from Massachusetts. He not only carries on the great work of TED KENNEDY, but he does it with the same passion and eloquence. . . .

Mr. KIRK. I thank the Senator. I am honored to be a Senator in this body. Back home, they think I am the 60th vote. I would like to believe we would have a more enlightened full body and that 60 would be a number we would pass through.

The American people are looking forward to debate on this issue. I think they believe they deserve many of the aspects that are contained in the bill. On behalf of my constituents in Massachusetts and those who, for so many years, revered and loved and elected and reelected Senator KENNEDY—I think they all, as we do, have him in our minds and hearts tonight, and we hope we can advance this bill to the American people, knowing his spirit and years of work are a reminder of our obligation. . . .

Ms. STABENOW. . . . I also thank the memory of a very important Senator named TED KENNEDY, who I know is here in spirit, for 40 years of dedication to this cause.

Proceedings
in the House of Representatives

TUESDAY, *September 8, 2009*

Ms. EDDIE BERNICE JOHNSON of Texas. Madam Speaker, I rise today to express my deep sadness and regret for the passing of Senator EDWARD KENNEDY. The world has lost a tremendous leader and an exceptional spirit. Senator KENNEDY's voice was a unique source of inspiration on the Senate floor, and he will be greatly missed for his public service and work to improve the lives of the less fortunate.

Senator KENNEDY was arguably one of the most influential Senators in U.S. history. He was an exceptionally accomplished legislator who authored roughly 2,500 pieces of legislation over the course of his career of more than 46 years in the U.S. Senate. More than 300 of Senator KENNEDY's bills went on to become law, and he had a rare ability to reach across party lines in the interests of passing important pieces of legislation. He was always well-versed on policy issues and highly prepared for committee hearings and floor debates.

As the chairman of the Senate Health, Education, Labor, and Pensions Committee, Senator KENNEDY courageously led the push to reform our Nation's failing health care system. He strongly believed that all Americans deserved to have access to affordable health care options and supported a number of initiatives, including America's Affordable Health Choices Act of 2009. Senator KENNEDY also helped enact the State Children's Health Insurance Program, the Medicare prescription drug benefit, the Ryan White Care Act and the Family Medical Leave Act.

Although health care was Senator KENNEDY's passion, he was also committed to combating discrimination. Even when it was politically unpopular, Senator KENNEDY believed in an America where ethnic minorities and women were treated equally. He supported Title IX, which outlawed discrimination on the basis of sex in institutions of higher education and the renewal of the Voting Rights Act, which banned racially discriminatory voting requirements.

My prayers go out to the Kennedy family in this time of profound grief. I ask my fellow colleagues to join me in remembering the life of a true American hero who dedicated his life to improving the lives of others.

WEDNESDAY, *September 9, 2009*

MESSAGE FROM THE SENATE

A message from the Senate by Ms. Curtis, one of its clerks, announced that the Senate agreed to the following resolution:

S. RES. 255

In the Senate of the United States, September 8, 2009.

Whereas the Honorable EDWARD MOORE KENNEDY was elected to the Senate in 1962 and served the people of Massachusetts in the United States Senate with devotion and distinction for nearly 47 years, the third longest term of service in Senate history;

Whereas the Honorable EDWARD MOORE KENNEDY became the youngest Majority Whip in Senate history at the age of 36;

Whereas the Honorable EDWARD MOORE KENNEDY served as Chairman of the Senate Judiciary Committee from 1979–1981 and as Chairman of the Senate Health, Education, Labor and Pensions Committee for nearly 13 years between 1987–2009;

Whereas the Honorable EDWARD MOORE KENNEDY made the needs of working families and the less fortunate among us the work of his life, particularly those of the poor, the disenfranchised, the disabled, the young, the old, the working class, the service member and the immigrant;

Wher[e]as his efforts on behalf of the citizens of Massachusetts and all Americans earned him the esteem and high regard of his colleagues;

Whereas more than 300 laws bear his name and he co-sponsored more than 2,000 others covering civil rights, health care, the minimum wage, education, human rights and many other issues; and

Whereas with his death his State and the Nation have lost an outstanding lawmaker and public servant: Now, therefore, be it

Resolved, That the Senate has received with profound sorrow and deep regret the announcement of the passing of the honorable EDWARD MOORE KENNEDY, the great Senator from the Commonwealth of Massachusetts.

Resolved, That the Secretary of the Senate communicate these resolutions to the House of Representatives and transmit an enrolled copy thereof to the Kennedy family.

Resolved, That when the Senate adjourns today, it stand adjourned as a further mark of respect to the memory of the deceased Senator.

The SPEAKER pro tempore. Under the Speaker's announced policy of January 6, 2009, the gentleman from Massachusetts (Mr. Markey) is recognized for 60 minutes as the designee of the majority leader.

Mr. MARKEY of Massachusetts. I ask unanimous consent that all Members may have 5 legislative days to revise and extend their remarks and include extraneous material on the subject of my Special Order.

The SPEAKER pro tempore. Is there objection to the request of the gentleman from Massachusetts?

There was no objection.

Mr. MARKEY of Massachusetts. Noting that Representative Neal from Massachusetts and Representative Capuano from Massachusetts want to, at this point, insert their written statements in honor of Senator KENNEDY, I made that unanimous consent request. But it is also so that any other Member seeking to be recognized can insert their comments at this point.

Mr. NEAL of Massachusetts. Mr. Speaker, with the passing of Senator EDWARD M. KENNEDY last month, the Commonwealth of Massachusetts lost its greatest champion, and the United States of America lost one of its strongest voices for fairness, equality, and justice. Personally, I lost a treasured friend. From civil rights to health care, from voting rights to Head Start, TED KENNEDY played a significant role in the passage of some of the most important legislation in our lifetime. I have often said his record in the U.S. Senate is unrivaled. And I believe history will remember him as the most effective individual to ever serve in that institution.

The TED KENNEDY his friends and colleagues knew was a kind, considerate, generous, funny, thoughtful, and hardworking person whose presence lit up the room. His personality and charisma were contagious. He loved his family and spoke about them with great pride. During good times and bad, he was always there with a phone call or a note. When it came to Western and Central Massachusetts, he always offered to help. He was a master of detail. His ability to work across the aisle was legendary. At the end of the day, TED KENNEDY made a difference in the lives of countless individuals.

For the past year he faced one of the most difficult challenges of his life. But he did so with characteristic dignity and grace. Whether it was sailing on Cape Cod in his beloved *Mya*, or throwing out the first pitch at Fenway Park, he taught us how to live life while facing adversity. And in the process he became an inspiration for us all.

I became interested in public service during John F. Kennedy's historic campaign for President nearly 50 years ago. Since then, I have been an outspoken and loyal supporter of the Kennedy family. It has been the honor of a lifetime to call TED KENNEDY my friend. His extraordinary life and legacy will never be forgotten. As we pay tribute to him tonight, my thoughts are with Vicki, Kara, Edward, Jr., Patrick, Curran, Caroline, and the rest of the Kennedy family. He will never be forgotten.

Mr. CAPUANO. Mr. Speaker, I rise today to honor a man who dedicated his life to the people of Massachusetts. The passing of Senator TED KENNEDY has left our Commonwealth without its principal champion, and while we grieve, we take solace in remembering the magnitude of his many accomplishments during almost 47 years in the U.S. Senate.

I am proud to have served with Senator KENNEDY as a member of the Massachusetts delegation and humbled when I recognize what we have lost. His work impressed me before I was elected to Congress, but it was in this context that I came to know Senator KENNEDY personally and witness his insight and intelligence and his formidable skills as a legislator. His ability to recognize an important and often daunting goal, and then effect legislation to achieve that end, was unparalleled. The testimonies we have heard from friends and colleagues in recent weeks bear witness to that.

TED KENNEDY's approach to government had been instilled in him from an early age—that we must, no matter our position in life, strive to help those in need and speak up for those whose voices cannot be heard. It is a lesson both he and his brothers took to heart and to which they gave their lives in service. Senator KENNEDY knew the people of Massachusetts needed his help, but his compassion did not stop there. He often championed national causes and shepherded major legislation with broad impact across the country: ensuring civil rights, expanding children's health insurance, establishing the Americans with Disabilities Act, strengthening education and service programs, and finally the effort he called "the cause of my life"—reform of our health care system.

Senator KENNEDY soared to great heights in the Senate. He achieved immense influence among his colleagues, both Republican and Democrat, while never compromising his progressive values or quenching his fighting spirit. The personal touch he lent to relationships with colleagues and constituents told of his deep connection to the work he was doing and his dedication to being the most effective Senator that Chamber has ever seen.

I can say I am a better person for having known TED KENNEDY. I am saddened by his loss, not only for myself and for the people of Massachusetts, but for the citizens of a grateful Nation. Indeed, the world mourns the loss of his passion for justice and peace. We must all strive to honor his legacy and continue fighting for the causes he defended with such vigor.

Lest it be forgotten or overlooked, TED KENNEDY was also a father and husband. I offer my deepest condolences to Vicki, Kara, Ted, Jr., Caroline, Curran, and of course my colleague Patrick. I thank each of you for allowing us to share this great man with you. He is, and will always be, greatly missed.

Mr. MARKEY of Massachusetts. We rise to honor our friend and our mentor, Senator EDWARD M. KENNEDY, one of the greatest Senators in the history of the United States. He will be on a very short list of the greatest who have ever lived and served our country. We gather tonight, noting that his son, Patrick, serves with us here in the House of Representatives, and we extend our best to him and to his sister, Kara, and to Teddy, Jr., as well as and especially to his beloved wife, Vicki, and to all of the other members of the Kennedy family.

He was, without question, "an idealist without illusions," in the words of his brother. He worked as best he could to achieve the goals that he set for our country while at the same time reaching across the aisle to find partners that he could work with in order to accomplish those legislative goals. Without question, it was our great honor, as the Massachusetts delegation, to work with him for all of those years.

Let me, at this point, turn and recognize the gentleman from Massachusetts (Mr. Frank), and then we will go through and recognize the other members of our delegation and other Members who have joined here to speak about the Senator. I recognize the gentleman from Massachusetts.

Mr. FRANK of Massachusetts. Madam Speaker, the gentleman who just recognized me, the dean of our delegation, has the distinction of having worked very closely with the late Senator KENNEDY for 33 years, for more than two-thirds of the Senator's term. And I know that Senator KENNEDY greatly valued his colleagueship, as all of us do who serve with him as the dean, and his work now in a number of the areas pays tribute. I do think it is important to note that the longer you worked with Senator KENNEDY, the more you came to admire what he did.

I would have one difference with my colleague with whom I rarely differ on things. He said Senator KENNEDY would be seen as one of the greatest Senators. I would say the best. And I know my colleague is gracious and may have a Senator or two he needs on the cap-and-trade bill, so he doesn't want to go too far. But I think we would all agree.

I was a fledging academic before I went into politics. I was studying for a Ph.D., and I then learned I had a personal characteristic which was a defect in academics but absolutely essential to serve in this body. I have a very short attention span. And it works to my advantage here and to my disadvantage in serious scholarship. But from both ends, I don't think there is much question about his greatness as a Senator.

Obviously, those of us in the delegation—and our great colleague and civil rights leader, the gentleman from Georgia (Mr. Lewis) whose work with Senator KENNEDY, goes back even before any of the rest of us in terms of colleagueship—agreed with his values, and that is a big part of it. But even those who didn't, and this is what's so striking and so needed in our country today, many Members of Congress who served with him who disagreed with him on most substantive issues, joined in the praise for his integrity and his character and his dedication.

We are at a time now where politics is held in low repute by a lot of young people. I would hope that younger people in particular would think back to the deep love for Senator KENNEDY that was expressed by so many people across the political spectrum. Think about the accomplishments that so many people attribute to him; think about the people who express the enormous gratitude for the difference he made in their lives. There could not be a better example of how you can get into this business of politics and do good. I would hope people would be encouraged by that.

Beyond that, there is one particular point that I want to stress. We have a besetting sin today in our politics where people think that you show your depth of commitment to a cause not just by rigidity, but by impugning the motives of those on your side who try to get something done. Compromise for its own sake is a very bad idea. People who talk about the "center" have to be clear what they mean. The "center" is not a place of value. It may be where you wind up. But you wind up there as you try to move the center. Yes, you want to try to be representative of a majority. Those who have as a goal finding the precise middle are giving up their own moral and intellectual capacity.

What Senator KENNEDY did was to start firmly from a set of moral principles and then work to get them accomplished the best that he could. And that is, unfortunately, a practice that today isn't as appreciated as it should be. Purity is a wonderful state, I am told. I do not say that from experience. But it doesn't make anybody any better off.

No one was more firmly committed to the ideals of fairness and equity than EDWARD M. KENNEDY, and he understood that the more firmly committed he was to them, the more he was morally obligated to make some progress on them.

I realize ideals help nobody, and I say that because he was at the same time one of the premier idealists of our time. No one better or more consistently articulated the goal of a society in which no one suffered unfairly, in which all were treated with dignity and had a certain minimum, at least, of substance. But while he was preeminent as a preacher of that set of moral virtues, he was also preeminent as a hands-on politician who could work with others within the democratic process and with other people elected who might have disagreed with him, and because of him, more of his goals were accomplished than were accomplished by anybody else. No one did more to advance those causes which he exemplified.

But he never got all he wanted. And I hope that is also an example; and the example is that, sure, you do not belong in politics unless you have a set of ideals. You don't have any business trying to gain influence over others unless it's to make this world a better place.

But once you have those ideals, your obligation is not simply to treat them in a way that makes you feel good; it is to get them accomplished.

I do not think in American history over the time of his Senate career that anybody did a better job for people of all incomes, for the victims of discrimination, whether it was based on race or sexual orientation, or gender, for the whole concept of what we think is the genius of America; namely, that when you're born, you're born with a chance to maximize your potential, and the economic circumstances or the prejudice of others or anything else don't hold you back.

This Nation is enormously indebted to Senator EDWARD KENNEDY for the work that he did and for the example that he set. And I thank my colleague, the dean of our delegation, for leading this Special Order.

Mr. MARKEY of Massachusetts. I thank the gentleman very much, and I turn and recognize now a good friend of the Senator, Bill Delahunt from Quincy.

Mr. DELAHUNT. Thank you.

I just want to pick up on a theme that Barney touched on. You know, TED KENNEDY might have had adversaries, but they were never his enemies. He treated everyone with respect and with dignity, and that character, that DNA, if you will, was the proximate cause of his success as a Senator who championed all of the great causes in the past 50 years.

You know, Tip O'Neill said that all politics is local. Well, with TED it was personal. It was based upon those personal relationships. I'm sure that there are literally thousands that considered TED KENNEDY a dear and close personal friend. I know I did.

I had the fun of being TED KENNEDY's Congressman, and as you all know here, in Massachusetts we had our own schtick. It was a great banter. And he would leave me messages on occasion on my cell phone at night, reminding me that the grass hadn't been cut and that the snow hadn't been shoveled out in Hyannis Port.

I frequently sailed with TED KENNEDY, our colleague, and his son, Patrick; his oldest son, Teddy, Jr.; his daughter, Kara; and his devoted wife and soulmate, Vicki Kennedy. He was an exceptional friend. I miss him terribly. But I know that my experience with him was multiplied by the thousands. He had a way of communicating with people that was unique. You could reveal to him your concerns. You could share with him your secrets, and you could always be assured that the advice that you received was sound, and it was in your best interests.

We're saddened by his death, those of us who have served with him, those of us who considered him a dear and close friend. But I guess for me the gift of that friendship was something that was so special that it overwhelms the sadness that we all share and that so many share.

We were indeed fortunate not just to serve with probably the most prolific Senator that ever served in the U.S. Congress—approximately 2,500 bills. I'm not going to touch on his public record, but we know that his record speaks for itself.

But what many in this country are only beginning to discover is that for TED KENNEDY, it was not about himself; it was about others. He had his share of pain and tragedy in his own life, and I dare say that provided him with an incredible capacity for empathy and to understand others better than anyone I've ever met in public life.

So let me conclude by saying I miss you terribly, TEDDY, but I know you're still with us. Sail on.

Mr. MARKEY of Massachusetts. I recognize the gentleman from Worcester, a good friend of the Senator's, Jim McGovern.

Mr. MCGOVERN. Thank you, and I thank my colleague for arranging this Special Order to honor an incredible leader and an incredible friend, TED KENNEDY.

In the McGovern household in Worcester, MA, the Kennedy name has always been magic. Our family admired and respected President Kennedy. We all supported him, were committed to Robert Kennedy and the causes that he stood for, and we always felt it a very special privilege to be represented in Massachusetts by TED KENNEDY. You know, all of us, especially the Massachusetts delegation, already miss Senator KENNEDY. We miss his humor, we miss his friendship, his advice, his leadership.

I tell my colleagues from outside of Massachusetts that I'm proud to call myself a TED KENNEDY Democrat, and a TED KENNEDY Democrat is somebody who's a believer in dynamic and efficient, bold and effective government, somebody who believes it is important to stand up for human rights and for civil rights, and Senator KENNEDY did so with incredible integrity and with incredible character.

I believe as has been said here that he is the greatest legislator in the history of the U.S. Senate.

On health care—every major piece of health care legislation that has been enacted into law has TED KENNEDY's fingerprints all over it. There are millions of children in America today who have health care because of TED KENNEDY.

And education—every major education bill to expand educational opportunities for people of every background is a result of TED KENNEDY's leadership.

In the area of workers' rights, he was a strong champion of organized labor, somebody who promoted and enacted major legislation that protected workers and workers' rights.

In the area of civil rights, you're going to hear from our colleague from Georgia, John Lewis, a hero in the civil rights movement who will talk to you about the fact that TED KENNEDY was the leader in the area of civil rights in the U.S. Senate.

And on the Iraq war, I have a special admiration and respect for his courage, for the stand he took against that war, when it was not popular to do so, but he took that stand because he believed it was the right thing to do. He thought that war should always be a last resort, not a first resort, and I think he was right on that war.

But to all of us in Massachusetts, he was our Senator who assembled the best staff you could possibly imagine. When somebody lost their Social Security check, they called TED KENNEDY in his office. When a veteran needed help, they called TED KENNEDY. When a local official needed funding for a local college or hospital or road project, they called TED KENNEDY's office. All phone calls were returned, whether it was from the Queen of England or Mrs. O'Leary who lived in a three-decker in Worcester.

But more than that, I appreciated very much his personal touch. I was grateful for that personal touch—the notes and the calls. When somebody was sick in your family, you got a phone call. When you got a special recognition or if you won an election, you got a note. If something great happened to you, he was the first to call.

When my son, Patrick, was born, the very first call we received was from TED KENNEDY, even before my mother and father called the hospital. The very first gift that we received was from TED KENNEDY, a blanket that had my son's name stitched into the blanket with the words, "Love, Vicki and TED." And the same thing happened when my daughter was born a couple of years later. Those are things that I will never forget and always treasure.

When he died, I said that nobody can ever fill his shoes, but we must try to follow in his footsteps, and I really believe that.

One of the things that Senator KENNEDY said was that the great unfinished goal of his life was health care. He believed

[214]

that everyone in this country deserves health care. He thought it was a national scandal that tens of millions of Americans are without health care. He believed that we could provide better health care to people, that we could put a greater emphasis on preventative care to keep people from getting sick. He believed we could come up with a health care system that would control costs so that families and small businesses wouldn't go broke trying to provide health care for their families or for their workers.

And so while he is no longer with us, we need to continue his work. He was the conscience of our country, and I believe that we need to continue to be inspired by his example. We need to continue to stand up for what's right. We need to continue to fight for what's right.

And I will say as my colleagues have said, I feel it has been a special privilege and an honor for me to be part of this delegation that for so many years was led by Senator KENNEDY, a great leader and a great friend. And the world is going to miss him. And I already do.

I thank my colleague for yielding to me.

Mr. MARKEY of Massachusetts. We thank the gentleman for his excellent comments.

Let me turn now and recognize the gentleman from Massachusetts, a good friend of the Senator's, John Olver.

Mr. OLVER. I thank the gentleman for yielding to me. I was still making changes in what I was intending to say, and usually I do that all the time.

I rise tonight to remember and honor the life and the life's work of a dear friend, Senator TED KENNEDY. There are few Americans alive today whose lives are not affected in some way by Senator KENNEDY's vast body of legislative achievements. He's credited with hundreds of laws enacted over his nearly 47-year Senate career, and many of those laws make up fundamental tenets of the social contract that is our modern society.

One of the best examples of Senator KENNEDY's impact on society can be seen in his ground-breaking Americans with Disabilities Act, which opened the door to jobs, housing, transportation, communications, and a better life for millions of citizens. It also fundamentally changed the way people viewed others who live with disabilities.

Providing opportunity was a great theme of Senator KENNEDY's work, as evidenced by his contributions to strengthening public education. Throughout his career, he fought for better teachers, better schools, more funding, and better methods to enhance learning for America's children.

For wage-earning Americans, TED KENNEDY will perhaps be best remembered for his refusal to accept minimum wage levels as they fell further and further behind in their purchasing power. When others balked or faltered on the issue, Senator KENNEDY had a knack for pushing through a deal to get everything he could for workers as soon as it could be achieved.

On the international front, when the great debate over America's waging a preemptive war arose at the outset of this decade, Senator KENNEDY used his stature and status as a national newsmaker to oppose the President and the Congress' transgressions, as he saw them, with the use of America's military power.

There are many other important accomplishments one could list, but the issue Senator KENNEDY himself labeled as the cause of his life, health care, probably stands out as his greatest area of achievement.

Senator KENNEDY extended COBRA coverage for workers in between jobs and eliminated preexisting condition restrictions for workers in group insurance plans. He fought for and won uncommon allies in his crusade to provide health coverage for all children, which he considered a moral obligation. He created the Family and Medical Leave Act and the Ryan White CARE Act for Americans living with HIV and AIDS.

Though his ultimate cause of universal health care was one he did not live to see enacted, we are where we are today because of KENNEDY's lifelong commitment to that cause. In a sense, the effort is still his effort. The gains that Congress will eventually pass will also be a part of his legacy.

Back in my part of Massachusetts, Senator KENNEDY was always a good friend to the First Congressional District. In recent years he championed the development of the University of Massachusetts' Pioneer Valley Life Sciences Institute and helped to support Holyoke Hospital, a critical health services provider in the Connecticut Valley. He was ever willing to exercise his seniority in the Senate when Massachusetts companies needed it, and when campaign season came around, no one could bring out and motivate as many workers as Senator KENNEDY. His stump speeches in remote corners of Massachusetts, for State or local candidates, were always an oratorical treat for those lucky enough to hear them.

To me personally, Senator KENNEDY was an inspiring and thoughtful friend. I could always count on an immediate and passionate response to whatever was on his mind and on my mind, and his attentive friendship came with a warm smile, a sense of humor and a caring heart. Senator KENNEDY's breadth and depth of leadership were unmatched in the Congress. He was a tireless worker for his constituents and all humanity, and I am honored to have known him and served with him.

Mr. MARKEY of Massachusetts. We thank the gentleman so much for his words. Next we recognize another great friend of the Senator, John Tierney, from the State of Massachusetts.

Mr. TIERNEY. I thank the gentleman for recognizing me and want to acknowledge before we start, Patrick, I know you're going to speak later, but I hope that this is somewhat fulfilling for you. It can never replace the loss of your dad, but hopefully it will at least let you know how much the people that served with him had the honor and pleasure of doing that, loved doing it and appreciated him every day. And my colleague, Bill Delahunt, was more than just the Congressman for the Senator, so I extend my sympathies to you as well; you were a friend, probably even closer than most of us were because you were there so often and spent so much time with him. And so I express those condolences to you. But it's a loss to all of us. The dean of the delegation, Ed Markey, of course, served many years with the Senator. I looked at a little factoid the other day that indicated that Senator KENNEDY was born on the 200th anniversary of George Washington's birthday. I thought if that's accurate, and I assume that it is, how interesting it was, because nobody appreciated history more than Senator KENNEDY, and nobody appreciated his role in history more than that.

I can remember Ed Markey at one point, at a function introducing Senator KENNEDY as one of the best U.S. Senators, only to be corrected by the Senator saying, "One of the best? The best." And while he was joking, I think he turned out to be absolutely right on that because he certainly has a record that you have heard from John Olver and others here that is just phenomenal. Jimmy McGovern expressed it as well.

I won't start to enumerate all of the things that the Senator did. We'd be here for far too long. And I think, after hearing my colleagues, most people finally start to appreciate that wherever you were in life, you benefited from him; whether you were cleaning hotel rooms or doing some other job that was difficult like that, you benefited from the minimum wage, health care, education, all the things that we care about. And frankly, when we are all looking to try and have the honor of serving here, listening to people in our constituencies, they're talking about those things that matter to them, the bread and butter issues, whether or not they're going to have a job, whether or not it pays well, whether or not they're going to be able to keep their family healthy; whether or not they're going to be able to give their children opportunity. This great Senator epitomized all of that.

One thing that I don't think has been mentioned so far that I just want to hit on is the fact that the Senator used to tell a story about being lectured by his father when he turned 21 or so about the fact that he was going to be the recipient of some resources that other people didn't have the benefit of; he could choose to be idle and do nothing with his time, or he could choose to be of service to others and to mankind. We all know which route he took. But that remains an inspiring story to all people even today.

During the course of this summer when the President had his Service to America campaign going on, many of us had the opportunity to go and visit a lot of these organizations that had volunteers. The Edward M. Kennedy Serve America Act that was signed into law earlier in the year by President Obama meant that now their role was stepping into his belief of service and doing something for their fellow citizens, doing something for America and no matter how small or large, no matter where it was, you could see the inspiration that they got from the Senator. It was from his life, from his acts, and from the fact that this law had passed because he motivated people to pass it and get it through.

This will remain as one of his great legacies, the fact that he spent his life serving others, that he was selfless in that regard, and that while he was serious about the business that he did, he was also never taking himself too seriously, and always willing to make people feel comfortable and to see the lighter side of things and to see the better part of humanity. In even people who were his political opponents, he saw a good part, and he was able to draw out of them a response that made them accept him and others and work on issues together.

I can remember being with the Senator when we would go out, particularly to senior citizen places where he just couldn't resist singing a song, particularly an Irish song, couldn't resist getting out and dancing if there was a ballroom dance going on. And, of course, I guess I must take myself too seriously, or just know how bad a singer or bad a dancer I am. I was always looking for the door, and he would never let that happen. He'd be the first one to force you on the floor, make a fool of yourself, but have some fun and go on that. That's the humanity of the man; that he loved everybody, he loved having a good time with them, could get them to go along with him; and then when it was time to get serious, he could do that in a heartbeat. He could make the case. He had great oratorical skills that carried the day over and over again. And he truly is a giant. I know that the story of his life is just jumping off the shelves right now because people are starting to remember all that he did.

Sometimes in the hustle and bustle of political jargon, when people are making attacks and going back and forth, people forget that when you separate all that out, whether you are a conservative, or whether you are a liberal, whatever your political opinion, there are things in your life that you have that you're grateful for that are a result of the work of Senator KENNEDY. I think the bottom line is that this Senator was a great Senator for America. He was a great friend to all of us. He was a great father and brother for people in Massachusetts. We sorely miss him. But none of us regret at all having had the opportunity to know him and to serve with him.

Mr. MARKEY of Massachusetts. I thank the gentleman very much. And the gentleman is so right. I could call Senator KENNEDY one of the greatest Senators in history. I could call him one of a small handful of the greatest Senators in history. But that would be inaccurate. That just wouldn't capture not only how history will record him, but how he wants to be recorded by history. And there will be an accurate reflection of that, I think, as people, as the gentleman pointed out, continue to focus upon his life.

Before I turn to the gentleman from South Boston, let me go back the gentleman from Quincy, Mr. Delahunt.

Mr. DELAHUNT. If the gentleman would yield for a moment before our friend, Steve Lynch, makes his remarks, this conversation, the colloquy between yourself and John Tierney, reminds me of an anecdote. I wasn't present and maybe Patrick could attest to its validity. When TED KENNEDY was described as one of the two most significant U.S.

Senators in that institution's history, the other being Webster, his response was, "Well, what did Webster do?"

Mr. MARKEY. I thank the gentleman.

No place played a more important role in the history of Massachusetts Irish politics than South Boston, the home of the next friend of Senator KENNEDY, Steve Lynch from South Boston, MA.

Mr. LYNCH. Mr. Speaker, I thank my friend, Mr. Markey, the dean of the New England delegation, for reserving this time in order for us to pay a special tribute to our friend and colleague, Senator TED KENNEDY. If you have been watching tonight, you will notice that the Members with the most seniority have been given the privilege to speak first, which is the way it works down here. The longer you are here, the more you appreciate that. However, I am one of the more junior members of the delegation, and unlike some of the fellows that have been around here forever, like Mr. Markey and Mr. Frank and Mr. Delahunt, I had a relatively short time, 8 years, to spend working with TED KENNEDY. And I cherish every one of those years. But in addition to working with TED, as a colleague—TED could get it done. I was always amazed at that.

But I also had a different perspective of TED KENNEDY. I saw him in action before I came to this House. I grew up in the public housing projects in South Boston, the Old Colony housing projects. And I can tell you that whether you lived in the housing projects in Old Colony in Southie or Bromley-Heath or Mission Main or Franklin Field, if you grew up, if your family struggled to make ends meet in public housing, no one in public housing had a better champion, a more valiant and noble champion, than TED KENNEDY. And that's really the first perspective that I had of TED KENNEDY, as someone who was working for our benefit as a family growing up in public housing and in pretty tough circumstances. He was there for us.

I also had a perspective of working as an ironworker for 18 years, strapping on a pair of work boots, becoming a union president for the ironworkers. I can say from that perspective as well, whether you were an ironworker, like I was, working in the building trades with a lot of my union brothers and sisters, or whether you worked on a factory floor, or maybe you were a nurse going out every day working double shifts and overtime, or you were a policeman or a fireman, no working person in this country had a more gallant champion to protect their rights and protect the conditions on the job than we had in TED KENNEDY. And the outpouring of love that we saw during the memorial service and the wake and the funeral and even during TED's illness reflected that collective experience of not only the people of Massachusetts but of New England and the United States. And it was something to see.

My mom raised us in public housing, and when the motorcade came along Carson Beach in the shadow of the housing project where we grew up, my mom insisted that I help her down there—she's not as young as she used to be, but I helped her down there just to give respect to the Kennedy family and to TED during that last part of his journey. There is a saying from the ironworkers, especially in the steelmills, that the strongest steel comes through the hottest fire. And really, when you looked at TED's life and saw what he accomplished and the challenges that he had; his brother, President of the United States, taken in violence; his brother, the Attorney General, candidate for the Presidency, taken from us in the same way. The huge challenges to TED—they were unthinkable, unimaginable, yet he worked through them, and not only did he overcome them, but he also reached out to other people and shared a strength that he gathered from those experiences.

I'll never forget—this is my only TED KENNEDY story that I'll relate tonight. I was a freshman—actually, it was very early in my career as a State representative, and we had six of our brave firefighters killed in a terrible fire in Worcester, MA. We all went to the Worcester Centrum for that ceremony. The families were there and every seat was taken, and every bit of space on the floor was taken. The place was filled to the rafters. And that's where I was sitting, far above the floor. But I remember TED's remarks. Here are six families that just lost their loved ones. And when TED KENNEDY spoke, you could have heard a pin drop in that Centrum that day.

He basically said to the families—I'll never forget his words. He said, "From my own experience, I have found that every once in a while life breaks your heart." And even though there were thousands of people in the Centrum that day, in reality, it was just TED and it was just those six families, and he was helping them through that. And that's a gift.

We all go to wakes and funerals and try to help families through tough times, but I never saw anybody carry it off with the grace and the profound empathy and love that TED was able to accomplish.

I just want to say that I'm delighted that we had an opportunity tonight to convey our thoughts and to share our concerns for TED's family, Patrick and the entire family. We know what they're going through.

I think the test of all of us who are born on this Earth, the true test of our time, however short it is on this Earth, is whether the work we do while we're on this Earth is going to live after us and is it going to positively affect the people that we leave behind.

By any measure, by any test, TED has passed that test with flying colors. He has left the power of his example for all of us to try to follow.

I want to thank you, the dean of our delegation, Ed Markey, for the opportunity to share my thoughts. My prayers and the prayers of my family go out to the Kennedy family.

Mr. MARKEY of Massachusetts. We thank the gentleman so much for his words.

In 1974, Paul Tsongas from Lowell was elected to the U.S. Congress. Today, these many years later, Niki Tsongas serves here in the Congress. So the Tsongas and the KENNEDY story goes back many years.

I'd like to recognize the gentlelady from Lowell, Niki Tsongas.

Ms. TSONGAS. I'd like to thank the dean of our delegation for hosting this Special Order so we can remember our most remarkable Senator.

As I was thinking about how best to talk about him—and we've heard some wonderful remembrances this evening—I was looking back to the early 1960s when I was, like so many of us, a student in high school, a beginning student in high school—I hate to give away our age—but the figures of the Kennedy family, in particular, President John F. Kennedy, were inspirational.

My husband, Paul, used to say that he was inspired by that Presidency to seek public office. But he had grown up in what he called a "disadvantaged household." His parents were Republicans. And it was the Presidency of John Kennedy that inspired him and so many others either to become a Democrat or to seek out public office, little knowing that some years later we would be serving with the man we remember tonight.

My first recollection, though, of Senator KENNEDY is in 1974, when Paul was a candidate for the seat that I now hold. Senator KENNEDY agreed to come to Lawrence, MA, to campaign for Paul, who was part of the great Watergate class in which there were many Democrats running across this country. Paul was running against an incumbent Republican.

Senator KENNEDY came to Lawrence, MA, to St. Mary's Church. He was accompanied by Barbara Souliotis, who many years later still serves as his State director. At the time, I think she was an advance person, and I remember her utter professionalism in keeping TED on track.

We've heard tonight what a great speaker he was, how he could really connect with the crowd. And so he did that evening. While TED was speaking, Paul looked at me like, "Now what on Earth do I do?," because he knew he could never compare with TED KENNEDY. And he didn't even try. But you could see then how fundamentally TED connected with people, because they trusted him, and they knew that he was working on their behalf.

I remember, again, TED in 1978, when he supported Paul against an incumbent U.S. Senator, somebody who was his colleague, a Republican, as he did so often; he kept his word, supported his colleagues, whether they were seeking the Presidency, as they in turn supported him.

Well, I haven't had the opportunity to serve, unfortunately, with TED as long as others here. I do have a couple of remembrances from the past several years. One was when he did agree to come and campaign for me, again, in Haverhill and Lawrence, MA, the cities of the Fifth District of Massachusetts.

This time, though, he came with a van. He brought Sunny and Splash, the dogs. Barbara Souliotis, who was with him in 1974, was there at his side yet again, along with Vicki. We started out in Haverhill. We went to an old diner that was owned by a Greek American family. Barbara's mother brought pastries that she cooked. TED sat there with a little demitasse of coffee, ate the pastries, and thoroughly enjoyed the morning.

Then we traveled on to a small school where we were going to read. It was an early reading program, a very good one, one that I think is a real model going forward. And TED, this remarkable Senator who has met with every imaginable world leader, sat and sang "Itsy Bitsy Spider" to the 2-year-olds and 3-year-olds that were in the room with him. He had a remarkable ability to connect with all of humanity.

My last conversation with him was around a point of legislation that we both jointly sponsored to protect a farm called Barrett's Farm. We've learned to know what a lover of history he is. I represent two parks: the Minute Man National Historical Park and the Lowell National Historical Park.

Barrett's Farm is a farm that played a very important role in the beginnings of the American Revolution. It was a farm that housed munitions that the Minutemen were going to use. And the British, learning of the new munitions, decided to march on Lexington and Concord, prompting Paul Revere's ride to warn that the British were coming.

The Minutemen got to Barrett's Farm and hid the munitions, so by the time the British arrived, the munitions were safely set aside where they could be used as we advanced our Revolutionary War effort, but the shot was heard round the world that changed the history of this country.

So we worked hard. My former Congressman, Marty Meehan, had initially filed the legislation to save the farm. I followed up on that, working with Senator KENNEDY. The bill finally was signed into law.

This April, I was sitting in my office and got a call. It was Senator KENNEDY on the line, and I picked it up and he said, "Niki, isn't it grand"? He could celebrate that small legislative act that protected such important history with the same joy and commitment that he did the grandest of efforts.

Senator KENNEDY's legislation has shaped American lives in ways we cannot even know. Every day our lives are different for all that he did. And we are so fortunate to have had his service, to have the great legacy of the Kennedy family, and to be serving today with Representative Patrick Kennedy, who continues that legacy as well.

We will miss him. We will miss him forever. But we will always remember him in the large acts and small kindnesses of his life.

Mr. MARKEY of Massachusetts. We thank the gentlelady so much for those words.

Now we turn to—and a number of Members have alluded to him—the great civil rights leader who knew the Kennedys in the 1960s and now serves here in the House of Representatives, Congressman John Lewis from the State of Georgia.

Mr. LEWIS of Georgia. Mr. Speaker, I want to thank my colleague Ed Markey and members of the Massachusetts delegation for holding this Special Order in honor of Senator KENNEDY. I rise today just to say thanks to Senator KENNEDY and to the Kennedy family.

During the 1960s, I had an opportunity to meet President KENNEDY, in June 1963, when I was only 23 years old, and then to see him at the end of the March on Washington when he invited us back down to the White House. I got to know Robert Kennedy, the Attorney General, meeting with him in his office and campaigning with him in Indiana, Oregon, and California.

I have known Senator TED KENNEDY for a long time. He was a very special man, a very special friend. I remember long before I came to Washington as a Member of Congress an occasion when we needed him to speak at a fundraiser for nonpartisan voter registration efforts in the South. He answered our call without hesitation. He spent time among us, honoring not just men and women of means, but everyday people and their little children.

Senator KENNEDY, this extraordinary man, was an elegant man who walked with kings, but never lost the common touch. As a colleague, he was generous and committed. He was our leader, our champion, our shepherd. He took up the causes of those who were weak and tried to make them strong. He stood tall and spoke with passion for all of those who have been left out and left behind—the people who had no voice in America.

TED KENNEDY never lost hope. He demanded justice for people of color when it came to civil rights and voting rights, and he also took a stand for seniors and for those with a different sexual orientation and for the disabled.

Senator KENNEDY was a man who lived his faith and tried to act on it every single day by doing good to help the least fortunate among us. At some of the most tragic and difficult moments in this Nation's history, Senator KENNEDY had the capacity, had the ability, to gather his strength and lead us toward a more hopeful future.

As a Nation and as a people, he encouraged us to build upon the inspirational leadership of his two brothers and use it to leave a legacy of social transformation that has left its mark on history.

I would say tonight, Mr. Speaker, to members of the Massachusetts delegation, to Patrick, and to other members of the Kennedy family, Senator KENNEDY was so thoughtful and so considerate. He was one of the most sharing, caring, giving human beings that I have ever met.

During July 2006, when the Senate was about to reauthorize the Voting Rights Act, he invited me over to the other side of the Capitol to be his guest on the Senate floor. When the last vote had been tallied, he gave me a copy of the tally sheet. Then he suggested that we walk out into an adjoining room, and he showed me the desk where President Lyndon Johnson had signed the original act on August 6, 1965.

He had a photographer to take a picture of the two of us standing near that desk. A few days later, I received the most beautiful copy of that picture with an inscription from Senator KENNEDY. It is hanging on the wall in my home in Atlanta. I will always cherish it as long as I live.

I remember in 1977 Senator KENNEDY came to Atlanta and we hosted a little reception for him at my home. He met a few of our friends, my wife Lillian, and our son John Miles. He spent so much time playing and talking with my young son, who was not quite a year old.

Senator KENNEDY had a heart full of grace and a soul generated by love that never forgot the spark of divinity that runs through us all, no matter whether you were his closest friend or his fiercest adversary.

A brilliant light has gone out that uplifted not just America, but the entire world community. During his life, Senator KENNEDY touched so many of us with his brilliant light. He touched more than Members of Congress, but also ordinary people. He touched our President and the leaders of tomorrow.

The spark of light that he gave to each one of us still burns brightly, and it is our duty, our obligation, to continue his legacy and pass that light on to unborn generations.

Senator KENNEDY will be deeply missed but not forgotten, and his legacy will live on in all of us. He was a wonderful friend, a wonderful colleague. He was like a brother.

Mr. MARKEY of Massachusetts. We thank the gentleman so much for his great words. For me, I had the honor of serving for 33 years out of the nearly 47 that TED KENNEDY served in Congress, here as his colleague. It was my great honor. For each of us, there are too many stories to retell.

But for me, it all begins with TED KENNEDY running for the Senate; and from that moment on, whenever he spoke about the war in Vietnam or health care or energy or injustice to any person, no matter where they were in the world, I listened. And not only did I listen, but tens of millions of other people listened as well because he took us on a journey to issues and people that we did not know of but he wanted us to know about and to respond to.

That was really his greatness, that when he spoke, he was true north. He was someone who you knew was speaking from his heart and speaking for issues that really only he had the capacity to draw attention to, and he used his power to do so. He used the special gift that he had been given to accomplish those goals.

I remember at the Democratic Convention in 1980, Senator KENNEDY had asked me and Henry Royce, who was chairman of the Banking Committee, to introduce his energy bill, which would be the counter to the incumbent President's energy bill. It called for solar and wind and conservation and higher fuel economy standards and a different direction for our country. Although his candidacy failed, and energy was the big issue at that time, I got a call to come up to his room right after he gave that great "The dream shall never die" speech. He was up in his room with his family—Patrick was there and others. In that room, there was not a defeated man. There was someone who had been a great victor. There was someone who had brought all of these issues to the American people.

In 1983, as Ronald Reagan had pulled out of all arms control negotiations with the Soviet Union—the first time in a generation—he called me, and he said, "Eddy, you know what I would like to do, I would like to work with you on a nuclear freeze resolution to end all production of new nuclear weapons in the world." And he said, "You know what would be a good idea, why don't we have it at American University, where my brother gave his speech to end all atmospheric nuclear testing?"

Then 1 month later, there was attention brought to this issue that changed that whole issue, and 3 months later, 1 million people were in Central Park calling for an end to the nuclear arms race. On every single issue he talked about in his entire life, it changed the whole dynamic of that issue because TED KENNEDY stood up and spoke to it. He inspired me; and he inspired, I think, millions of people across the planet to change the course of their lives.

So it has been a great honor for me and for all of the rest of our delegation to be able to work with him. It is an especially great honor to have as our concluding speaker this evening, his son, who is our colleague here in the House of Representatives, who in and of himself is a great U.S. Congressman and who continues the Kennedy tradition of fighting for those causes that other people do not want to fight for and to bring attention to those who are most in need of help in our country and in our world.

It is my great honor to recognize the great Congressman from the State of Rhode Island, Patrick Kennedy.

Mr. KENNEDY. I want to thank my good friend and colleague Ed Markey for organizing this Special Order and all of my colleagues for the wonderful tributes that they've given my dad tonight. I will just say that he loved people in public life because they were willing to go out and face the elements and weather the scorn of public opinion in order to stand up for what they believed in. That's why he really admired political figures, and especially in a time where political figures aren't very revered. They're pretty much down at the bottom of the public opinion polls in terms of most professions.

But he knew what a difference it meant to have people of good faith and conviction involved in the political process because he knew what a difference it made in terms of getting good policy done for the American people. He knew how easy it would be for most people to sit back and make criticisms from the sidelines, but it took a really special person to sacrifice a big part of their lives because it takes enormous sacrifice of their private lives to be in the public life, especially today.

So he always got energy out of the people that he served with. They were the ones who sustained him so much because he felt like he was part of a team effort. There is nothing that he loved more than being part of a team, whether it was playing sports or whether it was just being part of a family team, being part of a family. That was his politics. His politics was simple. It was being part of a group and making sure that nobody in the group was left behind. I think it's a great kind of a spirit that he brought to his politics. It was a family spirit that I saw over and over again in every issue that he faced. He wanted to treat everybody else the way he expected to be treated if he were a member of a family, and I was included.

He was brought up to believe that everybody had dignity and everybody had a place. You know, when I was growing up in my family, we all had a place. A lot has been said about his belief in everybody having an opportunity in society. Well, in an anecdotal way, I can tell you, in my life, he always made sure that I had an opportunity to participate.

The SPEAKER pro tempore. Under a previous order of the House, the gentleman from Massachusetts (Mr. Delahunt) is recognized for 5 minutes.

Mr. DELAHUNT. I yield the time to my friend and colleague.

Mr. KENNEDY. Thank you. I will just conclude now because I know my friends and colleagues have their time to speak.

I would like to say to each and every one of the folks who spoke tonight, thank you for being here to pay tribute to my father. To the folks on both sides of the aisle who have been so generous to me, it's a great thing, being part of this House, to have colleagues treat you as one of their own, as a part of a collegial family of sorts, in a professional way but also in a personal way.

What my dad loved so much about serving over in the Senate was the great friendships he developed there. I can tell you, having been through what I have been through in the last couple of weeks, I can appreciate personally what a difference it's made to have the friends that I've had in this Chamber be so supportive of me through this time. I want to thank all of my colleagues for their outpouring of support and affection from both sides of the aisle. It is in times like these where you really get to appreciate the fact that you work in a place where everybody appreciates and respects one another.

I think that is the thing my father would want most for our country right now, for people from very divergent points of view to respect one another and respect this country, which was founded on an appreciation for differences of opinion. The reason why he had worked so well across the aisle on so many occasions on important issues was because he understood that this country can't move forward unless people work together in good faith.

I think the thing that he found most distressing at any point in American history was when the country would stray from its foundation of believing that we could resolve our difficult problems through dialog. I think he knew personally, better than any other person in American history, what happens when people don't resolve their problems peacefully and, instead, resort to violence. I think that my dad is one of those people who believed in the democratic process. And at the end of the day, people saw what a difference his work made in their lives because of the work that he did within the democratic process, to make our country a better place for everybody to live in.

Even though he was from a different station in life from many people that he worked to help, he didn't look at it from the point of view of socioeconomic background. He looked at it from the point of view that we're all human beings, that we all have a spark of divinity in us, and we all ought to treat each other with the same respect that we would want to be treated ourselves, the golden rule, so to speak.

That's why it didn't matter what the issue was. He believed in fairness for everybody because he would want his family to be treated the same way he would want every other family to be treated. But there for the grace of God, he was lucky enough to come from a family that didn't have to worry about paying for health care, education, housing, or a pension to retire. He just knew that if he had come from a different family, he would hope that he wouldn't have to worry about the basic necessities of life that too many Americans have to worry about.

And I respect that about him because through the power of example he showed me that you could be a person of conscience and really try to work to make the lives of those who didn't have it as well off as you better through the work that you did in public life. Through that, I think he showed himself as a patriot in more than one way. He not only wore the uniform of this country in the Army, but he wore the uniform in the sense that he fought in the Senate to advance the lives of people in this country through the policy work that he did as a U.S. Senator.

So, again, let me thank all my colleagues for their great tributes. I look forward to paying him the biggest tribute that we could pay, and that is to make sure that the promise of health care for all is a promise that we ultimately achieve in this session.

Mr. DELAHUNT. Thank you for sharing that with us, Patrick. Thank you for your service, and know that we love you.

Speaking of reaching across the aisle, I'm going to introduce someone who had great love and affection for TED KENNEDY, your dad, and a wonderful guy for whom Senator KENNEDY had the highest respect, even though they agreed on very little. That's the senior Republican on the House Judiciary Committee, Lamar Smith.

Mr. SMITH of Texas. I thank my friend from Massachusetts, Congressman Delahunt, for yielding. I also want to thank my colleagues on both sides of the aisle for their forbearance tonight in not strictly enforcing the time limits.

The SPEAKER pro tempore. The time of the gentleman has expired. Under a previous order of the House, the gentleman from Texas (Mr. Smith) is recognized for 5 minutes.

Mr. SMITH of Texas. This gives me a second opportunity to thank my colleagues for their forbearance tonight.

Senator KENNEDY was a friend, as are members of his family, including his son Patrick who is here tonight. It was a privilege to have known him in lots of different ways. In my being a conservative Republican from Texas, and the Senator being a liberal Democrat from Massachusetts, many people wonder about this friendship. And therein lie many stories, but let me tell a couple tonight.

The first one goes back to when I was a fairly junior Member of Congress. I don't remember what the meeting was about, but there was a meeting in the Capitol in a small room. I was late getting to the meeting, and apparently so was Senator KENNEDY. When I walked in, there were no remaining seats around the table, but there were a couple of seats over by a window. In fact, there was only one seat empty, and it was next to Senator KENNEDY, whom at that point I had not met. I felt like I had nowhere else to go, so I sat by Senator KENNEDY.

After we had been there about a half hour and were bored by the discussion that was going on at the table, we started talking. I mentioned to Senator KENNEDY that, in fact, my grandmother had been from Boston, that I had enjoyed that part of the country many times on vacations, and we discovered that we had a mutual interest in sailing, although I have not gotten to do nearly as much of it as he has.

In any case, we spent the next hour just having a wonderful, friendly discussion. And that was the beginning of this friendship to which I refer.

Not long after that, I was at another meeting. Actually this was a conference meeting in the Capitol, where there were four or five Members of the House and four or five Members of the Senate in attendance trying to work out the differences on a particular piece of legislation. At that particular meeting I was at the table and so was Senator KENNEDY. In fact, he was directly across the table from me. And we had had a relatively mild discussion of the issues at hand, and it was time for Senator KENNEDY to speak.

[231]

He stood up at the table, proceeded to lay into us Republicans as if we knew nothing about the issues at hand, and made a very persuasive argument on his own behalf and on behalf of the issues that he cared about. The voice was so loud that, quite frankly, the walls of this small room were rattling. All the staff who were seated around the room were shaking. And I was wondering what I had gotten myself into. And here was the Senator with whom I had struck a friendship, and he was practically accusing all of us of not knowing what we were talking about on this particular legislation.

Well, the Senator talked for 5 or 10 minutes—completely dominated the room, and there really wasn't much else to say, or at least no one felt like saying anything in response to the Senator. Well, when he sat down, he picked up a piece of paper in front of them and grabbed a pencil, which I was absolutely sure he was going to break in half. But instead of breaking the pencil in half, he scribbled a note on this piece of paper. And everybody in the room was watching him. And he threw the piece of paper across the table to me. And I was thinking, what is going on?

So I picked up the piece of paper. This must have been around July of that particular summer. I looked at the piece of paper, and Senator KENNEDY wrote on the piece of paper, "Lamar, what are you doing for vacation this summer?"

You had to sort of be there to appreciate what had gone on in the previous 10 minutes and the friendship that this particular note to me showed.

I very quickly folded the note up and put it in my pocket so no one else would see it. And, of course, everybody in the entire room was now wondering what was it that Senator KENNEDY had written to the Republican across the table, Smith from Texas.

I never have revealed that note until right now. But that does show not only friendship, but both stories and many others that I could tell I think reveal a larger point. And that is, the public is probably not nearly as aware as they might be of the genuine friendships that occur in Congress between individuals who might not agree on many of the political issues but who can agree to be friends and appreciate each other's company.

(Mr. SMITH of Texas asked and was given permission to address the House for 1 minute.)

Mr. SMITH of Texas. Thank you, Mr. Speaker.

In this case, the idea that individuals can be friends from different sides of the aisle, and even if they disagree on some things political, occurs more often than a lot of people might expect. In fact, that's probably one of the unwritten stories of Congress. And I'm glad it exists.

Certainly on the surface there is an extreme partisanship. Sometimes that is regrettable. But underneath the surface, there are friendships that can occur, for which I think both sides and both friends can be grateful, and I am certainly in that category.

Mr. MARKEY. Will the gentleman yield?

Mr. SMITH of Texas. I will be happy to yield to the gentleman.

Mr. MARKEY. I thank the gentleman for his great words. And we thank all of the other Members for their participation in this Special Order.

The *Record* is going to remain open so any Member that wishes to make a comment about our great Senator TED KENNEDY may do so.

Mr. Speaker, I rise today to honor Senator EDWARD M. KENNEDY—a mentor, a friend, and the greatest Senator our country has ever known.

While it is still difficult to imagine these hallowed halls without TEDDY, today we honor the man who was an inspiration to all of us who have answered the call to public service. And while 1 hour is not nearly enough to pay tribute to the life and legacy of Senator KENNEDY, today we pause to celebrate the life of this extraordinary man.

Never afraid to "sail against the wind" in the name of justice, equality, and opportunity, TEDDY was a treasured friend, a tireless advocate for the people of Massachusetts, and a legislator without peer. Throughout his distinguished career, he helped bring health care to millions of children, enabled many young people to afford a college education and ensured that so many of our citizens could realize the American dream.

I am honored to serve with his son Patrick and to know his other children—Teddy, Jr. and Kara, his beloved wife Vicki, and all the members of the Kennedy family. And there is no doubt that his trusted friend and former staffer, Paul Kirk, will serve with distinction in his interim appointment.

TEDDY was "an idealist without illusions," as his brother, the late President John F. Kennedy, used to say. He came to the Senate to get things done. He was unafraid to reach

[233]

across the aisle to make a deal and he counted some of his staunchest ideological foes among his closest friends. But he never compromised his core beliefs in justice, equality, and access to the American dream.

From his first speech on the Senate floor in support of the Civil Rights Act until his valiant final fight for health care reform, when TED KENNEDY spoke, you knew you were hearing the "true compass" of a committed, principled progressive.

He transcended petty politics to become the lion of the Senate, a legislator like no other. TEDDY's was an unmatched legislative career, which included nearly 47 years in office, approximately 2,500 bills authored and scores of laws bearing his name.

On issues of war and peace there was no better moral compass than TEDDY. He picked up the banner of nuclear arms control from his fallen brother John and fought tirelessly to reduce the threat of nuclear weapons and make the world a safer place. Beginning in the 1980s, TEDDY worked closely with me to highlight the dangers of a nuclear arms race between the United States and the Soviet Union, and the need to prevent the proliferation of nuclear weapons.

In 1982, when I introduced the first nuclear freeze resolution in Congress to stop the buildup of nuclear weapons, no one thought we could do it. But it was TEDDY who led the fight for a freeze in the Senate, paving the way for a dramatic showdown with President Reagan that made it necessary for the Reagan administration to embrace nuclear arms control—a course it initially had rejected.

Our country is a better place because of TED KENNEDY. For the worker who struggled to make ends meet in a minimum wage job, TED KENNEDY was there. For the mother caring for a newborn, TED KENNEDY was there. For a family in need of health care for a sick child, TED KENNEDY was there. For a planet in peril due to the threat of nuclear war, TEDDY was there.

And now we must be there for the causes that Senator KENNEDY championed throughout his long and distinguished career.

In his final days, Senator KENNEDY wrote a letter to President Obama, reminding us all of just what is at stake in the health care debate. "What we face is above all a moral issue," he wrote. "At stake are not just the details of policy, but fundamental principles of social justice and the character of our society."

And there is no one who better understood those principles than TEDDY.

At the Democratic Convention in 1980, when it was clear that TEDDY's inspired campaign for the nomination had come to an end, he was still fighting for the issues he cared about.

Just hours after he delivered his famous speech declaring that the "dream shall never die," I went up to see him in his hotel room headquarters. And what struck me that night and stays with me to this day, was that instead of being heartbroken after coming up short in his quest for the Presidency, there was no defeat in that hotel room. Instead, TEDDY was triumphant. Despite the difficult day, he was still in high spirits.

Although he was a great Senator before that day, it was on that night that he truly began his transformation into the lion of the Senate, the master legislator fighting for the issues that mattered most: health care, civil rights, education, human rights, and others. That night, like so many other nights in his long career, he was able to transcend misfortune and shape something bigger. To commit to a cause larger than himself.

Above all, I will remember TED KENNEDY for his sense of hope. In rough seas and in calm, he always believed our better days were just ahead. In his final fight, the dignity and grace he showed were an inspiration to us all.

And throughout a long life of tragedy and triumph he never faltered in his belief in this country and its highest ideals. From landmark legislation like the Americans with Disabilities Act that touched the lives of millions, to simple gestures like reading to schoolchildren at a school near the Capitol, TEDDY believed in the American dream and helped so many to realize it.

And although the mighty lion has passed on, TEDDY's roar in defense of the disadvantaged and vulnerable will echo eternally in the halls and history of America, inspiring future generations to service, self-sacrifice, and a commitment to our country's highest ideals.

And as we pause to remember this great man, the task now is to follow TEDDY's immortal words and ensure that the causes which he championed shall endure, that his hopes will live on and his dreams of a better future for everyone shall never die.

Mr. RAHALL. Mr. Speaker, I rise today to recognize and remember the outstanding life and legislative achievements of U.S. Senator EDWARD M. KENNEDY.

[235]

I was first elected to the House of Representatives in 1976 and although that is over 33 years ago, TED KENNEDY had already been serving in the U.S. Senate for over a decade. The achievement of being the third longest serving Senator in our history is an accomplishment in its own right, but Senator KENNEDY affected public policy in such a substantial and enduring way that the length of his time in office is really only one achievement in his remarkable journey.

Senator KENNEDY boldly championed landmark legislation to improve the lives of all Americans. He fought fiercely for the poor and the disadvantaged. His legislative achievements include being a major player in a wide range of issues; from addressing funding for cancer research, health insurance reform, benefits for the mentally disabled, discrimination against disabilities, and the Children's Health Insurance Program to civil rights, and education reform. KENNEDY always considered health care the pinnacle issue of his legislative career, and it was a great achievement for him to see comprehensive health care reform moving further along in the legislative process than it ever has before. Five of the six committees handling the health care bill had passed it out of committee at the time of his passing.

One of his most recent achievements was the signing into law of the Edward M. Kennedy Serve America Act of 2009. This landmark legislation tripled volunteer opportunities across the country and created a new service corps for education, health care, energy, and veterans.

Although Senator KENNEDY was diagnosed last year with a malignant brain tumor, he continued to play a major role in the health care debate, and up until his final days he was truly the lion of the Senate, serving fiercely and passionately on behalf of so many Americans both in Massachusetts and around the country. August 25, 2009, was surely a sad day for all of us—but although KENNEDY's life was filled with tragedy, his life was also filled with triumph. His victories in life far surpass that of most men and women, and his story is one of humanity and progress.

Senator KENNEDY was a great statesman and a true leader who cared deeply about America's future, and I am honored to have served in the U.S. Congress with him. I extend my deepest sympathy and heartfelt condolences to Senator KENNEDY's wife and family, and hope they take comfort in knowing that his legend and legacy carry on in the hearts and memories of a grateful Nation.

Mr. HOLT. Mr. Speaker, what a remarkable life EDWARD M. KENNEDY lived. When I first met Senator KENNEDY in 1963, I mistakenly believed he was in office because of his family connections. As I watched and interacted with him over the subsequent decades of his great legislative career, he demonstrated a strong work ethic. No one worked harder. He had a deep commitment to freedom, fairness, and justice, and his persistent defense of the "little guy" was absolutely genuine. The result is a body of legislation that has brought equality, justice, and opportunity to millions. This towering figure was an inspiration to so many of his colleagues, and he showed each of us—from the most senior to the most junior—the highest level of consideration.

My thoughts go out to his family, including his wife Vicki and his son Patrick, who is a close friend of mine. EDWARD M. KENNEDY will live on in the accomplishments he leaves. May all of those close to him know we are grateful for his service to the Nation.

Ms. LEE of California. Mr. Speaker, today we gather to recognize the legacy of a man who will surely be remembered among the great legislators in our Nation's history—the lion of the Senate—Senator TED KENNEDY.

Senator KENNEDY was a champion for peace and justice throughout his entire career, and our Nation is undoubtedly a better place thanks to his leadership over the years—in particular on the issues of education, health care, and civil rights.

I vividly remember the first time I met TED KENNEDY.

I was interning in Washington, DC, in the summer of 1974, at a time when there were very few African American interns on Capitol Hill. My friend, the late Ron Brown, was working for Senator KENNEDY at that time, so I called him and requested a meeting with my fellow African American interns.

Senator KENNEDY immediately granted our request—we met with him a few hours later and knew immediately that we were truly in the presence of greatness.

More recently, I attended several election events with Senator KENNEDY during the primary election.

I had the pleasure of attending the American University rally for Senator Obama where Senator KENNEDY first announced his support and delivered one of the best speeches of the entire campaign.

A few weeks later, I attended an amazing rally at the Beebe Memorial Cathedral in Oakland where I was honored to introduce Senator KENNEDY before he delivered another amazing speech.

The line to get in the door seemed to stretch for miles as supporters waited with anticipation to see this great statesman and warrior for peace and justice.

Over the course of his career in public office, Senator KENNEDY underscored the meaning of the phrase "to whom much is given much is required."

His legislative legacy is unrivaled, and affects the lives of tens of millions of Americans every single day—especially the less fortunate among us.

But despite his countless achievements, there is one unfinished piece of business that was dear to his heart that we must continue to fight for: achieving universal health care in America, and doing so in a way that truly reforms our broken health care system.

In a letter written to President Obama shortly after learning of the terminal nature of his illness, Senator KENNEDY described our Nation's current health care crisis as a "moral issue"—which concerns "not just the details of policy, but the fundamental principles of social justice and the character of our country."

Senator KENNEDY knew, as we know, that health care is a fundamental human right.

Let us work to pass real health care reform, not just in remembrance of the cause that was this great man's life work, but because we see this issue as he saw it—as a test of our society's integrity.

Last week I had the honor, alongside my colleague, the Honorable Kendrick Meek, of presenting the late Senator KENNEDY with the Mickey Leland Award at the Congressional Black Caucus Foundation's Annual Legislative Conference Awards Dinner.

The award, received by his son, the Honorable Patrick Kennedy, was bestowed upon him in recognition of his lifetime's work in providing opportunities for society's less fortunate.

From civil rights, to education, and finally to health care, the late Senator KENNEDY is destined to be remembered as a true champion of equality and opportunity.

Our charge now is to keep this noble legacy alive by renewing our efforts to ensure that health care reform—his great, unfinished cause—provides each and every American with the universal and affordable coverage that was his vision.

I look forward to working with you in the weeks to come to do everything we can to make sure that happens.

WEDNESDAY, *September 30, 2009*

Mr. MEEK of Florida. Madam Speaker, I rise today with a poetic tribute penned by Albert Carey Caswell in honor of and in memory of a truly great American.

HEAVEN HOLDS A PLACE

Heaven holds a place!
For all of those who have so held such faith!
Who, no matter how dark the days ...
Somehow, always so kept pace!
Heaven holds a place!
For such men of love and grace ...
Who all the while, somehow always kept their smile ...
No matter the darkest of days!
All in what, they so faced ...
Yes, Heaven so holds a place!
For men of peace, and of such grace!
Who have so fought for the poor, the sick, and the old each day!
Heaven, so holds a place!
For those who gave warmth, even though the wind's turned cold they faced ...
For all those who have so loved children, our Lord God so holds a special place!
For a 77 year old man, who with the heart of a child who would stand ...
Who somehow ever wore a smile!
Who touched all those around him, all the while!
Yes, TEDDY ... Heaven so holds a place!
For heroes like you, who had to wipe those tears from your face!
Holding a family together, with your courage and grace!
Yes, for you TED ... Heaven so holds a place!
For men who have so fallen from grace ...
And, but asked for redemption, and so prayed and prayed ...
As our Lord so heard you calling, calling night and day ...
As such burdens, upon your own soul you placed!
As for redemption you so prayed!
Men who have taught love, not hate!
Why, Heaven so holds a place!
Who in the darkness cried out such tears, as the new day they faced ...
For all those with hearts like of a lion ...
Who for mankind, never stopped trying!
For you see, such things ... time can not so erase!
And for such men, Heaven so holds a place!

[239]

In loving memory of Senator EDWARD M. KENNEDY. May God bless you and your family ...

Ms. WOOLSEY. Madam Speaker, I rise today to honor Senator EDWARD KENNEDY, who passed away August 25, 2009, at age 77. A leader in the Senate for over 46 years, Senator KENNEDY dedicated his career to equality and justice for all.

Senator KENNEDY believed that the fight for quality and affordable health care was the cause of his life and nothing less than a moral obligation for us all. His courageous commitment to improving the welfare of all people was inspirational to me and millions of Americans. As chairman of the Senate Committee on Health, Education, Labor, and Pensions, he influenced nearly every piece of legislation that came before the Senate. Because of his deep concern for the treatment of mental health patients, he helped individuals suffering from mental health and substance abuse disorders receive adequate coverage and prompted the growth of America's community mental health centers. Senator KENNEDY was also committed to increasing access to health care for everyone. I wish he was with us long enough to see all his hard work come true.

Senator KENNEDY was a compelling advocate for equal access to education for all children. His leadership was instrumental in expanding the Head Start Program, and he devoted himself to improving teaching quality and equality across the country.

Senator KENNEDY fought tirelessly to ensure all students who wished to obtain higher education were able to do so. During the 110th Congress he helped enact the most substantial increase in student aid funding, making higher education more accessible and affordable to all.

Madam Speaker, Senator KENNEDY was a shining example of what the very best public servants can aspire to become, and his passion for helping others will live on through the lives he has touched. His legacy of hard work, compassion, and excellence will continue to impact America for generations to come.

Ms. ESHOO. Madam Speaker, "Be not afraid of greatness: some are born great, some achieve greatness, and some have greatness thrust upon 'em."—William Shakespeare, "Twelfth Night."

It is with a sense of proud sadness and deep gratitude that I am blessed to offer a few words about a man who was born to greatness, had it thrust upon him and achieved greatness—because, in the end, he was not afraid.

It is with an array of inexpressible emotions that I am blessed to call him an inspiration, mentor, and most valued friend.

To be TED KENNEDY's friend was to be wrapped in a special embrace, a golden aura of generosity and thoughtfulness, compassion and comradeship. It simply felt good to be around him.

I believe the highest praise bestowed on anyone is that he made the people around him better. This he did by calling all of us to the better angels of our nature.

It is said that to whom much is given, much is expected. No one expected more of himself than did TED KENNEDY, and no one gave more of himself to others.

No one bore greater burdens—some of them the result of cataclysmic events that damaged not only our Nation, but hurt him deeply and in ways that would have paralyzed any of us.

He carried on, shouldering the future of a young and sprawling family and the continuing hopes and dreams of our Nation.

In a speech in August 1968, mere weeks after the death of his brother Bobby, TEDDY said:

There is no safety in hiding. Like my brothers before me, I pick up a fallen standard. Sustained by the memory of our priceless years together, I shall try to carry forward that special commitment to justice, excellence and courage that distinguished their lives.

We met in 1978 in San Francisco when I was little more than a laborer in the vineyards of California Democratic politics. In 1979, I joined his campaign for President and was appointed to his State steering committee.

I soon found myself involved in decisions about who to seat at the 1980 Democratic Convention and in strategic discussions about how we might win the nomination against a sitting President.

In this way, he lifted the fortunes and the sights of so many, allowing us to find new challenges, to seek out new responsibilities and to broaden our own understanding of what we could do, who we could be and how we could help him achieve an America of justice, excellence, and courage.

It was at the convention, of course, that he gave what is widely regarded as his greatest single speech. The speech concluded with those words that have continued to ring out through the decades: "The work goes on, the cause endures, the hope still lives, and the dream shall never die."

Conventions have become prepackaged events with carefully staged "spontaneous" demonstrations of affection and support. At the 1980 convention, we were outsiders, there against the wishes of an incumbent President whose strategists controlled all the machinery of convention-like hoopla.

So, for an hour, we clapped and cheered, we cried and we chanted, "KENNEDY, KENNEDY."

In retrospect, we were enthralled not by the end of a campaign but by the promise of future fights and the certainty that our cause would go forward, as would our work on behalf of the downtrodden and the disaffected.

He said in 1985, with yet another Presidential election stirring, "The pursuit of the Presidency is not my life. Public service is."

He loved to be of service, and he reveled in all that it meant, taking joy in those things that would have seemed small and inconsequential to him—and spreading joy.

In 1986, while serving as a member of the San Mateo County Board of Supervisors, I was elected to the position of chairman of the board. The title was nice, but it was antiquated and was a vestige of an era when only men served in office. I asked the county council to take the necessary steps to change the title to president of the board.

It became a national news story that appeared in the *Wall Street Journal*, an article that included the headline: "Eshoo to become president."

TEDDY sent me a telegram that read: "I always wanted to be president, but I'm glad you got there first."

No one bore greater burdens—some of them self-inflicted. He faced them unflinchingly and with the hope that he would do better. In a scandal-besieged era, he was, again, an example to us of how to live in the public eye with humility, with humanity, and with yet another kind of courage.

He said:

I recognize my own shortcomings—the faults in the conduct of my private life. I realize that I alone am responsible for them, and I am the one who must confront them. I believe that each of us as individuals must not only struggle to make a better world, but to make ourselves better, too.

When others would have scrambled for the safety of obscurity, he stood at the helm and sailed the storms.

He was flawed, but in a way that makes his virtues stand even taller, for in our midst was a man who never thought of himself as a saint, but believed that the least among us deserve the greatest blessings this Nation can bestow.

He was generous. He was thoughtful. He was passionate. He was courageous beyond measure.

And so it is fitting that his last large moment on the national stage should be filled with hope. This is how he lived his life. This is the gift he gave to us.

At his final Democratic Convention, he harkened to his own past to paint an enduring vision of a better tomorrow that is uniquely TEDDY: "The work begins anew. The hope rises again. And the dream lives on."

So, we are saddened at his passing and in the knowledge we will never see his like again and that we will never be warmed by the sun in quite the same way.

But we are filled with the promise he believed and that he gave us, ready to do battle in his name and to extract a measure of joy from life, as he would do.

And we are comforted in the knowledge that he is with his family and his legions of friends and that he is at peace. May God grant this peace to Vicki, his great love, his precious children and his entire family.

As John Bunyan wrote in "Pilgrim's Progress":

When the day that he must go hence was come, many accompanied him to the riverside, into which as he went, he said, "Death, where is thy sting?" And as he went down deeper, he said, "Grave, where is thy victory?" So he passed over, and all the trumpets sounded for him on the other side.

TUESDAY, *October 13, 2009*

Mr. JACKSON of Illinois. Madam Speaker, I rise today to express my condolences to the family and friends of one of my most prestigious colleagues, Senator EDWARD M. KENNEDY.

Senator KENNEDY lived one of the most extraordinary lives in American political history. He was the last brother of one of America's most storied families; one of our all-time great Senators; and a champion for human rights. His legislative accomplishments have touched and improved the lives of virtually everyone who lived in this great country for the past half a century.

Albert C. Caswell approached me shortly after Senator KENNEDY's funeral with a poem he wrote titled, "Our Nation's Tears." My colleagues may recognize Mr. Caswell's familiar face, as he has served as a tour guide in the U.S. Capitol for the past 23 years. I was moved by Mr. Caswell's poem, and he has asked that I submit it in the *Congressional Record*. I ask unanimous consent to add my statement and his poem to the *Congressional Record*, and I encourage my colleagues to read it.

OUR NATION'S TEARS

(By Albert Carey Caswell)

Our ...
Our Nation's Tears ...
As so now lie here!
For one of America's finest sons, this oh so cherished one ...
A Champion, for Fathers, Mothers, Sisters, Brothers,
Daughters and Sons ...
For Seniors, and our most precious of all ones ... our Children ...
For America, and all of these ones!
Our Lion of The Senate TED, so very dear ...
As it's for or thee, we now so shed such tears ...
As down our quivering cheeks they now so run!
All for you TED, and your great American family my son ...
And that great love story, that our Lord God had so begun!
And that great Irish family, that came from far across those seas ...
But, for a better life to be ...
And that great void now so left, as upon our souls as now so etched ...
And that great hole in all our hearts, this abyss ...
Ah, but lies such depth ...
All in this great [season], with us you have so left ...
For this our nation, our TEDDY bear ... you have so blessed!
As our tears fall like the rains ...
As it's for you TEDDY, we now so cry out all in our pain ...
As comes from our swollen eyes ...
As it's for you, our shining Knight ... we now so weep ...
For in our hearts, you ... we shall so keep!
As we pray to our Lord above, that your soul he shall so reap!
For our True Champion, has so died!
As like Your Profiles in Courage, we too must so rise!
As you have so taught our nation, so over the many years ...
That out of such loss, such heartache ... and such swollen tears ...
That somehow, light too can come!
And that somehow, we must all so persevere!
With A Smile, With A Grin ...
With The Heart of A Child, and a work ethic so then!
And to cherish each new day, as it begins!
And make each new day count! Time and time, and time again!
And hold your families ever so close!
For this is life's full measure, that which so means the most!
Sail on my Son! We will hear your heart on the ocean's setting suns ...
Our beautiful brother from Boston!
For Heaven so holds a place, for our most precious one!
For such men, of such courage, kindness, style and grace ...

And who have worked and prayed for redemption, in all they've faced!
And live by such undying Faith!
Of such men so bright, who have all our hearts so bathed in all their light
. . .
As the baby bore the load, lesson's learned . . .
profiles in courage he so earned . . .
How, TEDDY raised his head each day . . . was but a lesson for all of us to
stay!
To take heart, to take pause . . . all in your pain, and
remember his life cause . . .
To remember his smile, and ever his heart of a child . . .
And that up in Heaven on this day . . .
Four brothers are so reunited, in a football game . . .
"And remember, that the work goes on!"
"The cause endures!"
"The hope still lives!"
"And the dream shall never die!"
TED, our most precious one . . . can you but not in Heaven hear my son?
All of Our Nation's swollen tears, these ones!
And for you, our Nation cry!

In loving memory of Senator EDWARD KENNEDY. May our Lord bless you, our warm son, and your family.

SATURDAY, *November 7, 2009*

Ms. ESHOO. Mr. Speaker, I come to the floor today to cast one of the most important votes of my congressional career— a vote in support of H.R. 3962, the Affordable Health Care for America Act. . . .

For so many of us, this long battle has had a singular, courageous champion who has fought like a lion for the sick, the elderly, the left behind and the left out. Our great achievement today will also be our greatest memorial to our friend, mentor and inspiration, Senator EDWARD KENNEDY.

Like Senator KENNEDY, many of us wondered—as the decades marched by—whether our efforts for comprehensive health care reform would ever be successful.

His unwavering commitment to decent health care for all Americans has paved the way for the bill before us today. It is on the shoulders of this giant that we stand, and I pledge my vote as a tribute to the late Senator. . . .

Mr. GEORGE MILLER of California. . . . The fight to reform this Nation's health care system has spanned nearly 100 years, across generations and many great leaders, from Teddy Roosevelt to Franklin Roosevelt to John F. Kennedy to President Clinton to my own personal hero, TED KENNEDY. . . .

Finally, I'd like to pay tribute to my mentor and friend, Sen. EDWARD M. KENNEDY.

Health care was the cause of TED's lifetime. Our effort would have been impossible had he not carried the torch of justice and equality for all those years.

I know I am not alone when I say that I sincerely wish TED KENNEDY could be with us today to see his dream of quality, affordable health care for all become a reality.

Madam Speaker, this is the most important bill I have ever worked on during my many years of service in Congress.

I could not be prouder to have helped to write this bill, to encourage each of my colleagues to support it, and to cast my vote in favor of the Affordable Health Care for America Act.

We stand at the doorstep of history.

Let us go in.

Ms. PELOSI. ... It's impossible to talk about health care reform in America without talking about Senator EDWARD KENNEDY. His leadership and his contribution to this debate are boundless. Health insurance reform was the cause of his life. He called it "the great unfinished business of our society." On this issue he said what is at stake "is the character of our country." When the President came to address the joint session, he quoted those comments by Senator KENNEDY from a letter that the Senator had sent to him. ... What the Senator also said in the letter that was sent to President Obama before he died was this:

I entered public life with a young President who inspired a generation and the world. It gives me great hope that as I leave, another young President inspires another generation and, once more on America's behalf, inspires the entire world.

He acknowledged President Obama's "unwavering commitment and understanding that health care is a decisive issue for our future prosperity."

MEMORIAL SERVICES

FOR

EDWARD MOORE KENNEDY

EDWARD MOORE KENNEDY

A Celebration of Life

John F. Kennedy Library and Museum
Boston, Massachusetts
August 28, 2009
7–9 PM

Paul G. Kirk, Jr.

Father Gerry Creedon, S.J.
Opening Prayer

"God Bless America"
Boston Community Chorus

Congressman Joseph P. Kennedy II

Senator Christopher J. Dodd

Nick Littlefield

Governor Deval L. Patrick

Senator John McCain

Video Tribute
Directed by Ken Burns and Mark Herzog

Senator John F. Kerry

Senator Orrin G. Hatch

"The Impossible Dream"
Sung by Brian Stokes Mitchell, soloist

Mayor Thomas M. Menino

Senator John C. Culver

"Just a Closer Walk with Thee"
Sung by Boston Community Chorus

Vice President Joseph R. Biden, Jr.

Caroline Kennedy

"When Irish Eyes Are Smiling"
Sung by Colm Wilkinson and John McCormack

MUSICAL PRELUDE: Borromeo String Quartet

WELCOME—PAUL G. KIRK, JR., chairman, John F. Kennedy Presidential Library: Good evening. It is my honor to welcome you all this evening and on your behalf, as well as mine, to offer sincere condolences to the entire Kennedy family, only recently pained by the loss of Eunice Kennedy Shriver, and now by the passing of Senator EDWARD M. KENNEDY; to their sister Jean; and to the Senator's children, Kara, Ted, Jr., and Patrick; his wife Vicki; and Curran and Caroline Raclin, each and all of whom brought such great happiness and pride to the Senator through the years; and, of course, to Vicki, whose love and devotion during their 17 years of marriage was the greatest joy of Senator KENNEDY's life, and whose caregiving these past 15 months was nothing less than heroic and inspirational. Our hearts are with you.

To lead us in a prayer for Senator KENNEDY's peace and the strength of his loved ones, I invite Father Gerry Creedon to offer an invocation, after which the Boston Community Chorus will open the celebration by singing "God Bless America," and I hope you will join them.

Rev. GERRY CREEDON, S.J., St. Charles Borromeo Catholic Church: Blessed are those who have eyes to see what you see and ears to hear what you hear. The work goes on. The cause endures. The hope still lives, and the dream shall never die. He knew sleep and wakeful nights, he had his nightmares, and, yet, he dreamed a dream that was dreamed of the heart and only his great heart could hold.

He gave flesh to that dream, the noble house of his thought where the sick were healed, the spear broken, and the stranger welcome. It is the age-old dream of the prophets, "Thy kingdom come." There will be a banquet yet for the last to feast. He goes ahead of us to lay the table of generosity. It is a dream of joy, an insoluble sign of the presence of God, the song of the roses, the music—"May flights of angels sing thee to thy rest."

"GOD BLESS AMERICA," Performed by the Boston Community Chorus:

God bless America, land that I love,
Stand beside her, and guide her,
Through the night, with the light, from above.
From the mountains, to the prairies,
To the oceans, white with foam.
God bless America, my home sweet home.
God bless America, my home sweet home.

[251]

PAUL G. KIRK, JR.: It was Senator KENNEDY who suggested that when the time arrived, there would be a gathering like this, and he selected as the venue this library where politics and public service are honored every day in the name of his brothers. Thinking back upon other times when we have felt the ache of emptiness, he was the one from whom we would draw comfort and strength, and I suspect tonight will be no different.

I have never met anyone whose spirits were not uplifted by being in the company of TED KENNEDY, and I hope you will feel that way once again when you leave his presence this evening. He wanted us to smile and be joyful as we remember and celebrate the depth of his faith, the quality of his character, the generosity of his heart, the love of his family and his friends, his patriotic service to his Commonwealth and country, and his countless contributions to the human spirit.

For myself, I can say that Senator KENNEDY was the most thoughtful, genuinely considerate human being I have ever known. He suffered from the constant pain of a shattered back, and he bore more hurt and heartache than most humans are ever asked to endure. But at every opportunity he brought hope and joy and optimism to more people than we will ever know. Each of you have your own memories, but all of us would agree TED KENNEDY was fun. He loved to laugh and he loved to make us laugh. He loved good music, and he loved to sing—conducting the Boston Pops and the Harvard Band, or leading the traditional July 4th or Thanksgiving Day sing-along with his friends and family at his home at the Cape.

He loved to tell a good story. One of his favorites that you no doubt have heard went back to when he was 30 years old and made his first run for the Senate. He was in a debate with his opponent who questioned his qualifications, and who pointed his finger at him and said, "You never even had a full-time job." And the next morning at one of these plants at 6 a.m., the Senator is out there greeting people and this big ironworker comes up and puts out his hand and says, "KENNEDY, I heard what they said about you last night, that you never worked a day in your life. Let me tell you something. You haven't missed a thing." He loved that story.

He hosted annual dinners for his aging Harvard football buddies, swapping stories of the glory days. He would laugh with that uproarious and unforgettable laugh and remind us that the older we get, the better we are—painting a seascape, enjoying the affection of his faithful dog, Splash, sailing on the *Mya* with family and friends. For those of us who were inspired by his unmatchable work ethic, to see him relax and enjoy the love of friends and family was our reward as well.

To know Senator KENNEDY well was to understand the quiet depth of the faith that guided him. He espoused the values of politics, but he practiced the politics of gospel values. He didn't preach about faith, but he was tireless in the practice of these tenets—the purpose of life is to live a life of purpose, to always be hopeful and make the most of every moment, to persevere and be strong no matter the adversity, to be the best you can be at what you choose to do, and to serve your neighbors with joy and love and make a positive difference in their lives.

During these last several months, Senator KENNEDY was gratified, as we all were, to have seen the outpouring of thanks for a lifetime of inspirational service and of love for him as a human being. He earned an honorary degree from Harvard, a knighthood from the Government of Great Britain, the John F. Kennedy Profile in Courage Award, an outpouring of contributions to the Edward M. Kennedy Institute for the U.S. Senate, and the Presidential Medal of Freedom. The list goes on. These honors are contemporary acknowledgments of what American history will ultimately record, that no individual legislator from any State of either House of Congress of any political party worked harder or longer, with great adherence to principle or with more political courage, for economic and social justice and for world peace than our own EDWARD M. KENNEDY.

He was the best at what he chose to do, and he left his indelible mark as the most accomplished and effective legislator in the history of this democracy. He believed and often said that America is a promise our Founding Fathers passed on to each succeeding generation to fulfill. He chose politics as the means to fulfill that promise, reminding us that to whom much is given, much is expected.

Gene Scheer gives voice to the life of selfless and patriotic service of our friend in these words of his hymn, "American Anthem."

All we've been given by those who came before,
the dream of a nation whose freedom would endure.
The work and prayers of centuries have brought us to this day.
What shall be our legacy? What will our children say?
Let them say of me I was one who believed
in sharing the blessings I received.

[253]

Let me know in my heart when my days are through.
America, America, I gave my best to you.

Be at peace, my friend. America will be in your debt forever.

Please join me in welcoming Senator KENNEDY's nephew, the oldest son of Senator Robert Kennedy and Ethel Kennedy, former Congressman Joseph P. Kennedy.

Congressman JOSEPH P. KENNEDY II: You know, ladies and gentlemen, one of the ways that I think Senator KENNEDY's life can be measured is by the kind of people that he was able to surround himself with. Everyone who has been a part of this library knows that TEDDY had one friend who stuck with him from the first day he ran until his last day in office and that was the fellow whom he selected to give that last talk. Let's just give Paul Kirk a big round of applause for the wonderful job that he does.

Thank you, Paul. You know, I just wanted to take a brief moment to thank each and every one of you for being here this evening. I wanted to thank you because every person in this audience was touched by TED KENNEDY in one way or another. All of you know the kind of person he was, what he stood for and how he looked out after one very large family. But he could only do that because of the kindness and generosity of his own family, and of Vicki, who in these last few days has shown a kind of grace and dignity and love and character that is simply beyond belief.

And thank you to Teddy and Kiki, whom I love so much, and their whole family, little Teddy and Kylie, Kara with Max and Grace, and my good friend Patrick who does such a terrific job following in his father's footsteps. Patrick, thank you. And thank you to Curran and Caroline, who have welcomed us as we have welcomed them. We just so appreciate their kindness and their love.

You know, it's very difficult to share a father with as big a family as the Kennedys are. Every single one of my brothers and sisters needed a father, and we gained one through Uncle TEDDY. Caroline and John were no different. The Smiths lost their father.

The truth of the matter is that for so many of us, we needed someone to hang on to. And TEDDY was always there to hang on to. He had such a big heart, and he shared that heart with all of us. But Teddy and Patrick and Kara, we want to let you know that we understand how much you gave to allow us to be cared for. And you had to share. So we just want to say thank you to TEDDY's entire family.

[254]

Every time I come to this library, I love to see the remembrances of my father and President Kennedy, and now we'll be able to come here and remember TEDDY. But of all the exhibits and the different aspects at this library, the one that I most appreciate is one that we can't see right at the moment, but is right around the corner.

It is the one thing outside of this building and that is the *Victura*, which most of you know as a boat that President Kennedy owned. From my point of view, that was TEDDY's boat. My father went out and bought me a boat—well, bought my mother a boat that I kind of tried to grab. I was supposed to go out and race against TEDDY. Every single weekend on Saturday and Sunday, I would see the butt end of that boat going over the horizon. TEDDY always came in first, second, or third. I like to think that I came in first, second, or third. The difference was I was third from last, second from the last, or just dead last.

I wanted to share with you a little story that I thought captured who TEDDY is. The reason that boat is out here in front of this library is the one time that I ever beat TEDDY. We were on the race course in Hyannis Port, and one of the crew said, "Hey, I actually think we're overtaking your uncle." I thought "Oh, my God, I can't believe it." So we got up next to him, and of course the reason why we were catching him was that he was up to his bellybutton in water, because the seams of the boat had opened up and the boat was sinking. So we passed TEDDY, my one victory, and after the race he came up to me and he said, "Listen, you don't have a boat. I don't have a boat. Maybe what we should do is buy a boat together and then on one weekend—one day of the weekend I'll crew for you," which was going to be interesting, "and on the other day of the weekend you crew for me."

The same was true for little Teddy and Patrick. So that was it—me, TEDDY, little Teddy, and Patrick. So off we go and the race starts. We race this boat non-stop, and then we get to the biggest race of the year, and there's like, 40 boats. We get up that morning, and it is a full-blown gale. It is blowing heavily. First they call the race off, and then all the skippers get together, and they say, "OK, we'll put the race back on."

Now, the race starts. We're going downwind, which means those big colorful sails called spinnakers are out in front. We start the race and it's about 5 miles to the first mark. I thought something was a little strange when the only boat in the entire fleet that set a spinnaker was ours, and I thought maybe they know something that we don't. Well, anyway, we came to find it out. So we start down toward the first mark, and we are now ahead, because we had this whole other sail. We had this huge advantage, and we are ahead by a country mile.

I am so happy. I am the happiest guy in the history of sailboat racing. What I haven't bothered to tell big TEDDY, little Teddy or Patrick is that I can't steer the boat at all, because it is going wherever the wind is taking it. I look out about 500 yards, and there is this 15-foot-high bell buoy, and we are headed right for it. And then it's 200 yards, and then it's 100 yards, and TEDDY looks around at me and says, "Hey, don't you think we should turn a little bit?"

I'm trying. But we hit that buoy. I thought we were all headed to Davy Jones' locker right there and then. They have this screwy rule in sailboat racing where if you hit the buoy, you can go back and sail around it three times. If you get around it three times without hitting it again, you can keep going in the race. So now we have to sail back to the buoy with 40 boats coming at us that are none too pleased with us.

There's a bit of screaming—none going on in our boat, of course. We somehow make it through this challenge. We get around the mark three times, and then we're going on to the second mark, and I feel like the biggest heel in the history of the world. There was no way that I could blame this on anybody but myself. I feel so terrible, and big TEDDY is up on the windward rail, and he is getting soaked, and it's not very pleasant right then.

He turned around to me, and he said, "Hey, Joe, if last night, before going to bed, I told you we were going to round the first mark in seventh or eighth place, how would you have felt?" I said, "Oh, I guess I would have felt pretty good." And he said, "Let's go win this race." And over the course of the next 3 hours, one after another, we picked off those boats, and we won the race.

Now, I don't tell you that because I think winning that particular race was important, although I think TEDDY would tell you it was important, because TEDDY liked to win. But TEDDY had this wonderful way about him; he would just sense in anyone when they needed a hand. He could just sense it, and I can't tell you how many times in my life it happened. I'm sure as I look around, and I see the people in this room who knew him so well, that every one of you has a story or two or three or five or ten of how TEDDY came and gave you a helping hand when you were down.

He was always there and that's what it was. He was telling me never, ever give up. You stay in the race. And if people don't have health insurance, you stay in the race. If people don't have adequate health care or adequate housing, you stay in the race. If people aren't being treated properly, you stay in the race.

I saw that man make phone calls to every single family in this State of those who died on 9/11. I saw him make the phone calls to every single family in this State who lost a son or daughter in the Iraq war or in Afghanistan. This was a man who cared so deeply about those on the outside of political and economic power, people who struggle, struggle each and every day to just get by.

He lived his whole life fighting for those people. That's why I think when you hear all these tributes, and you see Senator McCain and Senator Orrin Hatch and others here today from the other side of the aisle, they're here because they knew what kind of individual TEDDY was. They loved his laugh. They loved to spend time together. But at its core, they loved to be with an individual who stood for something.

And so, ladies and gentlemen, I am here today because I loved my uncle so very much. He did so much for me and my brothers and sisters and my mother when we needed a hand, and I tell you, ladies and gentlemen, there are thousands of others who lost a father or a mother or a sister or a brother or someone else in this life who turned to TED KENNEDY. We've lost such a human being. But, you know, ladies and gentlemen, he is going to want us to continue. He's going to want us to live as he lived. He came back after so much tragedy because of that heart, because of that drive and that determination. So I ask each one of you to rededicate yourself to the same goals and ideals that Senator TED KENNEDY lived his life for, because he lived to make this world a better place, and our country and our world are better places because of the life of TED KENNEDY. Thank you.

PAUL G. KIRK, JR.: You get a chance to cheer again when we welcome Senator KENNEDY's very good friend from the neighboring state of Connecticut, who served his State and country with honor and dignity. We're glad he's back from his "procedure," as I'll call it. Welcome everybody's good friend, Senator Chris Dodd.

Senator CHRISTOPHER J. DODD: Good evening, all. Vicki, let me begin by thanking you for the remarkable invitation to be here this evening and to stand at this podium and get a chance to express my feelings and my emotions about my dearest of friends, TED KENNEDY.

Tonight, of course, we gather to celebrate the incredible American story of a man who made so many other American stories possible, my friend TEDDY. And unlike his beloved brothers, his sister Kathleen, his nephews, TEDDY was granted the gift of time. He lived not just as the Irish poet suggested, to comb gray hair—but white hair.

And if you look at what he achieved in his 77 years, it seems at times as if he lived for centuries. Generations of historians will, of course, chronicle his prolific efforts on behalf of so many others around the world. I will leave that to them. Tonight I just want to share a few thoughts about my friend. And what a friend he has been, a friend of unbridled sympathy and empathy, of optimism, and of full-throated joy.

Examples, of course, of that friendship are legion. I remember many years ago a close friend of mine passed away. TEDDY didn't know him at all. I was asked to say a few words at the funeral. As long as I live, I'll never forget that as I stood at that pulpit and looked out over that gathering that day, there was TEDDY sitting in the back of that church. He obviously wasn't there for my friend. He was there for me at my time of loss. That was what it was like to have TEDDY in your corner.

When our daughters Grace and Christina were born, the very first call I received was from my friend TEDDY. When I lost the Iowa caucuses last year, not that anyone ever thought I was going to win them, the first call I received was from TEDDY and Vicki. When my sister passed away last month, the first call I received was from TEDDY, even though he was well into the final summer of his own life.

And 2 weeks ago, as I was coming out of surgery, I got a call from TEDDY, his unique voice as loud and booming as ever. "Well," he roared, "between going through prostate cancer surgery and doing townhall meetings, you made a great choice."

And though he was dying, of course, and I was hurting, believe me, he had me howling with laughter in the recovery room as he made a few choice comments I cannot repeat this evening about catheters.

As we all know, of course, TEDDY had a ferocious sense of humor. In 1994 he was in the political fight of his life against Mitt Romney. Before the first debate, held in Boston's historic Faneuil Hall, I was with TEDDY and Vicki and his team that evening, and along with everyone else we were offering our advice before the debate began.

"TEDDY," I cautioned, "We Irish always talk too fast. Even if you know the answer to a question, you have to pause, slow down, and at the very least appear to be thoughtful."

Well, out he went, and of course, the very first question was something like this: "Senator, you have served the Commonwealth of Massachusetts for nearly 35 years in the U.S. Senate. Explain, then, why this race is so close." TEDDY paused. And paused. And paused. Five seconds. Ten seconds. Finally, after what seemed like an eternity, he answered the question. After the debate I said, "Good Lord, TEDDY, I didn't mean pause that long after the first question. What in the world were you thinking of." He looked and said, "I was thinking that's a damn good question. Why is this race so close?"

In these last months of his life, I have just so treasured our conversations. At 6:30 a.m., on the morning of July 16, only a few weeks ago, the morning after his Senate Health Committee finished 5 weeks of exhausting work on a bill that he had written and that I believe will be one of the greatest of his many legacies, my phone rang in the morning. There was TEDDY, beyond ecstatic that we had finished our work and that his committee had been the first to report a bill. Always a competitor, of course. TEDDY was never maudlin during these last number of months or self-pitying about his health and his illness, but he was always fully aware about this happening to him. Over the last year or so, TEDDY got to enjoy what is, of course, every Irishman's dream—and that is to attend your own eulogies. That's why we Irish call the obituary page the Irish sports page.

I know he enjoyed a uniquely Celtic kick out of hearing people who abhorred his politics say incredibly nice thoughts about him along the way. Volumes, of course, will be published by those attempting to unlock the mystery of why TEDDY was such an effective legislator over the years. Was it his knowledge of parliamentary procedure? Was it his political instincts, his passionate oratory, his staff? What was it?

Please, let me save the pundits and the political scientists some time and all of you some money and tell you what TEDDY's secret was. People liked him.

He always had a great staff and great ideas, but that only counts for so much in the U.S. Senate if you lack the respect and admiration of your colleagues, and TEDDY earned that respect.

You'll recall he arrived in Washington as the 30-year-old brother of a sitting U.S. President and the Attorney General of the United States. Many people drew their conclusions about him before he spoke his first words in the U.S. Senate, and over the years, of course, he became a target of partisans who caricatured him as a dangerous liberal.

Now, liberal he was, and very proud of it, I might add. But once you got to know him, as his colleagues did in the Senate, you quickly learned TEDDY was no caricature. He was a warm, passionate, thoughtful, tremendously funny man who loved his country deeply and loved the U.S. Senate. If you ever needed to find TEDDY in the Senate Chamber, all you had to do was to listen for that distinctive thunderclap of a laugh echoing across the hallowed halls as he charmed his colleagues.

He served in the Senate, as all of you know, for almost half a century alongside liberals and conservatives, Democrats and Republicans, and he befriended all of them with equal gusto.

It's great to see his friends, Senator Orrin Hatch and Senator John McCain, here this evening. It is to their credit that they so often supported TEDDY's efforts. And I say in some jest it is to TEDDY's great credit that he rarely supported their efforts.

But TEDDY's personal friendships with Orrin and John and so many others over this half century weren't simply the polite working relationships that make politics possible in our country. They're the very real and lasting bonds that make the U.S. Senate of our Nation work. That's what made TEDDY one of our greatest Senators ever.

Some people born with a famous name live off it, others enrich it. TEDDY enriched his. As we begin the task of summing up all that he has done for our Nation and so many others around the world, perhaps we can begin by acknowledging this: John Fitzgerald Kennedy inspired our America, Robert Kennedy challenged our America, and our TEDDY changed America.

Nearly every important law passed in the last half century bears his mark, and a great deal of them, of course, bear his name. TEDDY was defined by his love of our country, his passion for public service, his abiding faith, and, of course, as

[260]

Joe has said, his family. His much adored Vicki, his children, Kara, Teddy, Patrick, Caroline and Curran, his grandchildren, nieces and nephews. All of you need to know, when you weren't around and I was, how often he talked about you and how much pleasure and joy, the unbounded joy and pleasure, you brought to him.

TEDDY, of course, was a man who lived for others, as Joe has pointed out. He was a champion for countless people who otherwise might not have had one, and he never quit on them. He never gave up on the belief that we could make tomorrow a better day. Never once.

Last August, in Denver, one year to the day before his passing, TEDDY spoke at our national convention. His gait, of course, was shaky, but his blue eyes were clear, and his unmistakable voice rang with strength. As he passed the torch to another young President, TEDDY said, "The work begins anew, the hope rises again, and the dream lives on."

He spoke of the great fight of his life, ensuring that every American, regardless of their economic status, be granted the right to decent health care in our country. We're deeply saddened that he did not live to see that battle won. But, in a few short days from now, we will return to our work in TEDDY's Senate. The blistering days of August will be replaced, I pray, by the cooler days of September, and we will prevail in the way that TEDDY won so many victories in our Nation—by listening to each other, by respecting each other and the seriousness of the institution to which we belong and where TEDDY earned an immortal place in American history.

As he so eloquently eulogized his brother, Bobby, 40 years ago, TEDDY doesn't need to be enlarged in death beyond what he was in life. We'll remember him for the largeness of his spirit, the depth of his compassion, his persistence in the face of adversity, and the breadth of his achievements. We'll remember him as a man who understood better than most that America is a place of incredible opportunity, of incredible hope, and a place of redemption. He labored tirelessly to make those dreams a reality for everyone.

Those dreams, the ones he spoke of throughout his life, live on like the eternal flame that marks President Kennedy's grave, that very flame that TEDDY and Bobby lit 46 years ago. In all the years that I have known and loved this man, that eternal flame has never failed to burn brightly in TEDDY's eyes. And now as he joins his brothers on that hillside in Arlington, may the light from that flame continue to illuminate our path forward, and with the work of our own hands and the help of Almighty God, inspired by TEDDY's example, may we lift up this Nation of ours that my friend TEDDY loved so much. I thank you.

PAUL G. KIRK, JR.: Senator Dodd and Senator KENNEDY had a good staff. An alumnus of his staff who worked tirelessly on the health issue while he was there and is now a distinguished attorney in the city of Boston is Nick Littlefield. In just a moment you'll learn more about Nick's other talents, but welcome him now to the podium, Nick Littlefield.

NICK LITTLEFIELD: I think that for the Senator, one of my most important attributes as staff director for the Labor and Human Resources Committee was that I could sing. You all know that he loved to sing, of course. Vicki and he and the family members and pianists that they invited always participated in these magnificent sing-alongs. I got to sing with the Senator in many different places over so many years. In Washington and Boston and the Senate and the Cape and Maine and always on the *Mya*, we sang. Those were magnificent times.

He even had me sing to Senator Hatch as they were wrapping up the deal on children's health. That was the Senator at his best. I learned that Senator KENNEDY liked the songs that he knew best. We sang "On the Street Where You Live" dozens of times, and "Sweet Adeline" was a close second.

When we sang to a crowd, if I got too loud, he'd give me a look, and I'd know I was in trouble.

Tonight I'm going to sing one of the songs he especially loved, and which we always sang every single evening when we got together to sing. We even sang this song the last time I saw him. I think he loved this song—I know he loved this song—because it said so much about him and Vicki.

If I could have an "E."

Love, love changes everything,
Hands and faces, earth and sky.
Love, love changes everything,
How you live and how you die.
Love can make the summer fly,
Or a night seem like a lifetime.
Yes, love, love changes everything.
How I tremble, at her name.
Nothing in the world will ever be the same.

Love, love changes everything.
Days are longer, words mean more.
Love, love changes everything,
Pain is deeper than before.

Love can turn your world around.
And that world will last forever.
Yes, love, love changes everything,
Brings you glory, brings you shame.
Nothing in the world will ever be the same.

Off into the world we go,
Planning futures, shaping years.
Love comes in and suddenly all our wisdom disappears.
Love makes fools of everyone.
All the rules we make are broken.
Yes, love, love changes everything,
Live or perish in its flame.
Nothing in the world will ever be the same.

PAUL G. KIRK, JR.: Don't go away, Nick. We're going to get you back before too long. What a gift.

Our next speaker is the chief executive officer of the Commonwealth of Massachusetts. Please join me in welcoming Governor Deval Patrick.

Governor DEVAL L. PATRICK: Good evening family and friends. Like a lot of people and some of you, I suspect—I knew TED KENNEDY before I ever met him. I knew him from the grainy black and white TV images of Camelot, when my mother used to say, to no one in particular, "I love me some Kennedy."

I knew him from the moving speeches, the eulogy of his brother Robert, the Democratic Convention speech of 1980. I got occasional sightings of him as I got older, like when he came to my high school graduation with the rest of his family when his niece, and my classmate Courtney, were graduating, or at Senate Judiciary Committee hearings when important civil rights laws were under review and I was working as a young staff lawyer at the NAACP Legal Defense Fund.

But the first time I actually met him was in 1993, when I was a finalist for the U.S. Attorney position in Boston. All three finalists were invited to Washington for a final interview with the Senator, and I was nervous. He was already long an icon by then, a legend of progressive politics. We met in his famous Capitol hideaway, just the two of us.

Before I got going, I said to him that whatever the outcome of the selection process, I wanted him to know that I knew that my path from the south side of Chicago to that interview was paved in large measure by his life's work, and that I was grateful for that.

Now, I have to say that in addition to being true and heartfelt, it was not a bad interview opener. But I still didn't get the job. And though he made a great choice, he felt awkward about letting me down. I know that, because the next time I met him—unexpectedly at a party on Nantucket the following summer—he blanched at first when he saw me, and sent Vicki across the lawn just to make sure the coast was clear before he came over to say hello.

In our time, he was a master of the Senate. When President Clinton sent my name to the Senate for a senior post in the Justice Department, TED took charge of the confirmation process in the way only a master could. The morning after the nomination was announced, he had me come up to the Capitol and he positioned me in the Vice President's ceremonial office just off the Senate floor. There was an early morning vote, and as Senators came off the floor, he steered colleagues, one by one, into that office so that they could shake my hand. His theory was, it's hard to demagogue someone you've actually looked in the eye and met.

I probably met 60 Senators coming off the floor after that vote, including most of the members of the Judiciary Committee. We had more than a few laughs later about my first impressions of his colleagues, and his more studied ones. For example, the importance of just smiling and nodding when speaking with Senator Howell Heflin of Alabama, even though it was sometimes impossible to understand just what he was saying. Or how not to worry about follow-up questions during the confirmation hearings from Senator Strom Thurmond, because he couldn't hear your answer to the first questions that he had asked you.

His observations were never harsh or sarcastic. He was never mean. He was a master of the Senate, not just because he knew his colleague's foibles, but because he so clearly respected their humanity. He knew their politics, yes, but he also knew them. Of course, he was a ham. He loved to sing, as Nick Littlefield was just saying. Two summers ago, TED and Vicki came out to Tanglewood for a Boston Pops concert of Broadway show tunes. The concert featured the famed Broadway ingénue Marin Mazzie and the Tony Award-winning baritone Brian Stokes Mitchell, whom we'll hear from tonight.

Now, this is significant, because Stokes is what TED thought he sounded like when he sang.

Diane and I had invited TED and Vicki for dinner at our house after the concert. About a week before, TED called to say he was bringing Pops conductor Keith Lockhart and his then-fiancée as well. Great. A few days later he called again to say that he was inviting Marin and Stokes to dinner as well. Delighted. But Vicki was horrified. She kept apologizing for TEDDY inviting all these add-ons, as she said, right up until we all sat down to dinner, when another stranger walked into the house. Vicki and I looked at each other, assuming we had to set another unexpected place at the table. Instead, our mystery guest started to set up a keyboard, because TEDDY had also invited the pianist from the Boston Pops, so we could have proper accompaniment after dinner. And we sang every show tune we knew until the wee hours of the morning.

That was the thing about TED. He was, in the same instant, larger than life and completely down to earth. His record of achievement and contribution is unrivaled in the U.S. Senate. His humanity, his compassion, his kindness in some ways had just as great an impact.

A friend of mine told me recently the story of TED's plans to attend the funeral of Yitzhak Rabin, the late Prime Minister of Israel. The day before he left for Jerusalem, he called the White House and asked if it would be appropriate to bring some soil from Arlington Cemetery. No one knew the answer. So that day, he went to the graves of his two brothers and scooped up some soil, and he carried that precious commodity in a shopping bag to the funeral of Rabin. And after the ceremony, after the crowd dispersed, away from the cameras and the press, he carefully, respectfully, lovingly spread that soil on Rabin's grave. No publicity; just a good man doing a sweet thing.

Everyone in this room has some quiet, private example of his or her own. What's even more powerful is to think how many thousands more—many of them lining the motorcade yesterday, or filing in through the doors of this library over the course of the last 2 days to pay their respects, or signing condolence messages around the world—have private, quiet examples of their own. No politician ever made me feel more that public life could be a noble calling, or better about who I was and where I came from. He loved the Commonwealth and this country. He loved the American people, but he also believed that we could be better. It was that vision of a better America that he went to work for every day, and millions of veterans and working men and women and people with disabilities and racial and ethnic minorities—millions of pragmatic idealists who want to believe that they can make the world better through public service—are in his debt.

So many I have heard from the last couple of days are asking how best to honor his legacy. I say we should live it. His legacy is to me about what we do in our own lives and communities to keep the dream alive, to make a great country even better.

It won't be easy, especially with the profound sadness we feel today that our standard-bearer has been taken from us. But it never was easy, even for our dear lost friend. TED KENNEDY sailed more often than not into the political wind, in search of that better America. And he did it with a skill and a grace so typical of him and his family. Let us honor his life and accomplishments by making his work our own.

God bless you Vicki, and all the family. Thank you.

PAUL G. KIRK, JR.: Thank you, Governor. The last time our next speaker was on the stage, he received the John F. Kennedy Profile in Courage Award—the distinguished American, the distinguished U.S. Senator from the State of Arizona. Please welcome John McCain.

Senator JOHN McCAIN: Thank you, Paul. As Paul mentioned, I was last in this wonderful library 10 years ago, when Russ Feingold and I were honored to receive the Profile in Courage Award. TED was very gracious to our family on that occasion. It was my son Jimmy's 11th birthday, and TED went out of his way to make sure it was celebrated enthusiastically. He arranged a ride for us on a Coast Guard cutter and two birthday cakes, and led a rousing rendition of "Happy Birthday," with that booming baritone of his drowning out all other voices, as it often did on the Senate floor.

He was good company, my friend TED. He had the Irish talent for storytelling and for friendship. At the lunch he hosted for us in the family quarters on the top floor of the library, he recalled an earlier episode in our friendship, a story he delighted in retelling.

It occurred on the Senate floor, when two freshman Senators, one a Democrat and the other a Republican, neither of whom would remain long in the Senate, were getting a little personal with each other as they debated an issue, which must have seemed important at the time, but which neither TED nor I were paying much attention to.

We both happened to be on the floor at the same time, and the heat of our colleagues' exchange eventually managed to get our attention. You might think that two more senior Members of the Senate would in such a situation counsel the two junior Members to observe the courtesies and comity which theoretically are supposed to distinguish our debates.

But TED and I shared the sentiment that a fight not joined was a fight not enjoyed, and, irresistibly, we were both drawn into a debate we had no particular interest in, but which suddenly looked like fun. I struck first, castigating the young Democratic Senator for abusing my Republican colleague. Before she could respond for herself, TED rode valiantly to her rescue. And, within minutes, he and I had forgotten why we were there and what the debate was all about. We had probably even forgotten the names of our two colleagues. As one of us spoke, the other would circle the floor agitated and anxious to fire back.

After a while, we must have thought the distance between our desks too great for either of us to hear each other clearly or that the pressure of the clerk transcribing our exchanges had become too distracting. As if we both had heard some secret signal, we put down our microphones simultaneously and walked briskly to the well of the floor, where we could continue in closer quarters and in language perhaps too familiar to be recorded for posterity, which regrettably was still audible enough to be overheard by a few reporters, who were now leaning over the railing of the Press Gallery trying to ascertain just what the hell was going on between McCain and KENNEDY.

After we both were satisfied and had sufficiently impressed upon each other the particulars of proper Senatorial comportment, we ended our discussion and returned to the business that had brought us to the Chamber in the first place. I'm happy to report we succeeded in discouraging our colleagues from continuing their intemperate argument. They both had deserted the Chamber with—I was later told, for I didn't notice their escape—rather puzzled if not frightened looks on their faces. When I saw TED ambling down a Senate corridor, he was bellowing laughter, that infectious laugh of his that could wake the dead and cheer up the most beleaguered soul.

He was good company, excellent company. I'm going to miss him more than I can say. We disagreed on most issues, but I admired his passion for his convictions, his patience with the hard and sometimes dull work of legislating, and his uncanny sense for when differences could be bridged and his cause advanced by degrees.

He was a fierce advocate, and no Senator would oppose him in a debate without at least a little trepidation, often more than a little. We all listened to him, of course. He was hard to ignore. When we agreed on an issue and worked together to make a little progress for our country on an important issue, he was the best ally you could have.

You never had even a small doubt that once his word was given and a course of action decided, he would honor the letter and the spirit of the agreement. When we worked together on the immigration issue, we had a daily morning meeting with other interested Senators. He and I would meet for a few minutes in advance and decide between us which members of our respective caucuses needed a little special encouragement or, on occasion, a little straight talk. If a member tried to back out of a previous commitment, TED made certain they understood the consequences of their action. It didn't matter to him that the offender was a member of his own caucus. He was the most reliable, the most prepared, and the most persistent Member of the Senate. He took the long view. He never gave up. And though, on most issues, I very much wished he would give up, he taught me to be a better Senator.

After Labor Day, I will go back to the Senate, and I will try to be as persistent as TED was and as passionate for the work. I know I'm privileged to serve there. But I think most of our colleagues would agree, the place won't be the same without him.

PAUL G. KIRK, JR.: Next, you will have the joy and the privilege of viewing a video tribute to Senator KENNEDY directed by Ken Burns and Mark Herzog. You have heard other people speaking tonight. Tonight, you will hear about the life of TED KENNEDY in his own words.

Senator KENNEDY: The sea for me has always been a metaphor of life. The sea is a constantly evolving, changing, shifting aspect of both nature and life. That sort of exposure to the sea is both enriching and enhancing, and it's fun.

VICKI KENNEDY: The sea, the wind, the outdoors, it is the most renewing, healing place for him and always has been.

Senator KENNEDY: That's a good job. Yes. Sweat it a little bit.

Senator JOHN KERRY: He loves getting out and sailing. I think he's never more at peace and perhaps in some ways never more in touch with his family and his roots and his brothers than when he's out there sailing.

Senator KENNEDY: I grew up in a family that wanted to achieve in the sense of making a difference in people's lives.

Senator KERRY: I know that TED KENNEDY has always been unbelievably sensitive to the accomplishments of his brothers. They were his inspiration.

Congressman JOHN LEWIS: He has a legacy. He's done his very best to pick up where his two brothers left off.

Senator KENNEDY: Like my three brothers before me, I pick up a fallen standard. Sustained by their memory of our priceless years together, I shall try to carry forward that special commitment to justice, to excellence, to courage that distinguished their lives.

Congressman LEWIS: He championed the cause of those who have been left out—the poor, the elderly, our children, those without education.

VICKI KENNEDY: He was brought up to believe that, you know, to those to whom much is given, much is required. But it's really bigger than that. He really feels a moral obligation to do everything possible to make this world a better place.

Congressman LEWIS: I have heard Senator KENNEDY say on many occasions that health care is not a privilege. It is a right.

Senator KENNEDY: As long as I have a voice in the U.S. Senate, it's going to be for that Democratic platform plank that provides decent quality health care, north and south, east and west, for all Americans, as a matter of right, and not a privilege.

Senator KERRY: Because of TED KENNEDY, people have things today, they're able to do things today, they're able to reach for the American dream in ways that they never imagined.

LAUREN STANFORD, witness at Kennedy Senate hearing: I first met the Senator at something called the Children's Congress through the Juvenile Diabetes Research Foundation. He asked me to come to testify in front of Congress about stem cell research and the support for that. If I could help someone almost as much as Senator KENNEDY's helped me, then I would be a very happy person.

Senator KENNEDY: City Year has given the opportunity for the best of our young people to serve in the community.

Senator KERRY: He deeply believes that national service ought to be part of the everyday life of every single American.

ALAN KHAZEI, co-founder of City Year: He committed right away to introduce new legislation to take programs like City Year to scale to make it possible for young people all over our country to serve our country.

VICKI KENNEDY: He deeply believes in service. Even as a United States Senator, he's read every Tuesday at a local school in Washington, DC, as part of the Everybody Wins! Program.

JASMINE HARRISON: We were signed up for this reading program, and I was assigned to read with Senator KENNEDY as my reading partner. It gave me someone to want to do well for and make proud. I'm going to Virginia Commonwealth University in Richmond, and I will be majoring in education.

Senator KERRY: We're talking about a man of incredible sensitivity. He has always been there for the troops. He's always been there, understanding the sacrifices that those troops made. He's been there for their families.

BRIAN HART: We met Senator KENNEDY for the first time in November 2003, when we buried our son John at Arlington National Cemetery.

VICKI KENNEDY: Their son was lost because his Humvee was not up-armored. And they have really dedicated their lives to making sure that other men and women don't suffer the same fate.

BRIAN HART: John died just after his 20th birthday. Senator KENNEDY agreed to call hearings. Within 6 months of those hearings, all troops in Iraq had body armor. And, for that, I owe the Senator.

Senator KENNEDY: Brian and his wife, Alma, turned that enormous personal tragedy into a remarkable force for change.

BRIAN HART: Senator KENNEDY had been there for his family before I was born. He remembers where his mother was, where his father was, when they came to tell him his brother Joseph was killed. We share a wound that doesn't heal and a deep and abiding love for this country. And Senator KEN-

NEDY taught me that government can function for the common man.

VICKI KENNEDY: His patriotism, his family, his faith, really, those three things are just intrinsic in who he is. And I think of him as this guy who's got really, really big shoulders. And he's strong for all of us. And he's funny. And he sort of leads the way. He's the Pied Piper in our family.

EDWARD KENNEDY III: How many sails are up?

Senator KENNEDY: Well, let's count them. What do we call the one that's way, way, way up at the tippy top?

EDWARD KENNEDY III: Oh, that? The halyard isn't it? Oh, no, no, the fisherman?

Senator KENNEDY: Fisherman.

EDWARD KENNEDY, JR.: Don't tell me you want to put the fisherman on the other side now, Dad.

President BARACK OBAMA: The year I was born, President Kennedy sent out word that the torch had been passed to a new generation of Americans. He was right. It had. It was passed to his youngest brother. From the battles of the 1960s to the battles of today, he has carried that torch, lighting the way for all who share his American ideals.

Congressman LEWIS: I see the day when President Barack Obama and TED KENNEDY would be moving progressive legislation through the Congress to help some of the most vulnerable people in our society.

Senator KENNEDY: We will break the old gridlock and finally make health care what it should be in America, a fundamental right for all, not just an expensive privilege for the few. The people in this country are going to respond to the hopeful in a positive way. It's going to be a very, very dramatic and important alteration and change. And it's one that I'm looking forward to being a part of. We're all set now!

PAUL G. KIRK, JR.: What a treat. I now have the privilege of welcoming a friend and colleague of Senator KENNEDY, and now the senior Senator of the Commonwealth of Massachusetts, John Kerry.

Senator JOHN F. KERRY: Vicki and Teddy, Kiki, Kara, Patrick, Curran, Caroline, thank you for the privilege of sharing some words here today about my friend and my colleague of a quarter of a century. From the moment of fateful diagnosis 14 months ago until he left us, we saw grace and courage, dignity and humility, joy and laughter and so much love and gratitude lived out on a daily basis that our cup runneth over.

How devastating the prognosis was as TED left MGH with his family waving to all in June a year ago. And that he lived the next 14 months in the way that he did—optimistic, full of hope, striving and accomplishing still—that he did that is in part a miracle, yes, but it's equally a triumph of the love and the care that Vicki and their children and all who cherished him gave him in such abundance.

In many ways, I think it's fair to say that this time—these last months—were a gift to all of us. The last months of his life were in many ways the sweetest of seasons, because he saw how much we love him, how much we respect him, and how unbelievably grateful we are for his stunning years of service and friendship.

And what a year he had, my friends. He accomplished more in that span of time than many Senators do in a lifetime—mental health parity, the Tobacco Act, a health care bill out of his committee. He spoke at the Democratic Convention. He wrote his memoirs. He was there for the signing of the Edward M. Kennedy Service America Act, and received the Medal of Freedom from the President and a knighthood from the Queen of England.

I think many of you who were there would agree with me that perhaps one of the most poignant moments of all was when he was awarded an honorary degree from Harvard. His staff through the years were gathered in the front. His friends and family and admirers were scattered throughout the audience and filled the room. Vice President-elect Biden was there.

You have no idea how hard TED practiced and worked to be able to speak at Harvard and at the convention and at the White House, and to make a speech that lived up to his high standards. He took the stage at Harvard and, for a few moments, we all worried that it would be difficult to pull off. And then, before you know it, his voice began to soar and the pace picked up, and he inspired us all again with a stunning restatement of his purpose in public life. When it was over, the applause never wanted to end. He stayed on the stage, reaching out to us and we to him, and we wanted him to stay there forever.

I first met TED KENNEDY when I was 18 years old as a volunteer for his first Senate campaign in the summer before I went to college. I met him again when I returned from Vietnam, and we veterans encamped on the Mall in Washington. It was TED KENNEDY who had the courage to come down to the Mall one night, and in a tent listen to us talk about Vietnam. We were controversial, but TED broke the barriers, and other Senators followed.

He worked his heart out for me in the Presidential race of 2004. And he made the difference in Iowa. When we were down in the polls and I was slugging it out there, TED brought his humor, his energy, and his eloquence to Davenport to help melt the snow of that State. There we were, just 2 weeks before the caucuses, and his voice boomed out in this room: "You voted for my brother. You voted for my other brother. You didn't vote for me." And as the crowd roared with laughter, TED bellowed, "But we're back here for John Kerry, and, if you vote for John Kerry, I will forgive you. You can have three out of four," he said, "and I will love you, and I will love Iowa."

And let me tell you, Iowa loved him. We had a lot of fun there. He would open an event, and he would come out and say: "I want to talk to you about a bold, handsome, intelligent leader, a man who should not only be President, but who should end up on Mount Rushmore. But enough about me. Now I will talk about John Kerry."

After that agonizing Tuesday night in November when we fell so short in one State, there were TED and Vicki on a Wednesday morning sitting with Teresa and me in the kitchen in Boston as we prepared to concede. He was always there when you needed him. And so were Sunny and Splash, incidentally, when you didn't.

Once, when we were at a Senate retreat, TED had just spoken, and then Joe Biden got up to make a point and rejoinder. As Joe got more forceful in his argument, he started to gesture, and he took steps toward TED. Boom! Sunny and Splash were up on their feet barking wildly, defending KENNEDY territory with a vengeance. And, ladies and gentlemen, for the first time in history, we witnessed a Biden rhetorical retreat.

I have to tell you, one of my really favorite moments was TED campaigning with my daughter, Vanessa, who is here. They were campaigning in New Mexico, visiting an Indian reservation, and the tribal medicine man wanted to bestow a blessing. He took a feather and he chanted, and he asked that TED and Vanessa stand side by side and extend their hands and bow their heads. With a sacred feather, he touched their feet and he touched their foreheads, and he touched their hands, all the while chanting away. And when he finished, TED leaned over to Vanessa and whispered, "I think we just got married." A couple of months later, she got a note from TEDDY which said, "No matter what happens, we will always have New Mexico."

One of the framed notes in TED's Senate office was a thank you from a colleague for a gift, a special edition of "Profiles in Courage." This is what it said. "I brought it home and reread it. What an inspiration. Thank you, my friend, for your many courtesies. If the world only knew." It was signed by Trent Lott, the Republican leader of the Senate.

Indeed, if everyone only knew. When George Wallace was wounded in an assassination attempt, the first to visit him was TED KENNEDY. When Joe Biden underwent brain surgery for an aneurysm, the first to board the train to Wilmington was TED KENNEDY. When Jesse Helms announced that he had to undergo heart valve surgery, Helms told his constituents back in North Carolina, "It's no piece of cake, but it sure beats listening to TED KENNEDY on the Senate floor." So, TED wrote a note to Jesse saying, "I would be happy to send you tapes of my recent Senate speeches if that will help your speedy recovery."

And just 2 weeks ago, when I was in the hospital after hip surgery, just like Chris Dodd, there was TED KENNEDY on the phone, asking how I was doing, with all that he was dealing with.

In his life, as we all know, TED knew the dark night of loss. I think that's why his empathy was global and deeply personal. After my father died of cancer just days before the convention in 2000, there was a knock at the door, completely unexpected, and standing there on the front porch was TED KENNEDY, dropping by to hug and talk and just to pass time with us.

For 25 years, I was privileged to work by his side, learning from the master. Over the years, I have received hundreds of handwritten notes from TED, some funny, some touching, a few correcting me, all of them special treasures now. He thanked me for my gift of a Catholic study Bible, commenting, "My mother would be very grateful to you for keeping me in line." He thanked me for a particularly challenging charter lift home after 9/11, when it was hard to get anything in the air. And he wrote: "Here's a riddle for you. What

[274]

do you get when you make three calls to the FAA, two calls to the Secretary of Transportation, and three calls to Signature Flight Support? You get a great trip to Boston." His way of saying thank you.

He thanked Teresa and me for the gift of a vintage bottle, concluding, "I just hope that I have aged as well as this wine."

The personal touch TED brought to life extended, as we know, well beyond Senate colleagues. It reflected the kind of man that he was and the kind of laws that he wrote. For 1,000 days in the White House, as Chris Dodd mentioned, President Kennedy inspired. For 80 days on the Presidential campaign trail, Robert Kennedy gave us reason to believe in hope again. And for more than 17,000 days as a U.S. Senator, TED KENNEDY changed the course of history as few others have.

Without him, there might still be a military draft. The war in Vietnam might have lasted longer. There might have been delays in granting the Voting Rights Act or in passing Medicare or Medicaid. Soviet Jewish refuseniks might have been ignored, and who would have been there to help them as TED did?

Without him, we might not have stood up against apartheid as forcefully as we did, and the barriers to fair immigration might still be higher today. If everyone only knew. Without TED, 18-year-olds might not be able to vote. There might not be a Martin Luther King Day, Meals on Wheels, student loans, increases in the minimum wage, equal funding for women's college sports, health insurance, the Family and Medical Leave Act, the Americans with Disabilities Act, workplace safety, AmeriCorps, children's health insurance.

If everyone only knew. He stood against judges who would turn back the clock on constitutional rights. He stood against the war in Iraq, his proudest vote. And for nearly four decades and all through his final days, he labored with all of his might to make health care a right for all Americans, and we will do that in his honor.

In these last months, every visit TED made to the Senate elicited an unstoppable outpouring of affection. Tears welled up in the eyes of Republicans and Democrats. Everyone missed his skills, his booming call to arms and conscience. On his last visit, Chris Dodd and I sat in the back row beside his desk and listened to TEDDY regale us with an imitation of his efforts to practice throwing out a ball for the Red Sox opening game. He laughed and he poked fun at how reluctant his hands and muscles were to obey his commands. I was in awe of this moment of humility and self-deprecating humor in the face of genuine frustration.

As he often said over the years, we have to take issues seriously, but never take ourselves too seriously. He was a master of that, too, and it was one of the great lessons that he taught me. In the end, his abiding gift was his incomparable love of life and his commitment to make better the life of the world.

In between his time changing the world, he found time to capture it in marvelous paintings. He was a talented, gifted artist—and as we know, an incurable romantic. Who else would have thought to hide their engagement ring on a coral reef in St. Croix as they were swimming and diving so Vicki could find it. It never occurred to him that the waters might wash the ring away. But one thing is certain, their love endured from then until now, and it will endure forever.

Massachusetts has always had its own glorious love affair with the sea. Like his brothers before him, saltwater was in his veins. TEDDY lived by the sea, and he lived joyously on it. The evening he passed away, I looked out at the ocean where gray sky met gray water. No horizon. The sky almost seemed to be in mourning. It was not a time for sailing. But the next afternoon as I sat at his home, I looked out at a perfect Nantucket Sound, and I thought to myself with certainty, "He's on a schooner now. He's sailing." Jack, Joe, Bobby on the foredeck, Rosemary, Eunice, Kathleen, Pat, trading stories with their parents, and TEDDY at the helm steering his steady course. Sail on, my friend. Sail on.

PAUL G. KIRK, JR.: The next speaker is one who has seen Senator KENNEDY's name and the names of his colleagues on legislation—another great American, who sat across the aisle and serves our country well in the U.S. Senate. Please welcome Senator Orrin Hatch.

Senator ORRIN G. HATCH: This is a tremendous honor to be in this wonderful city and this State where our revolution was begun. I'm just so grateful to be here.

Vicki, Teddy, Patrick, Kara, Ethel and Jean, and all the rest of the Kennedy family, it's a great honor for me to be here with you today, to talk about a man I have so much regard for, so much reverence for, with whom I've done battle for 33 years and have enjoyed every minute of it—like two fighting brothers, to be honest with you.

[276]

There are a lot of things I could say about TED KENNEDY's career, but what I'd like to do is just take a few minutes to talk about TED KENNEDY, the man, and TED KENNEDY, my friend.

By the time I came to the Senate in 1977, TEDDY was already a giant among Senators. As a Republican coming from Utah, I stated numerous times on the campaign trail that I planned to come to Washington to fight TED KENNEDY. In fact, I used to say that KENNEDY's name was my very best fundraiser in the country.

When I came to Washington, I hadn't the slightest idea that I would eventually have a strong working relationship with and love for the man that I came to fight. If you had told me that he would become one of my closest friends in the world, I probably would have suggested that you needed professional help. But that's exactly what happened. People called TEDDY and me the odd couple, which was certainly true. There are few men with whom I have had less in common.

TED was born in a famous well-to-do family in Boston. He attended private schools and Harvard University, was politically liberal and liberal in his lifestyle—at least until he married Vicki, who set him straight, by the way. I grew up in a poor working class family in Pittsburgh, PA. I attended public school and the Harvard of Utah, BYU.

Great school, Harvard. While TED often played the role of the affable Irishman, I was the teetotaling Mormon bishop. He was so proud one day to discover that I'm also Scots-Irish. Yet despite our differences, we were able to work out a lot of things together.

And that was due in large part to TEDDY's willingness to recognize and work with those who shared his goals, even if they had different ideas on how to reach those goals. One of the defining moments as a Senator came when I met two families from Provo, UT. The parents of these families were humble and hard working. They were prudent. They were frugal. And they were able to provide food and shelter for their children. But the one necessity they couldn't afford was health insurance. This is what inspired me to begin my work with TED in creating the SCHIP Program, which continues to provide health care and coverage for millions of children throughout the world. It passed with bipartisan support, even though it came at a seemingly inopportune time, politically speaking.

[277]

Over the years, TED and I worked successfully to get both Republicans and Democrats on board for causes such as assistance to AIDS victims. We passed the three AIDS bills and equal rights for the disabled. Our latest collaboration came just this year in the form of the Edward M. Kennedy Serve America Act, a new law that is designed to empower and encourage private citizens of all ages to volunteer in their communities. I named the bill after TED.

I don't think any of these bills could have passed if it were not for TEDDY's willingness to put bipartisanship ahead of partisanship. In 1962, President John F. Kennedy famously said:

> We must think and act not only for the moment but for our time. I am reminded of the story of a great French Marshal Lyautey, who once asked his gardener to plant a tree. The gardener objected that the tree was slow-growing and would not reach maturity for 100 years. The Marshal replied, "In that case, there is no time to lose. Plant it this afternoon."

The President's wisdom was not lost on his youngest brother. By force of will driven by the sense of immediacy that he brought to every endeavor, TED KENNEDY had the ability to take actions today that might not bear fruit until the distant tomorrow. Like all good leaders when they struck out on a mission, he was able to inspire many to follow him until the job was done, no matter how long it took or how hard the task was.

Now that is not to suggest that working with TED on a difficult piece of legislation was sheer drudgery, although sometimes it could be utterly fatiguing. More often—and this is what most of us who worked closely with him or against him will miss—TED KENNEDY would bring a sense of joy to even the most difficult, contentious legislative negotiating session.

While many of my more conservative constituents have run me over the coals for just being willing to sit in the same room with TEDDY KENNEDY, the truth is that he and I didn't agree on much. We didn't agree on a lot of things. We sat next to each other in the Health Committee for the better part of two decades. Some may not remember this, but there was a time when smoking was allowed during the committee meetings and hearings. And during that time, you could always tell when TEDDY and I were in an argument or were fighting by the amount of cigar smoke that he blew my way as a nonsmoking Mormon.

If there was a particularly strong disagreement, he would just sit back in his chair puffing smoke my way, giving me an actual headache to go along with the political headaches he gave to all of us on the Republican side. At other times in committee, or on the floor, or even in the press, TEDDY would lay into me with the harshest red meat liberal rhetoric you can imagine.

But just minutes later, he'd come over and put his arm around me and ask, "How did I do, Orrin?"

I will not tell you every response that I made to him. Of course, this wasn't spiteful. TEDDY just knew how to push people's buttons. It was one of the qualities that made him such an effective Senator. And for those who were lucky enough to become his friends, it was a source of no small amount of laughter.

It was in the late 1980s when I knew that I'd finally made it into TEDDY's inner circle. I was working out in the Senate gym one day in December when TEDDY came in and asked me if I was going to be at his party that night. Now I'm ashamed to admit that I'd been in the Senate for over a decade, and I hadn't heard about the annual Kennedy staff Christmas party. Those who have been to one or more of those parties will agree a different side of TEDDY was on display on those nights.

At the first party I attended, TEDDY came out and did a surprisingly accurate and hilarious impersonation of Elvis Presley—tight jumpsuit and all. He looked awful as far as I was concerned.

Then he joined the staff performing skits making fun of Ronald Reagan, Dan Quayle and even himself. It's really too bad that TEDDY was never asked to host "Saturday Night Live." But of course, serving in the Senate doesn't really leave you with enough time to do that sort of thing. Just ask John McCain.

Whenever TEDDY and I would introduce a bill together, TEDDY would tell reporters that if he and I were on the same bill, it was obvious that one of us hadn't read it. It always got a huge laugh, and I was just left there grinning, pretending it was the first time I'd ever heard him say that.

So one time I decided to come prepared. Right after TEDDY made his remark, I pushed out a copy of the bill that was heavily highlighted and said, "Here you go, TED, you can have my copy. The important parts are already underlined." TED got a big laugh out of that, and so did all the reporters who were there.

Complementing TEDDY's sense of humor was his personal generosity. On one occasion after a particularly late night in the Senate, I have to say that TEDDY was feeling no pain at that time. He was with his friend, Chris Dodd—my friend.

I did what my former AA asked me to do. He called me one day—it was Frank Manson and he had just become the Mormon Church Mission president in Boston, MA, presiding over 200 young Mormon missionaries.

When he called me, Frank Manson said, "Could I ask you a favor?" And I said, "Sure." He said, "Would you be willing to come to speak to my 200 young missionaries up here in Boston?" I said, "Well, for you, Frank, I will." He said, "Can I ask you another favor?" I said, "Sure." He said, "Would you ask TEDDY KENNEDY to come and speak, too?" I said, "Well, I don't know. But I'll ask him."

He said, "Well, can I ask another favor?" I said, "My gosh, what's that?" He said, "Will you ask TEDDY to get Faneuil Hall for the meeting?" I said, "Oh my goodness. Well, I'll ask him."

So that evening, when TEDDY and Chris were feeling no pain, I walked off the floor and TEDDY put his arm around me and he said, "Oh, Orrin, I want you to come up to Hyannis Port and I want you to go sailing with me. I want you to do that." I said, "Great."

I said, "TEDDY, I have a favor to ask of you." He said, "You do? So what's that?" I said, "Do you remember Frank Manson, my administrative assistant?" He said, "Oh, yes, good guy, good guy."

I said, "Well, he's now the mission president in the Mormon Church. He's asked that you and I come and speak to over 200 young Mormon missionaries in Boston." He said, "Done." Just like that.

I said, "Well, I have another favor to ask of you. He would like you to get Faneuil Hall." He said, "Done."

So the next day I got into the office, and I sent a nice letter thanking TEDDY and got it over to him. I saw him later in the day, and he was holding that letter and his hands were shaking. He said, "Orrin, what else did I agree to last night?"

After telling these things, my eyes start to water. My nose starts to run. It was just a mess, I tell you. But in any event, TEDDY KENNEDY and Orrin Hatch appeared before 200 young Mormon missionaries in Faneuil Hall, and they will never forget the tremendous altruistic talk that he gave to them on that day.

All I can say is, it was really something. He didn't try to weasel out of it. Instead, he produced the hall, and he gave that beautiful speech. I was impressed as usual, and those missionaries will never forget that. Though they were of a different faith, he commended them for their willingness to serve a cause bigger than themselves and thanked them for their selflessness. This is just one example of the graciousness of my dear friend, TED KENNEDY.

There was another time when the Mormon Church was nearing completion of its temple here in Boston. I was approached by several people working in the temple and informed that the city would not allow a spire to be placed on the top of the temple with an angel on top of it as is customary on Mormon temples. I immediately called TED and asked for help. Not long after the conversation, he called me back and said, "All of Western Massachusetts will see the Angel Gabriel on the top of the Mormon temple."

Though I was tempted to leave it alone, I had to inform TEDDY it was actually the Angel Maroni, a prominent figure in the LDS faith. At that point, TEDDY replied, "Does this mean I'm going to get another Book of Mormon for Christmas?" Of course he did. Of course, TEDDY was always respectful of my faith and that of others, but everyone around us knew that I liked to give him a hard time.

One thing that has been recounted in the tributes of the last few days has been TEDDY's dedication to his family, what he has been to his own children, to his mother, to his nieces and nephews and to his siblings. I can attest to this. After I spent some time getting to know the Kennedy family, Eunice started interceding for me when TED and I disagreed. I love to this day Eunice Kennedy Shriver and Sargent Shriver, and I love their family. Let me just say Bobby is one of my best friends and so are the other Shriver family members. What they do for this country and what Eunice did is just beyond belief.

Well, when TED and I weren't getting along one day, Eunice told TEDDY, "I don't want you mistreating that nice, young Senator Hatch from Utah."

I'm only a couple years younger than TED. But, it was just wonderful to have her stand up for me. And when he and I had really tough trouble reaching agreement on really important occasions, and he'd get really recalcitrant and bull-headed, and his back would go in the air, I would say, "All right, TEDDY, I'm going to see Eunice." He'd say, "No, no, no. Don't do that. We'll work it out." Well, Eunice had a great effect on both of us and we loved her very, very much.

The love TEDDY had for his family provided him with insight and empathy for others. This was reflected in his policy and in his dealings with his friends.

When TEDDY lost his wonderful mother, I snuck up here to Boston. I didn't tell him I was coming. I just thought I would sneak into the back of this beautiful Catholic Church and pay my respects. But they caught me, and he moved me right up closer to the family.

When I lost my parents, TED was there with empathetic words and sincere sympathy. TED was a man experienced with facing family tragedy, having grieved more than his share. And yet he became stronger for it. He and Vicki flew to Utah to attend my mother's funeral. I didn't know they were coming. It was a gesture that will always mean a great deal to me.

It was in a humble Mormon Church, and I had to give the eulogy. So, he was right in the front row with my family, and I just gave him the business as much as everybody else. But it was wonderful, and I'll never forget it.

I love Vicki Kennedy as well. She's been a tremendously wonderful wife to my friend, TED. I've said publicly that I've been present to witness two major changes in TED KENNEDY's life and career. The first was after the elections of 1980. Freed from the pressures that come from Presidential ambitions, TEDDY returned to the Senate with a singular focus on accomplishing his legislative goals, on building consensus and doing good for the American people.

The second change was, for those who knew TEDDY, I think much more profound. It's when he met and married Vicki. Vicki was the love and light of TEDDY's life. Their marriage in many respects saved TEDDY. He was forever a different man. He was still the fierce stubborn leader in the Senate he always was, but it was clear from that time on that he enjoyed his life and the role he played far more than he had in the past. TEDDY and Vicki's marriage made him a better man and a better Senator.

I remember one time he got mad as heck at me and demanded to come to the office. I brought him in and he started yelling at me. Finally, I just said, "Wait a minute." I said, "You know, I wrote a song for you and Vicki." He said, "You did?"

I said, "Yes. So you want to hear it?" He said, "Oh, yes." He forgot all about his anger. I just had a little cassette, and I played it for him. He said, "I've got to have that." It was called "Souls Along the Way." Actually that song was in

"Oceans 12." You can't hear it, but it was in there. I could hear it, barely.

Soon after that, I was working as usual, I think July 3 of that year in Salt Lake City, and I got this phone call from TED KENNEDY. He was out on his boat, as usual. And he said, "Orrin—I just played that song for Vicki. She's over there crying at the end of the boat. She loved it." I said, "That's great."

Then I said, "Why aren't you working like I have to work?" He just laughed, because he knew that his life was a far different one from mine. And I laughed, too, because I knew it as well.

On my way here today, let me just say that I thought about our relationship and how much I sorely miss him. A couple of months ago, we met for our last hour together, had pictures taken together. That meant so much to me, and I have to say it was a wonderful occasion.

I miss fighting with him in public, and joking with him in the background. I miss all the things that we knew we could do together and what he had to do with others as well.

On my way here today, I thought about the Apostle Paul, who shortly before his death wrote, "For I am now ready to be offered and the time of my departure is at hand. I fought a good fight. I have finished my course. I have kept the faith."

So as I came here, I just wanted to write a few thoughts down in my own handwriting. And I hope you won't mind if I read them to you just before I finish.

Some are weak and some are strong.
Some people go along to get along.

Some people are larger than life.
Some are born in poverty, some are born in wealth.
Some are like a flashing light that dissipates in air.
Some are like a gift of life who never find a spare,

Some fulfill their destinies.
Others lose each day.
Some are filled with daily joy, while others waste away.
Some are like my liberal friend.
God be with you till we meet again.

In the end, the good thing's won.
He leaves the Earth a better place.
In the end, we all can smile.
He cared for all the human race.

In the end, we all look back and see many things.
In the end, we all look up—he's carried there on angels' wings.
In the end, those in repose are greeting as we speak.
In the end, the darling rose no longer has to seek.

I will miss my Irish friend. God be with you till we meet again. God bless this family. God bless all of you. Thanks so much.

PAUL G. KIRK, JR.: We all know how much Senator KEN-NEDY loved songs. And now it's my pleasure to introduce the vocalist that he admired so very much, Brian Stokes Mitchell, accompanied by Vytas Baksys on the piano, with the song that captures a lot of what tonight is about.

BRIAN STOKES MITCHELL: Thank you. Senator KENNEDY really loved the arts as we all know. And those of us in the arts really have loved Senator KENNEDY also. It's how we met, through music, through singing. And it was rare that we wouldn't greet each other with not a hello but a sponta-neous duet of "Some Enchanted Evening" or "Oh What a Beautiful Morning." And I have to say to my heart and to my ear and to my mind, he is one of my favorite singers ever, because he sang with his heart.

Singing notes is easy. Singing from your heart is hard. And he sang as he lived his life and as he did everything else.

There's a song that I sang for him at one of his birthdays quite a few years ago. And I can't sing it now without think-ing of him. It is about an impossible dream or somebody who dreams the impossible, to make the impossible possible.

The quest is what's important. And I have to say now that Senator KENNEDY and this song will forever share a very special place in my heart.

"THE IMPOSSIBLE DREAM," from "Man of La Mancha," Music by Mitch Leigh, Lyrics by Joe Darion:

To dream the impossible dream,
To fight the unbeatable foe,
To bear with unbearable sorrow,
To run where the brave dare not go.

To right the unrightable wrong,
To love pure and chaste from afar,
To try when your arms are too weary,
To reach the unreachable star.

This is my quest,
To follow that star,
No matter how hopeless,
No matter how far.

To fight for the right,
Without question or pause,
To be willing to march into Hell
For a heavenly cause.

And I know, if I'll only be true
To this glorious quest,
That my heart will lie peaceful and calm
When I'm laid to my rest.

And the world will be better for this,
That one man, scorned and covered with scars,
Still strove with his last ounce of courage,
To reach the unreachable star

PAUL G. KIRK, JR.: Senator KENNEDY's grandfather, as you all know, presided over this city many years ago and the Senator enjoyed a working and friendly and warm relationship with the incumbent mayor of the city of Boston. We welcome him this evening, the Honorable Thomas Menino.

Mayor THOMAS M. MENINO: Thank you, Paul. Paul said he was going to ask me to sing. I got thrown out of the choir when I was in the eighth grade, and I haven't sung since.

Ted KENNEDY was my friend. I feel tremendous sadness today, but also a sense of pride. The history books will show that Boston wasn't just the cradle of liberty. It birthed its champions, too. Senator EDWARD M. KENNEDY was born here. The man of the Senate came from the Boston neighborhood of Dorchester, where he now rests.

Angela and I, together with all Bostonians, are mourning a native son. Many of our neighbors have met TED—some were immigrants from our ports, others were trained in our hospitals, or educated in our schools. They stepped foot onto the greenway, they knew his work.

Our thoughts and prayers are with Vicki and the entire Kennedy family. Your imprint across the city is indelible. The new Edward Kennedy Institute is another lasting legacy of the Kennedys from Boston.

I hate to say it in these tough financial times, but we need to buy some more red paint to extend the Freedom Trail.

I had the privilege of serving in the office that TEDDY's grandfather once held. Honey Fritz would have had a good laugh at TEDDY and me sitting together at Fenway Park. TEDDY called me up one day and he said, "Let's go to the ball game next week." It was a very cold night, but we decided to go. And I said, "TEDDY, I'll get a seat upstairs in the luxury boxes." He insisted we stay out of the skybox so we could be with the people.

By about the fourth or fifth inning, Senator KENNEDY finally leaned over to me and said, "Mr. Mayor, I love the people, but I'm freezing my bottom off."

I'll always be thankful that he worked so hard to bring the Democratic National Convention to Boston. Yes, because it put our city on display to the world, but also because it gave Senator KENNEDY and me reason to spend so much time together. We worked hard. We worked relentlessly. We had tremendous fun doing it. We played so much good cop/bad cop that I couldn't remember sometimes what role I was supposed to play. Senator KENNEDY would say to a person, "John, umm, I'd like to see $1.5 million from you folks." And within a half an hour later, this person would call me up and say, "Does he really mean that?" I'd say, "Well, if you gave us $1 million, we'd be happy." And that happened so often, it raised the money for the Democratic National Convention.

I know that one of the great highlights of his career was addressing that convention. TEDDY called Boston a place where every street is history's home. That's true of the old North Church and Faneuil Hall. It's true now of all the places Senator KENNEDY walked.

We have followed in his steps on a path to equality and opportunity. TEDDY was always out front on the issues. It's something I admired and tried to emulate. Sometimes it got us into trouble. Several years ago, at the beginning of the green revolution, we were supposed to go to a green event together. I had been driving around in a compact hybrid. I complained all the time it was tiny.

Well, our staffs thought—staffs always get you in trouble—our staffs thought it would be good for TEDDY and me to ride over to the event together in my hybrid. We're both small guys, by the way. Of course, it was really too small for me and certainly too small for the two of us. We were like two overgrown peas in a pod. We sought alternate transportation, but we never stopped fighting for progress together.

On the occasion of TEDDY's 70th birthday, I threw a party for him in Boston and made him an honorary Harbor Master. I mention it, because thinking about him that day makes me smile. The Senator took it a bit too seriously, but set out to try to actually direct traffic on Boston Harbor. I mention it, also, because I think it was a role suited to him. The Harbor Master is a guardian. He watches over the tired and the weary and the worn out. That was TED KENNEDY.

When the phone rings, I miss TEDDY's voice on the end of the line. When debates rage, I'm sad he won't echo in the well of the Senate. The sounds of schoolkids accepting diplomas, immigrants taking citizenship oaths, neighbors offering neighbors a helping hand—we'll forever hear his call for justice. I'll always hear the familiar tunes of a loyal friend.

He was a strong supporter of the Health Careers Academy in the city of Boston, one of our pilot schools. He was dedicated to health care. I sent a letter to the board of trustees the other day, and we're going to name that school after ED-WARD M. KENNEDY, because that's what they're about. They train kids to get into the health care field. And we know how much TEDDY loved health care, how he believed in it and how he led the charge. And shortly, we will have reforms in health care because of TED KENNEDY. I want to make sure that school in Boston reminds everybody how hard TEDDY fought for those things.

Vicki and family, thanks. Thank you for what you are. Thank you.

PAUL G. KIRK, JR.: John Culver was a Harvard classmate of Senator KENNEDY's and a football teammate. Worked in his Senate office. Went back home to Iowa. Served in the Congress of the United States, and then the Senate of the United States. Great friend for a long time—John Culver.

Senator JOHN C. CULVER: Thank you very much, Paul. To Vicki, who, Orrin Hatch said, really was the love of TED's life. To his sister, Jean Smith, who always told me that she was TED's favorite sister. And to all the children—Ted's children, Vicki's children, and all the extended Kennedy family. In a real sense, everyone here in this room, I think feels very strongly, a part of that extraordinary family.

It was in the winter, I believe, 1975, when TED called me and said, "I'd like you to come up to Boston with me. They've suggested several sites for the John F. Kennedy Museum and Library, and I'd like you to come along." So I did. And I remember it was a winter day, rather cold and overcast, and there was snow on the ground. When we came to this particular place and looked across Dorchester Bay, saw Boston, saw the water, TED turned to me and he said, "I think Jack would like this place." And, of course, it wasn't many years later that this library was built, and I think we all agree that Jack would really like this place.

But also, I was reminded, again, as I came here to the library, of that little sailboat out front, the *Victura*, which Joe Kennedy talked about.

I have a fond memory of the *Victura* myself. It was when TED and I were in summer school in 1953 at Harvard. TED turned to me one day, "You know, why don't you come with me this weekend. I'm going down to the Cape. It's a lot of fun. There's gonna be a sailboat race. It's called the Nantucket Regatta—it's a lot of fun. I want you to come down and be part of my crew on the sailboat race." I said, "TED, I'm sure that's an honor to be invited to be part of your crew on a sailboat race, but I've never been on a sailboat. I think I've seen a picture of a sailboat." I continued, "I come from Iowa, and the only boats I ever saw were barges on the Mississippi River." "Well," he said, "There's nothing to it." How many times have we all heard TED say, "There's nothing to it?"

At that time we were both young. I didn't quite understand that comment, but I grew to understand it later. I said, "OK." So we got in the car and TED and I were driving down to the Cape. He turned on the car radio, and we were enjoying the trip, listening to some music. This was on Friday afternoon.

Suddenly, the radio broadcast was interrupted with a bulletin, and the bulletin said, "Serious storm warnings. Danger at sea. Don't anyone go out in the ocean." I said, "Well, TED, I guess the sailboat trip is off." "Ugh," he said, "There's nothing to it." I said, "Well the fellow on the radio thought there was something to it." He said, "There's nothing to it." I thought, he must know what he's doing. He lives down there, and I've never been on the ocean.

When we got down to the Kennedy house, it was about 3 or 4 o'clock in the afternoon. There were dark black storm clouds gathering. I said, "TED, doesn't it look kind of scary?" He said, "Nothing to it." So I said, "Well, I'm hungry." He said, "I'm hungry too." It was about 3, and we'd missed lunch. We went right to the kitchen, where I often went with him when we were there. The cook was still there, and he said, "I'm just finishing up here, but I have some leftover salmon salad mix, and I could make you boys some sandwiches, if you'd like." We both thought that was a good idea. We didn't have a whole lot of time, so I only had two salmon salad sandwiches, and I had a quart of milk with it. I would've had more, but we didn't have time. TED said, "Come on, we gotta get going now." It was about 4 o'clock.

So we went out. In those days, they didn't have all the fancy docks and everything, even around the family compound. It was a beach, as I remember. He said, "We gotta get in this boat." I looked out on the horizon for the boat, and I said, "Where's the boat?" He said, "There's the boat." Well, if any of you have seen the *Victura* out front—that was the boat. That's the boat he pointed out, and said we were going on a sailboat race with it. It's 26 feet long. TED and I both at the time weighed over 200 pounds. We were both over 6 feet tall.

He said, "Yep, that's the boat. Let's get it out into the water." So I did what I could to help get it out into the water. There were huge waves now. There was thunder. There was lightning. The sky was black. I could hardly get in the boat, it was bouncing so much and he's at the till. Suddenly, I realized, this "friend" of mine I thought I knew quite well, started screaming at me. Shouting at me. I was terrified.

After a while I was more terrified of him than the storm. I didn't know this man. He kept screaming at me—"the spinnaker, the gib, portside, secure that." As you know, TED's not always easy to understand, even when you know what he's talking about. And now, with his roar, with the incredible roar of the ocean and the waves, and this little, tiny boat bouncing all over like a cork—it's my fault! I'm just hanging on for dear life. We'd gotten about 200 miraculous yards out, and I lost the sandwiches. I thought I was going to die! I've never been so miserable—hanging over the side of the boat, and he's screaming at me. Do you think he said, "Hey, I'm sorry you feel bad?" Forget it. Somehow I pulled myself together. Somehow we rode this boat in that incredible storm—unbelievable. I'm still scared even thinking about it.

We finally, finally, got all the way to Nantucket. It's 11 o'clock at night, and I'm saying to TED, "Which hotel do we stay in?" and TED said, "We're not staying in a hotel." I said, "We're not? We're all wet, we're all cold—where are we staying, TEDDY?" "We're staying on the boat," he said.

I realized then that I was with something out of Captain Ahab, "Moby Dick." Believe it or not, there were four cushions, and they were of course all wet. He took two. I wanted to take three, but he took two, I took two. There were 3 inches of cold seawater, seaweed, everything. We pulled the boat up on the beach, and that's where we spent the night.

Well, this was a lot of fun so far. The next day we got up. "We need a third man on our crew," TED said. I didn't have any idea what we needed, but I needed a lot more than one more man.

So we went walking in Nantucket, and sure enough, there was a poor little guy who was a salesman at the Andover shop in Cambridge. TED went up to him and said, "Would you like to go sailing with us today?" and the poor kid said, "Yeah, I'd like to."

We shanghaied him. We took him, just like I was taken. TED pulled him on the boat, and pulled me on the boat, and off we go for the races. The races started and from that point on all I remember is TED yelling, yelling to me to get up on the right side, the front of the boat, or the left side. He always claims that when I was to rotate with the other guy, I said, "You heard him, get up there!" Of course, it was really my turn to go up.

I didn't see anything but this cold water, sunburn, T-shirt—it was a nightmare. I didn't even see any of the other boats, but we kept going around, around, around.

Finally, this thing was mercifully over, and TED seemed satisfied. I had no idea, but probably I was satisfied too—I lived through it. I looked out and it was like a mirage. Here's this great, big yacht. And it was the *Honey Fitz*. TED wanted to surprise me. We all know how much fun TED has making his friends uncomfortable at times. He hadn't told me. But Ambassador Kennedy had come out to watch the race, and had brought three or four friends along, and they were out there in the big *Honey Fitz*, named after TED's grandfather. I never saw anything that looked so good to me as that boat.

TED said, "Now we're gonna board the boat. They're gonna tow the *Victura* back behind the boat." I thought, "My God this is OK!" So we come alongside the *Honey Fitz*. I remember, it was just like Eddie Rickenbacker in "South Pacific." I'd been on the boat, starving to death on the water. Cold. Miserable.

Ambassador Kennedy had a megaphone, and he leaned over the boat and said, "Good race, good race, TEDDY. But I got some bad news for you. The captain says the sea is far too rough to tow you boys back on that boat. So you'll have to sail back."

I couldn't believe my ears. I wanted to jump out of the boat and take my chances they'd pick me up. He said, "I have something for you in this container." Clam chowder, hot, vacuum-packed with the clam things on it. He's lowering it with a rope. TEDDY always claimed that I grabbed it, tore the rope off, ripped off the top without even opening it—just tore the top—then proceeded to chug-a-lug the whole canteen. The only thing I missed was what went down my T-shirt, I said, "Boy that was good!" and TEDDY said, "What about me? I'm supposed to have some of that."

I don't think it was entirely true that I drank all of it, but I drank most of it. Anyway, they pull the rope up, and we're on our own again. I'm 24 hours on this boat. Now we head back home. Fortunately the trip back wasn't that bad after what I'd been through. It was fairly calm. We get in sight of Hyannis after many hours. You can see the lights on the house. Probably a half-mile away. I'm thinking, "Boy, we'll be in a hot shower in no time."

Suddenly, the boat stopped—no wind. I said, "TEDDY, no wind." I could see the house. I didn't know how we were gonna get there. It was too far to swim. I said, "TEDDY, what do you do now?" He said, "We get out of the boat." I said, "We get out of the boat?" "Yeah," he said, "one of us has gotta push, and the other pull—pull the rope ahead of the boat." You can't believe it, can you? I couldn't believe it.

After 24 hours on this boat, its 11 or midnight. We climb out of the boat and into the water again. He's pulling and I'm pushing, and after a while we finally make it to shore. When we were back at summer school, it was a whole week before I could get the seaweed taste out of my mouth.

In the following years I was fortunate to take many, many sailboat trips with TED, not only around Hyannis and the island, but to Maine, the Caribbean, and to the Greek islands. Those were some of the most memorable, really truly enjoyable, pleasurable memories I ever had. Always full of fun, always full of joy and full of laughter. TED was awfully good about it. I never learned how to sail, but TEDDY always gave me a pass on those voyages, and for that I'm always grateful, and for those memories I'm always grateful.

Smooth sailing, TEDDY. Thank you.

"JUST A CLOSER WALK WITH THEE," Performed by the Boston Community Chorus:

Just a closer walk with Thee,
Grant it, Jesus, is my plea,
Daily walking close to Thee,
Let it be, dear Lord, let it be.

I am weak, but Thou art strong,
Jesus, keep me from all wrong,
I'll be satisfied as long
As I walk. Let me walk close to Thee.

Through this world of toil and snares,
If I falter, Lord, who cares?
Who with me my burden shares?
None but Thee, dear Lord, none but Thee.

When my feeble life is o'er,
Time for me will be no more,

Guide me gently, safely o'er,
To Thy kingdom's shore, to Thy shore.

PAUL G. KIRK, JR.: Our next speaker is Vice President Joseph R. Biden, Jr.

JOSEPH R. BIDEN, JR., Vice President of the United States: Thank you very much, Paul, Vicki and all the children. John used to regale us like that all the time at lunch in the Senate Dining Room. John is acting like TEDDY always took advantage of him. You should have seen it when they both teamed up on somebody else.

John, I remember we were talking about Angola once. And you and TEDDY were working out a deal with some of our more conservative friends. And you agreed on a particular course of action. You and your colleague Dick Clark and TEDDY and myself were in TEDDY's office. And being naïve as I was as a young Senator, we started talking about how we were going to approach this issue on the Senate floor. TEDDY said, "We've got to do this." And I said, "But that's not what we said. We told these guys we were going to do that."

And TEDDY very politely tried to say to me, "Well, no, we're going to do the other thing." This went on for a few minutes. And finally, John in a roaring voice said, "Biden, what the hell do you think this is? Boys State?" That was my introduction to the squeeze of KENNEDY and Culver. What the hell do you think this is? Boys State?

We're all here today to celebrate the life of an incredible man. But I want to first say to the whole Kennedy clan, I want to give thanks—thanks for your father; thanks for your husband; thanks for your uncle; thanks for your brother, who, in an astonishingly and totally unexpected way, ended up playing an important part in every critical moment of my adult life.

It was literally an accident of history. But he crept into my heart, and before I knew it, he owned a piece of it. Today, I was thinking about how I wouldn't be standing here if it were not for TEDDY KENNEDY. I wouldn't be standing here as Vice President of the United States. I wouldn't have been a U.S. Senator, were it not for TEDDY KENNEDY.

He was the catalyst for my improbable win as a 29-year-old kid running for the Senate, in a year when Senator McGovern got only 34, 35 percent of the vote in my State for President. I was running against a fellow who was extremely popular, the incumbent Senator.

Although it surprised the hell out of people, I was coming astonishingly close. We needed something else. And out of the blue, literally, about 8 days before the election, TEDDY KENNEDY showed up. He showed up in a neighborhood that we referred to as Little Italy in Wilmington, DE, and drew a crowd of a couple thousand people at a dinner. It was a community that would vote nationally for the Democrats, but on all of the statewide offices always voted Republican, including for the Senate and the House seats.

I ended up winning that neighborhood. I ended up winning the election by 3,100 votes. Although I don't know for certain, it seems highly unlikely, Congressman Kennedy, I would have ever won, were it not for your father energizing people the way he did at the very end.

I remember what he said. He ended his speech by saying, "I have only one problem with Joe Biden. I think he's a little too young to be a Senator." And literally, the next day, the *Wall Street Journal* played it straight, "KENNEDY Says Biden Too Young for U.S. Senate."

Seven weeks later, my wife and daughter were killed in an automobile accident, and my two boys were very badly injured and hospitalized. One of them is with me today, Hunter. The other is in Iraq.

I got a call from your dad. And I didn't know your dad too well. I had just met him that one time. Here I was, an Irish Catholic kid from Scranton, PA, who only thought of TEDDY KENNEDY and the entire Kennedy family in distant terms, hushed tones. And here he was on the phone.

And not only was he on the phone, but he called me in that hospital almost every day. And about every other day, whenever I turned around, there was another specialist from Boston, MA, one of your great hospitals, sitting next to me, who I never asked for and didn't know I needed, but I needed.

He was the prod. He convinced me to go to the Senate. I had told my Governor that he should appoint someone else. I didn't want to go to the Senate. And it was your father who came to see me to tell me that I owed it to my deceased wife and children to at least be sworn in and stay for at least 6 months.

When I got to the Senate, he would literally come by once or twice a week to my office in the middle of the afternoon. I didn't want to be there. I wanted to get the hell home. I didn't want to be around.

[293]

He took me the first time I ever went to the Senate gym. He'd come by and take me to the Senate gym. I'll never forget the first time he took me. I hadn't met any of these famous players. I got sworn in late compared to the other Senators.

I'll never forget walking into the Senate gym and him introducing me to Senator Jack Javits and Senator Warren Magnuson, both of whom were stark naked when I met them. I remember one of them saying, "My God, Senator, how are you?" He took on the role of being my older brother. He just was there all the time. And I never had to ask.

I never could really understand, at first. I didn't understand why he was going out of his way for me this way. He got me on the committees that I ended up chairing. He was my tutor, exposing this kid from Scranton to a world that I had never seen and didn't fully understand.

I went home every night in the beginning, and I kept doing it. I went home every night for 36 years. I went home every night as soon as the Senate was out of session. And I never once accepted any invitation in Washington—not out of a desire not to be in Washington. I just wanted to get home.

One afternoon, TEDDY came to my office and said, "Joe, look, I've got to give you a piece of advice." He said, "I got a call from Pamela Harriman. This is the fourth invitation you've gotten from Governor Harriman to come to one of his dinners." I didn't know enough to know that was a big deal. I really didn't. I honest to God didn't.

He said, "Joe, you've got to go. It just doesn't look right— I'll go with you." I'll never forget going to the Harriman home in Georgetown. He was sitting in a winged chair. I was on a couch next to the chair nearest Harriman. TEDDY was next to me. Henry Kissinger was across from me and so was Paul Warnke—both arms control experts.

And I was this 30-year-old kid. Averell Harriman had a way of trying to include everybody in the conversation. They were talking about a complicated arms control agreement. It used to be the SALT Agreement. The discussion was going on, and all of a sudden, Averell Harriman looked at me and said, "Well, Joe, what do the young people think about this?"

I didn't know what the hell to say. I was scared to death. I didn't want to make a fool of myself. Here I was, a U.S. Senator. So I reached over and picked up an object on the coffee table. I was nervous, and I was flipping it back and forth with my hands, I guess, as I answered the question.

I noticed everyone stiffened up when I was talking. The butler came in and said, "Time for dinner." And everybody immediately got up and bolted for the dinner table. Your dad grabbed my arm and said, "Damn it, put that thing down. It costs more than your house." I'd been flipping a Faberge egg in my hands—the sophisticated kid from Delaware.

It seemed like every single thing I did, he was there. When my character was under attack, I sat with the committee and said, "Maybe I shouldn't chair this committee until this issue gets settled." And your father stood up and said, "No. You stay right where you are." And I said, "Let me explain." And he said before 10 of my colleagues, "We know you. You don't have to explain a single thing." We walked out of the conference room. We walked back into the hearing.

You have no idea what that meant to me at that moment, because my character had never, ever been questioned.

I was sitting in Wilmington, DE, after recuperating for 6 months from two cranial aneurysms and a major embolism, and feeling sorry for myself. And all of a sudden, up my old dusty driveway comes a cab. And out jumps TEDDY KENNEDY. And he had a great big picture frame under his arm, about 2½ by 3 feet.

I was sitting by a pool, and he walked over and he said, "Where can I change?" and he had a bathing suit with him. He put on his bathing suit and came back out. And he said, I want to give you this. He gave me a picture of a big Irish stag. And he said, "To my Irish chairman, come back, I need you." He sat there for 6 hours with me, then called a cab and went back on the train.

For 36 years, I had the privilege of every single solitary day going to work every morning with TEDDY KENNEDY. I had the privilege every day for 36 years to witness history. I had the privilege the last 20 of those years to sit literally next to him every single day.

In the process, he had an incredible impact on me, and, I noticed, on everyone around him. He'd constantly renewed my faith and optimism in the possible. I never once saw your father with a defeatist attitude. I never saw him petty. I never saw him act in a small way.

As a consequence, he made us all bigger, both his friends, his allies, and his foes. His dignity, his lack of vitriol, his lack of pettiness forced some of the less generous members of our community to act bigger than they were. He was remarkable to watch.

People say we all have our theories of why TEDDY was so successful as a legislator. I think one of them was that people didn't want to look small in front of him, even the people who were small. The astounding thing to me after 36 years of having as a consequence, as my mother would say, living long, I've gotten to meet almost every major political figure in the world. And that's not hyperbole. It's literally true.

Your father was one of the few who I ever met who, at the end of the day, it was never about him; it was always about you. A truly remarkable character trait. So many others, when it got down to the end, it was about them, not about others. With TEDDY, it was never, ever about him.

The interesting thing to me is that I think the legacy of TEDDY KENNEDY—it's presumptuous of me to say this, because who am I to judge?—but I think the legacy of TEDDY KENNEDY can be measured in no small part as a consequence of how we in America look at one another, how blacks look at whites, how gays look at straights, how straights look at gays, how we literally look at one another, and, in turn, how we look at ourselves.

When you were with him, you had to measure yourself against him. And it always required you to be larger than you were inclined to be.

His death was not unlike his life, as we all know—overcoming pain and loss with a sense of dignity and pride that is amazing. He met his death in the same brave, generous terms that he lived his life. Archie Ingersoll could have been thinking about your father when he wrote, "When the will defies fear, when duty throws the gauntlet down to fate, when honor scorns compromise with death, this is heroism."

Your father was a historic figure. He was a heroic figure beyond that. I will remember and celebrate his life every single time I see a young adolescent kid coping with, rather than cowering from, having to make a decision about his sexuality.

I'll celebrate your father every single time I see my granddaughter stand up with those boys and smack something over the second baseman's head. I'll think of your father every time a woman stands up and demands and is granted exactly what she's entitled to. I'll think of your father every time I see an individual walk out of recovery and start a new life, start over again. And Vicki, I'll think of you every time I recall those words of Christopher Marlowe, who said, "Come live with me and be my love, and we will all the pleasures prove."

[296]

It's exactly what the two of you did and everyone can see it. Now, the pundits are writing, and they mean well by it, that this is the end of an era, that this is the end of the Kennedy era. But I watched at Eunice's funeral. And I invite everyone to look around this room today and take a look at this incredible family. Take a look. I mean it. Take a look. Take a look at this generation of Kennedys. It possesses more talent, more commitment, more grit, more grace than any family I've ever seen. So when they say—and they say that this is a new era, the end of the Kennedy era—I want you to know I realize your parents collectively left America a lot more than this great library, a lot more than landmark legislation, a lot more than inspirational leadership.

They left us you. As maybe your pop would say, "Because of you, the dream still lives." Thank you for the honor of allowing me to be with you.

PAUL G. KIRK, JR.: Our final speaker is Senator KENNEDY's lovely niece. I've had the privilege of introducing her to this stage many times, and I'm pleased to do it now. The president of the Kennedy Library Foundation, Caroline Kennedy.

CAROLINE KENNEDY: Thank you, Mr. Vice President and all of the speakers tonight for the gifts of TEDDY that you have given to all of us. Thank you, Vicki, for loving him with all your heart for so many years, bringing him so much happiness.

To Kara, Teddy, Patrick, Kiki, Curran, and Caroline, you're making him so proud, bringing him so much joy. To Jean, I know you've lost your soulmate, because you and TEDDY lit each others' lives for your entire lives. And all your nieces and nephews are here to help you as best we can.

Welcome to this library that TEDDY built and brought to life with his spirit and dedication to public service. As many of you know, over the last few years, or really for most of my semi-adult life, one of my part-time jobs has been introducing TEDDY to crowds of people who already knew him incredibly well.

Although this was unbelievably stressful for me, it was just another one of the gifts that he gave me. When he saw that I was nervous, he would give me a pat on the back. When he knew that I was sad, he would call up and say: "I have got a great idea. There's a convention coming up. And maybe you would like to introduce me." And off I would go on another adventure in public speaking. But, no matter how nervous I was, I always knew that, when I stepped down from the podium, I would get a big kiss and hear him whisper, "Now I'm going to get you back."

I can't believe that's not going to happen tonight. The other night, after Vicki called, Ed and I went outside. It was a beautiful summer night. The moon had set. There was no wind. The sea was calm and the stars were out. I looked up, and there was this one star hanging low in the sky that was bigger than all the rest and brighter than all the rest, with a twinkle and a sparkle louder than all the others. I know it was Jupiter, but it was acting a lot like TEDDY.

His colleagues have spoken tonight about his work, his devotion to the Senate, the joy he took in helping others, his thoughtfulness and compassion, his inspirational courage, and his commitment to the ideals of peace and justice that his brothers gave their lives for and that he fought his entire career for.

In our family, we were lucky to see his passion, his self-discipline and his generosity of heart every single day. He had a special relationship with each of his 28 nieces and nephews and with the 60 people who called him Great Uncle TEDDY. He was there for every baptism, every school trip to Washington, every graduation, and every wedding with his big heart, his big shoulders, and a big hug.

He knew when we were having a tough time or a great time, and he would just show up and say, it's time to go sailing. He convinced us that we could ace the next test, make the varsity team, win the next race, whether it was sailing or politics.

And it was OK if we didn't, as long as we tried our best. He did it by letting us know that he believed in us, so we should believe in ourselves. He taught by example and with love. He showed us how to keep going, no matter how hard things were, to love each other, no matter how mad we got, and keep working for what we believe in.

He never told us what to do. He just did it himself, and we learned from his example. Though it was sometimes overshadowed by his other gifts, TEDDY was a creative spirit. He loved painting and singing, the natural world and the sea. He was always looking for new ways to bring people together to make a better world, to get things done.

And he was always doing things that other people could have done, but he was somehow the one who did it. It's as true in the Senate, as we have heard tonight, as it is in our family.

So, I thought I would tell you a little bit about one of the less-known examples, his creation of the annual family history trips. Visiting historical sites is something anyone can do, but TEDDY made it into something special.

He realized that a family reunion was wasted if it was just a cookout, so he made it a chance to learn and share the love of history that he got from his mother and Honey Fitz. In my childhood, these trips were relatively simple affairs, an occasional visit to the Nantucket Whaling Museum, or a Western Massachusetts campaign swing that included the Crane Paper Factory where dollar bills were printed, and the studio where Daniel Chester French created the statue of Abraham Lincoln.

No visit to grandma's house was complete without TEDDY's recitation of "The Midnight Ride of Paul Revere." When I was young, I thought TEDDY was just entertaining us, but, as I grew up, I realized he was passing down his belief that each of us has the chance to change the course of history.

TEDDY lived for the future. Though he loved the past, when a new generation came along, in typical TEDDY style, he decided to take it all to a new level. He wanted us all to share his love of being together, his passion for history, and to learn about the sacrifices upon which this country was built, so that we would understand our own opportunities and obligations.

He took this on with his enthusiasm and his organizational magic—helped, as always, by the extraordinary team that are all here tonight and will be working for him forever.

TEDDY illuminated the world around us and brought the past to life. The trips were open to everyone. Although there was always some pretrip moaning and groaning among the teenagers, no one ever wanted to stay home.

We visited the monuments of Washington by night, and Mount Vernon by boat. We walked the Civil War battlefields of Antietam, Fredericksburg, Manassas, Harpers Ferry, and Gettysburg. In Richmond, we saw the Tredegar Iron Works and the church where Patrick Henry made his immortal speech about liberty.

We went to Fort McHenry in Baltimore, Valley Forge, and Constitution Hall in Philadelphia. We walked across the Brooklyn Bridge and learned about the Battle of Long Island. But the culmination of this tradition was our trip to Boston.

We took a ride on the Old Cape Railway and learned about the building of the Cape Cod Canal. On the way to Boston, we went to Plymouth Rock. When we got to Boston, we visited the U.S.S. *Constitution*, saved by Honey Fitz, Bunker Hill, Paul Revere's House, the Old North Church, the Old South Meeting House, the house where grandma was born, and the spot where the Irish immigrants came ashore. We toured the Kennedy Library and had a picnic at the Boston Harbor Lighthouse.

Although the rule for history trips was that they were day trips only, we all knew that, to TEDDY, Boston was special. He had a surprise for us, which was that we were going to get the chance to camp out on Thompson Island.

He didn't tell us that for most of the year, this facility is used for juvenile detention, until after we had set up our tents in the dirt. It was about 98 degrees. The bugs were out. It smelled like low tide all night long. And the planes from Logan were taking off and landing right over our heads. We figured TEDDY was trying to teach us something, but, after a boiling hot 16-hour history day with 20 children under 10, we weren't quite sure what it was.

In any event, that was when TEDDY decided that even he had had enough of history, finally, and he snuck out under cover of darkness on his secret getaway boat and headed for the Ritz. Once again, he had it all figured out.

Yesterday, as we drove the same route up from the Cape, I thought about all the gifts that TEDDY gave us and the incredible journey he took. I thought about how lucky I am to have traveled some of that journey with him and with all the wonderful people that he embraced, so many of whom are here tonight. I thought about how he touched so many hearts and did so many things that only he could have done.

I thought, too, about all the things he did that we all could do, but we just figured TEDDY would do them instead. As we drove through the Boston that he loved, and saw the thousands of people who loved him back, I realized that it was our final history trip together. Now TEDDY has become a part of history. And we have become the ones who have to do all the things he would have done for us, for each other and for our country.

PAUL G. KIRK, JR.: Well, no celebration could close if it's in honor of Senator KENNEDY without a song, as he closed them many times. Oftentimes, he closed them with a song about his heritage of which he was so proud, "When Irish Eyes Are Smiling," Tonight, we have the distinct pleasure to have two Irish tenors lead us in that song, Colm Wilkinson and John McCormack.

"WHEN IRISH EYES ARE SMILING," by Chauncey Olcott and George Graff, Jr.:

There's a tear in your eye,
And I'm wondering why,
For it never should be there at all.
With such pow'r in your smile,
Sure a stone you'd beguile,
So there's never a teardrop should fall.
When your sweet lilting laughter's
Like some fairy song,
And your eyes twinkle bright as can be;
You should laugh all the while
And all other times smile,
And now, smile a smile for me.

When Irish eyes are smiling,
Sure, 'tis like the morn in Spring.
In the lilt of Irish laughter
You can hear the angels sing.
When Irish hearts are happy,
All the world seems bright and gay.
And when Irish eyes are smiling,
Sure, they steal your heart away.

For your smile is a part
Of the love in your heart,
And it makes even sunshine more bright.
Like the linnet's sweet song,
Crooning all the day long,
Come your laughter and light.
For the springtime of life
Is the sweetest of all.
There is ne'er a real care or regret;
And while springtime is ours
Throughout all of youth's hours,
Let us smile each chance we get.

When Irish eyes are smiling,
Sure, 'tis like the morn in Spring.
In the lilt of Irish laughter
You can hear the angels sing.
When Irish hearts are happy,
All the world seems bright and gay.
And when Irish eyes are smiling,
Sure, they steal your heart away.

E DWARD M OORE K ENNEDY

1932–2009

AUGUST 29, 2009

"For all my years in public life, I have believed that America must sail toward the shores of liberty and justice for all. There is no end to that journey, only the next great voyage. We know the future will outlast all of us, but I believe that all of us will live on in the future we make."

—SEN. EDWARD M. KENNEDY

A Mass of the Resurrection

Basilica of Our Lady of Perpetual Help
Roxbury, Massachusetts

August 29, 2009

———

PRINCIPAL CELEBRANT
Reverend J. Donald Monan, S.J.

CONCELEBRANTS
Reverend Mark R. Hession, Homilist
Reverend Raymond Collins
Reverend Gerry Creedon
Reverend Percival D'Silva
Reverend Donald MacMillan, S.J.

PROCESSIONAL HYMN   **Holy God We Praise Thy Name**
Words by Ignaz Franz

Holy God, we praise Thy name;
Lord of all, we bow before Thee!
All on earth Thy scepter claim,
All in Heaven above adore Thee;
Infinite Thy vast domain,
Everlasting is Thy reign.

Hark! the loud celestial hymn
Angel choirs above are raising,
Cherubim and seraphim,
In unceasing chorus praising;
Fill the heavens with sweet accord:
Holy, holy, holy, Lord.

Holy Father, Holy Son,
Holy Spirit, Three we name Thee;
While in essence only One,
Undivided God we claim Thee;
And adoring bend the knee,
While we own the mystery.

Thou art King of glory, Christ:
Son of God, yet born of Mary;
For us sinners sacrificed,
And to death a tributary:
First to break the bars of death,
Thou has opened Heaven to faith.

Therefore do we pray Thee, Lord:
Help Thy servants whom, redeeming
By Thy precious blood out-poured,
Thou hast saved from Satan's scheming.
Give to them eternal rest
In the glory of the blest.

Spare Thy people, Lord, we pray,
By a thousand snares surrounded:
Keep us without sin today,
Never let us be confounded.
Lo, I put my trust in Thee;
Never, Lord, abandon me.

OPENING PRAYER

LITURGY OF THE WORD

First Reading   **G. Curran Raclin, Jr.**

The Book of Wisdom 3:1–9

The souls of the just are in the hand of God,
   And no torment shall touch them.
They seemed, in the view of the foolish, to be dead:
   And their passing away was thought an affliction
   And their going forth from us, utter destruction.
But they are at peace.
For if before men, indeed, they be punished,
   Yet is their hope full of immortality;
Chastised a little, they shall be greatly blessed.
   Because God tried them
   And found them worthy of himself.
As gold in the furnace, he proved them,
   And as sacrificial offerings he took them to himself.
In the time of their visitation they shall shine,
   And shall dart about as sparks through stubble;
They shall judge nations and rule over peoples
   And the Lord shall be their King forever.
Those who trust in him shall understand truth,
   And the faithful shall abide with him in love:
Because grace and mercy are with his holy ones,
   And his care is with his elect.

The Word of the Lord.

Responsorial Psalm **Kara Kennedy**

Psalm 72

Reader: Justice shall flourish in his time, and fullness of
peace forever.

All: *Justice shall flourish in his time, and fullness of peace
forever.*

Reader: The mountains shall yield peace for the people, and
the hills justice. He shall defend the afflicted among
the people, save the children of the poor.

All: *Justice shall flourish in his time, and fullness of peace
forever.*

Reader: Justice shall flower in his days, and profound peace,
till the moon be no more. May he rule from sea to sea,
and from the River to the ends of the earth.

All: *Justice shall flourish in his time, and fullness of peace
forever.*

Reader: For he shall rescue the poor man when he cries out,
and the afflicted when he has no one to help him. He
shall have pity for the lowly and the poor; the lives of
the poor he shall save.

All: *Justice shall flourish in his time, and fullness of peace
forever.*

Reader: May his name be blessed forever; as long as the sun
his name shall remain. In him shall all the tribes of
the earth be blessed; all the nations shall proclaim his
happiness.

All: *Justice shall flourish in his time, and fullness of peace
forever.*

Second Reading   **Caroline R. Raclin**

Letter of Paul to the Romans 8:31b–35, 37–39

If God is for us, who can be against us? He who did not spare his own Son but handed him over for us all, how will he not also give us everything else along with him? Who will bring a charge against God's chosen ones? It is God who acquits us. Who will condemn? It is Christ Jesus who died, rather, was raised, who also is at the right hand of God, who indeed intercedes for us.

What will separate us from the love of Christ? Will anguish, or distress, or persecution, or famine, or nakedness, or peril, or the sword? No, in all these things we conquer overwhelmingly through him who loved us. For I am convinced that neither death, nor life, nor angels, nor principalities, nor present things, nor future things, nor powers, nor height, nor depth, nor any other creature will be able to separate us from the love of God in Christ Jesus our Lord.

The Word of the Lord.

Gospel   Matthew 25:31–32A, 34–40

When the Son of Man comes in his glory, and all the angels with him, he will sit on his throne in heavenly glory. All the nations will be gathered before him, and he will separate the people one from another . . .

Then the King will say to those on his right, 'Come, you who are blessed by my Father; take your inheritance, the kingdom prepared for you since the creation of the world. For I was hungry and you gave me something to eat, I was thirsty and you gave me something to drink, I was a stranger and you invited me in, I needed clothes and you clothed me, I was sick and you looked after me, I was in prison and you came to visit me.'

Then the righteous will answer him, 'Lord, when did we see you hungry and feed you, or thirsty and give you something to drink? When did we see you a stranger and invite you in, or needing clothes and clothe you? When did we see you sick or in prison and go to visit you?'

The King will reply, 'I tell you the truth, whatever you did for one of the least of these brothers of mine, you did for me.'

[309]

Homily   **Reverend Mark R. Hession**

THE PRAYERS OF THE FAITHFUL
Kiki Kennedy, Introduction
Kiley Kennedy
Grace Allen
Max Allen
Jack Schlossberg
Robin Lawford
Kym Smith
Anthony Shriver
Rory Kennedy
Teddy Kennedy

LITURGY OF THE EUCHARIST
Offertory	J.S. Bach, Sarabande from Cello Suite No. 6 Yo-Yo Ma, cello
Gifts	Kiley Kennedy Grace Allen Max Allen Teddy Kennedy

COMMUNION
—Franck "Panis Angelicus"	Placido Domingo, tenor Yo-Yo Ma, cello
—Brahms "Let Nothing Ever Grieve Thee"	Tanglewood Festival Chorus John Oliver, conductor
—Schubert "Ave Maria"	Susan Graham, mezzo-soprano James David Christie, organ

REMEMBRANCES	Ted Kennedy, Jr. Patrick J. Kennedy
EULOGY	President Barack Obama
FINAL COMMENDATION	His Eminence Seán P. Cardinal O'Malley Archbishop of Boston

RECESSIONAL HYMN   "America the Beautiful"

Words by Katharine Lee Bates
Melody by Samuel Ward

O beautiful for spacious skies,
For amber waves of grain,
For purple mountain majesties
Above the fruited plain!
America! America!
God shed his grace on thee
And crown thy good with brotherhood
From sea to shining sea!

O beautiful for heroes proved
In liberating strife.
Who more than self their country loved
And mercy more than life!
America! America!
May God thy gold refine
Till all success be nobleness
And every gain divine!

O beautiful for patriot dream
That sees beyond the years
Thine alabaster cities gleam
Undimmed by human tears!
America! America!
God shed his grace on thee
And crown thy good with brotherhood
From sea to shining sea!

PALLBEARERS

Kara Kennedy
Ted Kennedy, Jr.
Patrick J. Kennedy
G. Curran Raclin, Jr.
Caroline R. Raclin
Caroline Kennedy

Christopher Lawford
Ed Michael Reggie
Bobby Shriver
Stephen E. Smith, Jr.
Kathleen Kennedy Townsend

HONORARY PALLBEARERS

Melody Barnes
Stephen Breyer
David Burke
Ranny Cooper
Greg Craig
John C. Culver
Stephanie Cutter
Bill Delahunt
Christopher J. Dodd
Kenneth R. Feinberg
Lee Fentress

Wyche Fowler
Tim Hanan
Claude Hooton
Larry Horowitz
John F. Kerry
Paul G. Kirk, Jr.
Kathy Kruse
Nick Littlefield
Ed Markey
Eric Mogilnicki

Michael Myers
Carey Parker
Edmund Reggie
Don Riegle
Larry Ronan
Jim Sasser
Robert Shrum
Barbara Souliotis
John Tunney
Vince Wolfington

USHERS

Kevin Callahan
Heather Campion
Gene Dellea
Don Dowd
Bob Fitzgerald
Joe Gargan
Mary Jeka

Jeannie Kedas
Joe Kennedy
Matt Kennedy
Jackie Jenkins Scott
Susan Riley
Tracy Spicer

SPECIAL THANKS TO:
Photo Credit: ©Denis Reggie

MEMBERS OF THE BOSTON SYMPHONY ORCHESTRA:
Malcolm Lowe and Haldan Martinson, violins; Cathy Basrak, viola; Mihail
Jojatu, cello; William R. Hudgins, clarinet

Anthony Fogg, Artistic Administrator, Boston Symphony Orchestra

[Processional Hymn]

Rev. MARK R. HESSION, Our Lady of Victory Catholic Church: Good morning. In the name of the Very Reverend Father, Patrick Woods, the provincial superior of the Redemptors of Baltimore Providence and the entire Redemptors community, it is my privilege to welcome you this morning to the Basilica of Our Lady of Perpetual Help, affectionately known as Mission Church.

Most eminent Cardinal Seán O'Malley, Archbishop of Boston, welcome once again to this basilica. The Redemptors fathers and brothers are most grateful for the many occasions you've joined with us here and we look forward to many future visits.

We gather today with sadness, but with hope, as we mark the passing of the distinguished senior Senator from Massachusetts, the Honorable EDWARD MOORE KENNEDY.

To Mrs. Kennedy and all of the family, we offer our sincere condolences and prayers. In this place of faith and hope and healing, we come together with confidence that Senator KENNEDY has gone forth to eternal life in the presence and mercy of the Lord.

We are honored this morning to welcome President and Mrs. Obama, Vice President and Mrs. Biden, Honorable and former Presidents and First Ladies of the United States, Members of Congress, the representative of the British Prime Minister, the Secretary of State for Northern Ireland, Massachusetts Governor Deval Patrick, mayor of Boston Thomas Menino, and all of the distinguished guests.

As we begin our liturgy this morning for Senator KENNEDY, be assured that all of you are always welcome in this blessed and holy place. May each of us share in the gifts of strength and peace that Senator KENNEDY found as he came here to pray, especially at the altar of our Lady of Perpetual Help.

Rev. J. DONALD MONAN, Chancellor, Boston College: My dear friends, a few scant miles from here, the city on a hill stands less tall against the morning sky. The sea out toward Nantucket is a bit more forlorn at the loss of one of its most avid lovers. We welcome you to the Mass of the Resurrection, to commemorate the life of Senator KENNEDY.

I'm sure I speak for everyone in expressing our sincere sympathy to all of the Kennedy family, and especially to the Senator's wife, Vicki, to his sons Teddy and Patrick and his daughter Kara, and to his sister Jean. We share your sadness as we share your love and your pride for your husband and father and brother and friend.

In the church's solemn Liturgy of the Eucharist, sadness is softened with hope. Fear is banished by the faith in the love and compassion of Christ, our Lord, who, through his own death and resurrection, has overcome death. And so as a believing community, let us now pray.

Almighty God, our Father, it is our Christian faith that your son died, and rose to life. We pray for our dear friend and brother, TED KENNEDY, who has died in Christ. Through your love and compassion, raise him at the last day to share the glory of the risen Christ, who lives and reigns with you and the Holy Spirit, one God, forever and ever. Amen.

All be seated for the liturgy of the word.

[First Reading]

[Responsorial Psalm]

[Second Reading]

[Gospel]

[Homily]

Rev. HESSION: So, good morning, everyone. Once again there have been a series of introductions already. But certainly one to greet Your Eminence, Cardinal Seán, President and Mrs. Obama, President and Mrs. Bush, President Clinton and Secretary Clinton, President Carter and Mrs. Carter, and our Vice President and Mrs. Biden.

All of us in church today, dear friends of TED and especially you, Vicki, Curran and Caroline, and Kara, Teddy, and Patrick and your mother Joan; a sister everyone in the world would love to have in you, Jean, with your devotion; Dr. Larry Ronan and the great team of doctors and nurses, and so many helpers at Hyannis Port these last weeks and months. And most especially the youngest of TED's gang, Gracie and Max, Kylie and Teddy.

In the Catholic tradition, the Mass of Christian Burial weaves together memory and hope. The worship of the churches locates us precisely between a past we reverently remember, and a future in which we firmly believe. We gather today as a community drawn from across the Nation to entrust the life of Senator EDWARD KENNEDY into the hands of God, and to provide you consolation and support.

We bring with us treasured memories of TED KENNEDY, memories not only of a national leader and a master legislator, but of a beloved husband, a great father, a terrific grandfather, a sweet uncle, a dear friend, a trusted colleague, a wise mentor.

We enter this church with these memories acutely alive for each of us. We gather to treasure the memory and to share our sense of loss. The liturgy of the Mass, its scripture, its music and ritual are designed to acknowledge these memories to provide a context of prayerful and communal reflection in which they can be held as deeply personal and sacred.

But the liturgy does not leave us in the past alone. It points us in Christian hope to the future. Our prayer, expressed in confidence and hope, is about the destiny of our brother and friend, with his future with God. The biblical readings of the day, selected by TED and Vicki and his family, move us from memory to hope, from the past to the future.

Curran proclaimed the first lesson of the Mass, speaking the words of Wisdom, "The souls of the just are in the hand of God" in life and death. St. Paul states our case with his usual confidence, and Caroline proclaimed it with such beauty: "For I'm sure that neither death, nor life, nor angels, nor principalities, nor things to come, nor powers, nor height, nor depth, nor anything else in all creation will be able to separate us from the love of God in Christ Jesus our Lord."

That confidence, the triumph of life over death, is rooted in the central belief of Christian faith, the resurrection of Christ the Lord. The Christian conviction upon which all faith is built is that Christ, who passed through death to new life, will, as he promised, lead us through death to new life as well.

On this day, we hold the memory of the life of Senator KENNEDY with reverence and with respect. We also recognize that like all of us, his life has a destiny beyond history. The destiny of risen life in the Kingdom of God, the Gospel of Matthew from which I proclaimed, focuses our attention on this destiny by reminding us of the words of Jesus, and the tests he posed for entrance into that kingdom: "Oh, come, blessed of my Father, inherit the kingdom prepared for you from the foundation of the world. For I was hungry and you gave me food. I was thirsty and you gave me drink. I was a stranger and you welcomed me. I was naked and you clothed me. I was sick and you visited me. I was in prison, and you came to me."

[315]

In this text on this day, our memories and our hopes converge. These words of the kingdom were daily concerns of the public life of TEDDY KENNEDY. They were the fabric of his mind, heart, and hands, as he sought to realize them in a society dramatically more complex than the society in which Jesus spoke these words.

Our hope, our confident Christian hope, is that the fruits of his work as a political and public figure have well prepared him for God's kingdom. As we together reflect upon TED's life, the choice of this incredible Basilica Church as the place for his funeral provides a fitting context for our thoughts and prayers. This basilica reminds us of two important aspects of the Senator's life and work.

First, we've come to know in the days since his death that when critical illness threatened his own daughter, he came to this place daily to pray. He came here, like generations before him, seeking the healing hand of God. We're reminded that the most public personalities also live a very personal existence. This church was the place of private prayer for a public man.

Second, this church sits in the midst of the neighborhoods where the important issues that animated TED KENNEDY's career are so frankly visible—the needs of the poor—social justice, health care and education, housing and the minimum wage. The Senator's choice of this church for his funeral mass resonates with the meaning and the purpose of his life and work.

As I search for words which could capture his life, I've been struck by how many different perspectives could be brought to bear upon it by so many gathered today—by Vicki and their children, by the many members of the Kennedy clan, by the Presidents, by Members of both Houses of the U.S. Congress and of both political parties, by dedicated staff who served him over four decades, and, as we've seen these last days, especially by the citizens of Massachusetts whom he faithfully served. The extraordinary diversity of these many memories is rather overwhelming.

It is neither my place nor within my power to capture them all. I know TED and Vicki and their family as their parish priest. My sources of reflection are the Scriptures and the pastoral experience of ministering to TED and his family. My vision, like yours, can't encompass the totality of his life. My memories, seen through the lens of a Catholic parish priest, are about how one person, one man, a husband, a father, a public figure, a Catholic, and a citizen, tried to meet the tests of the kingdom of Matthew's Gospel.

To know him as a pastor was to be introduced to the Kennedy family. The Senator led the family. He was supported by it through a long and complex career, and he was sustained by his family as his life entered its final chapter.

All of us know by instinct the fundamental importance of our families. None of us expects to face the great responsibility of being the most visible figure in a family whose narrative is woven through the history of our Nation over the past century. As a priest, I saw him treasure and draw strength from his family. Like others here today, I watched as his role of this family's leader required that he sustain them all through life and death, through victory and tragedy.

It is not too much to say that his abiding political and legislative concern for the welfare of families, especially those at the socioeconomic edge of American life, was rooted in his own experience of a vibrant and caring family life. Senator KENNEDY was a tower of strength to his family, and a towering presence on the American public landscape.

Others are better suited than I to describe in detail his legacy. As a pastor, my description seeks to root his public life in his personal convictions. No person's faith is easily summarized. The broad demands of Christian discipleship are clear enough in principle. Few of us, if any, meet them all, but we're all called to pursue the full vision of faith, even as we recognize the inevitable gap between what we're called to, and what we, in fact, achieve. Indeed, most of us have a strong suit matched with gaps and struggles.

There are few passages which express this more pointedly, and more poignantly, than Senator KENNEDY's own eulogy for his dear brother, Robert, at St. Patrick's Cathedral 41 years ago, in 1968. There, he said, "My brother need not be idolized or enlarged in death, beyond what he was in life. To be remembered simply as a good and decent man who saw wrong and tried to right it, saw suffering and tried to heal it, saw war and tried to stop it."

Like both of his brothers, TED KENNEDY was a public man, with a public faith. His strong suit was a central stream of biblical faith, expressed both in the Hebrew and Christian Scriptures.

His strong suit was the faith of the great Hebrew prophets—Isaiah, Jeremiah, Amos. It was they who tied the quality of faith to the character of justice in the land. It was they who stood in defense of the widows, the orphans, and the refugees of their time. The striking resemblance of these groups to the women, children, families, and immigrants in poverty of our time did not escape TED KENNEDY's notice.

His public faith was reinforced and nurtured in the Christian Scriptures. We've heard Matthew today. Now we should remember the Gospel of Luke, commonly known as the Gospel of the Poor. The Jesus of Luke knew the poor of his time well. He was in their midst often. He advocated for them, defended them and reminded his disciples of God's special concern for them.

At the heart of Luke's Gospel stands the person of Mary, the mother of Jesus. Senator KENNEDY had a special respect for her great prayer, the Magnificat, a prayer which simultaneously glorified God for his blessings and promised God's protection of the poor. In his final days the Senator and Vicki and I pondered this prayer in terms of the meaning of his life's work.

Our blessed mother proclaims these sentiments: "God's mercy is from age to age to those who fear Him. He has shown might with his arm and dispersed the arrogant of mind and heart. He's thrown down the rulers from their thrones but lifted up the lowly. The hungry he's filled with good things; the rich he has sent away empty."

TED KENNEDY, of course, lived in a far more complex world than that of Jesus' time and place. But that challenge evoked from him his public gifts. He understood the complexity of the society in which he lived. He was renowned for his mastery of the data, for his sense of the possible, and for his genius in crafting law and policy in a way which benefited the widows and orphans of our time.

Again, he described the motivation of his public life in light of the legacy of his brother Robert's vision when he spoke these words, "Our future may be beyond our vision, but it is not completely beyond our control. It is the shaping impulse of America that neither fate nor nature nor the irresistible tides of history, but the work of our hands, matched to reason and principle that will determine our destiny."

Every public figure has a uniquely personal life, distinct from, but not totally separated from, the public world of work and achievement. Others have remembered in the past week and will address this morning the record of achievement of TED KENNEDY.

I'd like to close with this reflection. As one lives more toward the final moments of life, the public character fades, and the deeper personal convictions and commitments which have sustained a person through a long and complex life come to occupy the center stage.

This was the case in the last few weeks and months, as TED and Vicki together faced the last measure of his life. Like any priest would be, I was present for them, and with them. The faith, which had sustained a visible historic presence, now became the faith which teaches us how to see this life in light of the next life.

The gift of the Eucharist, which Jesus promised would nourish us in this life and would carry us to eternal life, became a source of even greater strength and comfort for TED and Vicki. As the end approached, the convictions that sustained Senator TED KENNEDY through so many public struggles became the source of quiet confidence in a truth taught by his church at the Second Vatican Council in these words:

We do not know the time for the consummation of the Earth and of humanity, but we are taught that God is preparing a new dwelling place and a new Earth where justice will abide, and whose blessedness will answer, and surpass all the longings for peace which spring up in the human heart.

Today, at this holy Eucharist, we pray, we are confident that TED KENNEDY has entered this new dwelling of God. For as the liturgy today inspires us, Lord, for your faithful people, life is changed, not ended. When the body of our earthly dwelling lies in death, we gain an everlasting dwelling place in heaven. May he rest in peace.

[The Prayers of the Faithful]

KIKI KENNEDY (Introduction): Now we pray to the Lord, not only for TEDDY, but for all of us he leaves behind. Among his brothers and sisters, he was the youngest. So now his grandchildren, his younger nieces and nephews and the youngest child of one of his nieces will offer the intercessions. Each time, please respond, "Lord, hear our prayer."

TEDDY served for nearly 47 years, and he summoned us all to service. And so these intercessions are in his words, for the work of his life is our prayer for our country and our world.

KILEY KENNEDY: For my grandfather's commitment and persistence were not for outworn values but for old values that will never wear out. The poor may be out of political fashion, but they are never without human needs. Circumstances may change but the work of compassion must continue. We pray to the Lord.

CONGREGATION: Lord, hear our prayer.

[319]

GRACE ALLEN: For my grandpa that we will not in our Nation measure human beings by what they cannot do, but instead value them for what they can do. We pray to the Lord.

CONGREGATION: Lord, hear our prayer.

MAX ALLEN: For what my grandpa called the cause of his life, as he said so often, in every part of this land, that every American will have decent quality health care, as a fundamental right, and not a privilege. We pray to the Lord.

CONGREGATION: Lord, hear out prayer.

JACK SCHLOSSBERG: For a new season of hope that my Uncle TEDDY envisioned, where we rise to our best ideals, close the book on the old politics of race and gender, group against group and straight against gay. We pray to the Lord.

CONGREGATION: Lord, hear our prayer.

ROBIN LAWFORD: For my Uncle TEDDY's call to keep the promise that all men and women who live here, even strangers and newcomers, can rise, no matter what their color, no matter what their place of birth; for workers out of work, students without tuition for college, and families without the chance to own a home; for all Americans seeking a better life and a better land; for all of those left out or left behind. We pray to the Lord.

CONGREGATION: Lord, hear our prayer.

KYM SMITH: For my uncle's stand against violence, hate, and war, and his belief that peace can be kept through the triumph of justice, and that true justice can come only through the works of peace. We pray to the Lord.

CONGREGATION: Lord, hear our prayer.

ANTHONY SHRIVER: As my Uncle TEDDY once told thousands and millions, "May it be said of us in dark passages and bright days, in the words of Tennyson that my brothers quoted and loved that have a special meaning for us now: 'I am part of all that I have met. Though much is taken, much abides. That which we are, we are. One equal temper of heroic hearts, strong in will, to strive, to seek, to find, and not to yield.'" We pray to the Lord.

CONGREGATION: Lord, hear our prayer.

RORY KENNEDY: For the joy of my Uncle TEDDY's laughter, the light of his presence, his rare and noble contributions to the human spirit, for his face that is in heaven, his father, his mother, his brothers and sisters and all who went before him will welcome him home. And for all the times to come when the rest of us will think of him, cuddling affectionately on the boat, surrounded by family as we sailed in Nantucket Sound. We pray to the Lord.

CONGREGATION: Lord, hear our prayer.

TEDDY KENNEDY III: For my grandfather's brave promise last summer that the work begins anew, the hope rises again, and the dream lives on. We pray to the Lord.

CONGREGATION: Lord, hear our prayer.

Rev. MONAN: Lord our God, giver of peace and healer of souls, hear the prayers of the redeemer, Jesus Christ, and the voices of your people whose lives were purchased by the blood of the lambs. Forgive the sins of all who sleep in Christ and grant them a place in your kingdom. We ask this through Christ our Lord, amen.

CONGREGATION: Amen.

[Offertory: Bach, Sarabande from Cello Suite No. 6, Yo-Yo Ma, Cello]

[Presentation of Gifts of Bread and Wine by Kiley Kennedy, Grace Allen, Max Allen, and Edward M. Kennedy III]

Rev. MONAN: My dear father, may your sacrifice with ours be acceptable to God the Almighty Father.

CONGREGATION: May the Lord accept the sacrifice at our hands, and the praise and glory of his name for our good and the good of all his church.

Rev. MONAN: Lord, accept this sacrifice we offer for our brother, TED KENNEDY, on the day of his burial. May your love cleanse him from his human weakness and forgive any sins he may have committed. All of this we ask through Christ, our Lord, Amen. The Lord be with you.

CONGREGATION: And also with you.

Rev. MONAN: Lift up your hearts.

CONGREGATION: We lift them up to the Lord.

Rev. MONAN: Let us give thanks to the Lord our God.

CONGREGATION: It is right to give God thanks and praise.

Rev. MONAN: Father, all powerful and ever living God, we do well always and everywhere, to give you thanks through Jesus Christ our Lord. In Him who rose from the dead, our hope for resurrection dawned. The sadness of death gives way to the bright promise of immortality.

Lord, through your faithful people, life has changed, not ended. In the body of our earthly dwelling we lie in death. We gain an everlasting dwelling place in heaven. And so with all the choir of angels in heaven, we proclaim your glory and join them in their unending hymn of praise:

Holy, holy, holy, Lord, God of power and might. Heaven and earth are full of your glory. Hosanna in the highest. Blessed is he who comes in the name of the Lord. Hosanna in the highest.

Lord, you are holy indeed and all creation rightly gives you praise. All life, all holiness, comes from you, through your son, Jesus Christ our Lord, by the working of the Holy Spirit. From age to age, you gather a people to yourself, so that from east to west, a perfect offering may be made to the glory of your name.

And so, Father, we bring you these gifts. We ask you to make them holy by the power of your spirit, that they may become the body and blood of your son, our Lord Jesus Christ, at whose command we celebrate this Eucharist.

On the night he was betrayed, he took bread and gave you thanks and praise. He broke the bread and gave it to his disciples and said, "Take this, all of you, and eat it. This is my body, which will be given up for you."

When supper was ended, he took the cup. Again, he gave you thanks and praise. He gave the cup to his disciples and said, "Take this, all of you, and drink from it. This is the cup of my blood, the blood of the new and everlasting covenant. It will be shed for you and for all so that sins may be forgiven. Do this in memory of me."

Father, calling to mind the death your son endured for our salvation, his glorious resurrection and ascension into heaven, and ready to greet him when he comes again, we offer you in thanksgiving this holy and living sacrifice. Look with favor on your church's offering and see the victim whose death has reconciled us to yourself. Grant that we who are nourished by his body and blood may be filled with his Holy Spirit and become one body, one spirit in Christ.

Rev. DONALD A. MacMILLAN, Campus Minister, Boston College: May he make us an everlasting gift to you and enable us to share in the inheritance of your saints with Mary, the Virgin Mother of God, with Joseph, her husband, the apostles, the martyrs and all your saints. On his constant intercession, we rely for help.

Rev. HESSION: Lord, may this sacrifice, which has made our peace with you, advance the peace and salvation of all the world, strengthen in faith and love your pilgrim church on Earth, your servant Pope Benedict, our Cardinal Archbishop Seán and all of the bishops with the clergy, and the entire people your Son has gained for you. Father, hear the prayers of the family who has gathered here before you.

Rev. MONAN: In a special way, Lord, remember our dear friend, TED. In baptism, he died with Christ. May he also share his resurrection when Christ will raise our mortal bodies and make them like his in his own glory. Welcome into your kingdom our departed brothers and sisters and all who have left this world in your friendship.

There we hope to share in your glory, when every tear will be wiped away. On that day, we shall see you, our God, as you are. We shall become like you and praise you with every thought, through Christ our Lord from whom all good things come, through him, with him, in the unity of the Holy Spirit, all glory and honor is yours, Almighty Father, forever and ever. Amen.

And let us pray now together in the words that our Father taught us. Our Father, who art in heaven, hallowed be thy name, thy kingdom come, thy will be done, on Earth as it is in heaven. Give us this day our daily bread and forgive us our trespasses, as we forgive those who trespass against us. And lead us not into temptation, but deliver us from evil.

Deliver us, Lord, from every evil and grant us peace in our day. In your mercy, keep us free from sin and protect us from all anxiety as we wait in joyful hope for the coming of our savior Jesus Christ. For the Kingdom, the power and the glory are yours, now and forever.

Lord Jesus Christ, you said to your apostles, "I leave you peace. My peace I give you." Look not on our sins but on the faith of your church and grant us the peace and unity of your kingdom where you live forever and ever. Amen.

The peace of the Lord be with you.

CONGREGATION: And also with you.

Rev. MONAN: Let us offer each other a sign of Christ's peace.

Lamb of God, you take away the sins of the world. Have mercy on us. Lamb of God, you take away the sins of the world. Have mercy on us. Lamb of God, you take away the sins of the world. Grant us peace.

Lord Jesus Christ, with faith in your love and mercy, we ate your body and drank your blood. That does not bring us condemnation, but health in mind and body. This is the Lamb of God, who takes away the sins of the world. Happy are those who are called to his supper.

Lord, I am now worthy to receive you. Only say the word and I shall be with you. May the body of Christ bring us to everlasting life.

[Communion]

[Franck, "Panis Angelicus," Placido Domingo, Tenor, Yo-Yo Ma, Cello]

[Brahms, "Let Nothing Ever Grieve Thee," Tanglewood Festival Chorus, John Oliver, Conductor]

[Schubert, "Ave Maria," Susan Graham, Mezzo-Soprano, James David Christie, Organ]

[Remembrances]

EDWARD M. KENNEDY, JR.: My name is Ted Kennedy, Jr., a name I share with my son, a name I shared with my father. Although it hasn't been easy at times to live with this name, I've never been more proud of it than I am today.

Your Eminence, thank you for being here. You've graced us with your presence. To all the musicians who have come here, my father loved the arts and he would be so pleased by your performances today.

My heart is filled, and I first want to say thank you. My heart is filled with appreciation and gratitude to the people of Massachusetts and my father's loyal staff—in many ways my dad's loss is just as great for them as it is for those of us in our family—and for all of my father's family and friends who have come to pay their respects.

Listening to people speak about how my father impacted their lives and the deep personal connection that people felt with my dad has been an overwhelming emotional experience.

My dad had the greatest friends in the world. All of you here are also my friends and his greatest gift to me. I love you just as much as he did.

Sarah Brown, the Taoiseach, President Obama, President Clinton, Secretary Clinton, President Bush, President Carter, you honor my family by your presence here today. I remember how my dad would tell audiences years ago, "I don't mind not being President; I just mind that someone else is."

There is much to say and much will be said about TED KENNEDY, the statesman, the master of the legislative process and bipartisan compromise, workhorse of the Senate, beacon of social justice, and protector of the people.

There's also much to be said and much will be said about my father, the man, the storyteller, the lover of costume parties, the practical joker, the accomplished painter.

He was a lover of everything French—cheese, wine, and women. He was a mountain climber, navigator, skipper, tactician, airplane pilot, rodeo rider, ski jumper, dog lover and all-around adventurer. Our family vacations left us all injured and exhausted.

He was a dinner table debater and devil's advocate. He was an Irishman, and a proud member of the Democratic Party.

Here is one you may not know. Out of Harvard, he was a Green Bay Packer recruit, but decided to go to law school instead.

He was a devout Catholic, whose faith helped him survive unbearable losses, and whose teachings taught him that he had a moral obligation to help others in need.

He was not perfect, far from it. But my father believed in redemption. And he never surrendered, never stopped trying to right wrongs, be they the results of his own failings or of ours.

But today, I'm simply compelled to remember TED KENNEDY as my father and my best friend.

When I was 12 years old, I was diagnosed with bone cancer. A few months after I lost my leg, there was a heavy snowfall over my childhood home outside Washington, DC. My father went to the garage to get the old Flexible Flyer, and asked me if I wanted to go sledding down the steep driveway.

I was trying to get used to my new artificial leg. The hill was covered with ice and snow. It wasn't easy for me to walk. The hill was very slick, and as I struggled to walk, I slipped and I fell on the ice, and I started to cry. I said, "I can't do this." I said, "I'll never be able to climb up that hill." And he lifted me up in his strong, gentle arms and said something I will never forget. He said, "I know you can do it. There is nothing that you can't do. We are going to climb that hill together, even if it takes us all day."

Sure enough, he held me around my waist and we slowly made it to the top. And you know, at age 12, losing your leg pretty much seems like the end of the world. But as I climbed onto his back and we flew down the hill that day, I knew he was right. I knew I was going to be OK.

You see, my father taught me that even our most profound losses are survivable. It is what we do with that loss, our ability to transform it into a positive event, that is one of my father's greatest lessons.

He taught me that nothing is impossible. During the summer months when I was growing up, my father would arrive late in the afternoon from Washington on Fridays, and as soon as he got to Cape Cod, he would want to go straight out and practice sailing maneuvers on the *Victura*, in anticipation of the weekend's races.

We'd be out late. The sun would be setting, and the family dinner would be getting cold. We'd be out there practicing our jibes and our spinnaker sets, long after everyone else had gone ashore.

One night, not another boat was in sight on the summer sea. I asked him, "Why are we always the last ones on the water?" "Teddy," he said, "you see, most of the other sailors that we race against are smarter and more talented than we are. But the reason why we're going to win is that we will work harder than them, and we will be better prepared." He wasn't just talking about boating. My father admired perseverance. My father believed that to do a job effectively required a tremendous amount of time and effort.

Dad instilled in me also the importance of history and biography. He loved Boston, and the amazing writers and philosophers and politicians from Massachusetts. He took me and my cousins to the Old North Church and to Walden Pond and to the homes of Herman Melville and Nathaniel Hawthorne in the Berkshires.

He thought that Massachusetts was the greatest place on Earth. He had letters from many of its former Senators, like Daniel Webster and John Quincy Adams, hanging on his walls, inspired by things heroic.

He was a Civil War buff. When we were growing up, he would pack us all into his car or a rented camper, and we would travel around to all the great battlefields. I remember he would frequently meet with his friend, Shelby Foote, at a particular site on the anniversary of a historic battle, just so he could appreciate better what the soldiers must have experienced on that day. He believed that in order to know what to do in the future, you had to understand the past.

My father loved other old things. He loved his classic wooden schooner, the *Mya*. He loved lighthouses and his 1973 Pontiac convertible.

My father taught me to treat everyone I meet, no matter what station in life, with the same dignity and respect. He could be discussing arms control with the President at 3 p.m. and meeting with a union carpenter on fair wage legislation or a New Bedford fisherman on fisheries policy at 4:30.

I once told him that he had accidently left some money— I remember this when I was a little kid—on the sink in our hotel room. He replied, "Teddy, let me tell you something. Making beds all day is back-breaking work. The woman who has to clean up after us today has a family to feed." And that's just the kind of guy he was.

He answered Uncle Joe's call to patriotism, Uncle Jack's call to service, and Uncle Bobby's determination to seek a newer world. Unlike them, he lived to be a grandfather. And knowing what my cousins have been through, I feel grateful that I have had my father as long as I did.

He even taught me some of life's harder lessons, such as how to like Republicans. He once told me, "Teddy, Republicans love this country just as much as I do." I think he felt like he had something in common with his Republican counterparts—the vagaries of public opinion, the constant scrutiny of the press, the endless campaigning for the next election, but most of all, the incredible shared sacrifice that being in public life demands.

He understood the hardship that politics has on a family and the hard work and commitment that it requires. He often brought his Republican colleagues home for dinner. He believed in developing personal relationships and honoring differences. One of the wonderful experiences that I will remember about today is how many of his Republican colleagues are sitting here right before him. That's a true testament to the man.

He told me to always be ready to compromise, but never compromise about your principles. He was an idealist and a pragmatist. He was restless, but patient. When he learned that a survey of Republican Senators named him the Democratic Legislator that they most wanted to work with and that John McCain called him the single most effective member of the U.S. Senate, he was so proud, because he considered the combination of accolades from your supporters and respect from your sometime political adversaries as one of the ultimate goals of successful political life.

At the end of his life, my dad returned home. He died at the place he loved more than any other, Cape Cod. The last months of my dad's life were not sad or terrifying, but fulfilled with profound experiences, a series of moments more precious than I could have imagined. He taught me more about humility, vulnerability, and courage than he had taught me in my whole life.

Although he lived a full and complete life by any measure, the fact is, he wasn't done. He still had work to do. He was so proud of where we had recently come as a Nation. Although I grieve for what might have been, for what he might have helped us accomplish, I pray today that we can set aside this sadness and instead celebrate all that he was and did and stood for.

I will try to live up to the high standards that my father set for all of us when he said, "The work goes on; the cause endures; the hope still lives; and the dream shall never die." I love you, dad. I always will, and I miss you already.

Representative PATRICK J. KENNEDY: President and Mrs. Obama, distinguished guests, friends of my father, all of you. While a Nation has lost a great Senator, my brothers and sisters and I have lost a loving father. When I was a kid, I couldn't breathe. Growing up, I suffered from chronic and crippling asthma attacks. The medications I had to take were very difficult and gave me a throbbing headache every night that I had to use my bronchial nebulizer.

Now, obviously, I wish that I did not have to suffer those attacks and endure those headaches. Nor did I like having to grow up having a special non-allergenic, non-smoking room reserved for me whenever we went on family vacations. But as I now realize years later, while asthma may have posed a challenge to my physical health, it propped up my emotional and mental health, because it kept my father by my bedside.

My dad was always sure to be within reach of me, and the side effects of the medications meant that he was always holding a cold, wet towel on my forehead until I fell asleep again from my headache.

As far as the special effort that was made to ensure that I had a proper room to sleep in while we were on vacations as a family, this usually meant that I got the nicest room and it also ensured that dad was my roommate.

I couldn't have seen it at the time, but having asthma was like hitting the jackpot for a child who craved his father's love and attention. When his light shined on me alone, there was no better feeling in all the world.

When dad was away, I often didn't know when he'd return, and as a young boy, I didn't know why he wasn't around at Christmastime, when Santa came to the house. And I really wondered why Santa had the same two moles on his face that my dad had, and in the same place as my dad. Even after I figured out that he was my dad and the costume finally came off, he still remained to me a magical figure.

As a little kid, I didn't look like much of a sailor, but my dad thought otherwise. You see, in sailing there are rules as well, much like government. Tireless, mundane rules that will surely make you seasick. The rule was four people on the boat to race, just four. But my dad, of course, dug around until he found a rule around the rule. Sound familiar to you who served with him in the Senate? Kids under 12, he found out, especially scrawny little redheads like me, could tag along. My dad found that rule that meshed with his mission. He refused to leave me behind.

He did that for all of those around the world who needed a special voice as well. When we raced in foul weather, there was lots of saltwater and lots of salty language. Those experiences not only broadened my vocabulary, sure, but also built my self-confidence. I saw a lot of political philosophy in those sailboat races. One thing I noticed was that on the boat, as in this country, there was a role for everybody, a place for everybody to contribute. Another, in the race as in life, it didn't matter how strong the forces against you were, so long as you kept driving forward. There was nothing to lose. Maybe you would even come out a winner.

My dad was never bowed. He never gave up, and there was no quit in dad. And looking out in this audience and looking out at the tremendous number of people who aligned themselves along the roadways coming up from the Cape, and throughout Boston when we went around, or who waited in line for hours to see his casket as they came through the JFK Library, there's no doubt in my mind that my dad came out a winner.

I want to thank all of you for the amazing tribute that you've given my father in the last several days. Just as I was proud to be a crew on his sailboat, I am forever grateful for

[329]

the opportunity to have worked with him in the U.S. Congress as his colleague.

I admit I used to hang onto his T-shirt and his coat sleeve in the Capitol when I was just a little boy. So, when I got a chance to serve with him on Capitol Hill, all I needed to do was set my compass to the principles of his life.

My father and I were the primary sponsors of the Mental Health Parity and Addiction Equality Act, which was signed into law last year. This bill represented not only a legal victory for 54 million Americans with mental illness who are being denied equal health insurance, but as one of those 54 million Americans, I felt he was also fighting for me to help ease the burden and stigma and shame that accompanies treatment.

I will really miss working with dad. I will miss my dad's wonderful sense of self-deprecating humor. When the far right made dad their poster child for their attack ads, he used to say, "We Kennedys sure bring out the best in people." And when he was in the Senate, and my cousin Joe was a Member of Congress and I came to Congress, dad finally celebrated saying, "Finally after all these years when someone says, 'Who does that damn KENNEDY think he is?' There's only a one in three chance they're talking about me."

Most Americans will remember dad as a good and decent hard-charging Senator. But to Teddy, Curran, Caroline, Kara, and me, we will always remember him as a loving and devoted father. In the 1980 campaign, my dad often quoted Robert Frost at the conclusion of every stump speech to indicate that he had to go on to another political event. He would paraphrase the line from "Stopping by Woods on a Snowy Evening":

The woods are lovely, dark and deep,
But I have promises to keep,
And miles to go before I sleep,
And miles to go before I sleep.

Well, dad, you've kept that promise both literally and figuratively to be your brother's keeper. Now, it's time for you to rest in peace. May your spirit live forever in our hearts, and as you challenged us so many times before, may your dream for a better, more just America never die. I love you dad, and you will always live in my heart forever.

[Eulogy]

President BARACK OBAMA: Your Eminence, Vicki, Kara, Edward, Patrick, Curran, Caroline, members of the Kennedy family, distinguished guests, and fellow citizens:

Today we say goodbye to the youngest child of Rose and Joseph Kennedy. The world will long remember their son EDWARD as the heir to a weighty legacy; a champion for those who had none; the soul of the Democratic Party; and the lion of the U.S. Senate—a man who graces nearly 2,000 laws, and who penned more than 300 laws himself.

But those of us who loved him, and ache with his passing, know TED KENNEDY by the other titles he held: Father. Brother. Husband. Grandfather. Uncle TEDDY, or as he was often known to his younger nieces and nephews, the "Grand Fromage," or the "Big Cheese." I, like so many others in the city where he worked for nearly half a century, knew him as a colleague, a mentor, and above all, as a friend.

TED KENNEDY was the baby of the family who became its patriarch; the restless dreamer who became its rock. He was the sunny, joyful child who bore the brunt of his brothers' teasing, but learned quickly how to brush it off. When they tossed him off a boat because he didn't know what a jib was, 6-year-old TEDDY got back in and learned to sail. When a photographer asked the newly elected Bobby to step back at a press conference because he was casting a shadow on his younger brother, TEDDY quipped, "It'll be the same in Washington."

That spirit of resilience and good humor would see TEDDY through more pain and tragedy than most of us will ever know. He lost two siblings by the age of 16. He saw two more taken violently from a country that loved them. He said goodbye to his beloved sister, Eunice, in the final days of his life. He narrowly survived a plane crash, watched two children struggle with cancer, buried three nephews, and experienced personal failings and setbacks in the most public way possible.

It's a string of events that would have broken a lesser man. And it would have been easy for TED to let himself become bitter and hardened; to surrender to self-pity and regret; to retreat from public life and live out his years in peaceful quiet. No one would have blamed him for that.

But that was not TED KENNEDY. As he told us, "[I]ndividual faults and frailties are no excuse to give in— and no exemption from the common obligation to give of ourselves." Indeed, TED was the "Happy Warrior" that the poet Wordsworth spoke of when he wrote:

[331]

As tempted more; more able to endure,
As more exposed to suffering and distress;
Thence, also, more alive to tenderness.

Through his own suffering, TED KENNEDY became more alive to the plight and the suffering of others—the sick child who could not see a doctor; the young soldier denied her rights because of what she looks like or who she loves or where she comes from. The landmark laws that he championed—the Civil Rights Act, the Americans with Disabilities Act, immigration reform, children's health insurance, the Family and Medical Leave Act—all have a running thread. TED KENNEDY's life work was not to champion the causes of those with wealth or power or special connections. It was to give a voice to those who were not heard; to add a rung to the ladder of opportunity; to make real the dream of our founding. He was given the gift of time that his brothers were not, and he used that gift to touch as many lives and right as many wrongs as the years would allow.

We can still hear his voice bellowing through the Senate Chamber, face reddened, fist pounding the podium, a veritable force of nature, in support of health care or workers' rights or civil rights. And yet, as has been noted, while his causes became deeply personal, his disagreements never did. While he was seen by his fiercest critics as a partisan lightning rod, that's not the prism through which TED KENNEDY saw the world, nor was it the prism through which his colleagues saw TED KENNEDY. He was a product of an age when the joy and nobility of politics prevented differences of party and platform and philosophy from becoming barriers to cooperation and mutual respect—a time when adversaries still saw each other as patriots.

And that's how TED KENNEDY became the greatest legislator of our time. He did it by hewing to principle, yes, but also by seeking compromise and common cause—not through dealmaking and horse trading alone, but through friendship, and kindness, and humor. There was the time he courted Orrin Hatch for support of the Children's Health Insurance Program by having his chief of staff serenade the Senator with a song Orrin had written himself; the time he delivered shamrock cookies on a china plate to sweeten up a crusty Republican colleague; the famous story of how he won the support of a Texas committee chairman on an immigration bill. TEDDY walked into a meeting with a plain manila envelope, and showed only the chairman that it was filled with the Texan's favorite cigars. When the negotiations were going well, he would inch the envelope closer to the chairman. (Laughter.) When they weren't, he'd pull it back. (Laughter.) Before long, the deal was done. (Laughter.)

It was only a few years ago, on St. Patrick's Day, when TEDDY buttonholed me on the floor of the Senate for my support of a certain piece of legislation that was coming up for a vote. I gave my pledge, but I expressed skepticism that it would pass. But when the roll call was over, the bill garnered the votes that it needed, and then some. I looked at TEDDY with astonishment and asked how had he done it. He just patted me on the back and said, "Luck of the Irish." (Laughter.)

Of course, luck had little to do with TED KENNEDY's legislative success; he knew that. A few years ago, his father-in-law told him that he and Daniel Webster just might be the two greatest Senators of all time. Without missing a beat, TEDDY replied, "What did Webster do?" (Laughter.)

But though it is TEDDY's historic body of achievements that we will remember, it is his giving heart that we will miss. It was the friend and the colleague who was always the first to pick up the phone and say, "I'm sorry for your loss," or "I hope you feel better," or "What can I do to help?" It was the boss so adored by his staff that over 500, spanning five decades, showed up for his 75th birthday party. It was the man who sent birthday wishes and thank you notes and even his own paintings to so many who never imagined that a U.S. Senator of such stature would take the time to think about somebody like them. I have one of those paintings in my private study off the Oval Office—a Cape Cod seascape that was a gift to a freshman legislator who had just arrived in Washington and happened to admire it when TED KENNEDY welcomed him into his office. That, by the way, is my second gift from TEDDY and Vicki after our dog Bo. And it seems like everyone has one of those stories—the ones that often start with "You wouldn't believe who called me today."

TED KENNEDY was the father who looked not only after his own three children, but John's and Bobby's as well. He took them camping and taught them to sail. He laughed and danced with them at birthdays and weddings; cried and mourned with them through hardship and tragedy; and passed on that same sense of service and selflessness that his parents had instilled in him. Shortly after TED walked Caroline down the aisle and gave her away at the altar, he received a note from Jackie that read, "On you, the carefree youngest brother, fell a burden a hero would have begged to been spared. We are all going to make it because you were always there with your love."

Not only did the Kennedy family make it because of TED's love—he made it because of theirs, especially because of the love and the life he found in Vicki. After so much loss and so much sorrow, it could not have been easy for TED to risk his heart again. And that he did is a testament to how deeply he loved this remarkable woman from Louisiana. And she didn't just love him back. As TED would often acknowledge, Vicki saved him. She gave him strength and purpose; joy and friendship; and stood by him always, especially in those last, hardest days.

We cannot know for certain how long we have here. We cannot foresee the trials or misfortunes that will test us along the way. We cannot know what God's plan is for us.

What we can do is to live out our lives as best we can with purpose, and with love, and with joy. We can use each day to show those who are closest to us how much we care about them, and treat others with the kindness and respect that we wish for ourselves. We can learn from our mistakes and grow from our failures. And we can strive at all costs to make a better world, so that someday, if we are blessed with the chance to look back on our time here, we know that we spent it well; that we made a difference; that our fleeting presence had a lasting impact on the lives of others.

This is how TED KENNEDY lived. This is his legacy. He once said, as has already been mentioned, of his brother Bobby that he need not be idealized or enlarged in death because of what he was in life—and I imagine he would say the same about himself. The greatest expectations were placed upon TED KENNEDY's shoulders because of who he was, but he surpassed them all because of who he became. We do not weep for him today because of the prestige attached to his name or his office. We weep because we loved this kind and tender hero who persevered through pain and tragedy—not for the sake of ambition or vanity; not for wealth or power; but only for the people and the country that he loved.

In the days after September 11, TEDDY made it a point to personally call each one of the 177 families of this State who lost a loved one in the attack. But he didn't stop there. He kept calling and checking up on them. He fought through red tape to get them assistance and grief counseling. He invited them sailing, played with their children, and would write each family a letter whenever the anniversary of that terrible day came along. To one widow, he wrote the following:

As you know so well, the passage of time never really heals the tragic memory of such a great loss, but we carry on, because we have to, because our loved ones would want us to, and because there is still light to guide us in the world from the love they gave us.

We carry on.

TED KENNEDY has gone home now, guided by his faith and by the light of those that he has loved and lost. At last he is with them once more, leaving those of us who grieve his passing with the memories he gave, the good that he did, the dream he kept alive, and a single, enduring image—the image of a man on a boat, white mane tousled, smiling broadly as he sails into the wind, ready for whatever storms may come, carrying on toward some new and wondrous place just beyond the horizon.

May God bless TED KENNEDY, and may he rest in eternal peace.

Rev. MONAN: Let us pray. Lord God, your son Jesus Christ gave us the sacrament of His body and blood to guide us on our pilgrimage to your kingdom. May our dear friend TED, who shared in the Eucharist, come to the banquet of life Christ prepared for us. We ask this through Christ our Lord, Amen.

CONGREGATION: Amen.

Rev. MONAN: His Eminence Cardinal Seán O'Malley will conduct the final commendation.

SEAN P. CARDINAL O'MALLEY, Archbishop of Boston: Mr. President, we thank you for your presence and for your words of appreciation for the life and work of Senator KENNEDY. We've gathered here today to pray for a man who has been such an important part of our history and our country.

We are here because TED KENNEDY shares our belief in prayer and in eternal life. Vicki, you and the family surrounded TED with love at the end of his life and gave us all an example of love and compassion in the face of suffering and death. We die with dignity when we are surrounded by love and such care.

And now, let us commend TED's soul to God's loving mercy. Before we go our separate ways, let us take leave of our brother. May our farewell express our affection for him. May it ease our sadness and strengthen our hope. One day, we

[335]

shall joyfully greet him again through Christ, which conquers all things and destroys even death itself.

Into your hands, Father of Mercies, we commend our brother EDWARD in the sure and certain hope that together with all who have died in Christ, we shall all rise with him on the last day. We give you thanks for the blessings which you bestowed upon EDWARD in this life. They are signs to us of your goodness and of our fellowship with the saints and Christ.

Merciful Lord, turn toward us and listen to our prayers. Open the gates of paradise to your servants and help us who remain to comfort one another with assurances of faith until we all meet in Christ and are with you and with our brother forever. We ask this through Christ our Lord.

CONGREGATION: Amen.

CARDINAL O'MALLEY: In peace, let us take our brother to his place of rest.

[Recessional Hymn]

Edward Moore Kennedy

Service at the U.S. Capitol

Senate Steps

August 29, 2009

Rev. DANIEL P. COUGHLIN, Chaplain of the House of Representatives: Mrs. Kennedy, we gather with you, the family, and dear friends, to express our solidarity with you at this time. Some Members of both Chambers of the Congress, officers, co-workers, collaborators, and especially former and presently serving staff of the Senator are gathered here on the steps. Here we are to briefly pray with you—to offer our sympathy, and to thank you for sharing the Senator and so much of his life with us. Thank you also for your love and your care throughout the years, especially during the time of illness and these last moments. Be assured of our prayers and anything we can do for you as you move on.

Let us pray.

Though in the sight of people, your servant Senator TED KENNEDY suffered greatly and took on enormous tasks, Lord, you knew his hopes were unquenchable, full of immortality. You knew his strengths and his limitations. He knew you, Lord. He knew you could use anyone or anything to accomplish your purpose and draw people closer to one another and to His divine presence. Grounded in faith, fashioned by family values, and once expanded to a world vision, true contemplative leadership would draw staff and friends to new depths of human understanding. Embraced with compassion, such a vision would inspire people around the world to believe, to believe with all their hearts that peace and justice will conquer violence and division, and competition can be converted to collaboration. Although burdened by the weight of his passing, Lord, help his co-workers and collaborators raise the torch of his convictions and commitments for a new generation, one yet even to be born, and for all in all those parts of this Nation and the world who are still untouched by the social responsibility inherent in every aspect of human freedom. Faithful servant of the people and longtime spokesman for government of the people, go now to your place of rest and meet the Lord, your God. We thank you, Lord, for the short time you have given us to work together, to be together. To you, be all honor, power, glory, and praise now and forever. Amen.

Now I would like to introduce Samuel Bonds, choral director of the Duke Ellington School of Music, who will lead all of us in singing "America the Beautiful."

O beautiful for spacious skies,
For amber waves of grain,
For purple mountain majesties
Above the fruited plain!
America! America!

God shed his grace on thee
And crown thy good with brotherhood
From sea to shining sea!

Rev. COUGHLIN: Thank you very much for attending. Eternal rest bring unto him, O Lord, and let perpetual light shine upon him. May he rest in peace. May his soul and all the souls of the faithfully departed to the mercy of God rest in peace. Amen.

Representative PATRICK J. KENNEDY: I just want to say on behalf of my brother and sister how proud my dad was to serve here in the Senate and most of all for you to know that he could not have done it without all the people that he worked with. He knew that he was only great because he had great people supporting him, and he knew the value of good staff. That's why he was so successful.

I know that all of you, having watched what happened the last 3 days, have to feel good that you were part of his life. This country has outpoured its soul and heart these last few days to say what a difference he's made in the life of this country. I think you all today should be feeling that you were part of that, too, because of all that you have done to be part of the same legacy that he wanted for this country.

I hope you feel some consolation that the many hard hours you put into the nitty-gritty of legislating and policymaking give you some sense of satisfaction at having done a really important job for this country, because that is the legacy he would want you to feel good about.

He would be very proud to see you all out here today paying a final respect and tribute to his memory. I thank you on behalf of my family for being here.

EDWARD MOORE KENNEDY

Burial Service

Arlington National Cemetery

August 29, 2009

THEODORE CARDINAL McCARRICK, Archbishop Emeritus of Washington, DC: There is a certain fittingness in having a burial at the dying of the day, because we know that the sun will come back again tomorrow. As we think of TEDDY, we know that his new life begins, and as we look at this great family, we're sure that new life is already beginning, and that new great things are happening.

Mr. Vice President, Vicki, members of the family: It is for all of us a very special time in our own lives, in your life, and the life of our country. And so we begin in the name of the Father, and of the Son, and of the Holy Spirit.

ALL: Amen.

CARDINAL McCARRICK: Dear friends in Christ, in the name of Jesus and his church, we gather together to pray for EDWARD MOORE KENNEDY, that God may bring him to everlasting peace and rest. We share the pain of loss, but the promise of eternal life gives us hope, and therefore, we comfort one another with these words.

[Reading of Letter of Paul to the Philippians, 3:20–21]

KARA KENNEDY: Our citizenship is in heaven, and from it we also await a savior, the Lord Jesus Christ. He will change our lowly body to conform with his glorified body by the power that enables him also to bring all things into subjection to himself.

CARDINAL McCARRICK: Thanks be to God.

May I, for just a moment, be the voice of so many, all around the world, to pay a final tribute to Senator TED KENNEDY, and to offer our heartfelt condolences to his wife Vicki, to his sister Jean, to his children and grandchildren, and to all the Kennedy family, and also to that extended family that must probably include most of America.

May I also add a word that we who were privileged to watch the very beautiful funeral Mass this morning had to be touched by the wonderful part in that liturgy played by the younger generation of Kennedys. The warm and very personal tribute in the eulogies of TEDDY's sons, and even that of the President of the United States, whose warmth and whose friendship for TED are obviously so powerful. That, together with the splendid homily of Father Hession, TED's parish priest, made our farewell to Senator KENNEDY unforgettable.

On learning of his death last Wednesday morning, tributes to his half century of leadership in American life and politics came in from all over the globe. May I offer my own short one again.

They called him the lion of the Senate, and indeed that is what he was. His roar and his zeal for what he believed made a difference in our Nation's life. Sometimes, of course, we who were his friends and had affection for him would get mad at him when he roared at what we believed was the wrong side of an issue. But we always knew and were always touched by his passion for the underdog, for the rights of working people, for better education, for adequate health care for every American. His legacy will surely place him among the dozen or so greats in the history of the Senate of the United States.

Shortly before he died, Senator KENNEDY wrote a very moving letter to the Holy Father, and took advantage of the historic visit to the Vatican by President Obama to ask the President if he would deliver it personally, which President Obama gladly did. A couple of weeks later, the Pope replied with a fatherly message of concern for the Senator's illness, and a prayer for his progress.

When Vicki and I and others began to talk about the organization of this brief service, the happy thought emerged of using parts of these two letters to commemorate the faith of TED KENNEDY and the warm and paternal spirit of Pope Benedict XVI. I want to quote from that letter. It begins:

Most Holy Father, I asked President Obama to personally hand deliver this letter to you. As a man of deep faith himself, he understands how important my Roman Catholic faith is to me, and I am so deeply grateful to him.

I hope this letter finds you in good health. I pray that you have all of God's blessings as you lead our church and inspire our world during these challenging times.

I am writing with deep humility to ask that you pray for me as my own health declines. I was diagnosed with brain cancer more than a year ago, and although I continue treatment, the disease is taking its toll on me. I am 77 years old, and preparing for the next passage of life.

I have been blessed to be a part of a wonderful family, and both of my parents, particularly my mother, kept our Catholic faith at the center of our lives. That gift of faith has sustained and nurtured and provided solace to me in the darkest hours. I know that I have been an imperfect human being, but with the help of my faith, I have tried to right my path.

I want you to know, Your Holiness, that in my nearly 50 years of elective office, I have done my best to champion the rights of the poor and open doors of economic opportunity. I've worked to welcome the immigrant, to fight discrimination and expand access to health care and education. I have opposed the death penalty and fought to end war. Those are the issues that have motivated me and have been the focus of my work as a U.S. Senator.

I also want you to know that, even though I am ill, I am committed to do everything I can to achieve access to health care for everyone in my country. This has been the political cause of my life. I believe in a conscience protection for Catholics in the health field and I will continue to advocate for it as my colleagues in the Senate and I work to develop an overall national health policy that guarantees health care for everyone.

I have always tried to be a faithful Catholic, Your Holiness, and though I have fallen short through human failings, I have never failed to believe and respect the fundamental teachings of my faith. I continue to pray for God's blessings on you and on our church, and would be most thankful for your prayers for me.

Two weeks later, the reply came back from the Vatican, and in part, it read as follows:

The Holy Father has read the letter which you entrusted to President Obama, who kindly presented it to him during their recent meeting. He was saddened to know of your illness, and asked me to assure you of his concern and his spiritual closeness. He is particularly grateful for your promise of prayers for him, and for the needs of our universal church.

His Holiness prays that in the days ahead you may be sustained in faith and hope, and granted the precious grace of joyful surrender to the will of God, our merciful Father. He invokes upon you the consolation and peace promised by the risen Savior to all who share in his sufferings and trust in his promise of eternal life.

Commending you and the members of your family to the loving intervention of the blessed Virgin Mary, the Holy Father cordially imparts his apostolic blessing as a pledge of wisdom, comfort and strength in the Lord.

With the prayers of our Holy Father, Pope Benedict, added to our own prayers, we entrust the body of EDWARD MOORE KENNEDY, Senator TED, to his resting place, until the Lord calls us forth, until the end of time. Amen.

And now, let us pray.

Lord Jesus Christ, by your own 3 days in the tomb, you hallow the graves of all who believe in you, and so made the grave a sign of hope that promises resurrection, even as it claims our mortal bodies.

Lord, grant that our brother may sleep here in peace until you awaken him in glory, for you are the resurrection and the life. Then he will see you face to face and in your light will see light and know the splendor of God, for you reign forever and ever.

ALL: Amen.

CARDINAL MCCARRICK: I'm going to ask Father Gerry Creedon, an old friend of the family, to do the intercessions for us. He will be saying some prayers and then adding, "Lord, in your mercy," and our response is, "Lord, hear our prayer."

FATHER GERRY CREEDON: Lord, in your mercy.

ALL: Lord, hear our prayer.

FATHER GERRY CREEDON: Gracious Lord, forgive the sins of those who have died in Christ. Lord, in your mercy.

ALL: Lord, hear our prayer.

FATHER CREEDON: Remember all the good they've done. Lord, in your mercy.

ALL: Lord, hear our prayer.

FATHER CREEDON: Welcome them into eternal life. Lord, in your mercy.

ALL: Lord, hear our prayer.

FATHER CREEDON: Let us pray for those who mourn; comfort them in their grief. Lord, in your mercy.

ALL: Lord, hear our prayer.

FATHER CREEDON: Lighten their sense of loss with your presence. Lord, in your mercy.

ALL: Lord, hear our prayer.

FATHER CREEDON: Increase their faith, strengthen their hope. Lord, in your mercy.

ALL: Lord, hear our prayer.

FATHER CREEDON: Let us pray also for ourselves and our own pilgrimage through life. Keep us faithful in your service. Lord, in your mercy.

ALL: Lord, hear our prayer.

FATHER CREEDON: Kindle in our hearts a longing for your kingdom of justice and peace, a longing for heaven. Lord, in your mercy.

ALL: Lord, hear our prayer.

CARDINAL McCARRICK: In the sure and certain hope of the resurrection to eternal life through our Lord Jesus Christ, we commend to Almighty God our Brother TED, and we commit his body to the ground, earth to earth, ashes to ashes, dust to dust. May the Lord bless him and keep him, may the Lord make his face to shine upon him and be gracious to him, may the Lord lift up his countenance upon him and give him peace.

Let us join now in praying that prayer that Jesus taught us:

Our Father, who art in heaven, hallowed be thy name, thy kingdom come, thy will be done, on Earth as it is in heaven. Give us this day our daily bread, and forgive us our trespasses, as we forgive those who trespass against us. And lead us not into temptation, but deliver us from evil.

And now I will say again the prayers with which his Eminence Cardinal O'Malley ended the Act of Commendation, because they are fitting for this moment as well.

Before we go our separate ways, let us take leave of our Brother TED. May our farewell express our affection for him. May it ease our sadness and strengthen our hope. One day, we shall joyfully greet him again, when the love of Christ, which conquers all things, destroys even death itself.

Into your hands, Father of Mercies, we commend our Brother TED in the sure and certain hope that together with all who have died in Christ, he will rise with Him on the last day. We give you thanks for the blessings which you bestowed upon him in this life. They are signs to us of your goodness and of our fellowship with the saints in Christ.

Merciful Lord, turn toward us and listen to our prayers. Open the gates of paradise for your servant. And help us, who remain, to comfort one another with assurances of faith, until we meet in Christ and are with you and with our Brother TEDDY forever. We ask this through Christ our Lord.

FATHER CREEDON: Amen.

Let us now bow our heads and pray for God's blessing. Merciful Lord, you know the anguish of the sorrowful. You are attentive to the prayers of the humble. Hear your people who cry out to you in their need. And strengthen their hope in your lasting goodness. We ask this through Christ, our Lord. Amen.

And may the peace of God, which is beyond all understanding, keep your hearts and minds in the knowledge and love of God and of his Son, our Lord Jesus Christ, and may Almighty God bless you, the Father, and the Son, and the Holy Spirit. Amen.

And now I know that two of TEDDY's grandchildren are going to come and be with us, and say something about grandpa.

[Three Volley Salute; Taps]

KILEY KENNEDY: My name is Kiley Kennedy, and I'm the oldest of the four grandchildren of TED KENNEDY. When most people think of TED KENNEDY, they think about the man who changed the lives of millions of people by fighting for better health care. When I think about him, vibrant memories of sailing, laughing, Thanksgiving dinner, talking on the front porch and playing with Splash come to mind.

To me, all the things he has done to change the world are just icing on my grandpa's cake of a truly miraculous person. You see, my grandpa was really a kid. If you ever saw him conducting the Boston Pops, that's what he was like all the time with me. He knew how to joke, laugh, and have fun, like the time we played games with all the cousins at my 14th birthday party. I remember him smiling, playing, and dancing that day. And I'll never forget everyone's smile that he had made.

I will always remember the times we spent sailing on *Mya*, when I could tell that he was the happiest in the world, even when he was yelling, "Get that fisherman up!" But what I will miss the most are the times I woke up at 6:30 a.m. and would go to the front porch, where my grandpa would be sitting with Splash and gazing out to sea. It would be just us on the porch for awhile, and we talked and talked. And I would get a feeling that the world was just right. It was me and him sitting on his porch, watching a new day unfold as we stared into the sea of freedom and possibilities. I love you so much, grandpa, and I always will.

GRACE ALLEN: Hi. I'm Grace Allen. I'm the second oldest grandchild. I just want to say a few words about my grandpa. Our favorite time of the year was Thanksgiving, because we were all together as a family, sailing and eating together at the table, all of us, including Caroline Kennedy and her family. I just want to give thanks to my grandpa, because he's the best grandpa I've ever had, and the best in the world.

○

www.ingramcontent.com/pod-product-compliance
Lightning Source LLC
Chambersburg PA
CBHW070841300326

41935CB00039B/1340